Pali Text Society
TRANSLATION SERIES, No. 25

THE BOOK OF THE GRADUAL SAYINGS
(ANGUTTARA-NIKĀYA)
OR MORE-NUMBERED SUTTAS

VOL. III
(THE BOOKS OF THE FIVES AND SIXES)

TRANSLATED BY
E. M. HARE

WITH AN INTRODUCTION BY
MRS. RHYS DAVIDS, D.Litt., M.A.

"Say on, sayers! sing on, singers!
Delve! mould! pile the words of the earth!
Work on, age after age, nothing is to be lost,
It may have to wait long, but it will certainly come in use;
When the materials are all prepared and ready, the architects shall appear!"

WALT WHITMAN.

THE PALI TEXT SOCIETY, OXFORD

1988

First published – – 1934
Reprinted – – – – 1952
Reprinted – – – – 1961
Reprinted – – – – 1973
Reprinted – – – – 1988

ISBN 7100 7671 1 (1973 reprint)
ISBN 0 86013 0169 (1988 reprint)

PRINTED IN GREAT BRITAIN BY
ANTONY ROWE LTD, CHIPPENHAM, WILTS

INTRODUCTION

The Pali Text Society during its fifty-two years of life has had its ups and downs, and these have reverberated in the spiritual thermometers of its Presidents. The present work, being the first appearance among us of Edward Hare, known to us hitherto as a generous donor, now to be better known as an equally disinterested fellow-worker of high merit, counts as a very decided 'up.' Financial stringency is counting, as I have elsewhere reported, as a heavy 'down,' yet it would be with us sheer bankruptcy and nothing less, before we could bring ourselves to suspend the completing of these translations of the four Collections of the Suttas, of which this volume is the last number save two, so useful do we hold they should be for a better knowledge of Buddhism. Mr. Woodward, who has given us five of such volumes, and who may yet give us the last of this, the Anguttara Collection, has handed over this and the next volume to Mr. Hare. And it has been for me a task of deep interest to follow the latter's renderings and annotations, and now to introduce the same at his insistent request. This is not to say that I endorse every word of either; but I do say, that in nearly every case I should be proud were the translation my own.

I propose, as usual, to resolve my Introduction into a few notes, designed to bring into relief the historical changes between the birth and the later growth of the Buddhist movement, such as seem to be reasonably inferable from what these Sayings tell us. This is as yet not the way in which as a rule writers on Buddhism envisage these Pāli scriptures. Even when such writers cite context after context from the originals (and not, as is sometimes the case, from contexts as cited by earlier writers on them), the references are usually treated as being all equally authoritative. If, for instance, in one of such references the Founder (whether he be called Exalted One, Bhagavan, Tathāgata, Buddha, or Gotama) is recorded as having said this, and in another reference he is also recorded as having said that, it is accepted without comment that (*a*) this is true of both, whether the Sayings are mutually concordant or not, and (*b*) he is as likely to have said the one as the other. Now, that professing Buddhists should in these cases make no critical comment is scarcely to be expected, nor are we in a position, if we be followers of Christianity or of Islam, to find fault with them for accepting such Sayings *en bloc*. But it is surely better for the reader who is not bound by the shackles of well-meaning piety, that he should take for his guide historic truth rather than edification. And it is this reader to whom the following points are addressed.

Variant Versions.—I explained the historic interest I saw in these in my Introduction to the preceding volume, and will not repeat myself here. In this third volume the reader will also find a large number of such variants, and I have drawn up a table of them at the end. They are chiefly in pairs, but now and then they run to larger groups. Now it is the 'text' that varies, now and then the expositions or the verses vary; more often it is a varied exposition of a common text. For me these variants are a lively reminder of (*a*) the long-lived oral nature of the teaching, (*b*) the tether long permitted to the exponent to *make his own exposition*, (*c*) the various and mutually isolated conditions of place under which the teaching went on, (*d*) the felt need of revision to which such conditions would eventually give rise.

And here I am fain to be again referring to my preceding Introduction—namely, where I refer to a slight but possibly significant variety in the prose and verse of the Sutta: 'World' (Vol. II, pp. 43-45). I was re-reading the Sutta one day, when as in a flash it dawned upon me, that to fit word to context we must discard the word 'buddha' altogether, and substitute the original word 'suddha.'

I must remind the reader that to the question, 'As what

do you, sir, expect to be reborn ?',[1] the Founder, in replying, is said to explain that just as a water-lily gets no smear from the water, so he gets no smear from contact with the world; as it has grown up in and above the water, so has he grown up in and above the world, both of them clean, or, more literally, 'cleansed': *suddho.* The context does not call for the word *buddha* ('wise,' or 'wake,' or 'enlightened'); it *does* call for the word 'unsoiled' (*an-upalitta*), or the positive equivalent *suddha.*

How, then, did 'buddha' come to be substituted ?

In the first place there was growing up, in the second and third centuries after the Founder's death, the cult of him as a super-man, a super-god. Belief in personal Divinity, in Vishnu and Shiva, was renascent in India, modifying the immanent theism dominant at the birth of Buddhism. And in the growing Buddhist world there will have been a renascence no less strong in the felt need for a supreme Being. There will have been a predisposition, where teaching was still carried on through the ear, not through the eye, to get *buddha* where *suddha* had been spoken, not read.

In the second place, with a grown mass of oral mandates, there was growing the need of sorting this mass into the kind of arrangement we see in the Sutta-Piṭaka. Somehow it came about that, in the ten Sayings now known as 'Wheel,' this 'World' Sutta followed one called 'Vassakāra' (No. 35), in which a man of certain qualities is reputed to be 'wise (*buddho*), great sage, great man.' There is here no specific reference to the Founder; but it is possible that the *juxta-position* of the two Suttas may have, as by an echo, brought about the insertion of *buddha* for *suddha.*

The Buddhist 'Church,' be it never forgotten, was not alone in seeking, not to relate the true, but to edify the votary. *Suddho* had once meant, or still meant, in Indian idiom, 'having salvation,' 'being safe as to the hereafter.' But here was a newer, a more engrossing theme:—the Person of the Founder, bringing, in the one word, the edification we

---

[1] Lit. 'Will his reverence *become* (x, y or z) ?'

ascribe, in gentle humour, to 'that blessed word Mesopotamia.' We too have clung to the edifying, where the context required a different meaning, such as we admit in the present 'Revised Version'—we have, *e.g.*, preferred the imperative: 'Search the scriptures,' when the context required: 'Ye search the scriptures . . . but ye will not come to *me*.'

A Changed Category.—In Chapter XIII of my book *Sakya*, I put forward tentatively the theory that the category known as the *chal-abhiññā(yo)*, or Six Superknowings, had been originally one of *five only*. I have, in this translation of the Book of the Fives, come the better to see that the theory is right. And that in a very interesting case of monastic editing. Let the reader turn to Sutta 23, p. 11. Here the Category, called elsewhere the Five Hindrances (*Nīvaraṇāni*), is treated of under the figure of physical 'debasements' (*upakkilesā*). As so treated, it is finished on p. 12, line 8. But in the longer, more important Suttanta 2 of the Dīgha, the Hindrances are followed by the description of the Five Psychic Gifts, later called the Superknowings. To these, both there and here, *is appended a sixth item*, which has nothing in common with the Five: the extirpation of the three Āsavā, or Cankers, viz. of desire, rebirth, ignorance. (Elsewhere in the Canon a fourth is often added: that of views or opinions.)[1]

Now here we have an apparently sixfold category thrust, as it were, into a Book of Fives, with an incongruous sixth item. It should have been among the Sixfold Categories. *It is not to be found there.* And this is for me conclusive. I suggest that, when the Book of Fives was compiled there were just these Fivefold Psychic Gifts; that they made a distinct Sutta in that Book; that the sixth item *came to be added*, making the Sutta of the Six out of place among the Fives; that the Sutta was therefore *tacked on* to the preceding Sutta, following its already traditional order in the Teaching (Dīgha); that thus a further insertion of the Category as sixfold under the Sixes was deemed unnecessary. I do not see this as the only possible conclusion. But it strengthens

---

[1] *Dialogues of the Buddha*, i, pp. 82-93, and *n*. on p. 93.

the case for seeing, in the so-called Six Abhiññās, an original Five. I may add that the compound 'chalabhiññā-' occurs once only in this work, in a way suggestive of insertion, and that, in Saṃyutta-Nikāya II, pp. 216, 222, we have, in naïve confusion, first 'five abhiññās' referred to, then 'six,' then again 'five.'[1]

Certain Renderings.—(1) From Suttas and Category to Words. Mr. Hare's return to an English rendering of *Āsavā*: 'cankers,' with which I readily concur, is on the whole the best. In it we lose the liquid meaning, the permeation, as of ink on blotting-paper, and which is kept in view in 'intoxicants,' 'drugs,' 'floods,' 'poisons.' The scholastic description may be consulted in my *Buddhist Psychological Ethics*, § 1096, *n.*, and Maung Tin's *The Expositor*, p. 63 *f.*[2] We can see how much the term appealed to monastic Buddhism in the way it 'permeates' this volume. With the decline in the conception of 'the man,' with the wilting of any positive ultimate outlook for him, we can understand how the purging of this 'miserable sinner' became a more central teaching than the *original view of him. This* was to see a Seeker after the divine riches of his potential nature, an ultimate Winner of the Thing Needed which was at the end of the Way in the worlds.

(2) By 'Thing Needed' I refer to the original term for the *summum bonum* : *attha.* This word is here translated now by 'goal,' now by 'weal.' Few Pāli words are so hard to translate. In the Suttas a man needing, seeking something, say 'heart of oak,' is called '*sār' attha-ko, -atthiko*'; at the same time *attha* is often used emphatically in the sense of highest object, saintship won.[3] The first mission was to be

---

[1] This is not well handled in my translation, *Kindred Sayings*, ii, pp. 146, 150. On p. 146 read: 'And similarly . . . for the *five* Superknowledges.' (This is followed by 'six Superknowledges'), and p. 150, 'the five Superknowledges of me.'

[2] Pali Text Society's Translations.

[3] As object, aim, whether ordinary or highest, it is so used in the Upanishads. Early monastic Buddhism saw in *attha* perfected manhood already won here on earth. Original Buddhism saw in it something *uttariṃ*, 'beyond,' not realizable on earth. *Cf.* p. 72, Sutta 74.

undertaken 'for the "*attha, hita, sukha*" of devas and of men.' And in my *Manual of Buddhism*, p. 115, I pointed out how, in the first so-called 'sermon,' the word *attha*, required in the context, has been shelved for four inadequate substitutes, probably through the later literary pre-emption of the word for 'meaning' as opposed to 'letter.' The earlier higher force in the word rarely, if ever, occurs in later Pāli. It is all the more interesting to come across, in the present volume, the compound discarded in the 'sermon': *attha-saṃhita*, 'concerned with or about the Goal,' with its negative complement (retained in the 'sermon') of 'not about the Goal' (p. 145).

(3) It is good to have a term from one of those *abhiññās* used at last in its literal meaning. This is 'dwelling(s),' replacing the more usual 'births' or 'lives' in the reminiscence of one's past previous to this life:—*pubbe-nivās' ânussati* (p. 13, etc.). This apparently curious choice made by the Buddhist teachers has a significance which will not strike a European. What is that ?

Why the choice of 'dwelling,' when in Pāli we have 'birth,' 'rebirth,' 'life,' 'world' ? I see it thus: Consider first the formula (p. 13), or its more formal, more usual wording (p. 296):—'he remembers manifoldly appointed dwellings in the past.' This is followed by an exposition, careful as to the 'dwelling' being as inmate of a body, a society, a world, extravagant as to length and number, in which 'births' (*jātiyo*) is freely used. But the very usual word (in later years) for 'lives' and 'worlds,' *bhavā*, is not used. What may be the explanation ? I suggest the following:

(i) The formula 'he . . . the past' is the *original fixed wording*, or 'text.'

(ii) The exposition, long left to the exponent, became appended, in its odd medley, later.

(iii) When (i) was first listed, the word rendered 'dwellings' meant, not merely a house, but a 'nest,' a 'settlement,' an 'ingress';[1] on the other hand, the word *jāti* did not fit

---

[1] These are all old Vedic meanings.

for 'life.' It meant (*a*) birth on earth, (*b*) rank in the brahman, (*c*) happening, (*d*) a producing or source. Later on, the plural in the sense of 'new lives' became permissible.

(iv) The word for 'life' (*jīvita*) was never used in the plural; the word for 'world' (*loka*) in the plural is very hard to find till in later Pāli.[1]

(v) The word that came to be used for both 'lives' and 'worlds,' 'becomings' (*bhavā*), had *not so come into use* when the exposition (ii) was finally worded.

(vi) Original Buddhism taught that man was a wayfarer *in many worlds.*

Hence I come to this:—recollection of the past was of former homes, stations, rests, stages, rather than of 'births' or of 'lives'; hence *nivāsā.*

(4) Lastly, a word in passing on the frequent occurrence in this volume of the term *bhāvanīyo*, with or without the prefix *mano-* (mind). Here we have the compound *for the first time* translated rightly. Let the reader consult p. 225, and *n.* 1. The Commentarial definition *ettha manaŋ vaḍḍheti* means 'herein one makes the mind grow.' It was at the very heart of original Buddhism, that the very man, spirit, soul, should be 'made to grow,' made to become. And the mind was *not the very man*, as the second so-called 'sermon' warned men. But there had been growing a new culture of 'the mind' in India, due to Kapila, *fl.* probably a generation or two before Buddhism began. And experts in this culture, members of the Sakyan Order, are probably meant by the compound term. Its immense influence on Buddhism I have discussed elsewhere. We note this in the fairly obvious gloss with which the mainly ancient Dhammapada begins:

Things are forerun by mind, have mind as best, are compounds of the mind.
If with corrupted mind a man do speak or act,
therefrom ill follows him as wheel the foot of drawing beast.[2]

---

[1] There is *one* plural in this volume: *lokāsu.*

[2] So for the following verse.

Here the couplet proper, 'If . . . beast,' is in keeping with the Upanishads—the man acting 'with his mind.' But the *inserted superfluous first line* is the new note due to Kapila's influence; yet not altogether new, but in a way an echo and revival of the high importance seen in mind (*manas*) in the earlier Brāhmaṇa books of ritual; sayings—for so they then were—which may have inspired Kapila.

Bhāvanīyo without the *mano* is at times a very hard word to translate. Not on p. 192, where 'becomes not what he ought to become' (*a-bhāvanīyo hoti*) is unexceptionable; so p. 87. This is literally correct, but in the compound, the 'participle of necessity' in *-iyo* seems to me not here at all; we have the affix of agency: *-iko* or *-iyo*. This gives us a 'mind-making-becom-er,' an uncouth compound which is fairly well rendered by 'student of mind.'[1] Let the reader not think I comment on trifles. In the wording of growth, of a making to grow, making become, we have the one central driving force that arose with Buddhism. That man 'is' was not enough. Man must become a More, else never will he attain to his full stature as God:—here is original Buddhism carrying out to the Many the torch drooping in the hands of the Brahman teaching of the Few.

Fate.—Let the reader not be misled by 'fate' being used as a variant for 'death'—*e.g.*, p. 211. *Kāla-kiriyā* ('accomplishment of earth-time') is synonymous with 'dying.' No determinist doctrine is implied.

The Test of the Self's Reality.—I come to two features of great interest. The one is the Sutta entitled 'Self-acting' (*atta-kāro*, or *vv.ll. atta-kārī*) (p. 237). I commend it much to the reader's attention, for surely few Sayings have been so overlooked, and few Sayings can Buddhists and others so little afford to overlook. In it we have a man (said to be a brahman —which is obviously impossible) stating it as his opinion, that in a man's actions the doing is not rightly to be called 'by the self' or 'by another.' The statement might equally

---

[1] So *vaḍḍhan-iyo*, the Commentary's equivalent a 'grow-er.' (*See* p. 192, *n*. 3.)

well be rendered 'there is no self-agent, no other-who-is-agent': *-kāro, -kārī* may mean either agent or agency. We then have Gotama's reply, that he had '*never even heard or seen such an opinion*'! The 'seen' is baffling, since it can only refer to a written opinion;[1] and this could not be the case till about 400 years after the Founder's demise. Yet Gotama's refutation of the opinion is of the bedrock of his teaching, and wipes out the doctrine of *anattā*, no-self, as being his! He gives 'initiative,' literally the 'datum of having-started,' or 'begun' an act, as *the criterion of the active presence of the very man or self.* Here is verily a very live-wire of teaching; here is a very doctrine of will, of choice, such as I see buried in the First Address, without the needed words in which to tell of it. I regret profoundly I was among the overlookers of it till the translator's MS. came into my hands. It is not, as is said in the note, Makkhali's doctrine.[2] That was a denial of effective causation. This is a denial of the causer, the man, the invisible spiritual being, the soul, the self. And we have Gotama denying all knowledge of this denial, which he is by most writers declared to have made his central doctrine! But the chief interest lies in the testing of agency by 'initiative.' This was a great word.

Man the Seeker.—The other intensely interesting (and also unique) Saying is that called 'Gavesin, the Seeker' (No. 180, pp. 158 *ff.*). Here we have the Man of radiant will, as elsewhere smiling, and asked by Ānanda, why the smile? And there follows a story laid in the days of the preceding 'Buddha,' in which the teller himself gives no personal memory. The details of the story are very monkish, suggesting a tradition of generations of monk-tellers, giving as stages in the Seeker's progress, and that of those he helps along, the values of the cloister. But the real worth of the tale lies in its essential features of Man as seeking ever a Better, of Man as ever Becoming: 'This is but a matter of levels; there's nothing

---

[1] Unless 'seen, heard' is to be taken as an inclusive assertion parallel to the familiar 'know, see'; but I have not come across such an idiom elsewhere.

[2] *Cf.* my *Buddhism* (Home Univ. Library), p. 85.

More; well, then, I'm for the More!' And the moral of the story comes as a very Crown:—'In this way train yourselves: from beyond to beyond, from good to good endeavouring, let us realise *that* which has no beyond.' '*That*' in the text is the monastic ideal of India: 'release,' but it will not have been the Founder's ideal. In his day '*That*' was the God in Man. And this is the way in which I hear him teaching Man-as-the-Seeker to his world.

I have by no means mentioned all that this book contains of interest and value. There is the charming talk of Gotama to his friend Uggaha's daughters (Sutta No. 33, p. 28 *f.*), wise guidance meet to rank beside the talks to Sigāla in the Dīgha, and to Visākhā, in the first of these three volumes—precious survivals in a monk-swamped literature. There is the epithet, given to some men, of 'incurable' (*atekiccha*, pp. 112, 286), occurring also in the Majjhima Collection (I, 393), with the fearful implication, possibly monkish, of a Buddhist hell that is unending. There is the interesting context about Licchavis and Vajjians, suggesting that the former were not, as is supposed, included in the latter (p. 62). Here we have agreed that the rendering *bhavissanti*, like that of *bhavissati* in Vol. II, p. 44, should be literal—'will become'—and not a colloquially expressed assumption, such as I do not find we are warranted in tracing in Pāli idiom.

But I have already said more than enough, and will end on one very lovely note that brings the great Helper very near (p. 61): 'And in him reflecting hereon the Way comes into being; and that Way he follows, makes become, makes more. . . .'

Now am I bound to become one turning no more back;
I shall become a Further-Farer in the life divine.

C. A. F. RHYS DAVIDS.

CHIPSTEAD, SURREY,
September, 1933.

THE TRANSLATOR'S PREFACE

SINCE Mrs. Rhys Davids has kindly written the Introduction to this volume, it is only necessary for me to add here a few remarks.

The translation is based on the P.T.S. edition, but I have noted—and here and there adopted—many of the readings of the 1915 Colombo Sinhalese edition by T. D. Sri Devamitta, referred to in my notes as *S.e.* No *roman* edition of Buddhaghosa's Commentary, *Manorathapūraṇī*, on these two Nipātas was available, but Mr. F. L. Woodward kindly transliterated for me the appropriate sections of the Sinhalese edition of that work.

This volume very naturally does not follow, word for word, the renderings of other translators of the stock similes, paragraphs and phrases that recur here. That these are numerous will be seen from the references in my notes, and, excepting the similes, many more in most cases could be given. A departure in word-rendering, calling for comment, is the adoption of Lord Chalmers' 'canker' (see *Further Dialogues*) for the hitherto generally untranslated *āsava*: 'that which flows.' Some rendering seemed desirable, since the Pāli word in many contexts can convey little or nothing to the English reader unversed in Pāli-Buddhist terms; and canker, though not a precise etymological equivalent, has the meaning in one sense of a disease with a discharge.

As a matter of interest to students of comparative religion, I would draw attention to the parallel passages of sentiment and simile in the Bible, referred to in the footnotes; I give also a few found in Brāhmanic literature, and these, no doubt, could be greatly extended. The interesting references to the German translation by Nyāṇatiloka have been inserted by Mrs. Rhys Davids.

In Index IV of Pāli words, I have listed words occurring in the text and Commentary that are either not found in the P.T.S. Dictionary or are used in a sense not noted there.

I would here express my thanks to both Mrs. Rhys Davids and Mr. Woodward for reading through my typescript and for their advice and help, which have been invaluable. Owing to my return to Ceylon, I have not been able to see the proofs of the Indexes through the Press; I am much indebted to Mrs. Rhys Davids for undertaking this.

E. M. HARE.

WELLINGTON CLUB,
1933.

CONTENTS

THE BOOKS OF THE FIVES AND SIXES

PART III

(The Book of the Fives)

(The Book of the Sixes)

Indexes

CORRIGENDA

Note by Mrs. Rhys Davids.—On p. viii the sentence *It is not found there* needs thus much of modification: It is true that six items elsewhere, but not here, called *abhiññā* occur twice in the Book of the Sixes, but the occurrence in both cases has features which rather endorse than contradict the hypothesis that they were originally a set of Five. (*a*) They do not occur *as a set* of six things (*dhammā*, etc.). (*b*) In the former occurrence they are called, in an *alternative version*, a set of qualities 'worthy of offerings'; in the latter occurrence they are called collectively (but without number) 'variety of iddhi' (*iddhividhā*), and this Sutta *is omitted* from the *Uddāna* (list of contents).

Page 6, note 4, *delete* See Introduction.

Page 7, line 5, *read* that is to say.

Page 9, § vii, *for* perfect,-ed *read* accomplished.

Page 39 *f.*, 'to think much of it,' is lit. to take delight in it.

Page 57, line 2, *for* Tho' *read* Ay (or Yea).

Page 58, line 8, *more lit.* 'I will make become one who has guarded sense-doors.'

Page 124, note 6, *add* 2nd ed., p. 320.

Page 146, note 2, Rhys Davids has recorded on the fly-leaf that he, and not H. Oldenberg, was responsible for this portion (*S.B.E. Vinaya Texts*). Also the passage cited, p. 183, note 4.

Page 148, note 2. *Add to* lxxxii: 2nd ed., p. xc *f.*

Page 153 *f.*, *for* neither by us *read* neither by me (*mayā*). In the Sixes, p. 215, the Pāli is again *mayā*.

Page 155, 'very purposive' is on p. 101 rendered 'very mental.'

Page 155, also 174, 179, well gone *may also be rendered* well going.

Page 161, note, *before* Sallekha *insert* (note) 3.

Page 171, note 2, *read* Es' âhaŋ.

Page 178, 'has stepped' *may also be rendered* are stepping.

Page 221, lines 3-5. *Cf. G.S.* i, p. 132.

Page 227, *for* existences *read* dwellings (*as on* p. 13). *Cf.* p. 203.

Page 230, *for* godly man *read* brahman.

Page 243, note 1. *Cf.*, however, *K.S.* v, p. 320, as more modern in outlook.

Page 284, verse. Fausböll translates 'who does not stick in the middle.' 'Sage' is here *mantar.*

Page 291, note 2. *To first citation add* 2nd ed., p. 269, note.

Page 304, note 6. *To* trsl. 267 *add* 2nd ed., p. 245, note 2.

Three or four inaccuracies in accents are not mentioned here.

THE BOOK OF THE GRADUAL SAYINGS

(*ANGUTTARA-NIKĀYA*)

THE BOOK OF THE FIVES AND SIXES

PART III

THE BOOK OF THE FIVES

Chapter I.—The Learner's Powers.[1]

§ i (1). *The powers in brief.*

Thus have I heard: Once the Exalted One dwelt near Sāvatthī, at Jeta Grove, in Anāthapiṇḍika's Park; and there he addressed the monks, saying: 'Monks.'

'Yes, lord,' they replied; and the Exalted One said:

'These are the five powers of a learner. What five?

The power of faith, of conscientiousness, of fear of blame, of energy and of insight.

These, monks, are the five powers of a learner.

Wherefore, monks, train yourselves thus:

We will become possessed of the learner's power called the power of faith; we will become possessed of the learner's power called the power of conscientiousness; we will become possessed of the learner's power called the power of fear of blame; we will become possessed of the learner's power called the power of energy; we will become possessed of the learner's power called the power of insight.

Thus should ye train yourselves, monks.'

§ ii (2). *The powers in detail.*

'Monks, these are the five powers of a learner. What five? (*Reply as in* § 1.)

And what, monks, is the power of faith?

---

[1] *Balāni.* As *Indriyāni* this set recurs at *A.* ii, 150; as *Balāni* at *D.* iii, 25 3; *M.* ii, 12, below V, § 204.

Herein, monks, the Ariyan disciple has faith and believes in the enlightenment of the Tathāgata: Of a truth he is the Exalted One, arahant, fully enlightened, abounding in wisdom and right, the well-gone, the world-knower, the incomparable tamer of tamable men, the teacher of devas and men, the Buddha, the Exalted One. This, monks, is called the power of faith.

And what, monks, is the power of conscientiousness?

Herein, monks, the Ariyan disciple is conscientious; he feels conscientious scruple when acting wrongly in deed, word and thought; on entering on evil and wrong states. This, monks, is called the power of conscientiousness.

And what, monks, is the power of the fear of blame?

Herein, monks, the Ariyan disciple is afraid of blame; he is afraid of the blame that comes when acting wrongly in deed, word and thought; on entering on evil and wrong states. This, monks, is called the power of the fear of blame.

And what, monks, is the power of energy?

Herein, monks, the Ariyan disciple, abiding in active energy, puts away all wrong things and takes to right things; steadfast and strenuous, he shirks not the burden of right things. This, monks, is called the power of energy.

And what, monks, is the power of insight?

Herein, monks, the Ariyan disciple has insight; he is endowed with insight into the way of growth and decay, with Ariyan penetration of the way to the utter destruction of Ill. This, monks, is called the power of insight.

These, monks, are the five powers of a learner.

Wherefore, monks, ye should train yourselves thus:

We will become possessed of the learner's powers. . . .

Thus train ye yourselves, monks.'

§ iii (3). *Ill.*

'Monks, possessing five qualities a monk, in this very world, lives ill at ease, vexed, troubled, pained; on the breaking up of the body, after death, an ill-faring may be expected[1] for him. What five?

[1] *Cf. It.* 22 *f.*; *S.* iii, 8; *A.* i, 202, below VI, § 75.

Monks, herein a monk is without faith, unconscientious, has no fear of blame, is indolent and lacking in insight.

Monks, possessing these five qualities . . . an ill-faring may be expected for him.

Monks, possessing five qualities a monk lives wholly at ease in this world, free of vexation, trouble and pain; on the breaking up of the body, after death, a well-faring may be expected for him. What five ?' (*The opposite qualities.*)

§ iv (4). *Due.*[1]

'Monks, possessing five qualities a monk is duly[2] cast into hell. What five ?

Herein a monk, faithless, unconscientious, reckless of blame, is indolent, is without insight.

Possessing these five a monk is duly cast into hell.

Monks, possessing five qualities a monk is duly set in heaven. What five ?' (*The opposite qualities.*)

§ v (5). *The training.*

'Monks, whatsoever monk or nun disavows the training and returns to the lower life,[3] five matters for self-blame and reproach[4] from the standpoint of Dhamma come to him here-now. What five ?

In you[5] (he thinks) there was verily no faith in right things, no conscientiousness, no fear of blame, no energy and no insight into right things.

Monks, whatsoever monk or nun disavows the training and returns to the lower life, these five matters for self-blame and reproach from the standpoint of Dhamma come to him here now.

Monks, whatsoever monk or nun lives the godly life in perfect

---

[1] Our text reads *bhataŋ*, but *Sinh. edit. kataŋ*; see *G.S.* i, 6 *n.* 2 on *yathābhataŋ*.

[2] *Yathābhataŋ*. *Cf.* below V, § 115.

[3] See notes on this phrase at *G.S.* i, 143; *Dial.* i, 223.

[4] The *Sinh. edit.* reads *vādânupātā*, our text *vādânuvādā*.

[5] *Te.*

purity, though with tearful face he cries in pain and distress, five matters for self-praise from the standpoint of Dhamma come to him here now. What five?

(He thinks) in you, verily, there was faith in right, conscientiousness, fear of blame, energy and insight.

Monks, these five matters for self-praise . . . come to him here now.'

§ vi (6). *The stepping in.*

'Monks, there is no stepping in of wrong, so long as faith is set on right things; but when faith has vanished, disbelief prevails and stays; then there is a stepping in of wrong.

Monks, there is no stepping in of wrong, so long as conscientiousness . . . fear of blame . . . energy . . . or insight is set on right things; but when insight has vanished, lack of insight prevails and stays; then there is a stepping in of wrong.'[1]

§ vii (7). *Of pleasures.*

'Almost all beings find delight in pleasures,[2] monks; and of the clansman, who has laid aside sickle and pingo[3] and gone forth from the home to the homeless life, it is right to say: By faith has the clansman gone forth. And why? Pleasures, monks, are gotten in youth; yea, those of all kinds. Moreover, monks, low pleasures and the middling sort and those that are high-pitched,[4] they are all just reckoned pleasures.

Monks,[5] suppose a foolish baby boy, sprawling on his back, were, owing to the carelessness of his nurse, to put a piece of stick or stone in his mouth; with what utmost haste would she at once attend to the matter and quickly remove it. And if she could not get at it at once she would clasp him round the

---

[1] The text gives in full.

[2] *Kāmesu palāḷitā*, so *Sinh. edit.* and *Comy.*, explaining: *vatthukāma-kilesakāmesu abhiratā*; see *DhS. trsl.* 43 *n.*

[3] *Comy.* The sickle to cut grass and the pingo to carry it away.

[4] *Comy.* apportions these pleasures to low-class people, middle-class and rajahs, respectively.

[5] This simile recurs at *M.* i, 395; the opening phrase is stock, *cf. M.* i, 324, ii, 24; *Mil.* 40.

head with her left hand, and with her right, crooking her finger, fetch it out, even though she drew blood. And why? Monks, such a thing is a danger to the child; it is not harmless, I say. Moreover, monks, such an act ought to be done by the nurse out of love, seeking the child's good, from pity and compassion. But when that boy is older and sensible, then, monks, she no longer looks after him, knowing: "The lad is now self-warded, has done with remissness."

In just the same way, monks, so long as right things are not done by a monk by faith, conscientiousness, fear of blame, energy and insight, that monk must be watched over by me; but when right things are so done, then I no longer look after him, knowing: "The monk is now self-warded,[1] has done with remissness."'

§ viii (8). *He falls away.*

'Monks, possessed of five things a monk falls away, finding no support in Saddhamma.[2] What five?

Without faith a monk falls away, finding no support in Saddhamma; without conscientiousness . . . without fear of blame . . . being indolent . . . and without insight a monk falls away, finding no support in Saddhamma.

Monks, possessed of these five . . . a monk . . . finds no support.

Monks, possessed of five things a monk falls not away, finding support in Saddhamma. What five?' (*The opposite qualities.*)[3]

§ ix (9). *No respect.*

'Monks, possessed of five things an unruly[4] monk, lacking in respect, falls away, finding no support in Saddhamma. What five?

---

[1] *Attagutto. Dhp.* 379.

[2] On this emphatic term (usually rendered 'good' dhamma) see Vol. I, ix *ff.*

[3] The text repeats in full.

[4] *Appatisso,* the *Comy.* explains: *ajeṭṭhako anīcavutti,* 'having no senior, not of humble conduct.'

Without faith, an unruly monk, lacking in respect, falls away, finding no support in Saddhamma. . . .' (*Repeat* § 8 *with changes and for the converse.*)[1]

§ x (10). *Without respect.*

'Monks, possessed of five things an unruly monk, lacking in respect, cannot attain to growth, increase and fulness in this discipline of Dhamma.[2] What five ?

Without faith, an unruly monk, lacking in respect, cannot attain to growth, increase and fulness in this discipline of Dhamma. . . .' (*Continue as in* § 8 *with changes and for the converse.*)

Chapter II.—The Powers.

§ i (11). *Things unheard of.*

'Monks, I claim to have reached supreme mastery in things not heard of formerly.[3]

Monks,[4] for a Ṭathāgata these are the five powers of one who has won through to the truth, possessed of which a Tathāgata claims the chief place, roars the lion's roar among the peoples and sets rolling the Divine Wheel. What five ?

The power of faith, the power of conscientiousness, the power of the fear of blame, the power of energy and the power of insight.

Monks, for a Tathāgata these are the five powers. . . .'

---

[1] The text repeats in full.

[2] This is a stock phrase; *cf. A.* ii, 26; *It.* 113; *Vin.* i, 60.

[3] *Cf. M.* ii, 211 for this phrase, suggestive, where it stands, of later insertion; *Comy.* for *dhammā*: things, glosses with *catusaccadhammā*.

[4] This passage recurs at *M.* i, 69; *S.* ii, 27; *A.* ii, 9; v, 33, etc., where generally ten powers are referred to, and are totally different from these five. As a set these five do not appear to occur except in this Section; they are included in the *Sevens*; see *A.* iv, 3, also *D.* iii, 253. It is difficult to see how they are the powers of a Tathāgata. *Comy.* observes: *Yathā tehi gantabbaŋ tath' eva gatāni pavattāni ñāṇabalāni.* See Introduction.

§ ii (12). *The peak.*

'Monks, there are these five powers of a learner. What five?

The power of faith, conscientiousness, fear of blame, energy and insight.

Monks, these are the five. Monks, of these five learner's powers this is the chief, this is the binder, this is the tie, that to say: the power of insight.

Monks,[1] just as in a house with a peaked roof, this is the chief, this is the binder, this is the tie,[2] that is to say: the peak; even so, monks, of these five learner's powers . . . this is the chief . . . to wit: the power of insight.

Wherefore, monks, train yourselves thus:

We will become possessed of the learner's powers. . . . (*Continue as in* § 1.) Train yourselves thus, monks.'

§ iii (13). *The powers in brief.*

'Monks, there are these five powers. What five?

The power of faith, the power of energy, the power of mindfulness, the power of concentration and the power of insight.

Monks, these are the five powers.'

§ iv (14). *The powers in detail.*

'Monks, these five . . . (*as before*). And what is the power of faith? (*Repeat as in* § 2.)

And what is the power of energy? (*Repeat as in* § 2.)

And what is the power of mindfulness?

Herein, monks, the Ariyan disciple is mindful; he is endowed with the highest mindfulness and discrimination; he remembers and calls to mind what was said and done long ago. This, monks, is called the power of mindfulness.

And what is the power of concentration?

Herein, monks, the Ariyan disciple,[3] aloof from sensuous appetites, aloof from evil ideas, enters and abides in the first

---

[1] This simile recurs at *M.* i, 322; for allied similes see below VI, § 53.

[2] *Sanghātaniya*, so *Comy.* and *S.e.*; *M. sanghātanika*, but see p. 557. *P.E.D.* does not notice the former.

[3] See *DhS. trsl.* 43 *ff.* and full notes there.

musing, wherein applied and sustained thought works, which is born of solitude and is full of joy and ease; suppressing applied and sustained thought, he enters and abides in the second musing, which is self-evolved, born of concentration, full of joy and ease, free from applied and sustained thought, and there the mind becomes calm and one-pointed; free from the zest for joy, mindful and self-possessed, he enters and abides in the third musing, and experiences in his being that ease whereof the Ariyans declare: He that is tranquil and mindful dwells at ease; by putting away ease and by putting away ill, by the passing away of happiness and misery he was wont to feel, he enters and abides in the fourth musing, which is utter purity of mindfulness, which comes of disinterestedness and is free of ease and ill. This, monks, is called the power of concentration.

And what is the power of insight? (*Repeat as in* § 2.)

Monks, these are the five powers.'[1]

§ v (15). *Where to be seen.*

'Monks, there are these five powers. What five? (*Repeat as in* § 13.)' And where, monks, is the power of faith to be seen? In the four factors[2] of Streamwinning. There is the power of faith to be seen.

And where, monks, is the power of energy to be seen? In the four right efforts.[3] There is the power of energy to be seen.

And where, monks, is the power of mindfulness to be seen? In the four uprisings of mindfulness.[4] There is the power of mindfulness to be seen.

And where, monks, is the power of concentration to be seen? In the four musings.[5] There is the power of concentration to be seen.

---

[1] This set is found throughout the Canon—*e.g.*, *M.* ii, 12; *S.* v, 219; referred to at *D.* ii, 120.

[2] For one set see below V, § 179; *K.S.* ii, 49; *Dial.* ii, 99 (as the Mirror of Dhamma), but see *D.* iii, 227 for another, probably here referred to.

[3] *K.S.* v, 219 *ff.*

[4] See *K.S.* v, 119 *ff.*, there called 'stations.'

[5] As in § 14.

And where, monks, is the power of insight to be seen? In the four Ariyan truths.[1] There the power of insight is to be seen.

These, monks, are the five powers.'

§ vi (16). *The peak.*

(*Apply the simile in* § 12 *to these five powers.*)[2]

§ vii (17). *For whose good? (a).*

'Monks, possessed of five things a monk is set on his own good, but not the good of another. Of what five?

Herein, monks, a monk is perfect in virtue himself, but does not strive to perfect virtue in another; he is perfect in concentration himself, but does not strive to perfect concentration in another; his own release[3] is perfected, but he does not strive that another's should be; his own vision[4] and knowledge of release are perfected, but he does not strive that another's should be.

Monks, possessed of these five things a monk is set on his own good, but not the good of another.'

§ viii (18). *The same (b).*

'Monks, possessed of five things a monk is set on the good of another, but not his own good. Of what five?' (*The opposite of* § 17.)

§ ix (19). *The same (c).*

'Monks, possessed of five things a monk is neither set on his own good, nor the good of another. Of what five?'

(*In no case is he perfect himself, or strives to perfect another.*)

---

[1] Ill, its coming to be, etc.

[2] The text repeats in full.

[3] *Comy.* the fruit of arahantship.

[4] *Comy.* review (*paccavekkhana*) as in a mirror; *cf. M.* i, 415; *UdA.* 233.

§ x (20). *The same* (*d*).

'Monks, possessed of five things a monk is set on his own good, and the good of another as well. Of what five?' (*The opposite of* § 19.)[1]

Chapter III.—The Fivefold.

§ i (21). *Without respect* (*a*).

'Monks, that a disrespectful and unruly monk, not dwelling in harmony with his fellows in the godly life, will keep the minor precepts[2]—such a thing is not possible; that he will keep the learner's code[3] without keeping the minor precepts; the virtues[4] without the learner's code; right views without the virtues; right concentration without right views—such a thing is not possible.

But, monks, that a monk, respectful and obedient, dwelling in harmony with his fellows in the godly life, will keep the minor precepts—such a thing shall surely be; and that if he keep the minor precepts, he will keep the learner's code; if the learner's code, the virtues; if the virtues, right views; if right views, right concentration—such a thing shall surely be.'

§ ii (22). *The same* (*b*).

'Monks, that a disrespectful and unruly monk, not dwelling in harmony with his fellows in the godly life, will keep the

---

[1] The persons in these four suttas are called by the *Comy.* the virtuous, the wicked but learned, the unlearned and wicked, the learned arahant. The general form recurs elsewhere—*e.g.*, *A.* ii, 95 *ff.*; iv, 220; *D.* iii, 233.

[2] *Abhisamācārikaŋ dhammaŋ*. *Comy.* the highest conduct in accord with the duties (*vatta*, *Ch.* 557), the declared morality. *Cf. Vism.* 11.

[3] *Sekhaŋ dhammaŋ*. *Comy. sekha-sīlaŋ*, for which see *G.S.* i, 199. At *Vism.* 12 *n.* 3 (also *trsl.*) this passage is said to be quoted, but there '*ādibrahmacariyaka*' replaces our '*sekha*.' See below VI, §§ 67-8.

[4] *Sīlāni*. *Comy.* the four great '*sīlas*'; this seems to be a commentarial division; see Rhys Davids' note at *Q. of M.* ii, 57; moreover, the word '*mahāsīlāni*' does not seem to occur in the *Nikāyas*, though at *D.* i, 12 there is a subdivision called '*mahā-sīlaŋ*,' which is probably a late editorial addition. There is a fourfold division given at *Vism.* 11, also *J.* iii, 195; this is given at *Q. of M.* ii, 221, and is shown as being additional to the *sīlaŋ* of *D.* i, 4-12.

minor precepts—such a thing is not possible; that he will keep the learner's code without keeping the minor precepts; the whole body[1] of virtues without the learner's code; the whole body of concentrative exercises without the virtues; the whole body of insight without the concentrative exercises—such a thing is not possible.'

(*But the converse, monks, shall surely be.*)[2]

§ iii (23). *The debasements.*

'Monks,[3] there are these five debasements of gold by reason of which debased gold is neither pliable nor workable, nor bright, but is brittle and of no use for the best work. What five?

Iron, copper, tin, lead and silver.[4]

Monks, these five debase gold. . . .

But when gold is free of these five debasements, it is pliable and workable and bright, nor is it brittle, but fit for the best work; and whatever sort of ornament one wants, whether a signet-ring or an ear-ring, a necklace or a gold chain, it can be used for that.[5]

In just the same way, monks, there are these five debasements of the mind by reason of which a debased mind is neither pliable nor workable nor bright, but is brittle[6] and not rightly composed for the destruction of the cankers. What five?

Sensual desire, ill-will, sloth and torpor, flurry and worry, and doubt.[7]

---

[1] *Khandha*. *Comy*. *rāsi* (heap). The three constantly recur: *D*. iii, 229; *M*. i, 301; *A*. i, 291; *It*. 51; *Vin*. i, 62.

[2] The text repeats in full.

[3] *Cf*. the opening of this sutta with *K.S*. v, 77 (I think we ought to read 'easily broken up,' not 'nor . . .' there, as our text and *A*. i, 254) and the whole with *G.S*. i, 231 *ff*.

[4] This set is stock: *S*. v, 92; *D*. ii, 351; *J*. ii, 296 (*rajataṃ* for *sajjhuṃ* there, as our *Comy*.); *Mil*. 331. Our text reads *sajjhaṃ*, *S.e*. as *Comy*.

[5] This phrase recurs at *A*. i, 254 (quoted at *Vism*. 247), but there the reading is *paṭṭakāya* for our *muddikāya* (*S.e*. agrees).

[6] *K.S*. *loc. cit*. 'not'; our *Comy*. *ārammaṇe cuṇṇavicuṇṇabhāvūpagamanena bhijjanasabhāvaṃ*.

[7] For this set see *D*. i, 246; *M*. i, 60; *S*. v. 60; *A*. iv, 457, etc.

Monks, these five debase the mind. . . .

But when the mind is free of these five debasements, it is pliable and workable and bright, nor is it brittle, but is rightly composed for the destruction of the cankers; and one can bend the mind to the realization by psychic knowledge of whatever condition is realizable by psychic knowledge, and become an eyewitness in every case, whatever the range may be.[1]

Should one wish: I would experience psychic power in manifold modes—being one, I would become many; being many, I would become one; I would become visible or invisible;[2] I would go without let through walls, through fences, through mountains, as if they were but air; I would dive in and out of the earth, as if it were but water; I would walk on water without parting it, as if it were earth; I would travel cross-legged through the air, as a bird on the wing; I would handle and stroke the moon and the sun, though they be so powerful and strong; I would scale[3] the heights of the world even in this body[4]—one becomes an eyewitness in every case, whatever the range may be.

Should one wish: With the celestial means[5] of hearing, purified and surpassing that of men, I would hear sounds both of devas and mankind, both far and near—one becomes an eyewitness in every case, whatever the range may be.

Should one wish: I would compass and know with my mind the thoughts of other beings, other persons; I would know the passionate mind as such, the mind free therefrom as such; I would know the malignant mind as such, the mind free therefrom as such; I would know the infatuated mind as such,

---

[1] See *G.S.* i, 233; *M.* i, 494; *A.* iv, 421; the phrase is stock.

[2] See *Bu.'s* comment at *Vism. trsl.* 452.

[3] *Saŋvatteyyaŋ*. *S.e.*: *vasaŋ vatteyyaŋ*, see note at *K.S.* v, 233.

[4] This passage and the following are the stock sets of psychic power; in addition to the references given in *n.* 1 above see *Dial.* i, 88; *K.S.* v, 236. *S.e.* here does not give in full, but it reads at *A.* i, 255 (p. 154): *abhijjamāno*, see *P.E.D.* *s.v.*

[5] See *Vism. trsl.* 472 *ff.*

the mind free therefrom as such; I would know the congested mind as such, the mind free therefrom as such; I would know the diffuse mind as such, the mind free therefrom as such; I would know the lofty mind as such, the low mind as such; I would know the better mind as such, the inferior mind as such; I would know the controlled mind as such, the uncontrolled as such; I would know the liberated mind as such, the mind not freed as such—one becomes an eyewitness in every case, whatever the range may be.

Should one wish: I would call to mind many a previous dwelling, that is to say, one birth, two births, three births, four, five, ten, twenty, thirty, forty, fifty, a hundred births, a thousand births, a hundred thousand births, many an æon of progression, many an æon of destruction, many an æon of both progression and destruction; that in each such was my name, such my clan, such my caste, such my food, such my experience of happiness and ill, such my span of life; that faring on thence I arose there, when such was my name, clan, caste, and so forth, faring on thence I arose here; thus I would call to mind each detail and circumstance of my many previous dwellings—one becomes an eyewitness in every case, whatever the range may be.

Should one wish: With the celestial eye, purified and surpassing that of men, I would see beings faring on and being reborn, some low, some lofty, some beautiful, some ugly, some happy, some miserable; I would see them pass according to their works; thus these worthies were given over to evil ways in deed, word and thought, defamers of the Ariyans, holders of wrong views, reaping the reward accordingly, such, on the breaking up of the body after death, were reborn in hell, the wayward way, the ill way, the abyss, hell; or, those acted rightly in deed, word and thought, they were no defamers of the Ariyans, but held right views and reaped their reward accordingly, such, on the breaking up of the body after death, were reborn in heaven, that happy place of bliss; thus, with the celestial eye, purified and surpassing that of men, I would see beings faring on and being reborn, some low, some lofty and so forth; I would see them pass according to their works—

one becomes an eyewitness in every case, whatever the range may be.[1]

Should one wish: Having destroyed the cankers, I would enter and abide in the emancipation of the mind, in the emancipation of insight, which is free of the cankers, having realized that state by my own knowledge even in this very life—one becomes an eyewitness in every case, whatever the range may be.'

§ iv (24). *For the wicked.*

'Monks,[2] for the wicked, who lack virtue, right concentration is perforce destroyed; when right concentration is not, true[3] knowledge and insight are perforce destroyed in one who lacks right concentration; when true knowledge and insight are not, aversion[4] and dispassion are perforce destroyed in one who lacks true knowledge and insight; when aversion and dispassion are not, emancipated[5] knowledge and insight are perforce destroyed in one who lacks aversion and dispassion.

Monks, just as in the case of a tree, devoid of branches and leaves, its shoots come not to maturity, nor its bark, nor its sapwood, nor its core; even so in the wicked, who lack virtue, concentration[6] . . . and the rest are perforce destroyed.

Monks, in the moral and virtuous, right concentration perforce thrives; when there is right concentration, true knowledge and insight perforce thrive in one who has right concentration; when there is true knowledge and insight, aversion and dispassion perforce thrive in one who has true knowledge and insight; when there is aversion and dispassion, emancipated knowledge and insight perforce thrive in one who has aversion and dispassion.

Monks, just as in the case of a tree, possessing branches

---

[1] These five *came* to be known as the Abhiññā's, or super-knowledges, and a sixth, of a discrepant kind, was added. Inserted below, it is here out of place.

[2] *Cf.* below V, § 168; VI, § 50; *A.* iv, 99, 336; v, 4, 313.

[3] *Comy. taruṇa*: fresh insight, see *DhS. trsl.* 256 *n.*

[4] *Comy. balava-vipassanā.*

[5] *Comy. phalavimutti.*

[6] The text repeats in full.

and leaves, its shoots, its bark, sapwood and core come to maturity; even so in the moral and virtuous concentration[1] . . . and the rest perforce thrive.'

§ v (25). *Helped on.*

'Monks, helped on[2] by five things right view ripens to mind-emancipation and the advantages therefrom, ripens to insight-emancipation and the advantages therefrom. By what five?

Herein, monks, right view is helped on by virtue, by learning, by discussion, by tranquillity and by inward vision.[3]

Monks, helped on by these five things right view ripens to mind-emancipation and the advantages therefrom, ripens to insight-emancipation and the advantages therefrom.'

§ vi (26). *Release.*[4]

'Monks, there are these five spheres[5] of release wherein the unreleased mind of a monk, abiding zealous, ardent and resolute, finds release; or the cankers, not yet wholly destroyed, come to complete destruction; or the unsurpassed peace from effort, not yet attained, is won. What five?

Monks, take the case when the Master, or some fellow in the godly life who acts as teacher, instructs a monk in Dhamma—while he teaches, that monk partakes of both the spirit and the letter of this Dhamma; from this experience gladness[6] springs

---

[1] The text repeats in full.

[2] *Anuggahitā*. *Comy. anurakkhitā*, likening the matter to a man growing a mango tree: intuitive right view is the planting of a sweet mango seed; the care of it by virtue, making the boundary; learning is the watering; discussion, the root-cleaning; tranquillity, the clearing away of the insects, etc.; inward vision, the freeing of the cobwebs. As a tree, thus cared for, will grow quickly and bear fruit, so will right view, cared for by virtue, etc., grow quickly by reason of the Way and bear the fruit of mind-emancipation and insight-emancipation.

[3] The last four of this set recur at *A.* ii, 140 (with *savana* for *suta*).

[4] *Vimutti*. The whole sutta recurs at *D.* iii, 241; from the notes at *Dial.* iii, 229 it would seem that *D.A.* is much the same as our *Comy.*

[5] *Āyatanāni*. *Comy. kāraṇāni*. *Dial.* occasions.

[6] *Pāmujja*. *Comy. taruṇapīti*.

up; from that, zest;[1] in such a state his whole[2] being calms down; when he is calm, ease is experienced; and for him who dwells at ease the mind is composed.[3] Monks, this is the first sphere of release wherein the unreleased mind of a monk, abiding zealous, ardent and resolute, finds release; or the cankers, not yet wholly destroyed, come to complete destruction; or the unsurpassed peace from effort, not yet attained, is won.

Again, monks, when the Master, or some fellow . . . does not instruct him in Dhamma, but he himself instructs others in detail as he has heard it, as he has learnt it by heart —while he thus teaches, he partakes of this Dhamma and experiences gladness, zest, calm and ease, whereby his mind is composed. Monks, this is the second sphere of release. . . .[4]

Or else . . . he repeats Dhamma, as he has heard it, as he has learnt it; and while doing so . . . his mind is composed. Monks, this is the third sphere of release. . . .[4]

Or else . . . in his heart he ponders and reflects on Dhamma, as he has heard it, as he has learnt it; he reviews it carefully in his mind; and while doing so . . . his mind is composed. Monks, this is the fourth sphere of release. . . .

Or else . . . some concentration sign[5] is rightly grasped by him, rightly held by the attention, rightly reflected on, rightly penetrated by insight; and while this takes place, he partakes of both the spirit and letter of this Dhamma; from this experience gladness springs up; from that, zest; in such a state his whole being calms down; when he is calm, ease is experienced; and for him who dwells at ease the mind is composed. Monks, this is the fifth sphere of release wherein the unreleased mind of a monk, abiding zealous, ardent and

---

[1] *Pīti. Comy. tuṭṭhā kārabhūtā balavapīti.*

[2] *Kāyo. Comy. nāmakāyo,* 'name and shape.'

[3] Composed by the concentration which is the fruit of arahantship (*Comy.*). The passage is a stock one and recurs at *D.* i, 73; *M.* i, 37; *Vin.* i, 294.

[4] The text repeats in full.

[5] *Comy.* a concentration on one of the thirty-eight objects (*ārammaṇa-kasiṇa*); see *Vism. trsl.* 97; *Cpd.* 54.

resolute, finds release; or the cankers not yet wholly destroyed, come to complete destruction; or the unsurpassed peace from effort, not yet attained, is won.

Monks, these are the five spheres of release. . . .'

§ vii (27). *Concentration.*[1]

'Monks, being wise and mindful, make become immeasurable concentration; for in those who do, verily in each one of you, there shall arise a fivefold[2] knowledge. What fivefold knowledge?

"This concentration is verily a present ease and a source of ease for the future"—even in each this knowledge arises; "This concentration is Ariyan,[3] not of the flesh"—even this . . .; "This concentration is not the practice of base men"[4]—even this; "This concentration is the peace, the excellent thing,[5] the winning of calm, the attainment of one-pointedness, and the restraint that prevails is not a conscious restraint"—even this; "Self-possessed, I verily enter upon this concentration, self-possessed, I verily emerge from this concentration"—even in each this knowledge arises.

Monks, being wise and mindful, make become immeasurable concentration; for in each there shall arise this fivefold knowledge.'

§ viii (28). *The five-limbed.*

'Monks, I will teach you how to make become the five-limbed Ariyan right concentration; listen attentively and pay heed and I will speak.'

'Even so, lord,' they replied, and the Exalted One said:

'Monks,[6] take the case of a monk, who, aloof from sensuous appetites, enters and abides in the first musing; he steeps

---

[1] *Samādhi.*

[2] These five recur at *D.* iii, 278 (*Dial.* iii, 256), the fifth at *G.S.* i, 233.

[3] *Comy. kilesehi ārakattā ariyo*, but see *A.* iv, 145.

[4] But of Buddhas and great men (*Comy.*).

[5] *Comy.* not subject to satiety (*atappaniyaṭṭhena*).

[6] *Cf.* the whole of this sutta with *D.* i, 74 (*D.A.* i, 217 is materially the same as our *Comy.*), 232; *M.* i, 276; ii, 15; iii, 92.

and drenches and fills and suffuses this body[1] with a zest and ease, born of solitude, so that there is not one particle[2] of the body that is not pervaded by this lone-born zest and ease. Monks, just as a handy bathman or attendant might strew bath-powder in some copper basin and, gradually sprinkling water, knead it together so that the bath-ball gathered up the moisture, became enveloped in moisture and saturated both in and out, but did not ooze moisture;[3] even so a monk steeps, drenches, fills and suffuses this body with zest and ease, born of solitude, so that there is not one particle of the body that is not pervaded by this lone-born zest and ease. Monks, this is firstly how to make become the five-limbed Ariyan right concentration.

Or a monk, suppressing applied and sustained thought. . . . enters and abides in the second musing; he likewise steeps this body with zest and ease. . . . Monks, imagine a pool with a spring, but no water-inlet either on the east side or on the west or on the north or on the south, and suppose the (rain-) deva supply not proper rains from time to time—cool waters would still well up from that pool, and that pool would be steeped, drenched, filled and suffused with the cold water so that not a drop but would be pervaded by the cold water; in just the same way, monks, a monk steeps his body with zest and ease. . . . Monks, this is secondly how to make become the five-limbed Ariyan right concentration.

Again, a monk, free from the fervour of zest, . . . enters and abides in the third musing; he steeps and drenches and fills and suffuses this body with a zestless ease so that there is not one particle of the body that is not pervaded by this zestless ease. Monks, just as in a pond of blue, white and red water-lilies,[4] the plants are born in water, grow in water, come not

---

[1] *Kāya*, here *karaja-* (*Comy.*).

[2] *Comy.* instances, skin, flesh and blood.

[3] *Comy.* so that you can put it in your pocket (*ovaṭṭikāyaŋ*).

[4] *Uppala*, *paduma*, and *puṇḍarīka*. *Comy.* observes that the first may be any of the three colours; the second is white and has a hundred leaves (see *Kh.A.* 67 for the use of these); the last is deficient in these hundred leaves and is red (*Childers* the white lotus). *Cf.* *S.* i, 138 for this simile.

out of the water, but, sunk in the depths, find nourishment, and from tip to root are steeped, drenched, filled and suffused with cold water so that not a part of them is not pervaded by cold water; even so, monks, a monk steeps his body in zestless ease. . . . Monks, this is thirdly how to make become the five-limbed Ariyan right concentration.

Again, a monk, putting away ease . . . enters and abides in the fourth musing; seated, he suffuses his body with purity by the pureness of his mind so that there is not one particle of the body that is not pervaded with purity by the pureness of his mind. Monks, just as a man might sit with his head[1] swathed in a clean cloth so that not a portion of it was not in contact with that clean cloth; even so a monk sits suffusing his body with purity. . . . Monks, this is fourthly how to make become the five-limbed Ariyan right concentration.

Again, the survey-sign[2] is rightly grasped by a monk, rightly held by the attention, rightly reflected upon, rightly penetrated by insight. Monks, just as someone might survey another, standing might survey another sitting, or sitting might survey another lying down; even so the survey-sign is rightly grasped by the monk, rightly held by the attention, rightly reflected upon, rightly penetrated by insight. Monks, this is fifthly how to make become the five-limbed Ariyan right concentration.

Monks, when a monk has thus made become and thus made abundant the five-limbed Ariyan concentration, he can bend his mind to realize by higher knowledge whatever condition is so realizable, and become an eyewitness in every case, whatever the range may be.

---

[1] *Sasīsa.*

[2] *Paccavekkhanānimitta.* *Comy.* -*ñāṇă*, of which there are 19 (*UdA.* 336; in detail: *Vism.* 676, *trsl.* 829). It is noteworthy that this item is omitted from the *D.* and *M.* suttas referred to above; but see *D.* iii, 278 (*Dial.* iii, 255), where Mrs. Rhys Davids translates 'images for retrospective thought,' adding in a note 'insight on emerging from ecstasy.' (The five at *D.* differ in items 2 and 4 from our set.) See *Cpd.* 58 on 'reviewing' after *Jhāna.* Our simile does not appear to recur elsewhere.

Monks,[1] suppose a water jar,[2] brimful of water so that a crow could drink from[3] it, were set on a dish; as soon as a strong man rocked[4] it to and fro would the water spill ?'[5]

'Yes, lord.'

'Even so, monks, when a monk has so made become and made abundant the five-limbed Ariyan right concentration, he can bend the mind to knowledge . . . whatever the range may be.

Monks,[6] imagine a tank on a level piece of ground, with dykes built up on its four sides, brimful of water so that a crow could drink from it; as soon as a strong man loosened the sides here and there would the water flow out ?'[5]

'Yes, lord.'

'Even so, monks, when a monk has so made become . . . concentration, he can bend the mind to knowledge . . . whatever the range may be.

Monks,[7] suppose a carriage, harnessed with thoroughbreds, with goad hanging[8] handy, were to stand on the level,[9] where four main roads meet; as soon as the coachman, a capable trainer and driver of horses, had mounted and grasped the reins in his left hand and with his right seized the goad, he would drive on or back,[10] as and how he pleased. Even so, monks, when a monk has so made become and made abundant the five-limbed Ariyan right concentration, he can bend the mind to realize by higher knowledge whatever condition is so realizable and become an eyewitness in every case, whatever the range may be.

---

[1] This simile recurs at *M.* iii, 96.

[2] *Comy.* a jar with cords around it (*sa-mekhalā*).

[3] See *S.B.E.* xi, 178 *n.*; this expression recurs at *D.* i, 244; *S.* ii, 134; *Vin.* i, 230; *Ud.* 90.

[4] *Āvajjeyya*, so *S.e.*; *P.E.D.*, to cause to yield (?), but suggests the *v.l. āvatteyya*, to turn round.

[5] *Āgaccheyya.*

[6] *Cf. M. loc. cit.*

[7] This recurs at *M.* i, 124; iii, 97; *S.* iv, 176.

[8] *Odhastu. Comy. ālambana.*

[9] *Subhūmiyaṃ*, so *S.e.*, but *Comy. sa-*, glossing *sama-*.

[10] *Sāreyya pi paccāsāreyya*; see *Vism. trsl.* 355, where this phrase is used of racehorses.

Should[1] he wish to experience psychic power . . .; to hear deva sounds . . .; to thought-read . . .; to call to mind previous dwellings . . .; to see beings faring on according to their deeds . . .; to enter and abide, with the cankers destroyed, in the emancipation of the mind, in the emancipation of insight . . ., he becomes an eyewitness in every case, whatever the range may be.'

§ ix (29). *The alley-walk.*

'Monks, there are these five advantages of an alley-walk.[2] What five?

It hardens[3] one for travelling; it is good for striving; it is healthy; (its use) tends to good digestion after one has eaten and drunk, munched and crunched; the concentration[4] won from (the thought of) an alley-walk lasts long.

Monks, these are the five advantages of an alley-walk.'

§ x (30). *The venerable Nāgita.*

Once the Exalted One with a great company of monks, while wandering for alms among the Kosalese, came to the brāhman village of Icchānangala, belonging to them. And there the Exalted One dwelt in the Icchānangala woodland thicket.

Now the brāhman householders of Icchānangala heard of this. 'Mark you,' they said, 'the recluse, Master Gotama, the Sakya, gone forth from the Sakyan clan, has come to Icchānangala and dwells in our wood near by; and of this same Master

---

[1] *D.* and *M.* continue with all this (see references in the first note to this sutta); for full details see above, § 23. Our text is not in full.

[2] *Cankama* (pron. *chankămă*). Later, it became a cloister or terraced walk; see *Vin.* ii, 190 (*Vin Texts*, iii, 103 *f.*); but originally it must have been merely a clearing in the land about a monk's dwelling; see *Comy.* at *J.* i, 7, which gives the five defects (*Buddhism in Translations*, Warren; *cf.* Rh. Davids, *Bud. Birth-stories*, p. 89 [1925]).

[3] *Comy.* one is able to endure a long journey.

[4] At *A.* iv, 87 the Buddha exhorts Moggallāna to concentrate on his alley-walk to get rid of torpor. *Comy.* here observes: 'By fixing the attention on the alley-walk, a concentration of the eight attainments (*A.* iv, 410, omitting the last) is won.'

Gotama this excellent report goes abroad: He is the Exalted One, arahant, perfectly enlightened, endowed with wisdom and righteousness, one well-gone, a world-knower, the unsurpassed, a tamer of tamable men, a teacher, a Buddha of devas and men, the Exalted One! Having realized more-knowledge himself, he declares it to this world with its devas and Māras and Brahmās, to this earth with its recluses and brāhmans, its devas and men; and he teaches Dhamma, lovely in the beginning, lovely in the middle and lovely in the end; and sets forth the godly life, utterly pure and perfect, both in spirit and letter. Well indeed is it to see such arahants!' And when the night was over, they went to the wood, taking with them a great deal of hard and soft food, and stood outside the entrance,[1] making a great din and uproar.

Now at that time the venerable Nāgita was the Exalted One's personal attendant.

Then the Exalted One called to the venerable Nāgita and said: 'Who are these, Nāgita, that make this great din and uproar? Like fisherfolk, methinks, with a great haul of fish!'

'These men, lord, are the brāhman householders of Icchānangala, who wait outside the gateway. They have brought much hard and soft food for the Exalted One and for the Order.'

'I have naught to do with homage, Nāgita, nor has homage aught to do with me. Whosoever cannot obtain at will, easily and without difficulty this happiness of renunciation, this happiness of seclusion, this happiness of calm and this happiness of enlightenment, which I can obtain at will, easily and without difficulty, let him enjoy that dung-like happiness, that sluggish happiness, that happiness gotten of gains, favours and flattery.'

'Lord, let the Exalted One accept (their offerings)! Let the Well-gone accept; now, lord, is the time for the Blessed One to accept! For wheresoever henceforth the Exalted One shall go, the brāhman householders of town and country will be just as inclined (to give). Lord, just as when the (rain-) deva

[1] All this is a stock opening; see below VI, § 42; *D.* i, 87, etc. Here the *Comy.* is silent on Icchānangala.

rains big drops, the water flows with the incline; even so, lord, wheresoever the Exalted One shall henceforth go, the brāhman householders of town and country will be inclined. And why? Lord, it is because of the virtue and wisdom of the Exalted One.'

'Nāgita, I have naught to do with homage, nor has homage aught to do with me. Whosoever cannot obtain at will . . . this happiness of renunciation, seclusion, calm and enlightenment, which I can obtain; let him enjoy that dung-like happiness, that sluggish happiness, that happiness[1] gotten of gains, favours and flattery.

Verily, Nāgita, whosoever eats, drinks, munches and crunches must answer the calls of nature; such is the issue of it.

Whosoever loves, to him change and a state of otherness must come, grief, lamentation, suffering, sorrow and despair;[2] such is the issue of it.

Whosoever is bent on applying himself to the symbol of the unattractive,[3] in him disgust for the symbol of the attractive is established; such is the issue of it.

Whosoever abides seeing impermanence in the six spheres of touch,[4] in him disgust for touch is established; such is the issue of it.

Verily, Nāgita, whosoever abides seeing the rise and fall in the fivefold body of attachment,[5] in him disgust for attachment is established; such is the issue of it.'

---

[1] All this recurs at *A.* iv, 341; the *Comy.* here is materially the same. Regarding Nāgita, see *Dial.* i, 198; *Brethren*, lxxxvi, and p. 350.

[2] *Cf. S.* ii, 274; iii, 7; *M.* ii, 110.

[3] *Asubha* and *subha*, from *sobhati*, to shine, therefore attractive (*cf. Vism. trsl.*: 'as a moth falls into the flame of a lamp, and a man, greedy for honey-drops, licks the blade of a knife besmeared with honey' —it is to avoid such snares that *asubha*-meditation is enjoined). The word is more generally translated 'the foul'; see *DhS. trsl.* 69; *Vism. trsl.* 205 *ff.*; *Expos.* 264 *ff.*

[4] Contact with the five senses and the mind.

[5] That is, all that is 'not the self,' or very man, the skandhas: the physical parts, the feelings, the perceptions, the dispositions and the consciousness; see Mrs. Rhys Davids' *Buddh. Psych.* 40-56.

Chapter IV.—Sumanā.

§ i (31). *Sumanā, the rajah's daughter.*

Once the Exalted One was dwelling near Sāvatthī, at Jeta Grove, in Anāthapiṇḍika's Park; and there Sumanā,[1] the rajah's daughter, with a following of five hundred royal maidens in five hundred chariots, came and visited him; and, after saluting, sat down at one side. So seated, she spoke thus to the Exalted One:

'Lord, suppose two of the Blessed One's disciples were alike in faith, alike in virtue and alike in insight, but one was an alms-giver and the other was not. Both, on the breaking up of the body after death, would be reborn in the happy heaven world; but among the devas, lord, would there be a distinction, a difference, between them?'

'There would be, Sumanā,' and the Exalted One said:

'The alms-giver, when come to deva-state, surpasses the non-giver in five ways: in divine life-span, beauty, happiness, honour and power.[2] In these five ways, Sumanā, the alms-giver, when come to deva-state, surpasses the non-giver.'

'But if, lord, faring on thence, they should return to this state here; when become human, lord, would there be a distinction, a difference, between them?'

'There would be, Sumanā,' and the Exalted One said:

'The alms-giver, as man, surpasses the non-giver in five ways: in human life-span, beauty, happiness, honour and power. In these five ways, Sumanā, the alms-giver, as man, surpasses the non-giver.'

'But if both, lord, were to go forth from the home into the

---

[1] The *Comy.* relates how she made her resolve in a former life under the Buddha Vipassi. She was the sister of Pasenadi, rajah of Kosala (Nepal), and went forth and won arahantship when old; see *Sisters*, p. 19. Except here and at *A.* iv, 345 in a list of *upāsikās*, her name does not seem to recur in the four *Nikāyas*. The notice at *C.H.I.* i, 181, so far as she is concerned, refers to the trsl. of *S.* i, 69 (*K.S.* i, 94 *n.*), not the text; it is curious *S.A.* does not mention that she was present at the Buddha-Pasenadi talk. Dh'pāla on *Thig.* 16 has much to say; see *Sisters, loc. cit.*

[2] This is a stock set; *cf. D.* iii, 145; *S.* iv, 275; *A.* i, 115.

homeless life; when gone forth, lord, would there be a distinction, a difference, between them ?'

'There would be, Sumanā,' and the Exalted One said:

'The alms-giver, when gone forth, surpasses the non-giver in five ways:[1] he is often asked to accept a robe, he is not rarely asked; often to accept alms, not rarely; often to accept a lodging, not rarely; often to accept medicaments for sickness, not rarely; with whomsoever he dwells in leading the godly life, such folk mostly act towards him with cordiality in their ways of living, talking and thinking; it is rare for them not to act cordially, cordially they offer service,[2] seldom without cordiality. In these five ways, Sumanā, an alms-giver, when gone forth, surpasses the non-giver.'

'But, lord, if both win arahantship; in that state would there be a distinction, a difference, between them ?'

'In that case, Sumanā, I verily declare there is no difference whatsoever, that is to say, comparing emancipation with emancipation.'

'It is amazing, lord, it is wonderful, lord, how far-reaching is the effect of giving alms and doing good deeds, since they are a help and a boon to one as a deva, a help and a boon to one as a man, yea, a help and a boon when one has gone forth !'

'It is even so, Sumanā, it is even as you have just said . . . .'[3]

Thus spake the Exalted One; and when the Well-gone had thus spoken, the Master spoke again and said:

'As[4] stainless on her sky-bound course, the moon
Outshines in splendour all the stars' array:
Just so the virtuous, believing man
In charity outshines the mean on earth.
Ev'n[5] as the hundred cloud-peaked thunder-storm,
In lightning wreathed, the hills and hollows fills

---

[1] This paragraph recurs below V, § 104, and at *A.* ii, 87; see *G.S.* ii, 97, differently translated. *Cf.* also *Dial.* i, 76, § 35 *f.*

[2] *Upahāraŋ upaharanti.* *Comy.* on *A.* ii observes: *kāyika-cetasika-upahāraŋ upaharanti, upanīyanti.*

[3] Text repeats.

[4] *Cf.* below VI, § 53 for this simile.

[5] This recurs at *S.* i, 100; *cf.* *It.* 66.

And rains upon the foison-bearing earth:
So does the seer, disciple of the Best,
The all-enlightened One, wise man, o'ertop
Mean men in these five things: long life and honour,
Beauty and happiness, abounding wealth;[1]
And after death lives blissfully in heaven.'

§ ii (32). *Cundī, the rajah's daughter.*

Once the Exalted One was dwelling near Rājagaha, at the Squirrels' Feeding Ground[2] in the Bamboo Grove; and there Cundī,[3] the rajah's daughter, attended by five hundred maidens in a like number of chariots, came and visited him and, after saluting, sat down at one side. Thus seated, Cundī, the rajah's daughter, spoke to the Exalted One thus:

'Lord, our royal brother, Cunda, says this: When a woman or man has taken refuge in the Buddha, has taken refuge in Dhamma, has taken refuge in the Order, abstains from taking life, from taking what is not given, from carnal lusts, from lying and from indulging in spirituous liquor, causing idleness; he will surely arise, on the breaking up of the body after death, to a fair course, not to an ill one. But I, lord, would ask the Exalted One: With one's trust in what sort of teacher will one surely arise, on the breaking up of the body after death, to a fair course and not to an ill one? With one's trust in what sort of Dhamma . . . what sort of Order . . .? And what sorts of virtuous practices must one perform to arise, after death, to a fair course and not to an ill one?'

[4]'Whatsoever beings there are, Cundī, whether footless, two-

---

[1] *Bhogaparibbūḷho*; the word used above is *ādhipateyya* ('power').

[2] This 'park' was given to the Order by the rajah Bimbisāra of Magadha (*Vin.* i, 39); for the legend of its name see Rockhill's *Life*, 43; Watter's *Yuan Chwang*, ii, 157; it was the first of its kind.

[3] Except at *A.* iv, 347 in a list and here she does not seem to be mentioned; *Comy.* on *A.* iv: *rājakumārī*, merely; here we have no comment. She and her brother (not mentioned elsewhere) may have been the children of Bimbisāra, who had at least three wives; see *C.H.I.* i, 183. Pron. Choondee.

[4] Omitting the fourth clause, what follows recurs at *A.* ii, 34; *It.* 87, including the *gāthā*. See *G.S.* ii. 38.

footed, four-footed or many-footed, whether with bodies or without, conscious or unconscious or neither conscious nor unconscious, of them the Tathāgata, arahant, the perfectly enlightened One,[1] is declared the best;[2] whosoever put their trust in the Buddha, put their trust in the best, and unto them is the best reward.

Whatsoever Dhammas are formulated or not formulated,[3] Cundī, of them (the Dhamma of) dispassion is declared the best. I mean: the crushing of pride, the quenching of thirst, the rooting out of lust, the cutting off of rebirth, the destruction of craving, dispassion, making an end, Nibbāna; whosoever put their trust in (this) Dhamma, put their trust in the best, and unto them is the best reward.[4]

Whatsoever orders or communities there are, Cundī, of them the Order of the Tathāgata's disciples is declared the best, that is to say, the four pairs of men,[5] the eight persons, that Order of disciples of the Exalted One, which is worthy of offerings, worthy of gifts, worthy of oblations, meet to be reverently saluted, the world's peerless field for merit; whosoever put their trust in the Order, put their trust in the best, and unto them is the best reward.

Whatsoever virtuous practices there are, Cundī, of them those[6] loved by the Ariyans are declared the best, that is to say,

---

[1] This clause also recurs at *A.* v, 21; *Mil.* 217.

[2] *Agga*: tip, top, first, chief, illustrious.

[3] This clause is dealt with exegetically at *Vism. trsl.* 337, where *dhammā* is said to mean states, conditions; *sankhatā*, conditioned, compounded; see also *P.E.D. s.v. yāvatā*. But it is inconceivable that the B. should talk about 'things definite and indefinite' (*P.E.D.*) to a young woman who asks him: 'What is truth?' but with Marcus Aurelius he might well say: 'First and foremost, keep unperturbed!' (*To himself*, viii, 5; Rendall's *trsl.*, 1910); *cf. Vin.* iii, 20: *bhagavatā anekapariyāyena rāgavirāgāya dhammo desito, madanimmadanāya*, etc., as here.

[4] For these last three clauses *cf. D.* ii, 94; iii, 227; *S.* iv, 272, and *Vism. trsl.* 252 *ff.*

[5] Those on the four stages of the Way; see *Vism. trsl.* 253.

[6] *Comy.* inserts *sīlāni*, with two MSS., and observes: *magga-phala-sampayuttakāni sīlāni*; *D.A.* ii, 544: *pañca sīlāni*. I suppose it is because these five are mentioned that this sutta is included in the 'Fives.'

those unbroken and without a rent, untarnished and without blemish, bringing freedom, praised by the wise, incorrupt and conducive to concentration; whosoever perform the virtues, loved by the Ariyans, perform the best, and unto them is the best reward.

For pious men who truly in the best
Distinguish best;[1] who in the Buddha see
The gift-worthy, the unsurpassed, the best;
In Dhamma best the ease of passion's calm;
And in the Order best th' unrivalled field
For merit—yea, for those who alms bestow
In the best place best merit doth increase,
And life and beauty, honour, fame and power,
Best happiness. Who gives unto the best,
Wise man, in Dhamma best composed, as man
Or deva, with the best attained, finds joy.'

§ iii (33). *Uggaha, a householder.*[2]

Once the Exalted One dwelt near Bhaddiya in Jātiyā Wood; and there Uggaha, Meṇḍaka's grandson, paid him a visit and, after saluting, sat down at one side. So seated, he said to the Exalted One:

'Lord, let the Exalted One accept a meal at my house to-morrow, he as fourth (with us three).'[3]

---

[1] *Aggaŋ dhammaŋ*: the best thing.

[2] Meṇḍaka (the ram) was a fabulously rich man with magic powers, which his household were also supposed to possess (see *Vin.* i, 240; Warren, *B. in T.* 448); he fed the B. and Order on a journey, after which travelling rations were allowed. Reference is made to him and his family at *Vism. trsl.* 443 (see *note* 1, p. 444; the stories, with less exaggeration, are told at *Vin. loc. cit.*); *UdA.* 158; *DhpA.*: *Visākhāya vatthu* (Warren, *op. cit.*, 451). His granddaughter was Visākhā (*Sisters*, p. 16). The family lived at Bhaddiya (our *Comy.* -*ike*)—according to Warren, in Bengal, but probably Magadha, since Bimbisāra sent his minister to witness M.'s magic (*Vin.*). I cannot trace Uggaha elsewhere, our *Comy.* is silent. Of Jātiyāvana, *Comy.* observes that the forest was one continuous stretch up the slope of the Himâlayas.

[3] *Atta-catuttho*; *cf. M.* i, 393. *Comy.* says he did so fearing his girls would be nervous (*olīnamānā*) among the monks and not able to take in the Buddha's words.

The Exalted One accepted by his silence.

Then Uggaha, Meṇḍaka's grandson, seeing the Exalted One had accepted, rose from his seat, saluted, and took his leave, keeping the Exalted One on his right.

Now when the night was over, the Exalted One, robing himself in the morning, took bowl and cloak and went to Uggaha's house, and there sat down on the seat made ready. And Uggaha, Meṇḍaka's grandson, served and satisfied the Exalted One by hand with plenty of hard and soft food; and when the Exalted One had removed his hand from his bowl, he sat down at one side. Thus seated, he said:

'Lord, these girls of mine will be going to their husbands' families; lord, let the Exalted One counsel them, let the Exalted One advise them, for their good and happiness for many a day!' Then the Exalted One spoke to them and said:

[1]'Wherefore, girls, train yourselves in this way: To whatsoever husband our parents shall give us—wishing our weal, seeking our happiness, compassionate, because of compassion—for him we will rise up early, be the last to retire, be willing workers, order all things sweetly and be gentle voiced.[2] Train yourselves thus, girls.

And in this way also, girls: We will honour, revere, esteem and respect all whom our husband reveres, whether mother or father, recluse or godly man, and on their arrival will offer them a seat and water. Train yourselves thus, girls.

And in this way also, girls: We will be deft and nimble at our husband's home-crafts, whether they be of wool or

---

[1] These five and the *gāthā* recur at *A.* iv, 265.

[2] At *D.* ii, 175 these terms are applied to the ideal woman, *itthiratana*; at *D.* i, 60, *M.* ii, 84, *S.* iii, 113 to a servant or a slave; see *D.A.* i, 168. *Cf. Brihaspati Smriti*, xxiv, 6 (*S.B.E.* xxxiii, 368): 'Rising before others, paying reverence to the elders of the family, preparing food and condiments and using a low seat and bed—thus have the duties of women been declared.' Also *Proverbs* xxxi: 'She riseth while it is yet night . . . she seeketh wool and flax and worketh willingly with her hands . . . she looketh well to the ways of her household, and eateth not the bread of idleness.'

cotton,[1] making it our business to understand the work, so as to do and get it done. Train yourselves thus, girls.

And in this way also, girls: Whatever our husband's household consist of—slaves, messengers and workfolk—we will know the work of each by what has been done, their remissness by what has not been done; we will know the strength and the weakness of the sick; we will divide the hard and soft food, each[2] according to his share. Train yourselves thus, girls.

And in this way also, girls: The money, corn, silver and gold that our husband brings home, we will keep safe watch and ward over it, and act as no robber, thief, carouser, wastrel therein. Train yourselves thus, girls.

Indeed, girls, possessed of these five qualities, women, on the breaking up of the body after death, are reborn among the devas of lovely form.

Active,[3] alert to cherish him alway,
Not to that man who brings[4] her every joy
She offers slight; nor will a good wife[5] move
To wrath her husband by some spiteful word;
And she reveres all whom her husband honours,
For she is wise. Deft, nimble, up betimes,
She minds his wealth amid his folk[6] at work
And sweetly orders all. A wife like this,
Who with her husband's wish and will complies,
Is born again where lovely devas dwell.'

---

[1] Of the former *Comy.* observes: Combing, washing, dyeing, plaiting, working, etc., goat's hair; of the latter: ginning (*vaṭṭana*); *piñjana*, ? carding, *lit.*: painting, in *Sk.* also to bleach: *phoṭana*, ? spinning, *lit.* either to boil or shake; *kantana*, weaving, more generally spinning.

[2] *Comy.* with *v.l.* reads *c' assa*, as at *A.* iv.

[3] I take *yo* to refer to *mātugāmo*.

[4] With *A.* iv and *Comy.* reading *-haraṃ* for *arahaṃ*. *Comy. -dadaṃ*.

[5] *Sotthi, Comy. su-itthi.*

[6] *Parijjanā*: doubling the 'j' is no doubt for the sake of the metre, and this spelling has crept into the prose version at *A.* iv, 269; see *P.E.D. s.v.*

§ iv (34). *Sīha, the general.*[1]

Once the Exalted One dwelt near Vesālī, at the Gabled Hall, in Mahāvana; and there general Sīha paid him a visit, saluted him, and sat down at one side. So seated, the general said to the Exalted One:

'Is it possible, lord, to show the visible result of giving?'

'It is possible, Sīha,' and the Exalted One said:

'The almsgiver, Sīha, the liberal man, is good and dear to many folk; since he is so, Sīha, this is the visible result of giving.

Again, the good and wise follow him; since they do so, Sīha, this is the visible result of giving.

Again, a good report concerning him goes about; since such occurs, Sīha, this is the visible result of giving.

Again, whatever company he enters, be it of nobles, brāhmans, householders or recluses, he enters with confidence and untroubled;[2] since he does so, Sīha, this is the visible result of giving.

Again, the almsgiver, the liberal man, on the breaking up of the body after death, is reborn in the happy heaven world; since that is so, Sīha, it is hereafter the result of giving.'

When he had thus spoken, general Sīha said to the Exalted One:

'Lord, those four visible results of giving declared by the Exalted One—not as to them go I by faith in the Exalted One; I just know those things. Lord, I am a giver, a liberal man, and am good and dear to many folk; many good and wise men follow me; a good report concerning me goes about. People say: General Sīha is an almsgiver, a worker and a servant of the Order; whatever company of nobles and so forth I enter, I do so with confidence and untroubled. I do not go by faith in the Exalted One in regard to these things,

---

[1] He was general of the Licchavis, whose capital was Vesālī, and who built this hall for the Buddha; they belonged to a confederacy; see *Buddh. India.* Sīha was much given to questions like these; *cf. A.* iv, 79 *ff.* He was originally a supporter of the Jains.

[2] *Amaṅkubhūta.*

I just know them. But when the Exalted One says to me: Sīha, a giver, a liberal man, on the breaking up of the body after death, is reborn in the happy heaven-world—it is this that I do not know, and it is herein that I go by faith in the Exalted One.'

'It is even so, Sīha, it is verily just as you say. . . .

> Good is the giver, folk will follow him,
> Fame he attains and honours grow; 'mong men
> He walks untroubled, being liberal
> And confident. Wherefore the wise give gifts;
> They put aside the stain of stinginess
> And, seeking bliss, long in the Thrice-Ten[1] stay,
> Finding delight in deva-fellowship.
>
> Th' occasion made, the good deed done, hence fare
> They on, self-radiant devas, wandering
> In Nandana,[2] glad, happy and content
> Amid the fivefold pleasures of the sense,
> Joyed in the teachings of the Unattached,[3]
> In heaven disciples of the Man Well-gone.'

§ v (35). *The advantages from gifts.*

'Monks, there are these five advantages from gifts. What five?

He is good and dear to many folk; good and wise men love him; a good report is spread abroad about him; he strays not from the householder's Dhamma;[4] and, on the breaking up

---

[1] *Tidive*; in *Theragāthā*, *ver.* 534, *tidivasmi*, one of the names for the next world.

[2] A grove in the heaven of the Thirty Devas; see *K.S.* i, 8 *n.*, v, 296, where such joy is said to be the lot of a *rājā-cakka-vattī*; or it may be a grove in another group of devas, for *sabba-devalokesu hi Nandana-vanaṁ atthi yeva* (*J.* i, 49). In the Tusita grove of this name the Bodhisatta waited prior to rebirth.

[3] *Asita*: the quotation from the *Comy.* in the text note should read *ani-*, not *ati-*; see *Brethren*, 404 *n.* 2 on this word.

[4] *Gihidhammā anapeto. Comy. akhaṇḍa-pañcasīlā*, the Dhamma of a *Buddhamātā*, *J.* i, 49.

of the body after death, he is reborn in the happy heaven-world.

Monks, these are the five advantages from gifts.

> Dear is the giver, goodly the way he takes,
> Loved[1] by the good, God-goers,[2] self-restrained;
> They teach him Dhamma that dispels all Ill,
> That Dhamma he here having come to know,[3]
> He rid of cankers waneth utterly.'[4]

§ vi (36). *The timely gift.*

'Monks, there are these five timely[5] gifts. What five?

One gives to the new-comer; to one going away; to the sick; when food is hard to get; the first-fruits of field and orchard[6] he first sets before the virtuous.

Monks, these are the five timely gifts.

> Timely, unstinting give the very wise,
> The affable; their timely gift to such
> As they[7]—the noble upright Ariyan men—
> Is a rich offering[8] that brings man peace;[9]
> Nor they who laud,[10] nor they who do the deed
> Lack offering, but both in merit share.
> Give without let of mind where great the fruit,
> For living things (such) meritorious deeds
> Are in another world a footing sure.'

---

[1] *Comy.* reads *santo naŋ bhajanti, S.e. santo bhajanti sappurisā.*

[2] *Brahmacārayo*; see Mrs. Rhys Davids' *Gotama*, 95.

[3] The last two lines of the text recur at *Vin.* ii, 148, 164; *J.* i, 94; below, § 38.

[4] *Parinibbāti.*

[5] *Kāla. Comy.* glosses: *yutta-, patta-, anucchavika-.*

[6] *Nava-sassāni, -phalāni. Comy. ārāmato . . .*

[7] *Tādino. Tādī* is a term of reverence that came to be given to Founder and to arahants.

[8] *Dakkhiṇā*, among brāhmans, a sacrificial gift.

[9] *Cf.* verse 297 at *J.* i, 93.

[10] *Anumodanti. Comy. ekamante ṭhitā anumodanti* (*cf.* '*They also serve who only stand and wait.*')

§ vii (37). *The gift of a meal.*

'Monks, in giving a meal, a giver gives five things to an almsman. What five?

He gives life, beauty, ease, strength and wit;[1] but in giving these he becomes a partaker in each quality,[2] in heaven and among men.

Monks, these are the five things. . . .

> In giving life and strength and beauty, wit,
> In giving ease, wise men find happiness:
> Whoso shall give these gifts shall have long life
> And honour, wheresoe'er they be reborn.'[3]

§ viii (38). *The advantages of believing.*

'Monks, there are these five advantages for a believing clansman. What five?

Monks,[4] the good and wise in this world out of compassion first feel compassion towards the believer, never thus to the unbeliever; when visiting, they first approach the believer . . .; when receiving, they first accept alms of the believer . . .;[2] when teaching Dhamma, they first teach the believer, never thus the unbeliever. The believer, on the breaking up of the body after death, arises in the happy heaven-world.

Monks, these verily are the five advantages for a believing clansman.

Monks, just as in some pleasant countryside, where four main roads meet, the great banyan tree is a haven of rest[5] for all the winged creatures round about; even so, monks, the believing clansman is a haven of rest for many folk, for monks and nuns, lay-disciples both men and women.

---

[1] *Paṭibhāna. Comy. yutta-mutta-paṭibhāna*, which I suppose may mean apt and ready wit, understanding; Bacon's 'a ready man,' but see *P.E.D. s.v. mutta*, also *Pts. of Contr.* 379.

[2] The text repeats in full for each.

[3] *Cf.* below, § 44, where this line of the text recurs.

[4] *Cf. A.* iv, 79.

[5] *Paṭisaraṇaŋ.*

Lo! as a mighty leaf-clad banyan[1] tree,
A fruitful bower of branches, trunks and roots,
For the winged creatures is a resting-place,
And birds come home to that fair haunt[2] for shade
And fruit, each finding there his meed and want:
So, to the virtuous, believing man,
Humble and docile,[3] genial, friendly, mild,
Come arahants, devoid of lust, delusion,
Devoid of hate, earth's fairest field for merit,
Who teach him Dhamma that dispels all Ill.
That Dhamma here he coming thus to know,
He rid of cankers waneth utterly.'[4]

§ ix (39). *They desire a son.*

'Seeing[5] five things, monks, parents desire a son born in the family. What five?

He that is holpen he will help us; for us he will do what must be done; long will he keep up traditions; worthily possess his heritage; and make offerings to the petas when we are dead.

Monks, seeing these five things, parents desire a son. . . .

Wise folk who see these five desire a son:
Whoso is holpen, he will help; for us
He'll work, long the traditions keep,[6] fulfil
His heritage and peta offerings make—
Seeing these things the wise desire a son.
And the good and prudent, grateful and beholden,[7]

---

[1] *Mahāduma*, a great tree.

[2] This line is quoted and *āyatana: haunt* exegetically dealt with at *Expos.* 186; *Vism. trsl.* 569.

[3] *Nivātavuttiŋ atthaddhaŋ*; *cf. D.* iii, 192.

[4] Above, § 35.

[5] This sutta is quoted at *Pts. of Contr.* (the *gāthā trsl.* there is somewhat expanded). The five also recur at *D.* iii, 189 (*trsl.* omits fifth item).

[6] *Ṭiṭṭhe. S.e. ṭhassati.*

[7] *Kataññū katavedino*; see *G.S.* i, 78.

Cherish their parents, mindful[1] of the past;
They work for them as tho' it were a favour.
Who hearkens to instruction, holpen, helps,[2]
A son like that is praiseworthy indeed.'

§ x (40). *Sāl trees.*

'Monks,[3] the great sāl trees, supported by Himālaya, the mountain king, grow in five growths. What five?

They grow in branches, leaves and foliage; they grow in bark; in shoots; in pith; they grow in heart.

Monks, the great sāl trees, supported by Himālaya, the mountain king, grow in these five growths. Even so, monks, folk within a home, supported by a believing clan-chief, grow in five growths. What five?

They grow in faith, in virtue, in learning, in charity, they grow in insight.

Monks, folk within a home, supported by a believing clan-chief, grow in these five growths.

Where[4] rise Himālaya's rocky mountain slopes
The trees and forest-giants there find place
For growth amid the jungle's massy groves:
So in a virtuous, believing chief,
Wife, sons, kith, kin, friends, followers find place
For growth. The well-behaved, with wit to see,
Will emulate the virtues of that man,

---

[1] *Anussaraŋ*. *Comy.* explains: . . . *anussarantā.*

[2] *Bhata-posī*. *Comy. yehi bhato tesaŋ posako.*

[3] *Cf.* the whole sutta with *A.* i, 152 (*G.S.* i, 136); on sāl trees, see *K.S.* v, 266 *n.* These parts of a tree are stock; see above, § 25; *M.* i, 192; the five 'growths' for a layman recur below, § 46 *f.* and 63; in the 'Sevens' at *A.* iv, 4, *D.* iii, 163 as 'treasures.'

[4] I have ventured to translate this simile rather differently from *G.S. loc. cit.*, following the prose. The *gāthā* does not bring in Himālaya, and *A.A.* ii, 252 on *A.* i merely remarks that *selo* means made of rock, but in Sanskrit the word has a definite connection with Himālaya; see Macdonell's *Dict. s.v.*; Buddhaghosa would probably not be aware of this; see *P.E.D.* and Dr. Stede's *Afterword*, p. 203.

His liberal ways;[1] the way of Dhamma here
Will take which leads to heaven, and after dwell,
Joying in joy of devas, happy, glad.'

Chapter V.—Rajah Muṇḍa.

§ i (41). *On getting rich.*

Once the Exalted One was dwelling near Sāvatthī, in Jeta Grove, at Anāthapiṇḍika's Park; and there Anāthapiṇḍika, the householder, came and visited him and, after saluting, sat down at one side. So seated, the Exalted One said to him:

'Householder, there are these five reasons for getting[2] rich. What five?

Take[3] the case of an Ariyan disciple with riches gotten by work and zeal, gathered by the strength of the arm, earned by the sweat of the brow, justly obtained in a lawful way[4]—he makes himself happy, glad, and keeps that great happiness, he makes his parents happy, glad, and keeps them so; so likewise his wife and children, his slaves, work-folk and men. This is the first reason for getting rich.

Again, when riches are thus gotten, he makes his friends and companions happy, glad, and keeps them so. This is the second reason. . . .

Again, when riches are thus gotten, ill-luck from fire and water, rajahs and robbers, enemies and heirs[5] is warded off, and he keeps his goods in safety. This is the third reason. . . .

Then, when riches are thus gotten, he makes the five oblations,[6] that is to say: oblations to kin, guests, petas, rajahs and devas. This is the fourth reason. . . .

---

[1] The last two lines of the text recur at *It.* 112; with variation at *A.* ii, 62; the last *pāda* of the second line at *It.* 19; *Thag.* 242. (In the *uddāna.* with *v.l.* and *S.e.* we should read *putta-sālehi*, no doubt.)

[2] *Ādiya. P.E.D.* (*Ādiya*[1]), no doubt because of the confusion of *bhojanāni* with *bhogānaŋ* of the text, wrongly derives this word. It is presumably the gerundive of *ādiyati* (*P.E.D. Ādiya*[4]). *Comy. ādātabbakāraṇāni.*

[3] *Cf.* the whole sutta with *A.* ii, 67; *S.* i, 90; below V, § 227; the *Comy* refers to his remarks on *A.* ii.

[4] This passage recurs also at *A.* iv, 282.

[5] This is a stock set: *M.* i, 86; *A.* iv, 7.

[6] *Bali.*

Moreover, householder, when riches are thus gotten, the Ariyan disciple institutes offerings,[1] of lofty aim, celestial, ripening to happiness, leading heavenward, for all those recluses and godly men who abstain from pride and indolence, who bear all things in patience and humility, each mastering self, each calming self, each perfecting self. This is the fifth reason for getting rich.

Householder, there are these five reasons for getting rich.

Now, if the wealth of that Ariyan disciple, heeding these five reasons, come to destruction, let him consider thus: At least, I've heeded those reasons for getting rich, but my wealth has gone!—thus he is not upset. And if his wealth increase, let him think: Truly, I've heeded those reasons and my wealth has grown!—thus he is not upset in either case.

> "Bred,[2] borne and battened is my household all
> Upon my wealth; I've warded off ill-luck;
> Made five oblations; furnished those good men,
> Who lead the godly life composed, with gifts
> And offerings of lofty aim; that meed,
> The wealth wise householders should seek, by me
> Is won—whate'er befall there's no regret!"
> Whoso considers thus, that man firm set
> In Ariyan Dhamma here on earth they praise,
> And afterwards in heaven he finds delight.'

§ ii (42). *The good man.*

'Monks,[3] when a good man is born into a family it is for the good, welfare and happiness of many folk; it is for the good, welfare and happiness of his parents; of his wife and children; of his slaves, work-folk and men; of his friends and companions; it is for the good, welfare and happiness of recluses and brahmans.

Monks, just as good rains bring to perfection all crops for the good, welfare and happiness of many folk; even so a

---

[1] *Dakkhiṇā*; *cf. D.* iii, 61; *A.* iv, 45 for this passage.

[2] *Bhattā bhogā bhatā bhaccā* . . . This *gāthā* recurs at *A.* ii, 67.

[3] *Cf.* the prose of this sutta with *A.* iv, 244.

good man is born into a family for the good, welfare and happiness of many folk. . . .

> For many let the good man wealth pursue.
> Him Dhamma-warded doth a deva ward.
> For him well taught, moral and dutiful,
> Will honour never wane. On Dhamma standing,
> Virtuous, truth-speaking, conscientious,
> Of such a man who's fit to appraise the worth ?
> 'Tis even like red gold from Jambu's stream.
> Him devas praise, by Brahmā praised is he.'[1]

§ iii (43). *What is welcome.*

Then Anāthapiṇḍika, the householder, visited the Exalted One and, saluting him, sat down at one side; and so seated, the Exalted One spoke to him and said:

'There are these five things, householder, which are welcome, sought after, lovely, but hard to get in the world. What five ?

Long life, householder, is welcome, sought after, lovely, but hard to get in the world; beauty is welcome . . .; happiness is welcome . . . ; honour is welcome . . . ;[2] the heaven-worlds are welcome, sought after, lovely, but hard to get in the world.

Such, householder, are the five things, which are welcome, sought after, lovely, but hard to get in the world.

Now these five things, householder, are not to be got either by vows or prayers, I declare; for if they were, why would anyone languish here ? To bring about long life, householder, it is of no use for an Ariyan disciple, yearning for long life, either to pray for it or to think much of it; the way that leads[3] to long life must be wayfared by the Ariyan disciple, and when the way is wayfared by him, it leads to the winning

---

[1] The third line of the text recurs at *A.* i, 162; the two last lines at *Dhp.* 230, *A.* ii, 8 and 29, and are quoted at *Vism.* 48. For the simile *cf. S.* i, 65; *M.* iii, 102; *A.* i, 181; *J.* iv, 290.

[2] The text repeats in full.

[3] *Comy.* observes: *dāna-sīlâdikā puñña-paṭipadā. Paṭipadā* is the term used for the more usual, perhaps more genuine, Magga in the First (Benares) Utterance.

of long life, and he becomes a winner both of heavenly life and human life.

So too, of beauty . . . happiness . . . and honour. . . .[1]

Householder, to bring about (life in) the heaven-worlds, it is of no use for an Ariyan disciple, yearning for heaven, either to pray for it or to think much of it; the steps that lead to heaven must be stepped by the Ariyan disciple, and when those steps are stepped by him, they lead to the winning of heaven, and he becomes a winner of the heaven-worlds.

> Life,[2] beauty, honour, fame, high birth and heaven—
> Whoso, day in day out, again, again,
> Doth often pray for such, in him the wise
> Zeal in the acts that make for good commend.
> A twofold weal the wise, the zealous man attains:
> Good here and good hereafter. "Wise and sage"
> He's called who weal hath understood.'[3]

§ iv (44). *The giver of good things.*

Once the Exalted One dwelt near Vesālī, at the Gabled Hall, in Mahāvana. Now the Exalted One, robing himself before noon, went to the house of Ugga,[4] the Vesāliyan householder, and sat down on the seat ready there. And Ugga, the Vesāliyan householder, approached the Exalted One, saluted him and sat down at one side. So seated, he said to the Exalted One:

'From the mouth of the Exalted One have I heard this, lord; from his own mouth have I received this: The giver of good[5] things gains the good. Lord, to me the gruel[6] from sāl

---

[1] The text repeats in full.

[2] Except for the first line, this *gāthā* recurs at *S.* i, 87; *cf.* also 89; to suit the prose here I have varied the trsl. compared with *K.S.* i, 112. The last three lines of the text recur at *It.* 17, the last two at *D.A.* i, 32 (quoted), and the last at *A.* ii, 46.

[3] *Atthâbhisamayā.* *Comy. atthassa abhisamāgamena.* See *S.A.* i, 156.

[4] See *G.S.* i, 23; *A.* iv, 208 *f.*

[5] *Manāpa*, more usually translated lovely, as in § 43 above.

[6] *Comy.* calls it *yāgu* and says it is made by cooking stalks, leaves and filament with cummin seed in ghee. The Sinhalese today seem to use the nuts and bark of the sāl tree, but not to make a gruel.

flowers is good eating; let the Exalted One accept some from me out of pity.'

The Exalted One accepted out of pity.

'From the mouth of the Exalted One have I heard this . . .: The giver of good things gains the good. Lord, good is the flesh of pigs[1] with plenty of jujube fruit. . . .

. . . good is the oily tube-like vegetable. . . .[2]

. . . good is a mess of rice, cleaned of black grains, served with assorted curries and condiments. . . .[3]

. . . good are muslins from Benares. . . .

. . . good is a couch[4] with a fleecy cover, woollen cloth or coverlet, spread with rugs of deer-skins, with awnings over it and crimson cushions at either end, and though we know, lord, that it is not suitable[5] for the Exalted One: this sandal-wood plank of mine, worth more than a hundred thousand —yet let the Exalted One accept it out of pity.'

And the Exalted One accepted (each gift)[6] out of pity.

Then the Exalted One gave thanks to Ugga, the Vesāliyan, with this benediction:

> 'Who gives the good shall gain the good; he who
> To upright men gives willingly clothes, bed,
> Food, drink, the needful requisites; and what's
> Foregone, put by, obsesses[7] not the mind.

---

[1] *Sūkara-maŋsa*. *Comy.* pickled one-year-old pig's flesh with sweet-tasting jujube fruit and cummin condiment. *Cf. D.* ii, 127 and *trsl.* 137 *n.* on *sūkara-maddava*.

[2] *Nibbaddhatelakaŋ nāliyāsākaŋ*. *S.e.* with *v.l. nibbatta-*. *Comy. nibaddha*, glossing: *vinivaṭṭita-*. This may be 'ladies' fingers,' *Sinh. baṇḍakka*.

[3] This is a stock phrase; *cf. D.* i, 105; *M.* i, 31; *A.* iv, 231, etc.

[4] *Cf. D.* i, 7; *Vin.* i, 192, etc.

[5] *Cf. M.* ii, 116. *Comy.* observes that this plank was not very big, being two and a half cubits long and one and a half across.

[6] The text repeats each in full.

[7] The text reads *anuggahītaŋ*, but with *S.e.* and *Comy.* we should read *anaggahītaŋ*, from *agganhati* (*ā* $\sqrt{grah}$, not in *P.E.D.*, but see *Tr. Dict. s.v.*). *Comy.* observes: *anupekkhacittatāya cittena na aggahītan-ti*. *Cf.* below V, § 148.

Whoso in arahants doth find a field
For gifts, wise man, foregoing what is hard,
In giving thus, the good shall gain the good.'

And when the Exalted One had thus given thanks to Ugga, the Vesāliyan, he rose from his seat and departed.

Now in due course Ugga the householder died and thereafter arose in a certain inferable world.[1]

At that time the Exalted One dwelt near Sāvatthī, at Jeta Grove, in Anāthapiṇḍika's Park, and there, when the night was far spent, Ugga the deva, in lovely radiance, lighting up the whole of Jeta Grove, came and visited him and, after saluting, stood at one side. And the Exalted One spoke to him, standing there, saying: 'I hope, Ugga, things are with you as we hoped?'

'To be sure, lord,[2] things are as the Exalted One hoped.'

Then the Exalted One addressed this verse to Ugga, the deva:

'Who gives the good shall gain the good; who gives
The best shall best receive again; the choice,
The choice receive; the chief, the chief place win.
Who gives the best, the choice, the chief—that man
Has honour and long life where'er he rise.'[3]

§ v (45). *Yields in merit.*

'Monks,[4] there are these five yields in merit, yields in goodness, the food of happiness, heavenly, ripening to happiness, leading heavenward, conducive to what is welcome, sought after, to the lovely, to good and to happiness. What five?

Monks, whose robe a monk enjoys the use of, while entering

---

[1] *Manomayaṃ kāyaṃ. Kāya* is frequently used for *nikāya*; *cf. S.* i, 27 (*K.S.* i, 37). Or it may be the *body* of him that is to be inferred—viz., from his visit.

[2] *S.e.* so, but our text and *Comy.* omit.

[3] This line of the text recurs above, § 37.

[4] *Comy.* refers to *A.* ii, 54, where the whole sutta occurs, except that here lodging (*senāsana*) is expanded into lodging (*vihāra*) and bed and chair (*mañcapīṭhaṃ*), thus making the five heads required. *Cf.* also *A.* iv, 245; *S.* v, 391.

and abiding in limitless mind-concentration—unto him shall come unlimited yield in merit, yield in goodness, the food of happiness, heavenly, ripening to happiness, leading heavenward, conducive to what is welcome, sought after, to the lovely, to good and to happiness.

Monks, whose alms a monk enjoys . . . whose lodging . . . whose bed and bench . . . whose medicaments for sickness a monk enjoys the use of, while abiding in limitless mind-concentration—unto him shall come unlimited yield in merit, in goodness, the food of happiness. . . .

Monks, these are the five yields in merit, yields in goodness. . . .

Monks, of the Ariyan disciple, endowed with these five yields in merit, yields in goodness, it is not easy to grasp the measure of merit and to say: Thus much is the yield in merit, in goodness, the food of happiness . . . but this great mass of merit is reckoned incalculable, immeasurable.

Monks, just as it is not easy to grasp[1] the amount of water in the mighty ocean and to say: There are so many[2] pailfuls of water, or hundreds of pailfuls, or thousands of pailfuls, or hundreds of thousands of pailfuls of water, but the great mass of water is just reckoned incalculable, immeasurable; even so, monks, it is not easy to grasp the measure of merit of the Ariyan disciple endowed with these five yields of merit and goodness, and to say: Thus much is the yield in merit, the yield in goodness, the food of happiness, celestial, ripening to happiness, leading heavenward, conducive to what is welcome, sought after, lovely, good, and to happiness—but merely that this great mass of merit is reckoned incalculable, immeasurable.

> Vast deeps immeasurable, fearsome pool,
> The oozy home of sumless treasuries[3]—
> There flow the rivers, there to meet the sea,

---

[1] Our text and *S.e. gahetuŋ*; *S.* v, 400 *gaṇetuŋ*.

[2] Our text should read *udakâlhakānī ti*; see Rhys Davids' *Coins and Measures of Ceylon*, p. 19 *f.* *S.* v, *trsl.* gallon, but it seems to be more than that. For the simile see below VI, § 37.

[3] *Ratanagaṇānaŋ ālayaŋ* (from √lī, to stick); *cf. Henry V*, I, ii, 165.

Serving the needs of countless hosts of men:[1]
And to that man, wise almoner, who gives
Food, drink, clothes, bed, seat, mat, comes meed in torrents,
As rivers, bringing water, to the sea.'

§ vi (46). *The perfectings.*[2]

'Monks, there are these five perfectings. What five?

The perfecting of faith, of virtue, of learning, of charity and the perfecting of insight.[3]

Verily, monks, these are the five perfectings.

§ vii (47). *Treasures.*

There are these five treasures, monks. What five?

The treasure of faith, of virtue, of learning, of charity and of insight.[4]

And what, monks, is the treasure of faith?

Herein, monks, the Aṛiyan disciple has faith and believes in the enlightenment of the Tathāgata. . . . This, monks, is called the treasure of faith.

And what, monks, is the treasure of virtue?

Herein, monks, the Ariyan disciple abstains from taking life. . . . This, monks, is called the treasure of virtue.

And what, monks, is the treasure of learning?

Herein, monks, the Ariyan disciple has learning and a memory, retentive and well stored. . . . This, monks, is the treasure of learning.

And what, monks, is the treasure of charity?

Herein, monks, the Ariyan disciple, living the householder's life, is free in heart from the stain of avarice; given over to charity, open-handed, delighting in making presents, he is

---

[1] Our text reads *maccha-*, fish, but all other texts *nara-*.

[2] *Cf.* above, § 40.

[3] *Sampadā*, or accomplishments or achievements. 'Charity' is literally 'giving' (*dāna*); is in no way connected with love (*agapē*).

[4] *Cf. G.S.* i, 190, *D.* i, 163, and *A.* iv, 4 for seven. The text is thus abbreviated.

ready to comply with another's request and finds pleasure in almsgiving. This, monks, is called the treasure of charity.

And what, monks, is the treasure of insight?

Herein, monks, the Ariyan disciple has insight; he possesses insight into the way of growth and decay, and Ariyan penetration into the way to the utter destruction of Ill. This, monks, is called the treasure of insight.

These, monks, are verily the five treasures.

Faith[1] in the Tathāgata, unshaken, firm;
Fair virtue, praised and loved by Ariyans;
Serenity[2] in seeing upright men
And in the Order—he whose way is thus,
No beggar is he called, nor vain his life.
Wherefore faith, virtue and serenity,
Wise men, discerning Dhamma, e'er pursue,
Remembering the message Buddhas bring.'

§ viii (48). *States not to be got to.*

'Monks, there are these five states[3] not to be got to by recluse or godly man, by deva, Māra or Brahmā, nor by anyone in the world. What five?

Where ageing brings no old age—that state is not to be got to by recluse or godly man. . . . Where sickening brings no sickness . . . nor dying death . . . nor wasting destruction . . . nor ending brings the end—that state is not to be got to by recluse or godly man, by deva, Māra or Brahmā, nor by anyone in the world.

Monks, to the unlearned, average man, ageing brings old age; and when he is old, he reflects not thus: " Not to me only does ageing bring old age, but wheresoever there is a coming and going, a passing on and an arising of creatures, to all, ageing brings old age: and if, when old age comes, I should

---

[1] This *gāthā* recurs at *S.* i, 232; v, 384; *A.* ii, 57; *Th.* i, 506-9; for the last three lines of the text *cf.* *A.* iv, 4.

[2] Or satisfaction: *pasāda*; see note to *S.* i, *trsl.*, and *Bu.*'s gloss given there. I follow the more literal meaning.

[3] *Ṭhānāni.* *Comy.* glosses: *kāraṇāni.*

mourn[1] and pine, weep and wail and beat the breast and fall into distraction; food would not please me, ugliness would come upon my body,[2] affairs would be neglected, enemies would rejoice, while friends would grieve." And when old age comes, he mourns, pines, weeps, wails, beats his breast and falls into distraction. Monks, this man is called an unlearned average man; pierced by the poisoned dart of sorrow, he just torments himself.

Again, monks, to the unlearned, average man, sickening brings sickness . . . dying, death . . . wasting, destruction . . . and ending brings the end; and when the end is near, he reflects not thus: "Not to me only does ending bring the end, but wheresoever there is a coming and going of creatures, a passing on and an arising, to all, ending brings the end: and if, when the end is near, I should mourn and pine, weep and wail and beat the breast and fall into distraction; food would not please me, ugliness would come upon my body, affairs would be neglected, enemies would rejoice, while friends would grieve." And when the end is near, he mourns, pines, weeps, wails, beats his breast and falls into distraction. Monks, this man is called an unlearned average man; pierced by the poisoned dart of sorrow, he just torments himself.

To the learned Ariyan disciple also, monks, ageing brings old age; but when he is old, he does reflect in that foresaid way[3] . . . and when age comes, he does not mourn nor pine nor weep nor wail nor beat his breast nor fall into distraction. Monks, this man is called a learned Ariyan disciple; drawn[4] out is the poisoned dart of sorrow with which the unlearned average man torments himself; the sorrowless, dart-free, Ariyan disciple has cooled the self entirely.

So also, to the learned Ariyan disciple sickening brings sickness . . . dying, death . . . wasting, destruction . . . ending, the end; and when the end is near, he reflects in like manner. . . .[3] Monks, this man is called a learned Ariyan disciple; drawn out

---

[1] *Cf. Vism.* 529; most of this is stock.

[2] This phrase recurs at *It.* 76, of a deva.

[3] The text repeats in full.

[4] For this simile *cf. Th.* i, 404; *Sn.* 939; *M.* ii, 256.

is the poisoned dart of sorrow with which the unlearned average man torments himself; the sorrowless, dart-free, Ariyan disciple has cooled[1] the self entirely.

Monks, these are the five states not to be got to by recluse or godly man, by deva, Māra or god, or by anyone in the world.

Grieve[2] not, nor weep! It profits[3] not, e'en not a whit,
And enemies rejoice to see one's grief and pain;
But when the sage, skilled in the quest of good, ne'er quakes
Beneath misfortune's blows, his enemies are pained,
Seeing his face of old unchanged. By chant and charm,[4]
Well-worded speech, gifts and by customs rightly kept,
Where and whatever good may gotten be, just there
Let him exert himself for that. And when he knows:[5]
Neither by me nor other may this good be won—
Ungrieving, bearing all things, let him think: How now,
How shall I best apply my strength to what's at hand?'

§ ix (49). *The Kosalan.*

Once, while the Exalted One was dwelling near Sāvatthī, at Jeta Grove, in Anāthapiṇḍika's Park, rajah Pasenadi,[6] the Kosalan, paid him a visit and, after saluting, sat down at one side.

Now at that time Mallikā, the ranee, died.

Then a man approached rajah Pasenadi and whispered in his ear:

'Sire, the ranee Mallikā is dead.'

---

[1] *Parinibbāpeti.*

[2] This *gāthā* recurs at *J.* iii, 204 (*Pañcanipāta*) with some *v.l.* *Comy.* differs from *Mp.* It recurs in the Chinese version of *Sn.*; see *J.P.T.S.*, 1906-7, p. 51.

[3] *Attho.* *J. Comy. vaḍḍhi.*

[4] *Japena mantena* (*S.e.* and *Mp. jappena*). *J.Comy. mantaparijapanena; paṇḍitehi saddhiŋ mantagahaṇena.* *Mp. vaṇṇabhaṇanena; mahânubhāvamattaparivattanena.*

[5] *S.e.* and *J. yato ca jāneyya* for *sac' eva* . . . of our text.

[6] He was the same age as the Buddha (*F. Dial.* ii, 66). See *K.S.* i, 93 *ff.* for a whole set of suttas giving conversations he had with the B.; on *Mallikā*, p. 101 and *n.*; at *A.* iv, 348, her name appears in the list of *upāsikās*. For Kosala generally see *C.H.I.* i, 178-82.

And when the rajah heard this, he was sorely grieved and sick at heart, his shoulders drooped, his mouth fell and he sat brooding, unable to speak.[1]

And the Exalted One, seeing him thus . . . spoke to him and said:

'There are, Maharajah, five states not to be got to by recluse or godly man, by deva, Māra or Brahmā, nor by anyone in the world. . . .' (*And the Exalted One taught him the discourse aforesaid.*)[2]

§ x (50). *The venerable Nārada.*

One time the venerable Nārada[3] dwelt near Pāṭaliputta,[4] in the Cock's Park.[5] Now at that time Bhaddā, the dear and beloved ranee of rajah Muṇḍa,[6] died; and because of the loss of his dear ranee, Bhaddā, he neither bathed, nor anointed himself, nor partook of any food, nor concerned himself with any affairs, but day and night clung in grief to her body as though a-swoon.

After a while he summoned his treasurer, Piyaka, and said to him:

'Prythee, friend Piyaka, place the body of the ranee, Bhaddā, in an oil vessel made of iron and cover it over with another iron vessel,[7] so that we shall see her body longer.'

'Yes, sire,' Piyaka replied, and he did as he was ordered. . . .

Now Piyaka, the treasurer, thought to himself: Bhaddā, the dear, beloved ranee of rajah Muṇḍa, is dead; and because of this

---

[1] This is stock; see *Vin.* iii, 162 and references given at *K.S.* i, 155; here *Comy. pattakkhandho-ti, patita-*.

[2] The text is not in full.

[3] Except here and at *K.S.* ii, 81 *f.*, where he declares himself not arahant, I find no mention of him. Our *Comy.* is silent.

[4] Or Patna, the capital of Magadha; see *Buddh. India*, 262; *D.* ii, 87.

[5] See *K.S.* v, 14; *F.Dial.* i, 251. Here later Asoka built a monastery for 1,000 monks, *C.H.I.* i, 518; Watters, *Chwang*, ii, 98; Beals' *Records*, ii, 94.

[6] *C.H.I.* i, 189; *Mhvs. trsl.* 19: great-grandson of Ajātasattu, rājā of Magadha, a parricide; he does not seem to be mentioned elsewhere.

[7] Similarly for a *cakkavattin* and the Buddha see *D.* ii, 142 and 162; see *Dial.* ii, 155 *n.*

loss, the rajah not even bathes or anoints himself, nor eats food, nor concerns himself with his affairs, but clings in grief to her body as though a-swoon.[1] What if rajah Muṇḍa go and wait upon some recluse or godly man! When he had learnt Dhamma, he would pluck out the dart of sorrow.

And again he thought: Near Pāṭaliputta, in the Cock's Park, dwells this venerable Nārada; and of that same reverend sir this fair report is gone abroad: A sage is he, accomplished, wise, learned, an able speaker, of ready, gracious wit, both venerable and arahant.[2] Methinks, if rajah Muṇḍa were to go and wait upon the venerable Nārada, perhaps, after listening to the venerable one's Dhamma, he would pluck out the dart of sorrow.

So Piyaka, the treasurer, approached the rajah and said to him:

'Sire, this venerable Nārada dwells hard by Pāṭaliputta, in the Cock's Park; now of him a fair report has gone abroad, that he is a sage, accomplished, wise, learned, an able speaker, of ready, gracious wit, both venerable and arahant. Maybe, if my lord were to go and wait upon the venerable one, he could, after listening to the venerable Nārada's Dhamma, pluck out the dart of sorrow.'

'Very well, friend Piyaka, announce (my coming) to the venerable Nārada.' And he thought: How, I wonder, ought one like me to approach a recluse or godly man, previously unknown, dwelling in the kingdom?

'Yes, sire,' he replied; and Piyaka, the treasurer, went and visited the venerable Nārada and saluted him and sat down at one side. So seated, he spoke thus to the venerable one: 'Reverend sir, Bhaddā, the dear and beloved ranee of rajah Muṇḍa, has died; and because of his loss the rajah neither bathes nor anoints himself, eats food or does business, but

---

[1] *Ajjhomucchito. Comy.* swallowing and ending (in a faint)—(but I do not think the sense warrants such a literal interpretation; see *Tr. Dict.*; surely we should read *-niṭṭhāpetvā*)—possessed by ravening, excessive infatuation and craving.

[2] *Vuddho c' eva arahā ca*, aged and worthy; see note 3, p. 48; omitting these last two terms, the phrase recurs at *S.* iv, 375.

grieves over the body of the ranee. Good it were, reverend sir, if the venerable Nārada were to teach such Dhamma that rajah Muṇḍa, having heard, might pluck out the dart of sorrow.'

'Now is the time, Piyaka, for the rajah Muṇḍa to do as he thinks fit.'

Then Piyaka, the treasurer, got up from his seat, saluted the venerable Nārada and took his leave, keeping the venerable one on his right; and approaching the rajah, he said to him:

'Sire, I have made occasion with the venerable Nārada; sire, now is the time to do as you think fit.'

'Then, friend Piyaka, have our state carriages got ready.'

'Yes, sire,' he replied; and when he had done so, he told the rajah: 'Sire, the state carriages await you.'

Then rajah Muṇḍa got up into a state carriage and with many others went off in royal pomp and power to see the venerable Nārada at the Cock's Park. And having gone by carriage as far as the ground allowed, he got down and entered the Park on foot.[1]

And the rajah Muṇḍa approached the venerable Nārada, saluted him and sat down at one side; and the venerable Nārada spoke thus to him, so seated:

'Maharajah, there are these five states not to be got to by recluse or godly man, by deva, Māra or Brahmā, nor by anyone in the world. What five?

Where ageing brings no old age . . .; where sickening brings no sickness . . .; where dying brings no death . . .; where wasting brings no destruction . . .; where ending brings no end—these places are not to be got to by recluse or godly man, by deva, Māra or Brahmā, nor by anyone in the world.'

(*And thereafter the venerable Nārada taught him the discourse preached by the Exalted One in sutta* 48 *and said:*)

'Grieve not, nor weep! It profits not, e'en not a whit,
And enemies rejoice to see one's grief and pain;
But when the sage, skilled in the quest of good, ne'er quakes
Beneath misfortune's blows, his enemies are pained

[1] These expressions are stock; *cf. D.* ii, 73; *A.* iv, 181; v, 65.

Seeing his face of old, unchanged. By chant and charm,
Well-worded speech, gifts, and by customs rightly kept,
Where and whatever good may gotten be, just there
Let him exert himself for that. And when he knows:
Neither by me nor other may this good be won—
Ungrieving, bearing all things, let him think: How now,
How shall I best apply my strength to what's at hand ?'

And when he had thus spoken, rajah Muṇḍa said to the venerable Nārada: 'What, reverend sir, is this discourse of Dhamma called ?'

'It is called, maharajah, the Plucker Out of Sorrow's Dart.'

'In sooth, reverend sir, it is a very plucker out of sorrow's dart; in very sooth, reverend sir, it is a plucker out of sorrow's dart; for by me, who have heard this discourse of Dhamma, is sorrow's dart plucked out.'

Then rajah Muṇḍa summoned Piyaka, the treasurer, and said:

'Burn now, friend Piyaka, the body of the ranee, Bhadda, and build a cairn[1] for it; henceforth now we will bathe and anoint ourselves, eat food and go about our business.'

Chapter VI.—The Hindrances.

§ i (51). *A check.*

Thus have I heard: Once the Exalted One dwelt near Sāvatthī, at Jeta Grove, in Anāthapiṇḍika's Park; and there he addressed the monks, saying: 'Monks.'

'Lord,' they replied, and the Exalted One said:

'There are, monks, these five checks, hindrances, which overspread the heart, which weaken insight. What five ?

Sensual desire, monks, is a check, a hindrance, which overspreads the heart, which weakens insight; ill-will . . . sloth and torpor . . . flurry and worry . . . doubt, monks, is a check, a hindrance, which overspreads the heart, which weakens insight.'[2]

---

[1] *Thūpa*, dāgoba.

[2] *Cf. S.* v, 96; *D.* i, 246; *A.* iv, 457; *DhS. trsl.* 310.

These, monks, are the five checks, hindrances. . . .

Monks, that a monk, verily, without being rid of those five checks, hindrances, which overspread the heart, which weaken insight, without strength and weak in insight, shall know his own good, shall know another's good, shall know the good of both, or shall realize the excellence[1] of knowledge and insight proper to Ariyans, which goes beyond man's conditions—that cannot be.

Monks, suppose in the case of a mountain stream,[2] winding here and there, swiftly flowing, taking all along with it, a man were to open watercourses[3] into it from both sides; then indeed, monks, the flow in mid-stream would be disturbed, swirled about and diverted,[4] nor would the stream wind here and there, nor flow swiftly, nor take all along with it: even so, monks, that a monk, without being rid of these five checks, hindrances, which overspread the heart, which weaken insight, without strength and weak in insight, shall know his own good or another's or the good of both, or shall realize the excellence of knowledge and insight proper to Ariyans, which goes beyond man's conditions—that cannot be.

Monks, that a monk, being rid of these five checks, hindrances, which overspread the heart, which weaken insight, strong and with insight, shall know his own good, shall know another's good, shall know the good of both, or shall realize the excellence of knowledge and insight proper to Ariyans, which goes beyond man's conditions—that surely shall be.

Monks, suppose in the case of a mountain stream, winding here and there, swiftly flowing, taking all along with it, a man were to close the watercourses on both sides of it; then indeed, monks, the flow in mid-stream would not be disturbed, swirled about or diverted, but the stream would wind here and there, flow swiftly forward, taking all along with it: even so, monks, that a monk, rid of these five checks, hin-

---

[1] *Cf. G.S.* i, 7; *S.* iv, 300; *AA.* i, 58.

[2] *Cf. A.* iv, 137; *Vism.* 231.

[3] *Naṅgala-mukhāni. Comy. mātikā-*, explaining: *tāni hi naṅgala-sarikkhattā naṅgalehi ca katattā naṅgalamukhānī-ti vuccanti.*

[4] *Vyādinno*, no doubt for *vyādiṇṇo* with *Comy.*; *S.e. byādinno.*

drances, which overspread the heart, which weaken insight, strong and with insight, shall know his own good or another's or the good of both, or shall realize the excellence of knowledge and insight proper to Ariyans, which goes beyond man's conditions—that surely shall be.'

§ ii (52). *The heap.*

'"'Tis[1] a heap of bad things!" monks; and in saying this of the five hindrances, one would speak rightly. Indeed, monks, the whole is a heap of bad things, that is to say: the five hindrances. What five?

The hindrance of sensual desire, of ill-will, of sloth and torpor, of flurry and worry, and the hindrance of doubt.

"'Tis a heap of bad things!" monks; and in saying this of these five hindrances, one would speak rightly; for verily, monks, the whole is a heap of bad things, that is to say: these five hindrances.'

§ iii (53). *The limbs.*

'Monks, there are these five limbs of striving.[2] What five?

Herein, monks, a monk has faith, he believes in the enlightenment of the Tathāgata . . .; he has health and well-being, a good digestion, which is neither over-cold nor over-heated,[3] but even and suitable for striving; he is neither deceitful nor a make-believe, but declares himself to the Master or to his wise fellows in the godly life just as he really is; he lives striving hard to give up evil things, and to hold to good things; staunch and strong in effort, he shirks not the burden of righteousness; he has insight and is endowed therewith into the way of the rise and fall of things, with Ariyan penetration into the utter destruction of Ill.

These, monks, are the five limbs of striving.'

---

[1] This recurs at *S.* v, 145; for *akusalarāsi trsl.* there has 'heap of demerit.'

[2] This recurs at *D.* iii, 237; *M.* ii, 95, 128; *A.* v, 15; below V, § 135.

[3] *Comy.* observes that a digestion that is over-cold is 'cold-shy,' and similarly for the over-heated.

§ iv (54). *Times for striving.*

'Monks, there are these five wrong[1] times for striving. What five?

Herein a monk is old, overcome by old age. Monks, this is the first wrong time for striving.

A monk is ill, overcome by illness. Monks, this is the second . . .

There[2] is a famine, crops are bad, food is hard to get and it is not easy to keep oneself going by gleaning and favours. Monks, this is the third . . .

Fear is about, perils[3] of robbers, and the country-folk mount their carts and drive away. Monks, this is the fourth . . .

Again, monks,[4] the Order is rent; then there is reviling between one another, accusation between one another, quarrelling between one another, repudiation between one another; and they of little faith do not find faith there and the faithful become otherwise. Monks, this is the fifth wrong time for striving.

Monks, these are the five wrong times for striving.

Monks, there are these five right times for striving. What five?

Herein a monk is young, a mere youth, black-haired and blessed with the beauty of youth, the heyday of youth.[5] Monks, this is the first right time for striving.

A monk has health and well-being, a good digestion, which is neither over-cold nor over-heated, but even and suitable for striving. Monks, this is the second . . .

There is no famine and crops are good, food is easy to get,

---

[1] *Asamaya*, unseasonable.

[2] *Cf. Vin.* iii, 145.

[3] The text reads *aṭavisaṁkhepo, v.l.* and *S.e. -saṁkopo*, ? from √KŪP, the wrath of robbers. The whole phrase is stock; *cf. A.* i, 178 (*G.S.* i, 161), and below V, § 78.

[4] This section recurs at *It.* 11 almost word for word. *Cf.* below V, § 156.

[5] This is stock; see *D.* i, 115; *M.* ii, 66; *S.* i, 9; *A.* ii, 22.

and it is easy to keep oneself going by gleanings and favours. Monks, this is the third . . .

Men dwell in friendly fellowship together, as mingled milk and water, nor quarrel, but look upon one another with friendly eye.[1] Monks, this is the fourth . . .

Again, monks, the Order dwell in friendly fellowship together, finding comfort in one teaching;[2] when there is harmony in the Order, then there is no reviling one with another, nor accusation made, nor quarrelling, nor repudiation between one another, but there they of little faith find faith and the faith of the faithful is made become more.[3] Monks, this is the fifth right time for striving.

Monks, these are the five right times for striving.'

§ v (55). *Mother and son.*

Once, when the Exalted One was dwelling near Sāvatthī, at Jeta Grove, in Anāthapiṇḍika's Park, a mother and son[4] were both spending the rainy season in Sāvatthī, as monk and nun.

They longed to see one another often; the mother often wished for her son, the son his mother. And from seeing each other often, companionship arose; from companionship, intimacy; from intimacy, amorousness;[5] and without giving up the training[6] and making their weakness manifest, with their hearts inflamed, they gave themselves over to incestuous intercourse.

And a company of monks went to the Exalted One, saluted him and sat down at one side; and, so seated, they told the Exalted One all that had occurred. . . .

'What, monks, knows not this foolish man that a mother shall not lust after her son, nor son, verily, after his mother?

---

[1] See *M.* ii, 120; *S.* iv, 225; *A.* i, 70, more often of monks.

[2] *Ekuddesu phāsu.*

[3] *Cf.* below V, § 156; *It.* 12.

[4] In the Pāli we have *mātāputtā*, but *bhikkhu ca bhikkhunī ca*; and I keep this order.

[5] *Otāra*, proneness; *cf.* below V, § 226, where the passage recurs.

[6] It was a grave offence (*pārājika*) not to do so; see *Vin.* iii, 23-4.

Monks, I see no other single form so enticing, so desirable, so intoxicating, so binding, so distracting,[1] such a hindrance to winning the unsurpassed peace from effort—that is to say, monks, as a woman's form. Monks, whosoever clings to a woman's form—infatuated, greedy, fettered, enslaved, enthralled[2]—for many a long day shall grieve, snared by the charms of a woman's form.

Monks, I know no other single sound . . . perfume . . . taste . . . or touch, so enticing, so desirable, so intoxicating, so binding, so distracting, such a hindrance to winning the unsurpassed peace from effort—that is to say, monks, as the sound, perfume, taste and touch of a woman. Monks, whosoever clings to the sound, perfume, taste and touch of a woman—infatuated, greedy, fettered, enslaved, enthralled—for many a long day shall grieve, snared by a woman's charms.

Monks, a woman, even when going along, will stop to ensnare the heart of a man; whether standing, sitting or lying down, laughing, talking or singing, weeping, stricken[3] or dying, a woman will stop to ensnare the heart of a man.

Monks, if ever one would rightly say: It is wholly a snare of Māra,—verily, speaking rightly, one may say of womanhood: It is wholly a snare of Māra.[4]

Go parley with a man with sword in hand;[5]
Use question with a goblin;[6] sit ye close[7]
Beside th'envenomed snake, whose bite is death;
But never alone with a lone female talk!

Who mindfulness forgets, they fetter him
With gaze and smile, with sweet disordered dress,[8]

---

[1] *Cf. D.* ii, 337.

[2] *Ud.* 75; *UdA.* 364.

[3] *Ugghātitā. Comy. uddhumātā*, 'puffy,' but this word is generally used of corpses.

[4] Māra here is the Evil One; *cf. S.* i, 105; *It.* 56: 'the destroyer.'

[5] *Comy.* to cut off one's head with.

[6] *Pisāca. Comy.* a yakkha come to eat one.

[7] *Āsīde. Comy. ghaṭṭeyya.*

[8] *Dunnivatthena.*

Coy blandishments—ne'er cool,[1] content, that man
Tho' stricken, dead. These five lust-linking strands
Are seen in womanhood: her form, her sound,
Taste, perfume, touch—for each delights the mind;
And borne by flood of lusts, not seeing lust
In full, men, faring on, by deeds of old[2]
Induce in destined time this or that life
In worlds.[3] But they who lust have understood
Pursue their ways free of the thought: "Whence fear ?"
Crossed over, yea, on earth with sainthood[4] won.'

§ vi (56). *The preceptor.*

Now a certain monk approached his preceptor and said: 'My body, sir, is as it were drugged;[5] the quarters are not seen by me; things[6] are not clear to me; sloth and torpor compass my heart about and stay; joyless,[7] I live the holy life; and doubts about things are ever with me.'

So that monk with his fellow-monk went to the Exalted One and, an arrival, saluted and sat down at one side. So seated, the preceptor said to the Exalted One: 'Lord, this monk speaks thus: My body, sir, is as it were drugged; the quarters are not seen by me; things are not clear to me; sloth and torpor compass my heart about and stay; joyless, I live the godly life; and doubts about things are ever with me.'

(And the Exalted One said:)

'Monk, it is ever thus ! When one dwells with doors of the senses unguarded, with no moderation in eating, not bent on

---

[1] The text reads *svāsisaddo,* with *v.l. svāsaddo, savāsido*; *S.e. yavāsīdo*; the *Comy.* is silent. I do not know the meaning. Nyanatiloka slips past, omitting the whole line !

[2] *Purakkhatā. Comy. pure cārikā purato katā yeva*; the word in this meaning is somewhat unusual.

[3] *Bhavâbhavaŋ.* [4] *Āsavakkhayaŋ. Comy. arahattaŋ.*

[5] This recurs at *S.* iii, 106; *cf.* also v, 153; *D.* ii, 99 and notes at *S. trsls.* (At *K.S.* iii, 90 read *D.* ii, for i.) *Comy. Sañjātagarubhāvo.*

[6] *Comy. Samathavipassanādhammā me na upaṭṭhahanti*; see *DA.* ii, 547. Possibly 'faculties' as *Dial.* ii, 107 is the meaning.

[7] *Comy.* glosses: *ukkaṇṭhito,* with neck stretched out: with longings; *cf. Isaiah* iii, 16.

vigilance, not looking[1] for righteous things, nor day in day out[2] practise the practice of making become the things that are wings to enlightenment;[3] then is the body as though drugged, the quarters are not seen, things are not clear, sloth and torpor compass the heart and stay; joyless, one lives the godly life; and doubts about things are ever with one.

Wherefore, monk, train yourself thus:

I will make the guard-doors of the senses become more, I will be moderate in eating, bent on vigilance, look for righteous things and dwell, day in day out, practising the practice of making become the things that are wings to enlightenment.

Train yourself in this way, monk.'

Then that monk, admonished with this admonishment by the Exalted One, got up and saluted the Exalted One and departed, keeping him on his right.

And not long afterwards, dwelling alone, secluded, zealous, earnest and resolved, that monk entered and abode in that unsurpassed goal of the godly life, realizing it by personal knowledge even in this life; for the sake of which clansmen rightly go forth from the home into the homeless life; and he fully realized: Rebirth is destroyed, lived is the godly life, done is what had to be done, and there is no more of this state. And that monk was numbered among the arahants.[4]

Then that monk, with arahantship won, went to his preceptor and said: 'Sir, no longer is my body as it were drugged; the four quarters are visible; things are clear; sloth and torpor no longer compass my heart and stay; with joy I live the godly life; and I have no doubts about things.'

(*Then, as before, that monk goes with his fellow-monk to see the Exalted One, and they tell him of the matter, and the Exalted One repeats his previous declaration.*[5])

---

[1] *Avipassaka. Comy. avipassanta, agavesanta.*

[2] *Pubbarattâpararattaŋ:* previous to night, beyond night.

[3] *Comy.* here these are reckoned as 37. (Originally with the Way, *first*, not last, as One, They will have amounted to the more auspicious number of 30.) See *K.S.* v, Introduction, p. 1.

[4] A stock sentence.

[5] The text repeats in full.

§ vii (57). *Things to be contemplated.*

'Monks, these five things ought to be often contemplated by woman and man, by house-dweller and by him gone forth. What five?

Old[1] age can come upon me; I have not outstripped old age! —this ought to be often contemplated by woman and man, by house-dweller and by him gone forth.

Disease can come upon me; I have not outstripped disease! . . .

Death can come upon me; I have not outstripped death! . . .

All things near and dear to me are subject to variableness,[2] subject to separation! . . .

I am the result of my own deeds;[3] heir to deeds; deeds are matrix;[4] deeds are kin; deeds are foundation;[5] whatever deed I do, whether good or bad, I shall become heir to it!—this ought to be often contemplated by woman and man, by house-dweller and by one gone forth.

Monks, to what right end[6] ought the thought: Old age can come upon me; I have not outstripped old age!—to be often contemplated by woman and man, by house-dweller and by one gone forth?

Monks, beings in youth are obsessed with the pride of youth; vaunting[7] in that pride, they go about working evil in deed, word and thought. To one who often contemplates that thing,[8] that pride of youth in youth is either got rid of altogether or reduced.

---

[1] For the first three *cf. A.* i, 145 (*G.S.* i, 129); for the third *S.* i, 97; for the fourth *D.* ii, 118, 144, also *DA.* ii, 564.

[2] *Nānābhāvo vinābhāvo*; *cf. James* i, 17: 'Father of lights, with whom there is no variableness, neither shadow of turning.'

[3] *Kammassako.* *Comy. attano santakaŋ.* This passage is stock; see below V, § 161; *M.* iii, 203; *A.* v, 88; *Mil.* 65; *Vism.* 301. *Trsls.* of *M.* and *Vism.* render in the sense of possession.

[4] *Yoni.* *Comy. kāraṇaŋ.*

[5] *Paṭisaraṇo.* *Comy. patiṭṭho.*

[6] *Cf.* below V, § 144.

[7] *For the same idea cf.* Shakespeare's *Sonnet* xv.

[8] *Ṭhānaŋ*, that is, the thought of old age, etc.

Monks, to this end that thing ought to be often contemplated . . .

Monks, to what end ought the thought of disease to be often contemplated . . . ?[1]

Monks, beings in health are obsessed with the pride of health; vaunting in that pride they go about working evil in deed, word and thought. To one who often contemplates that thing, that pride of health in health is either got rid of altogether or reduced. Monks, it is to this end . . .

Monks, to what end ought the thought of death to be often contemplated . . . ?

Monks, beings in the fulness of life are obsessed with the pride of life; vaunting in that pride they go about working evil in deed, word and thought. To one who often contemplates that thing, that pride of life in the fulness of life is either got rid of altogether or reduced. Monks, it is to this end . . .

Monks, to what end ought the thought of variableness with and separation from those near and dear to be often contemplated . . . ?

Monks, beings are obsessed with a passionate desire for those who are dear; excited by that passion they go about working evil in deed, word and thought. To one who often contemplates that thing, that passionate desire is either got rid of altogether or reduced. Monks, it is to this end . . .

Monks, to what end ought the thought of being the result of (one's own) deeds and so forth to be often contemplated . . . ?

Monks, the ways of beings are evil in deed, evil in word and evil in thought. To one who often contemplates that thing, those evil ways are got rid of altogether or reduced. Monks, to this end ought the thought: I am the result of my own deeds, heir to deeds, deeds are matrix, deeds are kin, deeds are foundation; whatever deed I do, whether good or bad, I shall be heir to that—to be often contemplated by woman and man, by house-dweller and by one gone forth.

Monks,[2] the Ariyan disciple reflects thus: I am not the only one who is subject to old age, who has not outstripped old age;

[1] The text repeats in full here and similarly elsewhere.

[2] *Sace* of our text, in some MSS. and *S.e.* is omitted.

but wheresoever there are beings, coming and going, faring on and arising, all are subject to old age, none has outstripped it. And while he often contemplates this thing, the Way comes into being; and that Way he follows, makes become and develops; and in doing so the fetters[1] are got rid of, the tendencies[2] are removed.

So too, of the thoughts: I am not the only one subject to disease . . . to death . . . not to me only is there variableness with and separation from those near and dear. . . . I am not the only one who is the result of his deeds. . . . And while he often contemplates these thoughts, the Way comes into being; and that Way he follows, makes become and develops; and in so doing the fetters are got rid of, the tendencies are removed.

Having[3] these things: disease, old age and death—
As they, so men: repulsive is the thought to average man.
Not meet that I myself should be repelled
At creatures having these, seeing that I
Do lead my life no otherwise than he.

While living thus, I having come to know
Religion[4] wherein no substrate is found,
I who was wont to vaunt in health, youth, life,
O'ercame that pride and from the peace beheld
Renunciation's[5] coolth. Nibbāna seen,
Strength came to me. Ne'er now can I become
Addict of sense desires. I will become
A man who never turning back (hath ta'en)
The yonder-faring of the godly life.'[6]

---

[1] *Comy.* the ten; see *Dial.* iii, 225; *A.* v, 17.

[2] *Comy.* the seven; see *Dial.* iii, 237; *A.* iv, 9; *Cpd.* 172. (*Satta anusayā vigatattā paricchinnā parivaṭumā honti*; see *P.E.D. s.v. parivaṭuma.*)

[3] This *gāthā* recurs at *A.* i, 147, with some different readings; *AA.* ii, 242 is fuller than *Comy.* here.

[4] *Dhammaŋ nirūpadhiŋ. Comy. arahattamaggaŋ.*

[5] *Nekkhammaŋ daṭṭhu khemato* (*S.e. v.l. khemataŋ*, see *G.S. n.*). *Comy. Pabbajjaŋ khemato disvā.* This *pāda* also recurs at *Sn.* 424 and 1098 *SnA.* 385: *pabbajito 'mhi*; but at 598: *nibbānaŋ . . . kheman-ti disvā.*

[6] *Comy. magga-brahmacariya-parāyano.*

§ viii (58). *The Licchavi young men.*

At one time the Exalted One dwelt near Vesālī, at the Gabled Hall, in Mahāvana. And early one morning, after dressing, the Exalted One took bowl and robe and entered Vesālī for alms. And having gone his round, on his return, after the midday meal, he made his way into the great forest of Mahāvana, and sat down for the noonday rest at the foot of a tree.

Now at that time a company of Licchavi young men were out stalking and ranging in Mahāvana; they had their bows strung and were surrounded by a pack of dogs; and they saw the Exalted One seated at the foot of the tree. Then at that sight they cast aside their bows, called off their dogs and approached the Exalted One, saluted him and stood with hands upraised in silence reverencing him.

Just then Mahānāma,[1] the Licchavi, was stretching his legs in Mahāvana by walking up and down; and he saw those young Licchavis with upraised hands silently reverencing the Exalted One. And Mahānāma, the Licchavi, went to the Exalted One, saluted him and sat down at one side. So seated, he said with bated breath:[2]

'They will become Vajjians,[3] they will become Vajjians!'

'But why, Mahānāma, dost thou speak so: "They will become Vajjians!"?'

'Lord, these Licchavi young men are quick-tempered, rough, greedy fellows. Such presents as are sent[4] by clanfolk—

---

[1] We are not able to link up this Mahānāma with others of that name, either, *e.g.*, with him of the first five disciples, or the Sakyan lay-kinsman. It is possible that we have a name substituted, when *written* suttas involved many blurred words, for the forgotten name of a disciple. Rhys Davids lists Licchavis and Videhas as forming two branches of one Vajjian confederacy, but this sutta points to Licchavis as *not* Vajjians, a more cultured oligarchy. *Cf. Dial.* ii, p. 79 *ff.*; *Buddh. India*, ch. ii; *C.H.I.* i, 175.

[2] *Udānaŋ udānesi.*

[3] Or, as we might say, they will end by becoming Vajjians, their more cultured neighbours.

[4] *Pahiṇakāni pahīyanti.* I do not think the latter is from √*HĀ*, but from √*HI* and formed by false analogy. Thus as from *pajahati* the passive is *pahīyati*, *pp. pahīna*; so from *pahiṇati* (the Singhalese spell it with a dental, not lingual) the passive is *pahiyati* (so *S.e.*, not with text *pahīyati*) with an adj.-noun, *pahiṇa*.

sugar-cane, jujube fruit, sweet cakes, sweetmeats and lolly-pops[1]—they go about plundering and eating; they slap the women and the girls of the clan on the back.[2] Such are these fellows who now with upraised hands stand in silence reverencing the Exalted One.'

'Wheresoever these five conditions are found, Mahānāma, whether in a crowned warrior-rajah, or in a countryman living on his paternal[3] farm, or in a general of an army, or in a governor of villages,[4] or in a guild-master,[5] or in those who make themselves the one power among the clans, growth may be expected and not decline. What five ?

Take the case, Mahānāma, of a clansman who,[6] with wealth gotten by work and zeal, gathered by the strength of the arm, earned by the sweat of the brow, justly obtained in a lawful way, honours, reveres, venerates and reverences his parents. At once his parents, honoured, revered, venerated and reverenced, fondly regard him with loving thoughts and say: Long life to you, and may your long life be protected! To the clansman, Mahānāma, who has the fond regard of his parents, growth may be expected and not decline.

So too, Mahānāma, of his children and wife, his slaves, work-folk and men. . . .

. . . of the labourers in his fields and those whose business is with the boundaries. . . .[7]

---

[1] *Sakkhalakā.*

[2] *Pacchāliyaŋ khipanti. Comy. pacchato gantvā, piṭṭhipādena paharanti*, they go behind and kick them with the upper part of the foot (see *Vism. trsl.* 288 on *piṭṭhipādo*). *P.E.D.* suggests 'lap' or 'basket' for *pacchāliyaŋ*, but the word may be resolved into *pacchā* and *āli*, a dike; so: side, see *Childers.* As regards *khipanti*, in English we have the counterpart in the word 'chuck.'

[3] *Pettanika. Comy. pitaraŋ dattaŋ sāpateyyaŋ bhuñjati.*

[4] *Gāmagāmika. Comy. gāmānaŋ gāmika.* A *gāma* is more like our old term 'hundred' than the modern idea of village.

[5] *Pūgagāmaṇika. Comy. gaṇajeṭṭhaka.*

[6] *Cf.* above, § 41.

[7] *Sāmantasaŋvohāre, Comy. rajju-daṇḍehi bhūmippamāṇe gāhake saŋvohāre*, those who hold the office of measuring the ground with rope and rod—*i.e.*, surveyors.

. . . of the devas who are wont to receive oblations. . . .[1]

Moreover, Mahānāma, a clansman who, with wealth gotten by work and zeal, gathered by the strength of the arm, earned by the sweat of the brow, justly obtained in a lawful way, honours, reveres, venerates and reverences recluses and godly men, will at once by them, so honoured . . . be regarded with compassion, with benevolence, and they will say: Long life to you, and may your long life be protected! To the clansman, Mahānāma, who is regarded with compassion by recluse and godly man, growth may be expected and not decline.

Wheresoever these five conditions are found, Mahānāma, whether in a crowned warrior-rajah, a countryman living on his paternal farm, a general of an army, a governor of villages, a guild-master, or in those who make themselves the one power among the clans, growth may be expected and not decline.

To mother, father dutiful, to child and wife
A blessing ever, for the weal of both:
Of those within the home and those who live[2]
By him, moral and wise in word is he.
For him, for those gone on before, for such
As live e'en here,[3] for samaṇa and brāhman,
Breeder of welfare doth the wise become,
(In that) by Dhamma in the home he lives.
Author of lovely[4] (conduct) worshipful[5]
Doth he become, and worthy praise. E'en here
Men praise him, and to the hereafter gone,
In the bright world he dwells in happiness.'[6]

§ ix (59). *Hard to find* (*a*).[7]

'Monks, it is hard to find one, gone forth when old,[8] endowed with five qualities. What five?

---

[1] The text repeats all in full.

[2] The text and *S.e.* read *anujīvino*, but *Comy. upajīvino.*

[3] *Diṭṭhe dhamme ca jīvitaŋ. Comy. ye ca . . . jīvanti.*

[4] *So karitvāna kalyāṇaŋ.*

[5] We should read with *Comy.* and *S.e. pujjo*, I think.

[6] The last line of the text recurs above, § 41, and at *A.* ii, 5; *It.* 111.

[7] *Dullabho, lit.* hard to obtain.

[8] *Cf.* Harita's trouble at *Brethr.* 34.

Monks, it is hard to find one subtle-minded gone forth when old, hard to find one proper in deportment, very learned, a preacher of Dhamma, it is hard to find one who has the Discipline by heart.

Monks, it is hard to find one, gone forth when old, endowed with these five qualities.'

§ x (60). *The same* (*b*).

'Monks, it is hard to find one, gone forth when old, endowed with five qualities. What five?

Monks, it is hard to find one who speaks well, who grasps what is easily grasped, having the talent to grasp,[1] a preacher of Dhamma, it is hard to find one who has the discipline by heart.

Monks, it is hard to find one, gone forth when old, endowed with these five qualities.'

Chapter VII.—Thoughts.

§ i (61). *Thoughts* (*a*).[2]

'Monks,[3] these five thoughts, when made become, made an increase in, are very fruitful, of great advantage, merging in the deathless, having the deathless as their goal. What five?

The thought of foulness; the thought of death; the thought of peril; the thought of the cloying of food; the sense of distaste as to the world.

Verily, monks, these five thoughts, when made become, made an increase in, are very fruitful, of great advantage, merging in the deathless, having the deathless as their goal.'

---

[1] *Padakkhiṇaggāhī*, *lit.* grasping on the right. *Comy. dinn' ovādaŋ padakkhiṇato gaṅhanto.* The word recurs at *A.* v, 24, where the *Comy.* observes: *yathā ekacco ovadiyamāno vāmato gaṅhāti paṭippharati vā asuṇanto vā gacchati evaŋ akatvā ovadatha bhante anusāsatha tumhesu anovadantesu ko añño ovadissati-ti padakkhiṇaŋ gaṅhāti.* See *K.S.* ii, 137; below V, § 156.

[2] *Saññā*, as vague a term as is popularly our 'thought.'

[3] *Cf. D.* iii, 289; *S.* v, 132; *A.* i, 41, etc.

§ ii (62). *The same* (*b*).

'Monks, these five thoughts . . . What five ?

Of impermanence; of not-self; of death; of the cloying of food; of distaste as to the world.

Monks, these five . . .'

§ iii (63). *Growth.*[1]

'Monks,[2] growing in five ways of growth, the Ariyan disciple grows in Ariyan growth; he heeds what is essential and best for his whole being.[3] In what five ?

He grows in faith, virtue, learning, giving up and insight.

Verily, monks, growing in these five ways of growth, the Ariyan disciple grows in Ariyan growth; he heeds what is essential and best for his whole being.

> Whoso[4] in faith, in virtue makes a forward[5] growth,
> In learning, insight, giving up, alike:
> A very man like this, keen-eyed, lays hold
> E'en here upon the real in himself.'

§ iv (64). *The same.*

'Monks, growing in five ways of growth, the devout Ariyan woman grows in Ariyan growth; she heeds what is essential and best for her whole being. What five ?

(*Repeat as before. The last line of the gāthā alters to:*)

That woman, good, devout, heeds here the best for self.'

§ v (65). *Talk.*

'Monks, endowed with five qualities, a monk may[6] well talk to his fellows in the godly life. What five ?

Monks, herein a monk in himself has achieved virtue and

---

[1] *Vaḍḍhi.*

[2] *Cf. S.* iv, 250 (*K.S.* iv, Introd. xiv); and above, § 40.

[3] *Kāyassa.*

[4] Almost the same *gāthā* recurs at *A.* v, 137. *Cf.* the identical sutta § iv in *S.* iv, 250, with a varied translation in *K.S.* iv, 168 *f.*

[5] Here *pavaḍḍhati.*

[6] *Alaŋ. Comy. yutto*, fitting.

explains a question raised[1] by a talk on the achieving of virtue; so too, in regard to concentration . . . insight . . . emancipation; and in himself has achieved the knowledge and insight of emancipation and explains a question raised by a talk on the achieving of knowledge and insight of emancipation.

Verily, monks, endowed with these five qualities, a monk may well talk to his fellows in the godly life.'

§ vi (66). *An example.*[2]

'Monks, a monk, endowed with five qualities, is a fitting example to his fellows in the godly life. What five?'

(*The reply is as in* § 65, *but kataŋ*[3] *is used for āgataŋ.*)

§ vii (67). *Psychic power.*

'Monks,[4] whatsoever monk or nun make five things become, make an increase in five things, unto such one of two fruits may be expected: either gnosis here now or, being with some substrate left, the state of a Non-returner. What five?

Monks,[5] herein a monk makes become the psychic power which embraces desire-to-do, combined with concentration and resolution; the psychic power which embraces energy . . . thought . . . investigation, combined with concentration and resolution; and fifthly, just exertion.[6]

Monks, whatsoever monk or nun makes these five things become . . . either gnosis here and now or, being with some substrate left, the state of a Non-returner may be expected.'

---

[1] *Āgataŋ*. *Comy. pucchitaŋ.*

[2] *Sājīvan.* This word is explained at *Vin.* iii, 24 as *sikkhāpadaŋ*, a precept or rule of training. *Cf.* St. Paul to Timothy (I, iv, 12): 'Be thou an example of the believers, in word, in conversation, in charity, in spirit, in faith, in purity.' These suttas are preached by Sāriputta (below V, §§ 163-4).

[3] *Comy.* glosses: *abhisaŋkhataŋ*, prepared.

[4] This is a stock opening; *cf.* below V, § 122; *D.* ii, 314; *M.* i, 63; *S.* v, 129; *A.* v, 108; *It.* 39; *Sn.* p. 140. On *aññā*, gnosis, see *Brethr.*, p. xxxiii.

[5] For references see *D.* iii, 221; *K.S.* v, 225 *ff.* *S.e.* has '*pe*' between the terms.

[6] *Ussoḷhi.* *Comy. adhimatta-viriya*, extraordinary energy.

§ viii (68). *The same.*

'Monks, before I became enlightened, while I was still a bodhisat without complete enlightenment, I made five qualities become, I made an increase in five qualities. What five?

(*The aforesaid psychic powers and exertion.*)[1]

Monks, when I had made these qualities become, made an increase in them, I bent the mind to realize by psychic knowledge whatever is realizable by psychic knowledge, and I became an eyewitness in every case whatever the range might be.

Did I wish to experience psychic power in manifold modes? . . .'[2]

§ ix (69). *Disgust.*

'Monks, these five things, when made become, made an increase in, lead to complete disgust, dispassion, ending, calm, knowledge, enlightenment and to Nibbāna.[3] What five?

Monks, herein a monk abides perceiving the foulness of the body; is conscious of the cloying of food; is conscious of distaste as to the world; perceives impermanence in all compounded things; and the thought of death is by him inwardly well established.[4]

Monks, these five things, when made become, made an increase in, lead to . . . Nibbāna.'

§ x (70). *Destruction of the cankers.*

'Monks, these five things, when made become, made an increase in, lead to the destruction of the cankers. What five?

(*Just those aforesaid things.*)[5]

Monks, these are the five . . .'

---

[1] The text repeats.

[2] The text abbreviates; *cf.* above, § 23.

[3] This is stock; *cf. D.* i, 189; *A.* iv, 143; *Ud.* 36; *S.* ii, 223; *M.* ii, 82.

[4] *Cf.* below V, § 121.

[5] The text repeats.

Chapter VIII.—The Warrior.

§ i (71). *The fruits of mind-emancipation* (*a*).

'Monks, these five things, when made become, made an increase in, have as their fruits: mind-emancipation and the advantages thereof, insight-emancipation and the advantages thereof. What five ?

Monks, herein a monk abides perceiving the foulness of the body; is conscious of the cloying of food; is conscious of distaste as to the world; perceives impermanence in all compounded things; and the thought of death is by him inwardly well established.

Monks, these five things, when made become, made an increase in, have as their fruits: mind-emancipation and the advantages thereof, insight-emancipation and the advantages thereof.

Monks, when[1] indeed a monk is both mind-emancipated and insight-emancipated, that monk is said to have lifted the barrier,[2] filled in the moat, pulled up the pillar,[3] withdrawn the bolts, an Ariyan, with flag laid low, with burden dropped,[4] free of the fetters.[5]

And how, monks, has the monk lifted the barrier ? Herein by the monk ignorance is got rid of, cut down to the roots, made as a palm-tree stump, made so that it cannot grow up in the future, conditioned so that it cannot rise again. Thus, monks, has the monk lifted the barrier.

And how, monks, has the monk filled in the moat ? Herein

---

[1] This passage recurs at *M.* i, 139.

[2] *Cf. Dhp.* 398.

[3] *Abbuḷhesiko. Comy. esikātthambhaŋ luñcitvā. P.E.D.*, desire, but the *Comy.* regards all terms as analogues, so the literal trsl. is given.

[4] *Cf. Th.* i, 1021.

[5] The *Comy.* explains with much exegetical matter by a simile: Imagine two cities, one a city of robbers, the other a city of peace; and suppose some mighty soldier were to think: 'So long as the robbers' city exists, the city of peace is not free from fear.' So he dons his armour and attacks and burns that city and returns to rejoice at home. The skandha group is the robbers' city, Nibbāna is the city of peace, an earnest striver is the mighty soldier.

by the monk coming-to-be again, birth and faring on are got rid of, cut down to the roots. . . . Thus, monks, has the monk filled in the moat.

And how, monks, has the monk pulled up the pillar? Herein by the monk craving is got rid of, cut down to the roots. . . . Thus, monks, has the monk pulled up the pillar.

And how, monks, has the monk withdrawn the bolts? Herein by the monk the five lower fetters are got rid of, cut down to the roots. . . . Thus, monks, has the monk withdrawn the bolts.

And how, monks, is the monk an Ariyan, with flag laid low, with burden dropped, free of the fetters? Herein, monks, by the monk the conceit "I am" is got rid of, cut down to the roots, made as a palm-tree stump, made so that it cannot grow up in the future, conditioned so that it cannot arise again. Thus, monks, is the monk an Ariyan, with flag laid low, with burden dropped, free of the fetters.'

§ ii (72). *The same (b).*

'Monks, these five things, when made become, made an increase in, have as their fruits: mind-emancipation and the advantages thereof, insight-emancipation and the advantages thereof. What five?

The thought of impermanence, the thought of ill in impermanence, the thought of no-self in ill, the thought of renunciation, and the thought of dispassion.

Monks, these five things, when made become, made an increase in, have as their fruits: mind-emancipation and the advantages thereof, insight-emancipation and the advantages thereof.

Monks, when indeed a monk . . .'[1]

§ iii (73). *Living by Dhamma.*

Now a certain monk visited the Exalted One, saluted him and sat down at one side. So seated, he said to the Exalted

[1] Repeat as in the previous sutta.

One: 'Lord, they say: Living by Dhamma,[1] living by Dhamma! Lord, how does a monk live by Dhamma?'

'Monk, consider[2] the monk who masters Dhamma: the sayings, psalms, catechisms, songs, solemnities, speeches, birth-stories, marvels and runes[3]—he spends the day in that mastery; he neglects to go apart[4] (for meditation) and devotes not himself to calm of purpose of the self. Monk, that monk is said to be swift[5] to master, but he lives not by Dhamma.

Again, consider the monk who teaches others Dhamma in detail, as he has heard it, as he has mastered it—he spends the day in convincing[6] others of Dhamma; he neglects to go apart and devotes not himself to calm of purpose of the self. Monk, that monk is said to be swift to convince, but he lives not by Dhamma.

Again, consider the monk who gives in full a repetition of Dhamma, as he has heard it, as he has learned it—he spends the day in repeating it; he neglects to go apart and devotes not himself to calm of purpose of the self. Monk, that monk is said to be swift to repeat, but he lives not by Dhamma.

Then consider the monk who turns his mind to Dhamma, ponders over it, reflects on it, as he has heard it, as he has learned it—he spends his day in thinking about Dhamma; he neglects to go apart and devotes not himself to calm of purpose of the self. Monk, that monk is said to be swift to think, but he lives not by Dhamma.

But, monk, take the case of the monk who masters Dhamma: the sayings, psalms and so forth, and spends not the day in that mastery, neglects not to go apart and devotes himself

---

[1] *Dhammavihārī*. I have not been able to find this compound elsewhere. 'By Dhamma' comes nearest to the parallel term *dhammena*, frequently met with. The other form is *dhammaŋ*: *dhammaŋ cara*, met with both in Upanishad and in Sutta.

[2] *Idha*.

[3] This list recurs at *M*. i, 133; *A*. ii, 7; *Vin*. iii, 8. See *Expos*. 33; *DA*, i, 23 *ff*. for explanation and examples; below V, § 155.

[4] *Comy*. *ekībhāvaŋ vissajjeti*.

[5] *Bahulo*, much, full of.

[6] The text reads *-paññattiyā*, but *S.e.*, and *Comy*. *-saññattiyā*, the latter observing: *dhammassa saññāpanāya* (*v.l*. *paññāpanāya*).

to calm of purpose of the self. Verily, monk, such a monk is one who lives by Dhamma.

Monk, thus, verily, have I declared one swift to master, one swift to convince, one swift to repeat, one swift to think and one who lives by Dhamma.

Monk,[1] what should be done by a teacher for his disciples, seeking their good, from compassion and out of pity, that has been done by me for you ?[2] (Behold) these tree-roots, these empty places, monk ! Meditate, monk, and be not slothful; reproach not yourself afterwards ![3] This is our command to you.'

§ iv (74). *The same.*

(*Another monk approached the Exalted One and spoke in like manner; and the Exalted One said :*)

'Monk, consider the monk who masters Dhamma: the sayings, psalms and so forth—but knows not through insight the goal beyond.[4] Monk, that monk is said to be swift to master, but he does not live by Dhamma.'

(*Repeat the previous sutta with changes.*)[5]

§ v (75). *The warrior* (*a*).

'Monks, these five kinds of warriors are found in the world. What five ?

Monks, in one case there is the warrior who, just at the sight of the cloud of dust,[6] loses heart and falters and stiffens not,[7] nor is able to go down to battle.[8] Monks, there is here this

---

[1] This is a stock paragraph; see *M.* i, 46; *S.* v, 157.

[2] Both *Comy.* and *S.e.* read *vo.*

[3] *Comy.* seems to consider this was addressed to a young monk and the B. exhorted him to strive in youth and not wait till old age came; *cf. Ecclesiastes* xii, 1 for the same sentiment.

[4] *Uttariñ c' assa paññāya atthaŋ na ppajānāti. Comy. uttariŋ tassa dhammassa . . . cattāri saccāni na passati.*

[5] The text repeats in full.

[6] *Rajaggaŋ. Comy.* as *J.* v, 187: *rajakkhandhaŋ*: of elephants, horses, etc.

[7] *Na santhambhati. Cf. Hamlet* I, v: 'And you, my sinews . . . bear me stiffly up.'

[8] *Cf. Pug.* 65, below V, § 139 for this phraseology.

sort of warrior. This, monks, is the first kind of warrior found in the world.

Again, though another endure (the sight of) the dust cloud, just on seeing a standard lifted up,[1] he loses heart and falters and stiffens not, nor is able to go down to battle. Monks, there is here this sort of warrior. This, monks, is the second kind . . .

Again, though another endure the dust-cloud and the standard, at the sound of tumult[2] he loses heart . . . nor is able to go down to battle. Monks, there is here this sort of warrior. This, monks, is the third kind . . .

Though another endure the dust-cloud, the standard and the tumult, when struck[3] in conflict he fails. Monks, there is here this sort of warrior. This, monks, is the fourth kind . . .

Then there is one who endures the dust-cloud, the standard, the tumult and the conflict; victorious in battle, winning the fight, he continues at the head[4] of the battle. Monks, there is here this sort of warrior. This, monks, is the fifth kind of warrior found in the world.

Monks, these are the five kinds . . .

Even so, monks, these five kinds of persons, like warriors, are found among monks. What five?

Monks, in the case of the monk who on seeing the dust-cloud loses heart and falters and stiffens not, nor is able to stay the course[5] of the godly life—he declares his weakness,[6] gives up the training and returns to the lower life. And what for him is the dust-cloud? Monks, that monk hears: " Tis said,[7] in such and such a village or town there are women and girls, passing fair to look upon, lovely, with a wondrous lotus-like

---

[1] *Comy.* sẹt up on the backs of elephants, horses, etc., in chariots.

[2] *Ussādanaŋ*; so *S.e.* and *Comy.* explaining: the noise of elephants, etc.

[3] *Haññati*; both *S.e.* and *Comy.* read *āhaññati.*

[4] *Saṁgāmasīsa. Comy. taŋ yeva jaya-kkhandhâvāra-ṭṭhānaŋ.*

[5] *Santānetuŋ, v.l. sandhāretuŋ, S.e.* and *Comy.* as text; this form is not in *P.E.D. Comy.* explains: *brahmacariya-vāsaŋ anupacchijjamānaŋ gopetuŋ na sakkoti,* he cannot provide against uninterruptedly living the godly life.

[6] See above, § 55.

[7] *Nāma.*

beauty!"[1] And when he hears this, he loses heart and falters and stiffens not, nor is he able to stay the course of the godly life, but declares his weakness, gives up the training and returns to the lower life. This for him is the dust-cloud.[2]

Monks, just as the warrior on seeing the dust-cloud loses heart and falters and stiffens not, nor is able to go down to battle; like that, monks, I say, is this person. Monks, there is here this sort of person. This, monks, is the first kind of person, like a warrior, found among monks.

Again, monks, a monk endures the dust-cloud, but at the sight of the standard loses heart . . . and returns to the low(er) life. And what for him is the standard? In this case the monk does not merely hear that in such and such a village or town there are some lovely women and girls, passing fair to look upon, with wondrous lotus-like beauty—but he sees it for himself; and at the sight loses heart . . . and returns to the low(er) life. This for him is the standard.

Monks, just as the warrior endures the dust-cloud, but at the sight of the standard loses heart . . .; like that, monks, I say, is this person. Monks, there is here this sort of person. This, monks, is the second kind of person, like a warrior, found among monks.

Again, monks, a monk endures both the dust-cloud and the standard, but at the sound of the tumult[3] loses heart . . . and returns to the low(er) life. And what for him is the tumult? In this case, monks, some woman comes along, when he has gone to forest, tree root or lonely[4] place, and laughs him to scorn, rails[5] on him, snaps her fingers at him[6] and mocks[7] him; and being so treated by a woman he loses heart . . . and returns to the low(er) life. This for him is the tumult.

---

[1] This is stock; *cf. D.* i, 114; *S.* i, 95; *A.* ii, 203; *Vin.* i, 268.; *DA.* i, 282 is much the same as *Mp.* 632.

[2] *Rajo* (dust) is etymologically associated with *rajati*, sensuous excitement or pleasure. *Cf.* below, sutta 81: *rajanīya* (enticing).

[3] *Ussādanaŋ*. [4] *Suññā*, empty.

[5] *Ullapati*. *Comy*. merely *katheti*; in Sk. *ullāpa* means abuse.

[6] *Ujjhaggeti*; both *S.e.* and *Comy.* so, the latter observing: *pāṇiŋ paharitvā mahā-hasitaŋ hasitaŋ*; *lit.* to laugh out at.

[7] *Uppaṇḍeti*. *Comy. uppaṇḍena kathaŋ katheti* (!).

Monks, just as the soldier endures both the dust-cloud and the standard, but at the sound of the tumult loses heart . . .; like that, monks, I say, is this person. Monks, there is here this sort of person. This, monks, is the third kind of person, like a warrior, found among monks.

Again, monks, a monk endures the dust-cloud, standard and tumult, but being struck[1] in conflict, fails. And what for him is the conflict? In this case, monks, some woman comes along, when he has gone to forest, tree-root or some lonely place, and sits down close beside him, lies down close beside him and cuddles up to him;[2] and being treated thus by a woman, without giving up the training, without declaring his weakness, he gives himself over to fornication. This to him is the conflict.

Monks, just as the warrior endures the dust-cloud, standard and tumult, but, when struck in conflict, fails; like that, monks, I say, is this person. Monks, there is here this sort of person. This, monks, is the third kind of person, like a warrior, found among monks.

Again, monks, there is the monk who endures the dust-cloud, the standard, the tumult and the conflict; victorious in battle, winning the fight, he continues at the head of the battle. And what to him is victory in battle? Herein also, monks, some woman comes along, when the monk has gone to forest, tree-root or some lonely place, and sits down close beside him, lies down close beside him and cuddles up to him; but being treated thus by a woman, he disentangles and frees himself and goes off whithersoever he will.

And[3] he resorts to some secluded spot: forest, tree-root, mountain, glen, rock-cave, cemetery, wooded upland, open space or heap of straw; and come to forest, tree-root or empty hut, he sits cross-legged, with body erect, setting mindfulness in front of him. Putting away all hankering, he abides with heart free therefrom; he cleanses his mind of hankering:

---

[1] *S.e.* reads *ā-*, as above.

[2] *Comy.* having won him over, she sits down on the same seat or very near him.

[3] This passage recurs at *D.* i, 71; *M.* i, 269; *A.* i, 241; *Vin.* ii, 146, etc.

putting away ill-will and hatred, he abides with heart free therefrom; kindly and compassionate to all creatures, he cleanses his mind of ill-will and hatred: putting away sloth and torpor, he abides free therefrom; conscious of light, mindful and self-possessed, he cleanses his mind of sloth and torpor: putting away flurry and worry, he abides poised; with heart serene within, he cleanses his mind of flurry and worry: putting away doubt, he abides with doubt passed by; no more he questions Why? of right things; he cleanses his mind of doubt.

Putting away these five hindrances, when the mind's corruptions are weakened by insight, aloof from sensuous appetites . . . he enters and abides in the first musing[1] . . . he enters and abides in the fourth musing.

With[2] the heart thus serene, purified, cleansed, spotless, devoid of defilement, supple, ready to act, firm and imperturbable, he bends the mind to know the destruction of the cankers. As it really is, he understands: This is Ill—as it really is, he understands: This is the origin of Ill—as it really is, he understands: This is the ending of Ill—as it really is, he understands: This is the way leading to the ending of Ill. As it really is, he understands the thought: These are the cankers—This the origin of the cankers—This the ending of the cankers—This the way leading to the ending of the cankers.

Knowing this, seeing this, his heart is free from the canker of lust, free from the canker of becomings,[3] free from the canker of ignorance, and in the freedom comes the knowledge of that freedom, and he knows: Birth is destroyed; lived is the godly life; done is what had to be done; there is no more of this state. This to him is victory in battle.

Monks, just as the warrior endures the dust-cloud, the standard, the tumult and the conflict; and, victorious in battle, winning the fight, continues even at the head of the battle; like that, monks, I say, is this person. Monks, there is

---

[1] *Jhāna.*

[2] This is stock; see *D.* i, 83; *M.* i, 23; *A.* iv, 178.

[3] Bhavâsava, here *bhavānaŋ āsavo*, 'bhava' having the meaning of 'lives' or 'world.' See *Manual of Buddhism*, 1932, p. 127; *G.S.* i, 203.

here this sort of person. This, monks, is the fifth kind of person, like a warrior, found among monks.

These, monks, are the five kinds of persons. . . .'

§ vi (76). *The same (b).*

'Monks, these five kinds of warriors are found in the world. What five?

Monks, in one case a warrior, grasping his sword and shield, binding on his bow and quiver,[1] goes down into the thick of the fight; and there he dares and strives; but others strike him as he dares and strives and overpower him.[2] Monks, there is here this sort of warrior. This, monks, is the first kind of warrior found in the world.

Again, another, arming himself in like manner, goes down to the fight; and as he dares and strives the enemy wound[3] him. And they bear[4] him away to bring him to his relations; but while he is being carried by his kinsmen, ere he arrives, he dies on the way to his relations. Monks, there is here this sort of warrior. This, monks, is the second kind . . .

Another . . . wounded by the enemy, is carried to his relations and they nurse him and care for him, but he dies of that hurt. Monks, there is here this sort of warrior. This, monks, is the third kind . . .

Another . . . wounded by the enemy . . . nursed and cared for by his relations, is cured of that hurt. Monks, there is here this sort of warrior. This, monks, is the fourth kind . . .

Then, monks, there is the soldier who, grasping sword and shield, binding on bow and quiver, goes down into the thick of the fight; victorious in battle, winning the fight, he continues at the head of the battle. Monks, there is here this sort of warrior. This, monks, is the fifth kind of warrior found in the world.

Monks, these are the five kinds . . .

---

[1] This is stock; *cf. Vin.* ii, 192; *M.* i, 68; ii, 99.

[2] This recurs at *S.* iv, 308; our text with *S.* reads *pariyāpādenti*, *Comy. pariyādentī-ti*, *pariyādiyanti*, *S.e. pariyādiyanti*.

[3] *Upalikkhanti*, to scotch.

[4] *Comy.* they come with his own bed (stretcher).

Even so, monks, these five kinds of persons, like warriors, are found in the world. What five?

Monks,[1] take the case of a monk who lives dependent on some village or town—while it is yet early, he robes himself and with bowl and cloak enters that village or town for alms, just with his body under no restraint, with speech unrestrained, with mind unrestrained, without mindfulness being set up, with his faculties uncontrolled: and there he sees a woman with dress disordered or not properly dressed, and at the sight passion overwhelms his mind; in that state, without giving up the training, without declaring his weakness, he gives himself over to fornication.

Monks, just as the warrior, grasping sword and shield, binding on bow and quiver, goes down into the thick of the fight and there dares and strives; but the enemy strike and overpower him: like that, monks, I say, is this person. Monks, there is here this sort of person. This, monks, is the first kind of person, like a warrior, found among monks.

Again, in like circumstances . . . another sees the same sight . . . and passion overwhelms his mind; in that state he burns in body, he burns in mind; and the thought comes to him: What if I go to the Park and say to the monks: "Good sirs, I burn[2] with passion; I am overcome by passion; I cannot stay the course of the godly life; I declare my weakness and give up the training; I will return to the lower life." As he goes to the Park, ere he arrives, even on the way to the Park, he declares his weakness, gives up the training and returns to the lower life.

Monks, just as the warrior . . . wounded by the enemy, is carried to his relations, but dies on the way: like that, monks, I say, is this person. Monks, there is here this sort of person. This, monks, is the second kind . . .

Again, in like circumstances . . . another thinks to tell the

---

[1] For the whole of this para. see *S.* ii, 231, 271; *cf.* also iv, 122; below VI, § 60.

[2] Our text reads *rāgapariyuṭṭhito*, but *S.e.* and *Comy.* with *v.l.* *rāgāyito*, which I suppose is simply the *pp.* of the *denominative* of *rāga.*, *P.E.D.* omits; *Comy.* explains: *rāgena ratto.*

monks similarly, and actually does. . . . Then[1] they who live the godly life admonish him and warn him, saying: "Good sir, the Exalted One has said: But little satisfying[2] is this lust, fraught as it is with ill and tribulation, with perils worse to follow. Like a piece[3] of bone is lust, fraught as it is with ill and tribulation, with perils worse to follow . . . like a lump of meat[4] is lust . . . like a fire-stick made of grass . . . like a pit of glowing embers[5] . . . like a passing dream[6] . . . like some borrowed bravery is lust . . . like ripe fruit on a broken branch . . . like a chopper in the shambles[7] . . . like a spear and javelin[8] . . . like a hooded snake is lust, fraught as it is with ill and tribulation, with perils worse to follow—so the Exalted One has said. Find your delight, reverend sir, in the godly life; declare not your weakness, reverend sir, nor give up the training nor return to the lower life!"

And he thus admonished, thus warned, by those who live the godly life, replies thuswise: "Good sirs, although the Exalted One has said lust is but little satisfying, fraught as it is with ill and tribulation, with perils worse to follow; yet I am not able to stay the course of the godly life, but I will declare my weakness, give up the training and return to the lower life."

Monks, just as the warrior . . . wounded by the enemy, is carried off to his relations and they nurse him and care for him, but he dies of that hurt: like that, monks, I say, is this person. Monks, there is here this sort of person. This, monks, is the third kind . . .

Again, in like circumstances . . . they who live the godly

---

[1] These ten similes recur at *M.* i, 130; *Vin.* ii, 25; *J.* v, 210; *Thig.* 487-91. Seven are explained in full at *M.* i, 364 *ff.* In trsl. I have expanded a little. It is curious *Comy.* does not refer to *Majjhima.*

[2] *Cf. Dhp.* 186; *J.* ii, 313; iv, 118; *Vism.* 124.

[3] Text *-saṅkhala,* but *Comy.* and *S.e. kaṅkala,* with *v.l.*

[4] *Comy. Bahu-sādhāranaṭṭhena, cf. Mil.* 280.

[5] *Sn.* 396; *J.* iv, 118; *A.* iv, 224; v. 175; *cf. S.* iv, 188.

[6] *Cf.* Shakespeare's *Sonnet* 129.

[7] *Asi-sūnā. Comy. adhikuṭṭanaṭṭhena.*

[8] *S.* i, 128; *Thig.* 58; *Vism.* 341.

life speak to another in the same way . . . and he thus admonished, thus warned, replies: "Good sirs, I will dare and strive;[1] I will find my delight in the godly life; not now will I declare my weakness, nor give up the training, nor return to the lower life."

Monks, just as the warrior . . . wounded by the enemy . . . is nursed and cared for by his relations and cured of that hurt; like that, monks, I say, is this person. Monks, there is here this sort of person. This, monks, is the fourth kind . . .

Then, monks, there is the monk who lives dependent on some village or town. While it is yet early, he robes himself and with bowl and cloak enters the village or town for alms, with his body, speech and mind restrained, with mindfulness set up, with his faculties under control: and on seeing some form with his eye, he is not entranced with its appearance nor with any detail of it; since by abiding uncontrolled in the sense of sight, covetousness, dejection, wicked and evil states would flow in over him, he sets himself to control that sense; he restrains that sense and wins mastery over it. So too, of the sense of hearing . . . smelling . . . tasting . . . touching . . . and in respect of ideas that pass through his mind; since by abiding uncontrolled in any way . . . covetousness, dejection and wicked and evil states would flow in over him, he sets himself to control each sense; and he restrains each sense and wins mastery over it.[2]

And on his return from alms-gathering, when his meal is over, he goes off to some secluded spot: forest, tree-root, mountain and so forth . . . and come there, sets up mindfulness . . . cleanses his mind of the five hindrances . . . enters and abides in the first musing . . . the fourth musing . . . bends his mind to know the destruction of the cankers . . . understands Ill as it really is . . . and knows: Birth is destroyed; lived is the godly life; done is what had to be done; there is no more of this state.[3]

---

[1] *Comy.* and *S.e.* with *v.l.* read *dhārayissami.*

[2] This is a stock passage; see *D.* i, 70; *M.* i, 269; *A.* ii, 39; *DhS. trsl.* 351.

[3] See the previous sutta for details.

Monks, just as the warrior, grasping sword and shield, binding on bow and quiver, goes down into the thick of the fight and is victorious in battle, winning the fight; like that, monks, I say, is this person. Monks, there is here this sort of person. This, monks, is the fifth kind of person, like a warrior, found among monks.

Monks, these are the five kinds of persons. . . .'

§ vii (77). *Fear in the way (a).*

'Monks, there are these five fears in the way[1] from contemplating which the earnest, ardent, resolute monk, forest-gone, ought to live just to attain the unattained, to master the unmastered, to realize the unrealized. What five?

Take the case of a monk, forest-gone, who reflects thus: I am now quite alone in the forest; and living here alone, a snake may bite me, a scorpion may bite me, or a centipede may bite me,[2] and cause my death; and that would be a hindrance to me. Behold now, I will put forth energy to attain the unattained, to master the unmastered, to realize the unrealized.[3]

Monks, this is the first fear in the way from contemplating which the earnest, ardent, resolute monk, forest-gone, ought to live just to attain the unattained, to master the unmastered, to realize the unrealized.

Again he reflects: . . . I may stumble and fall; the food I have eaten may make me ill; bile may convulse me; phlegm choke me; wind within stab and shake me,[4] and cause my death; and that would be a hindrance to me. Behold now, I will put forth energy. . . .

Monks, this is the second fear in the way. . . .

Again he reflects: . . . an I consort with fearsome creatures: lion, tiger, leopard, bear or hyena[5]—they may take my life and cause my death; and that would be a hindrance to me. Behold now, I will put forth energy. . . .

---

[1] *Anāgata*, not come, future.

[2] This is a stock set; see *A.* ii, 73; iv, 320; *Vin.* ii, 110; below VI, § 20.

[3] *Cf. D.* iii, 255; *A.* iv, 332 for this passage.

[4] This set is at *A.* iv, 320 and below *loc. cit.*

[5] *Cf. J.* v, 416; *Mil.* 149 and *Vin.* iii, 58.

6

Monks, this is the third fear in the way. . . .

Again he reflects: . . . an I consort with thieves,[1] who either have done their deed or go about to do it,[2] they may take my life and cause my death; and that would be a hindrance to me. Behold now, I will put forth energy. . . .

Monks, this is the fourth fear in the way. . . .

Moreover, monks, the monk, forest-gone, reflects thus: I am now alone in the forest; and there are fearsome non-humans[3] here. They may take my life and cause my death; and that would be a hindrance to me. Behold now, I will put forth energy to attain the unattained, to master the unmastered, to realize the unrealized.

Monks, this is the fifth fear in the way from contemplating which the earnest, ardent, resolute monk, forest-gone, ought to live just to attain the unattained, to master the unmastered, to realize the unrealized.

Monks, these are the five fears in the way. . . .'

§ viii (78). *The same* (*b*).

'Monks, there are these (other) five fears in the way. . . .[4] What five?

Take the case of a monk who reflects thus: I am now young, a mere youth, black-haired and blessed with the beauty of youth, the heyday of youth,[5] the prime of youth; but time will be when old age shall touch this body: and when grown old and overcome by age, not easy is it to turn to the Buddhas' word, not easy things are forest-wilderness, the outland bed and seat, to seek. Ere[6] that state come to me—unwelcome, undesired, unloved—lo! I will put forth energy against that time even to attain the unattained, to master the unmastered,

---

[1] *Māṇavehi. Comy. corehi*; *cf. DA.* i, 36, quoting our passage.

[2] See *Vism.* 180. *Mp.* says they take the throat-blood (*gala-lohita*) and make an offering to the devas.

[3] *Comy.* harsh, evil *yakkhas.*

[4] This is the same as in the preceding sutta, but with *āraññaka*, forest gone, omitted.

[5] See above, § 54.

[6] Following the *Comy.* I have punctuated differently from the text.

to realize the unrealized, and of that state possessed I will dwell comforted even when old.

Monks, this is the first fear in the way. . . .

Again he reflects: I have health and well-being, a good digestion which is neither over-cold nor over-heated, but even and suitable for striving;[1] but time will be when sickness shall touch this body: and sick and ill, not easy is it to turn to the Buddhas' word . . . lo! I will put forth energy . . . and dwell comforted even when sick.

Monks, this is the second fear in the way. . . .

Again he reflects: Now is there no famine and crops are good, food is easy to get and it is easy to keep oneself going by gleanings and favours; but time will be when there is a famine, bad crops, and difficulty in getting food, nor will it be easy to keep oneself going by gleanings and favours; and the famine-stricken men will move to where there is ample food, and there one will dwell in a crowd and a throng: and where such conditions are, not easy is it to turn to the Buddhas' word . . . lo! I will put forth energy . . . and dwell comforted even in time of famine.

Monks, this is the third fear in the way. . . .

Again he reflects: Now men dwell in friendly fellowship together, as mingled milk and water, they do not quarrel, but look upon one another with friendly eye; but time will be when fear is about, perils of robbers, and the country-folk mount their carts and drive away, and the fear-stricken men will move away to where there is safety, and there one will live in crowds and throngs: and where such conditions are, not easy is it to turn to the Buddhas' word . . . lo! I will put forth energy . . . and dwell comforted even in time of fear.

Monks, this is the fourth fear in the way. . . .

Moreover, monks, the monk reflects thus: Now the Order lives in friendly fellowship together, finding comfort in one teaching; but the time will come when the Order will be rent: and when that happens, not easy is it to turn to the Buddhas' word, not easy things are the forest wilderness, the outland

---

[1] *Cf.* above, § 53 and § 54 for the following passages.

bed and seat, to seek. Ere that state come—unwelcome, undesired, unloved—lo! I will put forth energy against that time even to attain the unattained, to master the unmastered, to realize the unrealized, and of that state possessed I will dwell comforted even though the Order be rent.

Monks, this is the fifth fear in the way. . . .

Monks, these are the five fears in the way. . . .'

§ ix (79). *The same (c).*

'Monks, these five fears in the way, which have not yet arisen, will arise in the future. Be ye fully awake for them; and, being awake, strive to get rid of them. What five?

Monks, there will be, in the long road of the future, monks who have not made body become,[1] not made virtue become, not made mind become, not made insight become; and those who have not made this becoming . . . will cause the acceptance[2] of others, and verily they will not be able to lead them in the way of higher virtue, higher mind, higher insight: and they too will become monks who have not made body become, not made virtue become, not made mind become, not made insight become; and those who have not made this becoming will cause the acceptance of others, and verily they will not be able to lead them in the way of higher virtue, higher mind, higher insight: and they too will become monks who have not made body become, not made virtue become, not made mind become, not made insight become. Thus verily, monks, from corrupt Dhamma comes corrupt Discipline; from corrupt Discipline corrupt Dhamma.

Monks, this is the first fear in the way which, though not yet risen, will arise in the future. Be ye fully awake for it; and being awake, strive to get rid of it.

Again, monks who have not made this becoming . . . will give guidance[3] to others, and verily they will not be able to lead them in the way of higher virtue, higher mind, higher in-

---

[1] *Abhāvita-kāyā* = untrained in body.

[2] *Upasampādessanti*, they will cause their acceptance as full monks.

[3] *Nissayaŋ dassanti*, see *Childers*, 291; *P.E.D.* omits this expression. The period of tutelage is at least five years.

sight: and those too . . . who have not made this becoming will give guidance to others and will not be able to lead them . . . and they too will not make this becoming. Thus verily, monks, from corrupt Dhamma comes corrupt Discipline; from corrupt Discipline corrupt Dhamma.

Monks, this is the second fear in the way. . . .

Again, monks who have not made this becoming . . ., when giving a talk on More-Dhamma[1] or on the runes,[2] will not be fully awake (to the meaning), but will enter on a state of darkness.[3] Thus verily, monks, from corrupt Dhamma comes corrupt Discipline; from corrupt Discipline corrupt Dhamma.

Monks, this is the third fear in the way. . . .

Again, monks who have not made this becoming . . . will not listen, lend an ear, set up an understanding mind or deem such things should be grasped and mastered, when those sayings,[4] spoken by the Tathāgata, deep, deep in meaning, world-beyond, dealing with the void, are recited; but to the sayings of poets, mere poems, just a show of words and phrases, the works of outsiders, declaimed by their disciples—to such, when recited, they will listen, lend an ear, set up an understanding mind and deem such things should be grasped and mastered.[5] Thus indeed, monks, from corrupt Dhamma comes corrupt Discipline; from corrupt Discipline corrupt Dhamma.

Monks, this is the fourth fear in the way. . . .

Moreover, monks, there will be in the long road of the future monks who have not made body, virtue, mind or insight become; and those elders who have not made this becoming will become luxurious,[6] lax, prime-movers in backsliding,[7] shirking

---

[1] *Abhidhamma. Comy. uttama-dhamma.*

[2] *Vedalla, Comy. Veda-paṭisaṃyuttaṃ ñāṇa-missaka-kathaṃ.* See *Exp.* i, 33. They are suttas in the form of questions—*e.g.*, *F. Dial.* i, 213; *Dial.* ii, 229.

[3] *Kaṇhaṃ dhammaṃ*; *cf. Dhp.* 87; *A.* v, 253; *K.S.* v, 22. *Comy.* by looking for defects, mocking, preaching for gain and honour.

[4] *Suttantā*, an honorific way of referring to suttas.

[5] This passage recurs at *S.* ii, 267; *A.* i, 73; see *G.S.* i, 68.

[6] *Cf. M.* i, 14; iii, 6; *A.* ii, 148; below V, § 156.

[7] *Okkamane pubbaṅgamā.*

the burden of the secluded life; and they will put forth no effort to attain the unattained, to master the unmastered, to realize the unrealized; and the folk who come after them will fall into the way of (wrong) views:[1] and they too will become luxurious, lax, prime-movers in backsliding, shirking the burden of the secluded life, and will put forth no effort to attain the unattained, to master the unmastered, to realize the unrealized. Thus indeed, monks, from corrupt Dhamma comes corrupt Discipline, from corrupt Discipline corrupt Dhamma.

Monks, this is the fifth fear in the way which, though not yet risen, will arise in the future. Be ye fully awake for it; and being awake, strive to get rid of it.

Monks, these are the five fears in the way. . . .'[2]

§ x (80). *The same* (*d*).

'Monks, there are these (other) five fears in the way. . . . What five?

Monks, there will be in the long road of the future monks who long for fine[3] robes; and they, with this longing, will leave the ways of wearing rags, will leave the forest wilderness, the outland bed and seat; will move to village, town or rajah's capital[4] and make their dwelling there; and because of a robe, they will commit many things unseemly, unfit.[5]

Monks, this is the first fear in the way. . . .

Again, monks will long for rich[3] alms-food, . . . will leave the ways of the common round, the forest wilderness . . . and will move to village, town or rajah's capital . . . seeking out, as it were with the tip of the tongue, tasty morsels; and because of alms-food, they will commit many things unseemly, unfit.

---

[1] *Cf. Vin.* ii, 108; *S.* ii, 203.

[2] At *Dial.* i, xiii, Rhys Davids observes that this sutta is the one referred to by Asoka in his *Bhabra Edict*; but it is not clear why this of the four *Anāgatabhayāni* suttas is picked out.

[3] *Kalyāṇa. Comy. sundara.* [4] *Rājadhāni.*

[5] This passage recurs at *S.* ii, 194 (quoted at *Mil.* 401).

Monks, this is the second fear in the way. . . .

Again, monks will long for a goodly bed and seat, . . . will leave the ways of the tree-root abode, the forest wilderness . . . and will move to village, town or rajah's capital . . .; and because of a bed and seat, they will commit things unseemly, unfit.

Monks, this is the third fear in the way. . . .

Again, monks will live in company with nuns and novices in training; and when this shall be, it may be expected that the monks will take no delight in leading the godly life; and either they will commit some foul act or give up the training and return to the lower life.

Monks, this is the fourth fear in the way. . . .

Moreover, monks, there will be in the long road of the future monks who will live in company with the Park folk and novices; and when this shall be, it may be expected that they will live and feast themselves on the plenty of hoarded stocks[1] and will mark out their lands and crops.

Monks, this is the fifth fear in the way which, though not yet risen, will arise in the future. Be ye fully awake for it; and being awake, strive to get rid of it.

Monks, these are the five fears in the way. . . .'

Chapter IX.—The Elder.

§ i (81). *Enticing.*

'Monks, if an elder monk be possessed of five qualities, among his fellows in the godly life he becomes neither dear nor pleasant nor respected nor what he ought to become.[2] What five?

He[3] is enticed by the enticing; corrupted by the corrupting; infatuated by the infatuating; angered by the angering; maddened by the maddening.

---

[1] *Sannidhi-kāraka-paribhoga*; this was not permitted, see *Vin.* ii, 206 *ff.*; *D.* iii, 235 (impossible for arahants); *A.* iv, 370; *M.* i, 523.

[2] *Bhāvanīyo.* See Introduction.

[3] *Cf. Mil.* 386.

Monks, if he be possessed of these five qualities, he becomes . . . not what he ought to become.'

(*But the opposite obtains.*)[1]

§ ii (82). *Free of passion.*

'Monks, possessed of five qualities, the elder becomes not what he ought to become. . . . What five ?

He is not free of passion, nor of corruption, nor of infatuation, and is full of cant and deceit.

Monks, possessed of these five . . .'

(*But the opposite obtains.*)

§ iii (83). *The trickster.*

'Monks, possessed of five qualities, the elder becomes not what he ought to become. . . . What five ?

He is a trickster,[2] a ranter, an insinuator, a dissembler,[3] one who seeks to add gain to gain.

Monks, possessed of these five . . .'

(*But the opposite obtains.*)

§ iv (84). *Faith.*

'Monks, possessed of five qualities, an elder becomes not what he ought to become. . . .

He is without faith, modesty, fear of blame, lazy and lacks insight.[4]

Monks, possessed of these five . . .' (*By the opposite qualities he becomes what he ought to become.*)

§ v (85). *He cannot endure.*

'Monks, possessed of five qualities, an elder becomes not what he ought to become. . . .

He[5] cannot endure forms, sounds, smells, tastes and touches.

Monks, possessed of these five . . .' (*By the opposite qualities he becomes what he ought to become.*)

---

[1] The text repeats each in full.

[2] *Cf. Vism.* 23 (*trsl.* 27 *ff.*); *D.* i, 8 (*Dial.* i, 16); *DA.* i, 91.

[3] *Nippesiko. Comy. nippiŋsanak' atthāya samannāgato.*

[4] *Cf. M.* i, 43; *S.* ii, 159; *D.* iii, 252; below V, § 101.

[5] *Akkhama, cf.* below V, § 139. *Comy. rūpârammaṇaŋ anadhivāsako hoti tad-ārammaṇehi rāgâdīhi abhibhuyyati.*

§ vi (86). *Analysis.*

'Monks, possessed of five qualities, an elder becomes what he ought to become. . . .

He is a master of logical analysis; a master in analyzing causal relations; a master of grammatical analysis; a master in analyzing things knowable;[1] what things have to be done by his fellow-men, living the godly life, either great or small, therein he is able and active, alive to investigating such matters; ready to do and get them done.[2]

Monks, possessed of these five . . .'

§ vii (87). *Virtue.*

'Monks, possessed of five[3] qualities, an elder becomes what he ought to become. . . .

He is virtuous, abides restrained by the restraint of the Obligations, is perfect in conduct and habit, sees peril in the smallest fault, accepts the training and trains himself accordantly.[4] He is learned, with mind retentive and well stored; those things lovely in the beginning, lovely in the middle, lovely in the end,[5] which set forth in spirit and in letter the godly life of purity, perfect in its entirety—those are fully learnt by him, resolved upon, made familiar by speech, pondered over in the mind, fully understood in theory.[6] He has a pleasant voice, a good enunciation, is urbane in speech, distinct, free from hoarseness and informative.[7] At will, easily and without trouble, he attains to the four states of musing, which bring comfort both here and now, transcending thought. By destroying the cankers he enters and abides in the emancipation of the heart and of insight, which is free

---

[1] See discussion on these terms at *Pts. of Contr.* 377 *ff.* On these terms our *Comy.* observes: *pañcasu atthesu pabhedagatañāṇaŋ patto ; catubbhidhe dhamme* . . .; *dhamma-niruttisu* . . .; *tesu tīṇi ñāṇesu* . . .

[2] For this passage see above, § 33; *Vin.* i, 70; *A.* v, 24.

[3] *Cf.* below V, §§ 166, 232.

[4] *A.* iv, 140; *D.* iii, 78; *It.* 96 and *passim.*

[5] *Cf.* Mrs. Rhys Davids' *Sakya,* p. 73; *Manual,* p. 161.

[6] A. iv, 6; *D.* iii, 267, etc.

[7] *A.* iv, 279; *M.* ii, 166; *D.* iii, 115.

of the cankers, and this state he knows and realizes for himself, even in this life.[1]

Verily, monks, possessed of these five qualities, an elder monk becomes among his fellows in the godly life, dear, pleasant, respected and what he ought to become.'

§ viii (88). *The elder.*

'Monks, possessed of five qualities, the way[2] of an elder monk is not to the advantage of many folk, is not for the happiness of many folk, is not for the good of many folk; it is to the harm and ill of devas and men. Of what five ?

There is the elder, time-honoured[3] and long gone forth; well-known, renowned, with a great following of householders and those gone forth; a receiver of the requisites: the robe, alms, lodging and medicaments for sickness; who is learned, has a retentive and well-stored mind, and those Ḍhammas, lovely in the beginning[4] . . . are by him fully understood in theory; but he is a wrong viewer with a perverted vision. He turns away many folk from Saddhamma and sets them in what is not Saddhamma. Thus though he be an elder, time-honoured and long gone forth, through him they fall into the way of wrong views; though the elder be well known, renowned, with a great following of householders and those gone forth, through him they fall into the way of wrong views; though the elder be a receiver of the requisites . . ., through him they fall into the way of wrong views; though the elder be learned and has a retentive and well-stored mind, through him they fall into the way of wrong views.

Monks, possessed of these five qualities the way of an elder is not to the advantage of many folk. . . .

Monks, possessed of five qualities the way of an elder is to the advantage of many folk, is for the happiness of many folk, is for the good of many folk; it is to the advantage and happiness of devas and men. Of what five ?'

(*Just the opposite qualities.*)[4]

---

[1] *A.* iv, 140 for both clauses.

[2] *Paṭipanna.*

[3] *Rattaññū.*

[4] The text repeats in full.

§ ix (89). *The monk in training* (*a*).

'Monks, these five conditions lead to the decline of a monk in training. What five?

Delight in business;[1] delight in gossip; delight in sleeping; delight in company; and he does not reflect on the mind as freed.[2]

Monks, these are the five conditions. . . .

Monks, these five conditions do not lead to the decline of a monk in training. What five?'

(*Just the opposite conditions.*)[3]

§ x (90). *The same* (*b*).

'Monks, these five . . . What five?

Monks, take the case of a monk in training who is always busy and has much to do and is clever at work; he lets the time for going apart slip by, nor does he apply himself to calming the heart within. This, monks, is the first condition that leads to the decline of a monk in training.

Again, he spends the day in doing small things and lets the time for going apart slip by. . . . This, monks, is the second condition . . .

Or he lives in company with householders and those gone forth, in laymen's company which is not meet. . . .[4] This, monks, is the third condition . . .

Or he enters the village too early and leaves it too late. . . .[5] This, monks, is the fourth condition . . .

Moreover, monks, such talk as is austere and a help to opening the heart:[6] talk on wanting little, on contentment, on loneliness, on not keeping company, on strenuous endeavour,

---

[1] *Cf. A.* iv, 22; *It.* 72; below VI, §§ 14, 21. Business=*kamma.*

[2] *Yathâvimuttaŋ cittaŋ na paccavekkhati.* *Comy.* as if it were a mind freed (*yathâssa cittaŋ vimuttaŋ*); the faults got rid of and the good qualities won—he reflects on those, but makes no effort to win higher ones. *Cf.* below V, § 95 *ff.*

[3] The text repeats in full.

[4] *Cf. Vin.* ii, 7; below V, § 223; *Comy.* not in accord with (the Master's message).

[5] *Vin.* i, 70; *M.* i, 469; *S.* i, 201 (*K.S.* i, 256, the case of Nāgadatta).

[6] *Citta-vivaraṇa-saṅkhātānaŋ*; *cf. A.* iv, 352; v, 67; *M.* iii, 113; *Ud.* 36.

on virtue, on concentration, on insight, on emancipation and on the knowledge and vision of emancipation—that the monk in training cannot obtain at will, easily and without difficulty; and he lets the time for going apart slip by, nor does he apply himself to calming the heart within. This, monks, is the fifth condition that leads to the decline of a monk in training.

Monks, these are the five . . .

Monks, these five conditions do not lead to the decline of a monk in training. What five ?'

(*Just the opposite conditions.*)[1]

Chapter X.—Kakudha.

§ i (91). *Achievements.*

'Monks, there are these five achievements.[2] What five ?

The perfecting of faith, the perfecting of virtue, the perfecting of learning, the perfecting of charity, and the perfecting of insight.

Verily, monks, these are the five achievements.'

§ ii (92). *The same.*

'Monks, there are these five . . .

The perfecting of virtue, of concentration, of insight, of emancipation and the perfecting of the knowledge and vision of emancipation.

Monks, these are the five . . .'

§ iii (93). *Avowal.*

'Monks, there are these five avowals of gnosis.[3] What five ?

One will avow gnosis through folly and blindness;[4] one

---

[1] The text repeats in full.

[2] *Sampadā, cf. D.* iii, 235 and below V, § 130 for a different set. *Cf.* above, Nos. 46, 65. We have no coincident word for *sampadā*. 'Perfection' is too high in meaning. 'Success' might be fairly adequate, but has for us no religious associations. *Cf.* the saying, *Dial.* ii, trans., 'Work out your own salvation.' This is very free, but indicates the long arduous procedure.

[3] *Cf. Vin.* v, 189; *Brethr.* p. xxxiii.

[4] *Mandattā momūhattā*; our colloquial 'soft' is *manda*. *Cf. M.* i, 520; below V, § 141.

filled with evil desires and longings; one being foolish with mind tossed up and down;[1] one through overweening pride; and one will avow gnosis from the fulness[2] of knowledge.

Monks, these are the five avowals of gnosis.'

§ iv (94). *Comfort.*

'Monks, there are these five abodes of comfort.[3] What five?

Herein, monks, a monk, aloof from sensuous appetites, aloof from evil ideas, enters and abides in the first musing, wherein applied and sustained thought works, which is born of solitude and full of joy and ease. Suppressing applied and sustained thought . . . he enters and abides in the second musing . . . the third musing . . . the fourth musing; and by the destruction of the cankers, he enters and abides in the realization of mind-emancipation and insight-emancipation, which is free of the cankers, fully comprehending those states himself, even in this world.

Monks, these are the five abodes of comfort.'

§ v (95). *The immovable.*

'Monks, possessed of five qualities a monk in no long time will penetrate the immovable.[4] Of what five?

He is a master of logical analysis; a master in analyzing causal relations; a master of grammatical analysis; a master in analyzing things knowable;[5] and he reflects on the mind as freed.[6]

Monks, possessed of these five qualities . . .'

§ vi (96). *The learned.*

'Monks, possessed of five qualities a monk, practising awareness in breathing in and breathing out,[7] will in no long time penetrate the immovable. Of what five?

---

[1] *Cittakkhepā*, as the Psalmist (cix, 23). *Cf. S.* i, 126.

[2] *Samma-d-eva*. *Comy. hetunā, nayena, kāraṇena.*

[3] *Cf.* below V, § 105.

[4] *Akuppa, lit.* unshaking. *Comy. arahattaṃ.*

[5] Above, § 86.

[6] Above, § 89.

[7] *Ānāpānasati*, see *K.S.* v, 257 *ff.* and references there.

He is set on little,[1] busied in little, frugal, well content with life's necessities; taking food in little, he serves not his own belly;[2] slothful in little, he is heedful in vigilance; he is learned, with a retentive and well-stored mind; those things, lovely in the beginning, lovely in the middle and lovely in the end, which set forth in spirit and letter the godly life of purity, perfect in its entirety—those are fully learnt by him, resolved upon, made familiar by speech, pondered over in mind, fully understood in theory; and he reflects on the mind as freed.

Monks, possessed of these five qualities . . .'

§ vii (97). *Talk.*

'Monks, possessed of five qualities a monk, cultivating awareness in breathing in and breathing out, will in no long time penetrate the immovable. Of what five?

He is set on little . . .;[3] such talk as is austere and a help to opening the heart: talk on wanting little and so forth . . . —that he can obtain at will, easily and without difficulty; and he reflects on the mind as freed.

Monks, possessed of these five qualities . . .'

§ viii (98). *Forest.*

'Monks, possessed of five qualities a monk, making much of awareness in breathing in and breathing out, will in no long time penetrate the immovable. Of what five?

He is set on little . . .; is a forest-dweller with outland bed and seat; and he reflects on the mind as freed.

Monks, possessed of these five qualities . . .'

§ ix (99). *Lion.*

'Monks, at eventide the lion, king of beasts, leaves his lair; he stretches himself; he looks around on the four quarters; three times he roars his lion-roar; then he goes forth to hunt.[4]

---

[1] *Appaṭṭha; cf.* this first quality with *It.* 72; *Sn.* 144.

[2] *Anodarikattam anuyutto; cf. Romans* xvi, 18.

[3] The text gives in full. The repetition of *appamiddho* . . . is to be deleted.

[4] *Cf. A.* ii, 33; v, 32; *S.* iii, 84.

Monks, if he strike a blow at an elephant, he strikes verily with care, not without care; if he strike a blow at a buffalo . . . at an ox . . . at a leopard . . . if he strike a blow at any small creature, be it but a hare or cat, he strikes with care, not without care. And why? He thinks: Let not my skill[1] fail me!

A[2] lion, monks, that is a name for the Tathāgata, arahant, fully enlightened. Verily, monks, when the Tathāgata teaches Dhamma in assembly, that is his lion-roar; and if he teach Dhamma to the monks, he teaches with care, not without care; if he teach Dhamma to the nuns . . . to laymen . . . to lay-women, disciples, . . . if the Tathāgata teach Dhamma to the many folk, be they but fowlers who go about with grain,[3] he teaches with care, not without care And why? Filled with respect for Dhamma is the Tathāgata, monks, filled with reverence for Dhamma.'

§ x (100). *Kakudha.*

Now the Exalted One was once staying near Kosambī, in Ghosita Park; and at that time Kakudha,[4] a Koliyan[5]—the venerable Mahā Moggallāna's servitor—had just died and was reborn[6] in a mind-pictured body;[7] and the form that he took was such that it filled two or three Magadhan village fields;[8] yet that form caused suffering neither to him nor to another.

---

[1] *Yoggapatha.*

[2] *Cf. Sn.* 546, 572; *It.* 123; *S.* i, 28.

[3] *Annabhāranesādānaŋ.*

[4] At *D.* ii, 92 the B. tells of his faring-on, a Non-returner; at *S.* i, 54, as devaputta, he questions the B. as to whether he is glad or sad; the whole of our sutta recurs at *Vin.* ii, 185 (*S.B.E.* xx, 234 *ff.*); see also Rockhill's *Life* for the Tibetan version. There he is said to have been Kaundinya's son (Koṇḍañña), but Koṇḍañña seems to have been a Sākya; see *Breth.* 284; *J.* i, 56 (Warren, B. *in T.* 51, 69).

[5] For this clan see *C.H.I.* i, 177.

[6] *Upapanna*; at *A.* iv, 225 this word is used in contrast to *paccājāta* for beings reborn elsewhere than here.

[7] *Manomayaŋ kāyaŋ.* *Cf.* below, § 166; *G.S.* i, p. 17. Nyāṇatiloka: *geisterzeugten.*

[8] *Comy.* says this is *tigāvuta*, or about six miles!

And Kakudha deva visited the venerable Mahā Moggallāna, saluted him and stood at one side; and so standing, he spoke thus to the venerable one: 'Sir, in Devadatta has arisen this longing:[1] "It is I who will lead the Order of monks!" —and, sir, with the rising of that thought Devadatta's psychic power has declined.'[2] Thus spake the deva, Kakudha; and having spoken so, he saluted the venerable Mahā Moggallāna and, keeping him on his right, disappeared thence.

Then went the venerable Mahā Moggallāna to the Exalted One and, saluting him, sat down at one side. And he told the Exalted One all that had occurred. . . .[3]

(*And the Exalted One said:*) 'What, Moggallāna, have you with your mind so compassed[4] the mind of Kakudha deva as to know: Whatsoever Kakudha deva says, all that is just thus and not otherwise?'

'Lord, I have so compassed his mind. . . .'

'Then ward thou thy words, Moggallāna, ward thou thy words; for even now the foolish fellow (Devadatta) will betray himself!

Moggallāna, there are these five teachers found in the world. What five?

Take the case, Moggallāna, of some teacher whose ways are impure, but who thinks: "I am pure, pure are my ways, clean and stainless"—but his disciples know: "This worthy teacher is impure in his ways, but thinks just otherwise. . . .[5] If we tell the householders, he will not like it; and how can we do what he will not like? And he is honoured by gifts of the requisites: the robe, alms, lodging and medicaments. What the self shall do, even by that shall the self be known."[6] Mog-

---

[1] Our text and *S.e.* omit '*lābhasakkārasilokena abhibhūtassa pariyādinnacittassa*' of the *Vin.* version.

[2] See Thomas' *Life*, 132 *ff.*

[3] The text repeats in full.

[4] *Parieca* (wholly gone round), as in the formula of 'thought-reading,' above, p. 12.

[5] The text gives all in full.

[6] *Yaŋ 'tumo karissati, 'tumo 'va tena paññāyissati. Comy. yaŋ esa karissati, so eva tena kammena pākaṭo bhavissati.* 'By their fruits shall ye know them' (*Matt.* vii 20).

gallāna, the disciples ward such a teacher in his ways; and such a teacher expects this warding of his disciples.

Again, Moggallāna, some teacher's mode of livelihood is not pure . . . Dhamma teaching . . . exposition . . . knowledge and insight. . . . "What the self shall do, even by that shall the self be known." Moggallāna, the disciples ward such a teacher as to knowledge and insight; and such a teacher expects this warding of his disciples.

These, Moggallāna, are five teachers found in the world.

But I, Moggallāna, am pure in ways and know that I am pure; I know that my ways are pure, clean and stainless: my disciples ward not my ways, nor do I expect this warding of my disciples.

I am pure in my mode of livelihood . . . in Dhamma teaching . . . in exposition . . . and in knowledge and insight, and I know that I am pure; I know that these things are pure within me, clean and stainless: not as to them do my disciples ward me, nor do I expect this of my disciples.'

Chapter XI.—The Abodes of Comfort.

§ i (101). *The fearful.*

'Monks, these five things give confidence to a learner. What five?

Herein, monks, a monk has faith, is virtuous, learned, energetic and has insight.

Monks, what is fearful[1] to one of little faith is not fearful to the believer; wherefore this quality gives confidence to a learner.

Monks, what is fearful to the unvirtuous . . . him of little learning . . . the lazy . . . and to one who lacks insight, that is not fearful to the virtuous . . . learned . . . energetic . . . and to one with insight. Wherefore these qualities give confidence to a learner.

Verily, monks, these five things give confidence to a learner.'

---

[1] *Sārajja. Comy. domanassa, cf. Ephesians* iii, 12: '. . . We have boldness and access with confidence by faith. . . .'

§ ii (102). *Suspected.*

'Monks, a monk who follows after five things is mistrusted and suspected; he is thought of as an evil monk, yea, even though he has won to the immovable.[1] What five?

Herein, monks, a monk haunts a harlot's house;[2] a widow's house; the house of some fat maid;[3] where a eunuch lives; or haunts the nuns' premises.

Verily, monks, a monk who follows after these five things is mistrusted and suspected; he is thought of as an evil monk, yea, even though he has won to the immovable.'

§ iii (103). *The robber.*

'Monks,[4] a robber chief, pursuing five courses, breaks into houses, makes off with plunder, makes for lonely houses[5] or lies in wait in the highway. What five?

Herein, monks, a robber chief relies on the roughness of the way, the entanglements, and the powerful, he is a briber[6] and works alone.

And how, monks, does the robber chief rely on the roughness of the way? He relies on the rivers being unfordable and on the roughness of the mountains. Thus, monks, a robber chief relies on the roughness of the way.

And how does he rely on the entanglements? He relies

---

[1] The text reads *api kuppadhammo pi, v.l. akuppa,* and so *S.e.* and *Comy.* observing: even though he has destroyed the cankers he is suspected by others. On *akuppa* see above, § 95, *Tr. Dict. s.v.*

[2] This set recurs at *Vin.* i, 70; at *Vibh.* 246 (quoted at *Vism.* 17) and *Expos.* i, 201, quoting a *ṭīkā*, a sixth is given: a liquor shop. In the trsls. *gocara* is generally assumed to mean for alms; our *Comy.* glosses: *tāsaŋ gehaŋ abhiṅha-gamano.*

[3] *Thullakumārī-. Comy. mahallaka-*, elsewhere translated 'old maid,' but see *J.* iv, 219.

[4] *Cf. A.* i, 153 (*G.S.* i, 137) for the first three items of this sutta, *Vin.* ii, 89 for other five.

[5] *Ekâgārikaŋ karoti. Comy.* on *A.* i: rounding on a lonely house for plunder; *ekâgārika* has quite a different meaning at *D.* i, 166; see *Dial.* i, 229. The whole set is stock; *cf. D.* i, 52; *M.* ii, 88; *S.* iii, 208.

[6] *Bhogacāgī.*

on the entanglement of the grass, the trees, the thickets[1] and the great forest-wilderness. Thus, monks, a robber chief relies on the entanglements.

And how does he rely on the powerful? He relies on rajahs and their ministers. He thinks: If any question me, these rajahs or their ministers will tell a tale in my defence—and if any do question him, they speak up for him. Thus, monks, a robber chief relies on the powerful.

And how is he a briber? He is rich with great wealth and property; and he thinks: Should anyone question me, I'll make him friendly from now on by a bribe—and if anyone does question him, he acts in this way. Thus, monks, a robber chief is a briber.

And how, monks, does a robber chief work alone? Herein, monks, a robber chief deals with his loot[2] alone. Any why is that? He thinks: Let none plan the hiding place with me[3] and then embroil me! Thus, monks, a robber chief works alone.

Monks, pursuing these five courses a robber chief breaks into houses, makes off with plunder, makes for lonely houses or lies in wait in the highway.

Monks, in just the same way an evil monk, following five courses, goes about to dig[4] a pit to hurt himself; and he is blamed and censured by the wise and begets demerit. What five?

Herein, monks, the evil monk relies on roughness, relies on entanglements, relies on the powerful, and he is a briber and works alone.

And how, monks, does the evil monk rely on roughness? He is possessed of roughness in body-working, of roughness in word-working and of roughness in mind-working. Thus, monks, the evil monk relies on roughness.

---

[1] The text reads *rodhaŋ*, but *S.e.* with *v.l. gedhaŋ*; see *G.S.* i, 137 *n.*

[2] *Niggahaṇāni. Comy. parasantakānaŋ bhaṇḍānaŋ gahaṇāni.* I suppose the prefix here is *ni*; *P.E.D.* only gives the form with *nis* (*nir*).

[3] *Guyhamantā. Comy. guhitabbamantā.*

[4] *Khataŋ upahataŋ attānaŋ pariharati. Comy.* on *A.* i: *guṇakhaṇanena khataŋ*; *cf. Job* vi, 27; *Psalm* lvii, 6; more literally, possessed of five conditions, he carries himself round, dug, hurt. *Cf.* below, p. 274 text.

And how, monks, does he rely on entanglements? He is one of wrong views and he follows the views of the extremist.[1] Thus, monks, the evil monk relies on entanglements.

And how, monks, does he rely on the powerful? He relies on rajahs or their ministers; he thinks: If any question me, these rajahs or their ministers will tell a tale in my defence—and if any do question him, they speak up for him. Thus, monks, the evil monk relies on the powerful.

And how, monks, is he a briber? The evil monk is a receiver of the requisites: the robe, alms, lodging and medicaments; and he thinks: Should anyone question me, I will make him friendly from now on by a good turn—and if anyone does question him, he acts in this way. Thus, monks, the evil monk is a briber.

And how, monks, does the evil monk work alone? Herein, monks, he has a house built for himself alone in the country outskirts, and from there visits the families and gets gain. Thus, monks, the evil monk works alone.

Monks, following these five courses an evil monk goes about to dig a pit to hurt himself; and he is blamed and censured by the wise and begets demerit.'

§ iv (104). *He who graces.*

'Monks,[2] endowed with five qualities a monk is a recluse who graces recluses.[3] What five?

Herein, monks, a monk is often asked to accept a robe, not seldom; often to accept alms . . . lodging . . . medicaments, he is not seldom asked. And with whomsoever he has fellowship in the godly life, often they act cordially toward him, not

---

[1] *Antagāhika. Comy. Sassataŋ vā ucchedaŋ vā gahetvā ṭhitāya*, taking up the position of either the eternalists or the annihilationists. See the *Brahma-jāla* sutta (*Dial.* i).

[2] The whole of this sutta recurs as part of § 87 of the 'Fours,' *A.* ii, 87: see trsl. The third clause is stock; *cf.* *Ṡ.* iv, 230; *Mil.* 302; as diseases in the lists at *A.* v, 110; *Mil.* 112; the fourth and fifth, above, § 31.

[3] *Samaṇesu samaṇa-sukhumālo.*

seldom; often they speak cordially . . .; often they think cordially, not seldom; cordially they offer service, seldom without cordiality. And the pains that arise from bile, or from phlegm, or from wind, or the union of humours, or that come from seasonal changes, or from improper care, or from an attack (of some disease), or that come as a result of (former) deeds—they press not sorely upon him; he suffers little from ill-health. And he obtains at will, without trouble, without difficulty, both here and now, the abodes of ease: the fourfold musings, highly mental.[1] And by destroying the cankers, he enters and abides in the emancipation of the mind, the emancipation of insight, which is free of the cankers, realizing this state by his own knowledge even in this life.

Verily, monks, endowed with these five qualities a monk is a recluse who graces recluses.

Of him, monks, of whom in speaking rightly one may say: He is a recluse who graces recluses—verily of me, monks, in speaking rightly may one say that—He is a recluse who graces recluses.

I, monks, am often asked to accept a robe . . . alms . . . lodging . . . and medicaments, I am not seldom asked. With whomsoever I have fellowship in the godly life, unto me often they act cordially . . . speak . . . and think cordially, not seldom; cordially they offer service, seldom without cordiality. The pains that arise from bile, phlegm, wind, mixed humours, that come from seasonal changes, improper care, attack of disease and result of deeds, press not sorely upon me. The abodes of ease: the fourfold musings, I can obtain at will. . . . I enter and abide in the emancipation of the mind, in the emancipation of insight. . . .

Verily, monks, of him of whom in speaking rightly one may say: He is a recluse who graces recluses—even of me, monks, in speaking rightly one may say that—He is a recluse who graces recluses.'

---

[1] *Abhicetasikānaṃ*. The rendering is quite literal. The mental residuum from fourfold jhāna was *sati*-cum-*upekkhā*, mental alertness and poise.

§ v (105). *Comfort.*

'Monks, there are these five comfortable abodes.[1] What five?

Herein, monks, there is ever present in a monk amity in act of deed, in act of word, in act of mind when among his fellows in the godly life, both in open and in secret; and those virtues, unbroken, without a rent, untarnished, without blemish, bringing freedom, praised by the wise, incorrupt and conducive to concentration—in such he lives, one in virtue,[2] in open and in secret, among his fellows in the godly life; and that view, which is Ariyan, saving, and leads the doer thereof to the utter destruction of Ill—in that he lives, one in view, in open and in secret, among his fellows in the godly life.

Verily, monks, these are the five comfortable abodes.'

§ vi (106). *The venerable Ānanda.*

Once the Exalted One was dwelling near Kosambī in Ghosita Park; and there the venerable Ānanda came to him, saluted and sat down at one side. So seated, the venerable Ānanda spoke thus to the Exalted One:

'Lord, to what extent may the Order of monks, as they live, live comfortably?'

'When, Ānanda, a monk has achieved virtue by self and is no importuner[3] of another as to more-virtue[4]—to that extent, Ānanda, may the Order, as they live, live comfortably.'

'But, lord, might there be another way wherein the Order, as they live, may live comfortably?'

'There might be, Ānanda,' said the Exalted One. 'When, Ananda, a monk has achieved virtue by self and is no importuner

---

[1] The whole sutta recurs at *D.* ii, 88; *DA.* ii, 531 has much more to say than *Mnrp.*; for the fourth clause see above, § 32, below V, § 179; for the fifth *cf. M.* i, 69; *D.* i, 235. For a different set see above, § 94.

[2] *Sīlasāmaññagato. Comy. samāna-sīlataŋ gato, ekasadisa-sīlo hutvā-ti attho.*

[3] *Sam-pa-vattar.* The *Comy.* observes: *paraŋ sīlabhāve na garahati, na upavadati.*

[4] *Adhisīle.*

of another as to more-virtue, considers self[1] and does not consider another—to that extent, Ānanda, may the Order, as they live, live comfortably.'

'Lord, might there be yet another way . . . ?'

'There might, Ānanda. . . . When, thus having achieved and considering self . . ., a monk is neither famous nor vexed by lack of fame—to that extent may the Order live comfortably.'

'Lord, might there be still another way . . .?'

'There might, Ānanda. . . . When, so living . . . a monk obtains at will . . . the abodes of ease: the fourfold musings . . . —to that extent may the order live comfortably.'

'Lord, might there be some other way wherein the Order, as they live, may live comfortably ?'

'There might be, Ānanda,' said the Exalted One. 'Verily, Ānanda, when a monk has achieved virtue by self, and is no importuner of another as to more-virtue; considers self, does not consider another; is neither famous nor vexed by the lack of fame; obtains at will . . . the abodes of ease: the fourfold musings . . .; and enters and abides in the emancipation of the mind, in the emancipation of insight . . . verily, Ānanda, to that extent the Order of monks, as they live, may live comfortably.

And I declare, Ānanda, than this comfortable abode there is none higher, none loftier.'[2]

§ vii (107). *Virtue.*

'Monks, possessed of five things a monk is worthy of offerings, worthy of gifts, worthy of oblations, meet to be reverently saluted, the world's unsurpassed field for merit. Of what five ?

Herein, monks, a monk has achieved virtue, concentration, insight, emancipation and the knowledge and vision of emancipation.

---

[1] *Attânupekkhī*; so also St. Paul to the *Galatians* (vi, 1): ' . . . if a man be overtaken in a fault . . . restore (him) . . . considering thyself, lest thou also be tempted.'

[2] *Uttaritaro vā paṇītataro vā;* the latter is from *pra* $\sqrt{}$*nī*, and occurs everywhere in the Piṭakas.

Verily, monks, possessed of these five things a monk is worthy. . . .'

§ viii (108). *No need to train.*[1]

'Monks, possessed of five things a monk is worthy. . . . Of what five?

Herein,[2] monks, a monk is possessed of the whole body of virtue, with no need to train; with the whole body of concentration . . . of insight . . . of emancipation . . .; with the whole body of the knowledge and vision of emancipation, with no need to train.

Verily, monks, possessed of these five things a monk is worthy. . . .'

§ ix (109). *The four-regioner.*

'Monks, possessed of five things a monk is a four-regioner.[3] Of what five?

Herein, monks, a monk is virtuous, abides restrained by the restraint of the Obligations,[4] is perfected in conduct and habit, sees peril in the smallest fault, accepts the training and trains himself accordantly; and he is learned, with a retentive and well-stored mind, and those things lovely in the beginning, lovely in the middle, lovely in the end, setting forth in spirit and letter the godly life, perfect in its entirety, are learnt

---

[1] *Asekhiyā.*

[2] This recurs at *D.* iii, 279; *S.* i, 99 (*cf.* v, 162); *A.* i, 162 (*G.S.* i, 144); v, 16; below p. 271 of text; for 3 see *It.* 51. In this and following sutta Nyāṇatiloka suppresses several terms.

[3] *Cātuddiso. Comy. catusu disāsu appaṭihatacāro*, moving without let in the four quarters—and adds that a *khīṇâsava* is spoken of. The word as a technical term does not seem to recur elsewhere in the four Nikāyas. It occurs at *Sn.* 42:

Cātuddiso appaṭigho ca hoti
santussamāno itarītarena,

the second line conveying the idea of the third clause in our sutta. (*Cf.* our *Comy.* with *J.* i, 7, last line of page.) At *D.* i, 145: *cātuddisaŋ saŋghaŋ uddisa vihāraŋ karotī; Dial.*: the putting up of a dwelling-place for the Order in all four directions.

[4] *Pāṭimokkha.*

by him, resolved upon, made familiar by speech, pondered over in the mind, fully understood in theory;[1] and he is well contented[2] with any requisite: robe, alms, lodging and medicaments; and he obtains at will the abodes of ease: the fourfold musings . . .; and he enters and abides in the emancipation of the mind, in the emancipation of insight. . . .

Verily, monks, possessed of these five things a monk is a four-regioner.'

§ x (110). *The forest.*

'Monks, possessed of five things a monk is fit to follow the ways of the forest-wildernesses, the outland bed and seat.[3] Of what five?

Herein, monks, a monk is virtuous . . .; and he is learned . . .; and he abides in active energy[4] . . . shirking not the burden of righteousness; and he obtains at will the abodes of ease . . .; and he enters and abides in emancipation. . . .

Verily, monks, possessed of these five things a monk is fit to follow the ways of the forest-wildernesses, the outland bed and seat.'

Chapter XII.—Andhakavinda.

§ i (111). *The clan-goer.*

'Monks, pursuing five courses a clan-going monk becomes among clan folk neither dear nor loved nor revered nor what he ought to become. What five?

He is intimate with those who are unfamiliar;[5] interfering without warrant;[6] frequents the society of[7] dissenters; whispers[8] in the ear; and asks too much.

---

[1] For these first two *cf.* above, § 87.

[2] *Cf. M.* ii, 6; *S.* ii, 194; *A.* iv, 233; v, 25; below V, § 127.

[3] See *Breth.* p. xl. *Comy.* says a *khīṇāsava* is referred to.

[4] The text does not give in full; see above, § 2. Nyāṇatiloka renders *besitzt Willenskraft,* which gives India a term she did not possess, though Gotama used his best substitutes. *Viriya,* 'effort,' 'energy,' is a *mode of using* will.

[5] *Comy.* those who do not make friends with him.

[6] *Comy.* being no lord, he apportions as a lord, saying, Give this, take that. *P.E.D.* intentioning unruliness (?).

[7] *Vyatta.*

[8] *Cf. Romans* i, 29, also *Proverbs* xvi, 28.

Monks, pursuing these five courses a clan-goer is not dear to . . . clan-folk.'

(*But pursuing the opposite five he is dear.*)[1]

§ ii (112). *The recluse who walks behind.*

'Monks, acting in five ways a recluse[2] ought not to be taken to walk behind. What five?

He keeps too far behind or too near; takes not the alms-laden bowl;[3] restrains not one's speech from being overtaken in a fault; interrupts one, time and again, in speaking; and is dull-witted, stupid, an idiot.

Monks, acting in these five ways a recluse ought not to be taken to walk behind.'

(*But if he act in the opposite five ways he should be taken.*)[1]

§ iii (113). *Concentration.*

'Monks, possessed of five qualities a monk cannot enter and abide in right concentration. What five?

Herein, monks, a monk cannot endure[4] sights, sounds, smells, tastes and touches.

Monks, possessed of these five qualities a monk cannot enter and abide in right concentration.'

(*But possessed of the opposite five he can.*)[1]

§ iv (114). *At Andhakavinda.*

On one occasion, when the Exalted One was dwelling among the Magadhese at Andhakavinda,[5] the venerable Ānanda came to him, saluted and sat down at one side. And the Exalted One spoke thus to the venerable Ānanda, so seated:

---

[1] The text repeats in full.

[2] A junior; for the first four clauses see *Vin.* i, 46 (in different order); for the fourth *cf.* below VI, § 60; *Sn.* p. 107; *M.* ii, 122.

[3] *Patta-pariyāpanna.*

[4] *Cf.* above, § 85, below V, § 138.

[5] Our *Comy.* is silent; *S.A.* i, 220, a village. It presumably lay between Benares and Rājagaha; see *Vin.* i, 109, 220 and 224.

'Ānanda, the monks that are novices, lately gone forth, come newly to this Dhamma[1] and discipline—those monks, Ānanda, verily[2] must be made to take heed of, enter into, and stand fast in five things. What five?

Say thus: Come you, sirs, be virtuous; live restrained in the restraint of the Obligations,[3] perfected in conduct and habit; see danger in the smallest fault; and, in your endeavour, train in the steps of the training!—Thus must they be made to take heed of, enter into, and stand fast in the restraint of the Obligations.

And say thus: Come you, sirs, live with the sense-doors guarded, awake to the watch,[4] be wise in wakefulness,[5] with the ways of the mind[6] well watched, possessed of a heart that is awake and on watch!—Thus must they be made to take heed of, enter into, and stand fast in the restraint of the senses.

And say thus: Come you, sirs, be little in talk, make a limit to talk!—Thus must they be made to take heed of, enter into, and stand fast in the limiting of talk.

And say thus: Come you, sirs, be forest-dwellers, seek ye the ways of the forest-wilderness, the outland bed and seat! —Thus must they be made to take heed of, enter into, and stand fast in seclusion as to the body.

And say thus: Come you, sirs, be right in view,[7] seeing right! —Thus must they be made to take heed of, enter into, and stand fast in seeing right.

Ānanda, the novices, lately gone forth, come newly to this Dhamma and discipline, must be made to take heed of, enter into, and stand fast in these five things.'

---

[1] This is stock; see *Vin.* i, 40; *M.* i, 457; *S.* 1, 9.

[2] *Vo.*

[3] *Pātimokkha.*

[4] *Ārakkhasatino.* *Comy. dvāra-rakkhikāya satiyā samannāgatā.*

[5] *Nipakasatino* (text *nipakka*). *Comy. dvāra-rakkhanakena va ñāṇena samannāgata-satino.*

[6] *Sārakkhitamānasā*; *cf. Sn.* 63; *SnA.* 116; *Thag.* 729.

[7] Our text and *S.e.* read *sammādiṭṭhikā*, but *Comy. -diṭṭhino.*

§ v (115). *Begrudging.*[1]

'Monks, pursuing five courses a nun is surely cast into hell as a reward.[2] What five?

She begrudges sharing her lodging, a family's services, the gain therefrom, fame, and Dhamma.[3]

Monks, pursuing these five courses a nun is surely cast into hell as a reward.

Monks, pursuing five courses a nun is surely set in heaven as a reward. What five?' (*Just the opposite.*)[4]

§ vi (116). *Praise.*[5]

'Monks, pursuing five courses a nun is surely cast into hell as a reward. What five?

Without[6] testing or plumbing[7] the matter, she speaks in praise of the unpraiseworthy, in dispraise of the praiseworthy; without testing or plumbing the matter, she shows her faith in things unbelievable, her disbelief in things believable; and she rejects[8] the gift of faith.

Monks, pursuing these five courses a nun is surely cast into hell as a reward.'

(*Pursuing the opposite she goes to heaven.*)

§ vii (117). *Jealousy.*

'Monks, pursuing five courses . . .

. . . she is jealous, mean, and rejects the gift of faith. . . .'

§ viii (118). *Views.*

. . . she is wrong in views, wrong in purpose and rejects the gift of faith . . .'

---

[1] *Maccharī*; for this sutta *cf. D.* iii, 234; *A.* iv, 459; *DhS. trsl.* 299; *Vism.* 683; *Expos.* ii, 480.

[2] *Cf.* above, § 4.

[3] *Comy. pariyattidhammaŋ*, the dhamma of the texts. Nyāṇatiloka here leaves 'law' (*Gesetz*) and has 'spiritual things.' That the opposites are also set forth he entirely omits!

[4] The text repeats in full.

[5] *Vaṇṇanā.*

[6] *Cf.* below V, § 236; *A.* ii, 84; *Pug.* 49.

[7] *Apariyogāhetvā.*

[8] *Vinipāteti. Comy.* she gives it to another. *Cf.* below V, § 235.

§ ix (119). *Speech.*

. . . she is wrong in speech, wrong in action and rejects the gift of faith. . . .'

§ x (120). *Effort.*

'Monks, pursuing five courses she is cast into hell. . . .

Without testing or plumbing the matter, she speaks in praise of the unpraiseworthy, in dispraise of the praiseworthy; she is wrong in effort; wrong in mindfulness; and rejects the gift of faith.

Monks, pursuing these five courses . . .'

(*Pursuing the opposite courses she goes to heaven.*)[1]

Chapter XIII.—The Sick.

§ i (121). *A sick man.*

On one occasion, when he was staying near Vesālī, at the Gabled Hall in Mahāvana, the Exalted One, arising from seclusion at eventide, visited the hall of the sick.[2] And the Exalted One saw a monk, weak and ailing; and at the sight he sat down on the seat made ready.

And when he was seated, the Exalted One addressed the monks, saying: 'Monks, if five things forsake not anyone weak and ailing, for him this may be expected: ere long, by destroying the cankers, he will enter and abide in the emancipation of mind, the emancipation of insight, which is free of cankers, realizing this by his own knowledge even both here and now. What five?

Herein, monks, a monk abides seeing nothing attractive in the body; is conscious of the cloying of food; conscious of distaste as to the world; perceives impermanence in the compounded; and his inner self is well set on the thought of death.[3]

Monks, if these five things forsake not anyone weak and ailing, for him this may be expected: ere long, he will enter and abide in emancipation. . . .'

---

[1] The text repeats all in full.

[2] *Gilānasālā*; *cf.* *S.* iv, 210 for the same setting.

[3] *Cf.* above, § 71.

§ ii (122). *The arising of mindfulness.*

'Monks, whatsoever monk or nun make become five things, make an increase in five things, unto such one of two fruits may be expected: either gnosis here and now or, if he have some substrate left, the state of a Non-returner.[1] What five?

Herein, monks, mindfulness as to insight into the way of the rise and fall of things is well established within a monk; he abides seeing nothing attractive in the body; is conscious of the cloying of food; conscious of there being no real joy in the world; and perceives impermanence in the compounded.

Monks, whatsoever monk or nun make become these five . . . unto such . . . either gnosis is here and now or . . . the state of a Non-returner.'

§ iii (123). *On helping*[2] *(a).*

'Monks, possessing five qualities a sick man is an ill help to himself. What five?

He treats not himself with physic;[3] knows no measure[4] in his treatment; applies not medicaments; sets not out the extent of his illness to one who tends him in goodness of heart, saying: "In going it goes thus, when it returns it comes so, while it is with me it is just thus"; nor is he the kind of man who endures the onset of bodily aches and pains, racking, shooting, stabbing, bitter, galling, life-taking.[5]

Monks, possessing these five qualities a sick man is an ill help to himself.'

(*Possessing the opposite qualities he is a sure help.*)[6]

§ iv (124). *The same (b).*

'Monks, possessing five qualities one who waits on the sick is not fit to help the sick. What five?

---

[1] *Cf.* above, § 67.

[2] *Uddānaṃ* has *dve paṭṭhānā*; these two suttas recur at *Vin.* i, 302-3, but the 'five' are called *aṅgā*, for our *dhammā*.

[3] *Sappāya*, what makes for good; *cf. Mil.* 215, *trsl.* tonic; *P.E.D.* drug (? simple).

[4] *Sappāye mattaṃ*; *cf. D.* i, 205, where Ānanda cannot pay a visit owing to *bhesajja-mattā pītā*.

[5] *Cf.* below V, § 140 and references there. [6] The text repeats in full.

He cannot prepare medicaments; does not know physic from what is not physic, offers what is not, does not offer what is; in hope of gain[1] waits on the sick, not from good-will; loathes to move excrement, urine, puke and spittle; nor can he from time to time instruct, rouse, gladden and satisfy the sick with Dhamma-talk.

Monks, possessing these five qualities one who waits on the sick is not fit to help the sick.'

(*Possessing the opposite qualities he is fit to help.*)[2]

§ v (125). *Health shall spring forth* (*a*).

'Monks, not from these five things shall health[3] spring forth. What five?

He treats not himself with physic; metes out physic without intelligence; eats unripe things; goes about at unseemly times; and walks not the godly[4] way.

Verily, monks, not from these five shall health spring forth.'

(*But from the opposite five shall health spring forth.*)[2]

§ vi (126). *The same* (*b*).

'Monks, not from these five . . .

He treats not himself with physic; metes it out without intelligence; eats unripe things; is without virtue; and is a bad friend.

Verily, monks, not from these five shall health spring forth.'

(*But from the opposite five shall health spring forth.*)[2]

§ vii (127). *On withdrawing.*[5]

'Monks, pursuing five courses a monk is not fit to draw apart from the Order. What five?

---

[1] *Comy.* 'expecting (gifts) of robes, etc.' (forgetting the helper might well be a lay-disciple, *e.g.* Suppiyā, *A.* i, 26).

[2] The text repeats in full.

[3] *Āyussa*, leading to health or vitality, life; *Comy.* āyuvaḍḍhana.

[4] *A-brahma-cārī*, not a god-way-er.

[5] *Avappakāsa*, from the root √kṛṣ, a derivative of which means to plough. See *Brethr.* p. xxxix.

Herein, monks, a monk is not content with any robe, with any alms, with any lodging, or with any medicament, and he dwells full of lustful purpose.[1]

Monks, pursuing these five courses a monk is not fit to draw apart from the Order.'

(*But pursuing the opposite he is fit.*)[2]

§ viii (128) *The ills of a recluse.*

'Monks, these are the five ills of a recluse. What five?

Herein, monks, he is not content with any . . . of the four requisites and he finds no delight in leading the godly life.

Verily, monks, these are the five.

Monks, these are the five comforts.[3] What five?'

(*The opposite.*)[2]

§ ix (129). *Festering.*[4]

'Monks, five are the lost in hell who lie festering, incurable. What five?

(By him) has his mother been deprived of life; his father; an arahant; (by him), with evil thought, has the Tathāgata's blood been drawn; (by him) has the Order been embroiled.[5]

Verily, monks, these are the five lost in hell who lie festering, incurable.'

§ x (130). *Profit.*[6]

'Monks, there are these five losses. What five?

Loss of kin, loss of wealth, loss by disease, loss of virtue and loss of (right) view. Monks, not caused by loss of kin, wealth, or by disease do beings, on the breaking up of the body after death, arise in the wayward way,[7] the ill way, the

---

[1] *Kāmasaṅkappa*; the opposite here, as at *D.* iii, 215 (see *trsl. n.*), is *nekkhammasankappa*, renunciation-purpose.

[2] The text repeats.

[3] *Sukhāni.*

[4] *Parikuppo. Comy.* observes: *kuppana-sabhāvā*, as an old wound. *Kuppati* means to shake, to be agitated, to be angry (so in the English idiom).

[5] *Cf.* below VI, § 87; *Mil.* 214.

[6] *Sampadā*; *cf.* above, § 91. This sutta recurs at *D.* iii, 235.

[7] *Apāya.*

abyss, hell. Monks, caused by loss of virtue or by loss of view do beings, on the breaking up of the body after death, arise in the wayward way, the ill way, the abyss, hell.

Verily, monks, these are the five.

Monks, there are these five profits. What five?

Profit of kin, profit of wealth, profit of health, profit of virtue and profit of (right) view. Monks, not caused by profit of kin, wealth or health do beings, on the breaking up of the body after death, arise in the happy way, the heaven world. Monks, caused by profit of virtue or by profit of view do beings, . . . after death, arise in the happy way, the heaven world.

Verily, monks, these are the five.'

CHAPTER XIV.—THE RAJAH.

§ i (131). *The onward roll of the wheel* (*a*).

'Monks, endowed in five ways a rajah, rolling the wheel (of state), rolls on the wheel[1] by Dhamma;[2] and that wheel may not be rolled back by the hand of any hostile son of man. In what five ways?

Herein, monks, the rajah, rolling the wheel of state, knows good;[3] knows Dhamma; knows measure;[4] knows times;[5] and knows assembled[6] men.

Monks, endowed in these five ways a rajah, rolling the wheel of state, rolls on the wheel by Dhamma; and that wheel may not be rolled back by the hand of any hostile son of man.

Even so, monks, endowed in five ways, the Tathāgata, arahant, fully enlightened, rolls on by Dhamma the unsurpassed Dhamma wheel; and that wheel may not be rolled back by recluse, godly man, deva, Māra, Brahmā, or by any in the world. In what five ways?

---

[1] *Comy. āṇā-cakka*, the order-wheel.

[2] *Comy. dasakusaladhammena.*

[3] *Attha*, but *Comy. hetu.*

[4] *Comy.* in punishments and impositions; *cf. Jer.* xxx, 11: 'I will correct thee in measure.'

[5] *Comy.* times for pleasure, court-work and touring the country.

[6] *Comy.* whether they be nobles, brāhmans, etc.

Herein, monks, the Tathāgata, arahant, fully enlightened, knows good;[1] knows Dhamma;[2] knows measure; knows times;[3] and knows assembled men.

Verily, monks, endowed in these five ways the Tathāgata, arahant, fully enlightened, rolls on by Dhamma the unsurpassed wheel[4] of Dhamma; and that wheel may not be rolled back by recluse, godly man, deva, Māra, Brahmā, or by any in the world.'

§ ii (132). *The same* (*b*).

'Monks, endowed in five ways the eldest son of a rajah, who rolls the wheel (of state), keeps[5] rolling on by Dhamma the wheel his father set a-roll; and that wheel may not be rolled back by the hand of any hostile creature. In what five ways?'

(*He has these endowments of the rajah.*)[6]

'Monks, endowed in these five ways the rajah's eldest son keeps rolling on the wheel. . . .

Even so, monks, endowed in five ways Sāriputta keeps rolling on, just in the right way,[7] the unsurpassed wheel of Dhamma the Tathāgata set a-roll; and that wheel may not be rolled back by recluse, godly man, deva, Māra, Brahmā, or by any in the world. In what five ways?'

(*He has these endowments of the Tathāgata.*)

'Verily, monks, endowed in these five ways Sāriputta keeps rolling on the Dhamma wheel. . . .'

§ iii (133). *The same*[8] (*c*).

'Monks, the rajah who rolls the wheel (of state), a Dhamma man, a Dhamma rajah, rolls on indeed no[9] unroyal wheel.'

---

[1] *Comy. pañca atthe jānāti.* [2] *Comy.* the four.

[3] *Comy.* for going apart, attainment (in musing), teaching and touring.

[4] *Comy. seṭṭha-cakka,* the best wheel.

[5] *Anupavatteti,* in distinction from *pavatteti* previously.

[6] The text repeats in full. *Cf. Sn.* 557; *Thag.* 827.

[7] *Samma-d-eva.*

[8] This sutta for the Threes recurs at *A.* i, 109 (*G.S.* i, 94); it is fully commented on at *AA.* ii, 178, to which our comment refers.

[9] *A.* i. reads *so pi nāma arājakaṃ,* but *S.e.* both there and here, with *Comy.* and our text, *so pi na* . . ., which I follow.

And when he had thus spoken, a certain monk said to the Exalted One: 'But who, lord, is the rajah of the rajah, the roller of the wheel, the Dhamma man, the Dhamma rajah ?'

'It is Dhamma, monk !' said the Exalted One.

'Herein, monk, the rajah, the wheel roller, the Dhamma man, the Dhamma rajah, relies just on Dhamma, honours Dhamma, reveres Dhamma, esteems Dhamma; with Dhamma as his standard, with Dhamma as his banner, with Dhamma as his mandate, he sets a Dhamma watch and bar and ward for folk within his realm.

. . . he sets a Dhamma watch and bar and ward for warrior and camp follower, for brāhman and for householder, for town and country folk, for recluse and for godly man, for beast and bird alike.

Thus indeed, monk, that rajah . . . setting a Dhamma watch and bar and ward for . . . folk and creatures within his realm, rolls on the wheel by Dhamma; and that wheel may not be rolled back by the hand of any hostile creature.

Even so, monk, the Tathāgata, arahant, fully enlightened, a Dhamma man, a Dhamma rajah, relies just on Dhamma, honours Dhamma, reveres Dhamma, esteems Dhamma; with Dhamma as his standard, with Dhamma as his banner, with Dhamma as his mandate, he sets a Dhamma watch and bar and ward for monks, saying: "Follow ye such a practice in deed, not that other; follow ye such a practice in word, not that other; follow ye such a practice in thought, not that other; follow ye such a livelihood, not that other; seek ye such a town or village, not that other."

So too, . . . for nuns and lay-disciples, both men and women. . . .

Thus indeed, monk, that Tathāgata . . . setting a Dhamma watch and bar and ward for monk and nun, for lay-disciple, both man and woman, rolls on by Dhamma the unsurpassed wheel of Dhamma; and that wheel may not be rolled back by recluse, godly man, deva, Māra, Brahmā, or by any in the world.'

§ iv (134). *In every quarter.*[1]

'Monks, if he have five[2] qualities, a warrior rajah, anointed of head, in whatsoever quarter he abide, abides where he himself has conquered. What five?

Herein, monks, the anointed warrior rajah is well born on both sides, pure in descent as far back as seven generations both of mother and father, unchallenged and without reproach in point of birth;[3] he is rich with great wealth and resources and his treasuries and granaries overflow;[4] and his strength is in the four[5] divisions of his army, loyal and alert to commands; his minister is wise, intelligent, discreet, able to judge rightly the future from past happenings;[6] and these four things ripen to his glory; and with this fifth quality of glory, wheresoever he abide, he abides where he himself has conquered. And how is that? Verily, monks, it is just thus for conquerors of the conquered.[7]

Even so, monks, if he have five qualities, a monk, in whatsoever quarter he abide, abides released in heart. What five?

Herein, monks, the monk is virtuous, lives restrained in the restraint of the Obligations, perfected in conduct and habit, seeing danger in the smallest fault, in his endeavour, training himself in the steps of the training,—this is like the anointed warrior rajah's perfect birth.

He has heard much, bears in mind things heard, as it were lays up in store things heard; those things lovely in the beginning, lovely in the middle, lovely in the end, which set forth in spirit and letter the godly life of purity, perfect in its entirety—those are heard much by him, resolved upon, made familiar by speech, pondered over in mind, fully understood

---

[1] The *uddāna* reads *rājā yassaŋ disaŋ*, so also *S.e.*

[2] *Cf. D.* i, 137 for eight qualities; *Mp.* 639 *ff.* nearly equals *DA.* i, 281.

[3] *A.* i, 163; *D.* i, 113; *Sn.* p. 115; *J.* i, 2; below V, § 192.

[4] *Cf. D.* i, 134; *Vin.* i, 342.

[5] Elephants, chariots, cavalry and foot soldiers.

[6] At *D.* i, 137 this is a quality of the rajah; see *Dial.* i, 178 *n.*

[7] *Vijitāvīnaŋ*. *Comy. vijitavijayānaŋ, mahantena vijayena samannāgatānaŋ.*

in theory,—this is like the rajah's riches and overflowing treasuries and granaries.

He abides in active energy, putting away all unright things, taking to right things, steadfast and strenuous, shirking not the burden of right,—this is like the rajah's strength.

He has insight, being endowed with insight into the way of the rise and fall of things, with Ariyan penetration into the way to the complete destruction of Ill,—this is like the rajah's possession of a minister.

And these four things ripen to his release; and with this fifth quality that is release, wheresoever he abide, he abides released in mind. And how is that? Verily, monks, it is just thus for those whose minds are released.'[1]

§ v (135). *The aim*[2] *(a).*

'Monks, if he have five things,[3] an anointed warrior rajah's eldest son makes rule his aim. What five?

Herein, monks, he is well born . . . without reproach in point of birth; handsome, comely, amiable, he has a wondrous lotus-like beauty;[4] dear and lovely is he to his parents; dear and lovely to town and country folk; and in matters of skill that belong to anointed warrior rajahs: elephant, horse, chariot, bow and sword skill,[5] he is fully[6] trained.

And that he has these five things[7] . . . occurs to him; and he thinks: "Wherefore should I not make rule my aim?"

Monks, if he have these five things, the warrior rajah's eldest son makes rule his aim.

Even so, monks, if he have five things,[8] a monk makes the destroying of the cankers his aim. What five?

Herein, monks, a monk has faith, he believes in the enlightenment of the Tathāgata: He indeed is the Exalted One,

---

[1] *Vimuttacittānaṃ. Comy. pañcāhi vimuttīhi vimuttamānāsānaṃ.*

[2] *Patthanā, pa+√arth,* forward-good or goal.

[3] *Aṅgā.* *Cf.* above, § 75.

[5] *Comy.* the sixteen, adding: writing, sealing, arithmetic, etc. *Cf. Ud.* 31.

[6] *Anavayo. Comy. samattho, paripuṇṇo.*

[7] The text repeats in full.

[8] *Dhammā; cf.* above, § 53 for these, there *aṅgā.*

arahant, fully enlightened . . .; he has health and well-being, a good digestion . . .; he is not deceitful . . .; he abides in active energy . . .; and he is endowed with insight into the way of the rise and fall of things. . . .[1]

And that he has these five things[1] . . . occurs to him; and he thinks: "Wherefore should I not make the destroying of the cankers my aim?"

Verily, monks, if he have these five things, the monk makes the destroying of the cankers his aim.'

§ vi (136). *The same* (*b*).

'Monks, if he have five things, an anointed warrior rajah's eldest son makes viceroyalty[2] his aim. What five?

Herein, monks, he is well born . . .; handsome . . .; dear and lovely to his parents; dear and lovely to the army; and he is wise, intelligent and discreet, able rightly to judge the future from past happenings. And that he has these five things . . . occurs to him; and he thinks: "Wherefore should I not make viceroyalty my aim?"

Monks, if he have these five things, the rajah's son makes viceroyalty his aim.

Even so, monks if he have five things, a monk makes the destroying of the cankers his aim. What five?

Herein, monks, a monk is virtuous . . .; he has heard much . . .; he is firmly set in the fourfold stand of mindfulness;[3] he abides in active energy . . .; and he is endowed with insight. . . . And that he has these five things . . . occurs to him; and he thinks: "Wherefore should I not make the destroying of the cankers my aim?"

Verily, monks, if he have these five things, the monk makes the destroying of the cankers his aim.'

§ vii (137). *They sleep little.*

'Monks, these five sleep little by night, they are much awake. What five?

---

[1] The text repeats in full.

[2] *Oparajja*, see *C.H.I.* i, 488 *ff.*; *cf.* the stages of *Mahā Sudassana* (*D.* ii, 196): *kumārakiḷikaŋ kiḷi, oparajjaŋ kāresi* and *rajjaŋ kāresi.*

[3] Above, § 15: mindfulness as to body, feelings, mind and ideas.

A woman longing for a man sleeps little by night, is much awake; so too a man longing for a woman . . .; a thief longing for booty . . .; a rajah[1] bent on royal business . . .; a monk longing for bondage-release[2] sleeps little by night, is much awake.'

Verily, monks, these five sleep little by night, they are much awake.'

§ viii (138). *The eater of eatables.*[3]

'Monks, possessed of five things a rajah's elephant—a gross[4] eater, filling the ways,[5] spilling his dung,[6] grabbing his food[7]—is reckoned merely[8] a rajah's elephant. What five?

Herein, monks, the rajah's elephant cannot endure forms, sounds, smells, tastes or touches.

Monks, possessed of these five . . .

Even so, monks, possessed of five things a monk—a gross eater, filling the ways, tumbling his bed,[9] grabbing his food ticket—is reckoned merely a monk. What five?

Herein, monks, the monk cannot endure forms, sounds, smells, tastes or touches.

Verily, monks, possessed of these five things a monk—a gross eater, filling the ways, tumbling his bed, grabbing his ticket—is reckoned merely a monk.'

---

[1] The text reads *rājayutto*, but *v.l.* and *S.e.* simply *rājā*.

[2] *Comy. evaŋ nibbānajjhāsayo.*

[3] *Bhattâdā*, which I suppose is the *nom.* of *bhattâdar.*

[4] *Bhattâdako. Comy. bahu-bhatta-bhuñjo.*

[5] *Okāsa-pharaṇo*, space-pervading. *Comy. okāsaŋ pharitvā, aññesaŋ sambādhaŋ katvā, ṭhānena okāsapharaṇo.*

[6] *Laṇḍa-sādhano*, but *S.e. v.l.* and *Comy* .-*sāṭano*, observing: *tattha tattha laṇḍaŋ sāṭeti, pāteti.* See *P.E.D. s.v. saṭa*; I take *sāṭeti* to be the causative of √*śad.*

[7] *Salāka-gāhī. Comy. ettakā hatthī-ti, gaṇanakāle salākaŋ gaṇhati.*

[8] Prof. Hardy (*A.* v, 393) sums up the sutta as: a bh. who deserves this name is likened to a true royal elephant; but I think just the contrary must be the meaning, in view of the following sutta and above, §§ 85 and 113.

[9] *Pīṭha-maddano. Comy.* simply *nisīdana-sayana-vasena mañca-pīṭhaŋ maddati* ('by way of sitting and lying down he tumbles couch and chair').

§ ix (139). *He cannot endure.*

'Monks, possessed of five things a rajah's elephant is not worthy of a rajah, is no rajah's asset,[1] is not even reckoned a rajah's portion.[2] What five?

Herein, monks, he cannot endure forms, sounds, smells, tastes or touches.

And in what manner can he not endure forms? Take the case, monks, of a rajah's elephant going forth to fight, when he sees a force of elephants, horses, chariots or foot soldiers, he loses heart, falters and stiffens not and cannot go down to battle[3]—in this way an elephant, monks, cannot endure forms.

And how can he not endure sounds? Take the case . . . of when he hears the sound of elephants, horses, chariots, the noise and sound of tabor, drum, conch and tom-tom[4] and loses heart . . .—in this way he cannot endure sounds.

And how can he not endure smells? Take the case . . . of when he smells the smell of the dung and urine of those finely bred rajah's elephants, whose home is the battle-ground, and loses heart . . .—in this way he cannot endure smells.

And how can he not endure tastes? Take the case . . . of when he is disgusted by a single dole of grass and water, or by two, three, four or five doles, and loses heart . . .—in this way he cannot endure tastes.

And how, monks, can he not endure touches? Take the case, monks, of a rajah's elephant going forth to fight, when, pierced by the piercing[5] of arrows, he loses heart and falters and stiffens not and cannot go down to battle—in this way, monks, he cannot endure touches.

Monks, possessed of these five things a rajah's elephant is not worthy of a rajah, is no rajah's asset, is not even reckoned a rajah's portion.

---

[1] *Cf. A.* i, 244, 284; ii, 113, 170; iv, 188.

[2] *Aṅga.* [3] *Cf.* above, § 75.

[4] *Tiṇava*; the set recurs at *A.* ii, 117.

[5] Our text reads *-vegena*, but *S.e.* with *v.l. vedhena*, which makes better sense.

In just the same way, monks, possessed of five things[1] a monk is not worthy of offerings, worthy of gifts, worthy of oblations, is not meet to be reverently saluted, is not the world's peerless field for merit. What five?

Herein, monks, the monk cannot endure forms, sounds, smells, tastes or touches.

And how, monks, can he not endure forms? Take the case, monks, of the monk who, seeing forms with the eye, is lured[2] by alluring forms and cannot compose[3] his mind—in this way he cannot endure forms.

. . . who, hearing sounds with the ear, is lured by alluring sounds. . . .

. . . smelling smells with the nose, is lured by alluring smells. . . .

. . . tasting tastes with the tongue, is lured by alluring tastes. . . .

. . . who, touching touches with the body, is lured by alluring touches and cannot compose his mind—in this way he cannot endure these things. . . .

Verily, monks, possessed of these five things a monk is not worthy of offerings, worthy of gifts, worthy of oblations, is not meet to be reverently saluted, is not the world's peerless field for merit.' .

(*But possessed of the five opposite things a rajah's elephant is worthy of a rajah; and even so a monk, possessed of the five opposite things, is worthy of offerings.*)

§ x (140). *The hearers.*

'Monks,[4] possessed of five things a rajah's elephant is worthy of a rajah, is a rajah's asset, is verily reckoned a rajah's portion. What five?

Herein, monks, he is a hearer, a destroyer, a warder, an endurer and a goer.

And how, monks, is the rajah's elephant a hearer? Monks, as soon as the tamer of tamable elephants tasks him with a

---

[1] Here *dhammā*, but *aṅgā* of the elephant.

[2] *Rajanīye rūpe sārajjati.*

[3] *Samādahituṃ. Comy. sammā ṭhapetuṃ*, to rightly fix.

[4] *Cf.* the whole sutta with *A.* ii, 116.

task, whether done before or not; making it his business, setting his mind to it, bringing his whole heart to bear on it, he hears with bended ear. Monks, in this way the rajah's elephant is a hearer.

And how is he a destroyer? Monks, the rajah's elephant, gone forth to fight, destroys an elephant, destroys the rider, destroys a horse, destroys the rider, destroys a chariot, destroys the rider, and indeed destroys a foot soldier. Monks, in this way he is a destroyer.

And how is he a warder? . . . He wards his fore part, he wards his hind part, he wards his fore feet, he wards his hind feet, he wards his head, his ears, his tusks, his trunk, his tail, he wards his rider. Monks, in this way he is a warder.

And how is he an endurer? . . . He endures the blow of the spear, the blow of the sword, the blow of the arrow, the blow of the axe, the sound and noise of tabor, drum, conch and tom-tom. Monks, in this way he is an endurer.

And how is he a goer? Monks, as soon as his driver sends him to some place, whether it has been gone to before or not, he even quickly is a goer there. Monks, in this way the rajah's elephant is a goer.

Monks, possessing these five things he is worthy of a rajah. . . .

In just the same way, monks, possessed of five things a monk is worthy of offerings. . . . What five?

In this case also, monks, he is a hearer, a destroyer, a warder, an endurer and a goer.

And how is he a hearer? Monks, when the Dhamma-discipline, declared by the Tathāgata, is being taught; making it his object, setting his mind to it, bringing his whole heart to bear on it, he listens with bended ear. Monks, in this way he is a hearer.

And how is he a destroyer? Monks, he lets not the surge[1] of lustful thoughts abide, but voids[2] them forth, drives them

[1] *Uppanna*, and lower, *uppannuppanna*.

[2] *Pajahati*. For the phrase *cf. It.* 115; M. i, 11; *D.* iii, 226; *A.* ii, 118, where the whole section recurs, also *M.* i, 115 with *anabhāvaŋ gameti* omitted. (*P.E.D. s.v. anabhāvaŋ* considers this a late idiom [?].)

out, makes an end of them completely and makes them go where there is no becoming; so, too, of the surge of fell thoughts . . . cruel thoughts . . . the continuous surge of evil and wrong ideas,[1] he bids them not abide, but voids them forth, drives them out, makes an end of them completely and makes them go where there is no becoming. Monks, in this way he is a destroyer.

And how is he a warder? Monks, on seeing a form with the eye, he is not entranced[2] with its appearance or detail; since by abiding uncontrolled in the sight-sense, covetousness, dejection and wicked and evil thoughts would flow in over him, he sets himself to control that sense; he wards that sense and wins control over it. So too, on hearing a sound with the ear . . . smelling a smell with the nose . . . tasting a taste with the tongue . . . touching a touch with the body . . . apprehending an idea with the mind, he is not entranced with its appearance or detail; since by abiding uncontrolled in each . . . sense, covetousness, dejection and wicked and evil thoughts would flow in over him, he sets himself to control each sense; he wards each sense and wins control over it. Monks, in this way he is a warder.

And how is he an endurer? Monks, he endures cold, heat, hunger, thirst; the bite of gadfly, gnat, wind, heat and creeping thing, rough, unwelcome[3] ways of speech; he is the kind of man who abides the onset of bodily aches and pains that rack and shoot and stab, bitter, galling and life-taking.[4] Monks, in this way he is an endurer.

And how, monks, is he a goer? Monks, that quarter where in this long journeying on he has not been before, where there is rest for all things made, a complete pouring[5] away of all (rebirth) substance, a destruction of craving, a release from passion, an ending, Nibbāna[6]—verily he quickly is a goer thither. Monks, in this way the monk is a goer.

---

[1] *Dhammā.*

[2] *Cf.* above, § 76.

[3] *Durāgata.*

[4] *Cf. M.* i, 10; *A.* v, 132; *Vin.* i, 78; below IV, § 58; above, § 123.

[5] *Sabb' ûpadhi-paṭinissaggo,* from √sṛj, to pour out.

[6] *S.* iii, 133; *A.* ii, 118; v, 8.

Monks, possessed of these five things a monk is worthy of offerings, worthy of gifts, worthy of oblations, meet to be reverently saluted, the world's peerless field for merit.'

CHAPTER XV.—THREE-THORN GROVE.[1]

§ i (141). *He gives and despises.*

'Monks, these five persons are found living in the world. What five?

One who gives and despises a man; one who despises a man by living with him; one who has a mouth[2] to take in anything; one who wavers; and one who is foolish and mind-[3]tossed.

And how, monks, does a person give and despise a man? Herein, monks, a person to a person gives requisites: the robe, alms, lodging and medicaments, and thinks: I give; this fellow receives! He gives and despises him. Thus, monks, a person gives and despises a man.

And how, monks, does a person despise a man by living with him? Herein, monks, a person lives with a person for two or three years. By living with him he despises him. Thus, monks, a person despises a man by living with him.

And how, monks, has a person a mouth to take in anything? Herein, monks, a person, while another is being spoken of in praise or blame, just promptly[4] revels in it. Thus, monks, a person has a mouth to take in anything.

And how, monks, does a person waver? Herein, monks, a person is uncertain[5] in faith, uncertain in devotion,[6] uncertain in love, uncertain in goodness. Thus, monks, a person wavers.

---

[1] *Tikaṇḍaki*; so *S.e.*, but see *K.S.* v, 264 *n.*, 'Cactus Grove.'

[2] *Ādiyamukha*. *S.e.* with *v.l.* *ādiyya-*. *Comy.* *ādiyana-*, *gahaṇa-*; *pāliya pana ṭhapitamukho-ti attho*, adding: (his mouth) is like a hole dug in the road with water continually flowing into it. *P.E.D.* suggests gossip, but the literal meaning is the complement.

[3] Above, § 93.

[4] *Khippaŋ*.

[5] *Ittara*. *Comy.* *parittaka*.

[6] *Bhatti* = *bhakti*; see *DhS. trsl.* 345 *n.* and correct accordingly.

And how, monks, is a person foolish and mind-tossed? Herein, monks, a person does not know good conditions from bad; does not know blameworthy conditions from blameless; does not know low conditions from lofty; does not know whether conditions are evenly mixed with bright and dark qualities.[1] Thus, monks, a person is foolish and mind-tossed.

Verily, monks, these five persons are found living in the world.'

§ ii (142). *He does amiss.*

'Monks, these five persons are found living in the world. What five?

There is the case, monks, of a person who does amiss and is dejected[2] and knows not, as it really is, that mind-release, that insight-release, wherein for him these surges[3] of evil and wrong states end entirely; there is one who does amiss and is not dejected and knows not that mind-release . . .; one who does not amiss but is dejected and knows not that mind-release . . .; one who does not amiss and is not dejected and knows not that mind-release . . .; and there is one who does not amiss and is not dejected and knows, as it really is, that mind-release, that insight-release, wherein for him these surges of evil and wrong states end entirely.

There, monks, he who does amiss and is dejected . . . this may be said of him: Verily to the venerable one the cankers, born of doing amiss,[4] are discovered; born of dejection they wax: well were it for the venerable one to rid himself of the cankers, born of misdeeds, to drive out the cankers, born of dejection, and to make mind and insight more-become: then will the venerable one become the very same with this fifth person.

And he who does amiss and is not dejected . . . this may

---

[1] *Cf. Mil.* 379.

[2] *Ārabhati ca vippaṭisārī ca. Comy. āpatti-vītikkama-vasena ārabhati c' eva tappaccayā ca vippaṭisārī hoti. Ārabhati* is *lit.* to start (doing something); and *vippaṭisārī*: strongly remembering something against (oneself), so generally 'remorse.' *Cf. Pug.* 64.

[3] *Te uppannā.*

[4] The text reads *ārabbhajā*, but *S.e.* with *v.l.* and *Comy. ārambhajā.*

be said of him: Verily to the venerable one the cankers, born of doing amiss, are discovered; they wax not from dejection: well were it for the venerable to rid himself of the cankers, born of misdeeds, and to make mind and insight morebecome . . .

And he who does not amiss and is dejected . . . and he who does not amiss and is not dejected . . .' (*Reply as above with changes.*)[1]

'Thus verily, monks, these four persons with this fifth, being so exhorted, so counselled, gradually win to the destruction of the cankers.'

§ iii (143). *At Sārandada shrine.*

Once, while he dwelt near Vesālī, at the Gabled Hall in Mahāvana, the Exalted One early one morning, after dressing, took bowl and robe and entered Vesālī for alms.

Now at that time about five hundred Licchavis were met and seated at Sārandada[2] shrine and this chance talk occurred: 'Rarely are the five treasures[3] revealed in the world. What five? Rarely is the elephant treasure revealed in the world. rarely the horse treasure . . . the jewel treasure . . . the woman treasure . . . rarely the householder treasure. Rarely are these five treasures revealed in the world.'

Now these Licchavis had put a man in the road, saying: 'When, my man, you see the Exalted One coming along, come and tell us.'

And the man saw the Exalted One a good way off coming along, and went and told the Licchavis, saying: 'Sirs,[4] here comes this same Exalted One, arahant, fully enlightened; and now's the time to do what you meant!'

And the Licchavis approached the Exalted One, saluted him and stood at one side; and so standing they said: 'Lord,

---

[1] The text repeats all in full.

[2] A *yakkha* shrine; see *K.S.* v, 231 *n.*

[3] Generally seven, the other two being the wheel and the minister; see *Dial.* ii, 202-8; *A.* iv, 89.

[4] *Bhante.*

it were good if the Exalted One were to visit Sārandada shrine out of compassion!'

The Exalted One accepted in silence.

And when he had come to the shrine, he sat down on the seat they had made ready; and so seated he said this to the Licchavis: 'What talked ye of, O Licchavis, as ye sat here together just now; what talk between you was interrupted?'

'Lord, as we sat together the talk turned on how rarely the five treasures are revealed[1] in the world. . . .'

'Truly with you Licchavis, sense-enthralled,[2] talk between you turns just to things of the flesh! Five, O Licchavis, are the treasures rarely revealed in the world. What five?

The[3] Tathāgata, arahant, fully enlightened, is rarely revealed in the world; rare in the world is a person able to teach discipline and Dhamma, declared by the Tathāgata; rare a person able to recognize the teaching . . .; rare in the world is a person who has stepped his way[4] in Dhamma by Dhamma, recognizing the teaching, Dhamma and discipline, declared by the Tathāgata; rare in the world is a person who is grateful and thankful.[5]

Verily, O Licchavis, these are the five treasures rarely revealed in the world.'

§ iv (144). *At Three-thorn Grove.*

Once, while dwelling near Sāketa at Three-thorn Grove, the Exalted One addressed the monks, saying: 'Monks!'

'Lord,' they replied; and the Exalted One said:

'Monks, good is it for a monk from time to time to abide conscious of the distasteful in what is not distasteful;[6] . . . conscious of what is not distasteful in the distasteful; . . . conscious of the distasteful in both what is not and what is distasteful; . . .

---

[1] *Pātu-bhāvo*, the making become manifest.

[2] *Kamâdhimuttānaŋ*. *Comy. vatthu-kāma-kilesa-kāmesu adhimuttānaŋ*.

[3] *Cf.* below V, § 195; VI, § 96.

[4] *Dhammânudhamma-paṭipanno*.

[5] See *K.S.* ii, 183 and the Jackal simile, also *G.S.* i, 72 *n*.

[6] *Appaṭikkūle*. *Comy. -ârammaṇe*. *Cf. Dial.* iii, 107; *K.S.* v, 100 for the whole section.

conscious of what is not distasteful in both what is and what is not distasteful; monks, good is it for a monk from time to time, rid[1] of all that, both the distasteful and what is not, to abide in poise,[2] mindful and self-possessed.

Monks, pressing toward what good mark[3] should a monk abide conscious of the distasteful in what is not distasteful? "May the passion of impassioning things surge not within me!"—it is verily pressing toward this good mark that a monk abides conscious of the distasteful in what is not distasteful.

. . . (and in the converse)? "May the defilement of defiling things surge not within me!"—it is verily pressing toward this good mark. . . .

. . . abiding conscious of the distasteful in both what is not and what is distasteful? "May the passion of impassioning things . . . the defilement of defiling things surge not within me!"—it is verily this. . . .

. . . (and in the converse)? "May the defilement of defiling things . . . the passion of impassioning things surge not within me!"—it is verily pressing toward this good mark that a monk abides conscious of what is not distasteful in both what is and what is not distasteful.

Monks, pressing toward what good mark should a monk abide in poise, mindful and self-possessed, rid of both the distasteful and what is not distasteful? "May never anywhere,[4] in any place, in any way, within me surge the passion of impassioning things; may never anywhere, in any place, in any way, within me surge the defilement of defiling things; may never anywhere, in any place, in any way, within me

---

[1] *Tadubhayaŋ abhivajjetvā*, elsewhere translated avoiding; *cf. It.* 81.

[2] *Upekkhako. Comy. majjhatta-bhāve ṭhito. Cf.* the late Lord Northcliffe: 'The important thing is poise. . . . Poise in all things and at all times. So few men have it.' (*My Northcliffe Diary*, by Mr. Tom Clarke.)

[3] *Attha-vasaŋ paṭicca*; *cf.* above, § 57; on *attha* see Mrs. Rhys Davids' *Sakya*; *vasa* means originally, will, wish, desire; so: aim, purpose; *paṭicca* is the ger. of *pacceti*, to go against; *cf. Philippians* iii, 14.

[4] *Kvacini katthaci kiñcana. Comy. kismici ārammaṇe; kismici padese; koci appamattako pi.*

surge the confusion of confounding things!"—it is verily pressing toward this good mark that a monk abides in poise, mindful and self-possessed, rid of both the distasteful and what is not distasteful.'

§ v (145). *The way to hell.*

'Pursuing five things, monks, one is surely cast into hell as the reward. What five?

One destroys life, takes what is not given, lusts after evil, lies, and lives in the idleness of liquor and strong drink indulgence.

Verily, monks, pursuing these five things one is surely cast into hell as the reward.'

(*But abstaining from these five things one is cast into heaven.*)[1]

§ vi (146). *The friend.*

'Monks, seek ye not a monk for a friend whose ways are five. What five?

He works at (field)[2] work; busies himself in affairs;[3] is at enmity with eminent monks; spends his life taking the long way, the way without an object;[4] and cannot from time to time incite, arouse, gladden and satisfy one with Dhamma talk.

Verily, monks, seek not a monk for a friend whose ways are these.'

(*But seek for a friend whose ways are the opposite.*)[1]

§ vii (147). *Not a good man's gifts.*

'Monks, these five are not a good man's gifts. What five?

He[5] gives without deference; gives without thinking; gives not with his own hand; gives orts; he gives holding no views as to the future.[6]

Verily, monks, these are the five.'

(*But the opposite five are a good man's gifts.*)[1]

---

[1] *Sic.* The text repeats in full. [2] So *Comy.*

[3] *Comy.* the four; these can hardly be the four at *M.* ii, 247.

[4] *Ana-vattha. Comy. a-vavatthāna-. Cf.* below V, § 221.

[5] *Cf. A.* iv, 392.

[6] *Comy.* on the opposite: he gives believing in deed (*kamma: karma*) and result. *Cf.* below VI, § 92.

§ viii (148). *A good man's gifts.*

'Monks, these five are a good man's gifts. What five? He gives a gift in faith, with deference, in time, with unconstrained[1] heart, he gives a gift without hurt to self or others.

And in giving a gift in faith, wheresoever the full[2] result of that gift ripens, there comes wealth, riches and great property, and he is fair to look upon, handsome, with the wondrous beauty of the lotus.[3]

And in giving a gift with deference, wheresoever . . . that ripens, there comes wealth . . . and his[4] children and wife, his slaves, messengers and work-folk hearken diligently unto him, lend ear and serve him with understanding heart.[5]

And in giving a gift in time, wheresoever . . . that ripens, there comes wealth . . . and the goods that come to him in time[6] are abundant.

And in giving a gift with unconstrained heart, wheresoever . . . that ripens, there comes wealth . . . and he bends the mind to enjoy the fulness[7] of the fivefold joy of the senses.

And in giving a gift without hurt to self or others, wheresoever the full result of that gift ripens, there comes wealth, riches and great property, and never from anywhere comes hurt to his property either from fire or water, rajahs or thieves, or impious heirs.[8]

Verily, monks, these are the five gifts of a good man.'

---

1 Our text reads *anuggahitacitto*; so *S.e.*, but *Comy.* with *v.l. anaggahita-*, observing: *agahitacitto, muttacāgo hutvā.* See *DhS. trsl.* 301 *n.* and above, § 44 *n.*

2 *Vipāka.*

3 *Cf.* above, § 75.

4 *D.* i, 230; *A.* iv, 393; *Vin.* i, 10; above, § 79.

5 *Aññācittaŋ.*

6 *Kālāgatā c' assa atthā pacurā.* The *Comy.* is not very clear, but I think it means *atthā* come, not in old age (*vayo-vuddha-kāle*), but in the fit and proper time, in youth (*paṭhama-vayasmiŋ*).

7 *Uḷāra.*

8 *Cf.* below V, § 227.

§ ix (149). *Occasional release.*

'Monks, these five things lead to the falling away of a monk who is occasionally released.[1] What five?

Delight in (body) work, in gossip, in sleep, in company and he does not look at the mind apart[2] as released.

Verily, monks, these are the five. . . .'

(*But the opposite five do not lead to a falling away.*)[3]

§ x (150). *The same.*

(*Repeat* § 149, *substituting* 'delight in unguarded doors of the senses' *and* 'no moderation in eating' *for the last two* 'things.')

Chapter XVI.—Saddhamma.

§ i (151). *The Saddhamma way* (*a*).

(*The first half of this sutta is the converse of the following:*)

'Monks, pursuing five courses and hearkening unto Saddhamma he must become[4] one to enter the way,[5] the right way[6] in right things. What five?

He does not belittle[7] talk, nor belittle the talker, he does not belittle the self, hears Dhamma with unperturbed mind and with mind one-pointed, makes[8] thinking orderly.

---

[1] *Samaya-vimutta. P.E.D.* wrongly 'finally emancipated'; our *Comy.* just in momentary flashes (*appit' appita-khaṇe, appeti* means both to fix and to rush on) with the depravities discarded, there is a state of release; *cf. SnA.* 105; *SA.* i, 182. Were it not that the idea of 'temporary release' recurs at *Sn.* 54, one might judge it to be a late development. It occurs seldom. See *K.S.* i, 150 *n.* The sutta is quoted at *Pts. of Contr.* 70.

[2] *Paccavekkhati*, to view something *over against* (*paṭi*).

[3] The text repeats in full.

[4] *Bhabbo*, should or ought to become. ('Not "should do!" "Must, must, must do!" . . . "Should" is to-morrow, "must" is to-day!' —*Benito Mussolini the Man:* V. J. Bordeau.) See Mrs. Rhys Davids' *Sakya*, p. 324; *Manual*, p. 128.

[5] *Niyāma.*

[6] *Sammatta*, the state of *sam* $\sqrt{i}$, going along well.

[7] *Pari-bhoti* (*-bhavati*).

[8] *Manasikaroti.*

Verily, monks, pursuing these five courses and hearkening unto Saddhamma he must become one to enter the way, the right way in right things.'

§ ii (152). *The same* (*b*).

(*Repeat* § 151, *substituting* 'is filled with insight, no dullard or lack-wit' *and* 'not given[1] to thinking of his knowledge of the unknown' *for the last two terms.*)

§ iii (153). *The same* (*c*).

(*Repeat* § 152, *substituting* 'without unction[2] he hearkens to Dhamma, not unctuously prepossessed'; 'hearkens without captiousness,[3] without seeking flaws'; 'at Dhamma-teaching time his heart is not smitten[4] nor barren' *for the first three terms.*)

§ iv (154). *The confounding of Saddhamma* (*a*).

'Monks, these five things lead to the confounding,[5] the disappearance of Saddhamma. What five?

Herein, monks, carelessly[6] the monks hear Dhamma; carelessly they master it; carelessly they bear it in mind; carelessly they test the good of the things borne in mind; knowing the good and knowing Dhamma, carelessly they go their ways in Dhamma by Dhamma.

Verily, monks, these are the five things that lead to the confounding, the disappearance of Saddhamma.'

(*But[7] acting with care in respect to these five leads to its stability, to its being unconfounded, to its non-disappearance.*)

---

[1] *-mānī*, a causative formation from √*man*, to think; *a man*, opinionated, so conceited. *Cf. Brethr.* 336: 'Deeming they know the depths of truth.'

[2] *Makkha*, *lit.* to smear.

[3] *Upârambha-*. *Comy. niggahâropana-*.

[4] *Dhamma-desake anāhata°-akhilajāto*; *cf. Psalm* cii, 4: 'My heart is smitten and withered like grass.'

[5] *Sammosa.*

[6] *Na sakkaccaŋ*, not doing the right thing. From *sat-karoti*.

[7] The text repeats in full.

§ v (155). *The same* (*b*).

'Monks, these five things lead to the confounding, the disappearance of Saddhamma. What five?

Herein, monks, the monks master not Dhamma: the sayings, psalms, catechisms, songs, solemnities, speeches, birth-stories, marvels, runes.[1] This, monks, is the first thing that leads to the confounding, the disappearance of Saddhamma.

They teach not others Dhamma in detail, as heard, as learned. This, monks, is the second thing. . . .

They make not others speak it in detail, as heard, as learned. This, monks, is the third thing. . . .

They make no repetition of it in detail, as heard, as learned. This, monks, is the fourth thing. . . .

Again, monks, the monks do not in their hearts turn over and ponder upon Dhamma, they review it not in their minds. This, monks, is the fifth thing that leads to the confounding, the disappearance of Saddhamma.

Monks, these are the five things. . . .'

(*But acting in the converse manner in respect to the five leads to the stability of Saddhamma, to its being unconfounded, to its non-disappearance.*)

§ vi (156). *The same* (*c*).

'Monks, there are these five. . . . What five?

Herein, monks, the monks master an ill-grasped saying,[2] ill-arranged as to word and letter; monks, when it is so ill-arranged, the meaning[3] also is an ill deduction. This, monks, is the first thing. . . .

They are speakers of ill, whose ways make for unruliness, without endurance, with little talent for grasping instruction.[4] This, monks, is the second thing. . . .

---

[1] See *Expos.* i, 33 *ff.*; above, § 73. [2] *Suttanta*. *Cf.* above, No. 79.

[3] *Attha*. *Cf. A.* i, 59 for this section, and the whole sutta with *A.* ii, 147, where *suttanta*='text.' We see here *attha* having the import of 'meaning,' as a later preoccupation rather than that of 'weal' or 'thing-of-quest,' as in Nos. 57, 123, etc.

[4] *Appa-dakkhiṇa-ggāhino*. See *M.* i, 95; *K.S.* ii, 137, reading *apa-*.

And the monks who have heard much, to whom the traditional lore[1] has come down, the Dhamma-bearers, the Discipline-bearers, the Summary[2]-bearers; they make not another say a saying carefully; and because of them the saying becomes like a thing with its roots[3] cut and no refuge. This, monks, is the third thing. . . .

Again, the elders[4] are luxurious, lax, prime-movers in backsliding, who shirk the burden of the secluded life, nor put forth effort to attain the unattained, to master the unmastered, to realize the unrealized; and the folk who come after them fall into the way of (wrong) views; and they too become luxurious, lax, prime-movers in backsliding, shirking the burden of the secluded life, putting forth no effort to attain the unattained, to master the unmastered, to realize the unrealized. This, monks, is the fourth thing. . . .

Moreover, monks, the Order[5] is broken; then there is reviling between one another, accusation between one another, quarrelling between one another, repudiation between one another; and they of no faith do not find faith there and the faithful become otherwise. This, monks, is the fifth thing that leads to the confounding, the disappearance of Saddhamma.

Verily, monks, these are the five. . . .'

(*But acting in the opposite way leads to its stability. . . .*)[6]

§ vii (157). *Ill talk.*

'Monks, to five persons talk is ill talk when the appropriate person is confronted.[7] Of what five ?

Monks, to the faithless faith-talk is ill talk; to the virtueless virtue-talk is ill talk; to the little learned learned-talk is ill talk; to the mean generosity-talk is ill talk; to the lack-brain[8] insight-talk is ill talk.

---

[1] *Āgatâgamā*, what is handed down.

[2] *Mātikadharā*, *lit.* channels, the proto-*Abhidhamma*.

[3] *Chinna-mūlako appaṭisaraṇo.*

[4] Above, § 79.

[5] Above, § 54.

[6] The text repeats in full.

[7] *Puggalaŋ puggalaŋ upanidhāya. Comy. taŋ taŋ puggalaŋ upanikkhipitvā, sakkhiŋ katvā.*

[8] *Duppaññassa*, one without insight.

And wherefore, monks, is faith-talk to the faithless ill talk? Monks, the faithless, when faith-talk is talked, are roused,[1] angered, upset, made obstinate; they show temper, ill-will and sulkiness. And why? They perceive no achieving of faith in themselves and they get no joy and gladness therefrom. Therefore to the faithless faith-talk is ill talk.

So (likewise)[2] to the virtueless of virtue-talk. . . .

So (likewise) to the little learned of learned-talk. . . .

So (likewise) to the mean of generosity-talk. . . .

So (likewise) to the lack-brain; when insight-talk is talked, they are roused, angered, upset, made obstinate; they show temper, ill-will and sulkiness. And why? They perceive no achieving of insight in themselves and they get no joy and gladness therefrom.

Verily, monks, to these five persons talk is ill talk when the appropriate person is confronted.

Monks, to five persons talk is good talk when the appropriate person is confronted. Of what five?

Monks, to the faithful faith-talk is good talk . . .' *and so forth.*[2]

§ viii (158). *The fearful*[3] *heart.*

'Monks, possessed of five qualities a monk becomes of a fearful heart. Of what five?

Herein, monks, a monk is without faith, without virtue, of little learning, indolent and lacks insight.

Verily, monks, these are the five. . . .

Monks, possessed of five qualities a monk becomes confident. What five?' (*The opposite.*)[2]

§ ix (159). *The venerable Udāyin.*

Once, while the Exalted One was dwelling near Kosambī in Ghosita Park, the venerable Udāyin,[4] surrounded by a great gathering of laymen, sat teaching Dhamma.

Now the venerable Ānanda saw the venerable Udāyin so

---

[1] This is stock; *cf. D.* iii, 159; *A.* i, 124; *J.* iv, 22.

[2] The text repeats in full.

[3] *Cf.* above, § 101.

[4] *Comy.* does not indicate which Udāyin this is; see *Brethr.* 288.

seated, teaching, and thereat went to the Exalted One, saluted and sat down at one side. So seated, he said to the Exalted One:

'Lord, the venerable Udāyin, surrounded by a great gathering, teaches Dhamma.'

(And the Exalted One said:)

'Verily, Ānanda, not easy is it to teach Dhamma to others. In teaching others Dhamma, Ānanda, make[1] five things stand up within you, then teach others Dhamma. What five?

Teach others Dhamma, thinking: I will talk a talk on the gradual;[2] teach others Dhamma, thinking: I will talk a talk with the way[3] in view; teach others Dhamma, thinking: I will talk a talk out of kindliness;[4] teach others Dhamma, thinking: I will talk a talk not as a means for gain;[5] teach others Dhamma, thinking: I will talk a talk not to my own hurt nor to others.

Verily, Ānanda, not easy is it to teach Dhamma to others. In teaching others Dhamma, Ānanda, make these five things stand up within you, then teach others Dhamma.'

§ x (160). *Hard to make a push against.*[6]

'Monks, these five surges[7] are hard to make a push against. What five?

The passion-surge is hard to make a push against; so too is the ill-will-surge, the infatuation-surge, the ostentation-surge,[8] the surge of vagrant[9] thoughts is hard to make a push against.

Verily, monks, these are the five. . . .'

---

[1] *Upaṭṭhāpetvā*, a double causative: make these things stand to (attention); so at *D.* ii, 141 of *sati*, mindfulness, when women are about!

[2] *Anupubbikathaŋ*. That is the gradual advancement. *Comy.* by way of giving, virtue, heaven and the Way.

[3] *Pariyāyaŋ*. *Comy.* of whatsoever is good, showing the cause (*kāraṇaŋ idha pariyāyo*).

[4] *Anuddayataŋ paṭicca*; see above, § 144 *n.* [5] *Āmis' antaro.*

[6] *Dubbinodaya* and *duppaṭivinodaya*, the causative of *du-ppaṭi-vi-√nud.*

[7] 'Surge' is free for *uppanna*; 'uprisen thing.'

[8] *Paṭibhāna*. *Comy.* *kathetu-kamyatā vuccati.*

[9] *Gamika-cittaŋ*. *Comy.* is silent.

Chapter XVII.—Malice.

§ i (161). *The putting away of malice* (*a*).

'Monks, there are these five ways of putting away malice[1] whereby all malice arisen in a monk ought to be put away. What five?

Monks, in whatsoever person malice is engendered, in him amity ought to be made to become more. In this way malice in him ought to be put away.

Monks, in whomsoever malice is engendered, in him pity . . . poise ought to be made to become more. In this way malice in him ought to be put away.

Monks, in whomsoever malice is engendered, in that man[2] unmindfulness, inattention to it, ought to be brought about. In this way malice in him ought to be put away.

Monks, in whomsoever malice is engendered, in that man the fact that he is of his own making ought to be fixed in his mind; and he should think: This,[3] reverend sir, is of one's own making, the heir to deeds, deeds are the matrix, deeds are the kin, deeds are the foundation; whatever one does, good or bad, one will become heir to that. In this way malice in him ought to be put away.

Verily, monks, these are the five ways of putting away malice. . . .'

§ ii (162). *The same* (*b*).

Then said the venerable Sāriputta, addressing the monks: 'Reverend sirs!'

'Reverend sir,' they replied; and he said:

'Reverend sirs, there are these five[4] ways of putting away malice whereby all malice arisen in a monk ought to be put away. What five?

---

[1] *Aghāta-paṭivinayā.* *Comy.* glosses: *vūpasamenti*; the sutta is partly quoted at *Vism. trsl.* 345; for other sets see *D.* iii, 262; *A.* iv, 408; v, 151. *Cf. Ephesians* iv, 31. It is curious that, from the first three ways *muditā*, 'happiness,' the third of the four *brahmavihāras*, should be omitted. In *S. Nipāta*, 73, 'poise' is omitted and *vimutti* substituted.

[2] *Asati amanasikāro āpajjitabbo.* *Comy.* like a person hidden by a wall, etc., and does not appear.

[3] *Cf.* above, § 57.

[4] Quoted at *SnA.* 10.

There is the case, reverend sirs, of the person whose ways are impure in deed, but not in word—in such a person, sirs, malice ought to be put away.

And one whose ways are impure in word, but pure in deed . . .; and one whose ways are impure both in deed and word, yet from time to time obtains mental clarity, mental calm . . .; and one whose ways are likewise impure, but obtains no such clarity and calm . . .; and lastly, one whose ways are pure both in deed and word and who obtains mental clarity, mental calm—in (each), reverend sirs, ought malice to be put away.

Now of him whose ways are impure in deed, but not in word—how in him ought malice to be put away? Suppose, sirs, a monk, who robes himself in dust-heap rags, were to see a rag in the carriage-way; he would hold on[1] to it with his left foot and spread it out with his right and take and make use[2] of the best of it and go his ways. Just so, sirs, of one whose ways are impure in deed, but pure in word: the ways of deeds that may be impure ought not at that time to be thought on; let him think at that time on the ways that may be pure. In this way in him ought malice to be put away.

And of him whose ways are impure in word, but pure in deed—how in him ought malice to be put away? Suppose, sirs, a man, tortured by heat, by heat forspent, wearied, craving and thirsty,[3] were to come to a pond overgrown with mossy slime[4] and water plants; he would plunge into that pond, scattering with both hands the moss and plants hither and thither, and cup[5] his hands and drink and go his ways. Just so, sirs, of one whose ways are impure in word, but pure in deed: the ways of words that may be impure ought not then to be thought on; let him think then on the ways that may be pure. In this way in him ought malice to be put away.

---

[1] *Niggahetvā.* *Comy.* glosses: *akkamitvā.*

[2] *Paripācetvā.* *Comy. luñchitvā,* to pull out.

[3] This is a stock phrase; see *M.* ii, 74; *S.* ii, 110; *cf. D.* ii, 266.

[4] *Sevāla-paṇaka-pariyonaddhā.* *Comy. sevālena ca udaka-pappaṭakena ca paṭicchannā*; *sevala*=slimy, in *Skt.* *Cf.* below V, § 193.

[5] *Añjalinā pivitvā.* *P.E.D.* *s.v.* observes that *añjali* only occurs in stock phrases referring to salutations.

And of him whose ways are impure both in deed and word, yet from time to time obtains mental clarity, mental calm—how in him ought malice to be put away? Suppose, sirs, a man, tortured by heat and so forth, were to come upon a puddle in a cow's footprint;[1] he might think: Here's a cow's footprint puddle, but if I drink of it by hand or cup, I shall stir and churn[2] it up and make it unfit to drink; what if, crouched on all fours,[3] I were to lie and sup[4] as a cow sups and then go my ways?—and he does so. . . . Just so, sirs, of one whose ways are impure both in deed and word, yet from time to time obtains mental clarity, mental calm: neither the ways of deeds . . . nor the ways of words that may be impure ought to be thought on then, but the mental clarity, the mental calm, that he obtains from time to time, let him think then just on that. In this way in him ought malice to be put away.

And of him whose ways are likewise impure, but obtains no such clarity and calm—how in him ought malice to be put away? Suppose, sirs, a sick and ailing man, grievously ill,[5] were to go along the highway—it might be with no village near ahead or near behind—unable to get proper food, to get proper medicine, to get proper attention, to get a guide[6] to some village boundary; and suppose another man, also going along the road, were to see him; verily it[7] might raise pity in that man, raise compassion, raise commiseration, so that he might say to himself: Alas for this man! he ought to have proper food, proper medicine, proper attention; he ought to have a guide to some village. Wherefore? Lest he suffer even here wasting and destruction. Just so, sirs, of one whose ways are impure, who obtains no mental clarity, mental calm: in such a person verily pity ought to arise, compassion ought to arise, commiseration ought to arise, so that he say to himself: Alas for this venerable sir! he should

---

[1] *Cf. A.* iv, 102.

[2] *Khobhessāmi, lolessāmi. Comy. cālessāmi, ākulaŋ karissāmi.*

[3] *Catukuṇḍiko. Comy. jānuhi ca hatthehi ca bhūmiyaŋ patiṭṭhānena.*

[4] *Go-pītakaŋ pivitvā. Comy. gāviyo viyo mukhena ākaḍḍhanto pivitvā.*

[5] *Cf.* below V, § 194. [6] *Gam' anta-nāyakaŋ.* [7] *So.*

give up bad habits in deed and make good habits become more, give up bad habits in word . . ., give up bad habits in thought and make good habits become more. Wherefore ? Lest this venerable sir, on the breaking up of the body, after death, arise in the wayward way, the ill way, the abyss, hell. In this way in him ought malice to be put away.

And of him whose ways are pure both in deed and word and who obtains mental clarity, mental calm—how in him ought malice to be put away ? Suppose, sirs, a man, tortured by heat, by heat forspent, wearied, craving and thirsty, were to come to a pool,[1] clear, sweet, cool, limpid, a lovely resting-place,[2] shaded by all manner of trees; he would plunge into that pool, bathe and drink, and coming out, would sit and lie there in the shade of the trees. Just so, sirs, of one whose ways are both pure in deed and word, who from time to time obtains mental clarity, mental calm: the ways of deeds . . . the ways of words that may be pure at that time, let him think on them then; and the mental clarity, the mental calm, that he obtains from time to time, let him verily think on that then. In this way in him ought malice to be put away. Reverend sirs, when a person comes to be calm throughout,[3] the mind becomes calm.

Verily, sirs, these are the five ways of putting away malice whereby all malice arisen in a monk ought to be put away.'

§ iii (163). *Talk.*

Then said the venerable Sāriputta, addressing the monks: 'Reverend sirs.'

'Reverend sir,' they replied. (*And he repeated* § 65 *above.*)[4]

---

[1] *Cf. M.* i, 76, 283; below V, § 194; the phrases are stock; see *D.* ii, 129; *Vin.* iii, 108; *Ud.* 83.

[2] Our text *supatiṭṭhā*, which I follow; however, *S.e.*, *Comy.* and other texts *-tittha*, *Skt. tīrtha*; our *Comy. sama-*, level; *DA.* ii, 569 and *UdA.* 403 *sundara-*, good; *Dial. trsl.* easy to get down into.

[3] *Samantapāsādikaŋ . . . āgamma cittaŋ pasīdati*; on the first word see *G.S.* i, 19 *n.*, but here we have three derivatives of √sad: *pāsādika, pasāda* and *pasīdati*. On *āgamma* see *K.S.* i, 114, 318.

[4] The text repeats in full.

§ iv (164). *An example.*

(*The venerable Sāriputta repeats* § 66 *to the monks.*)[1]

§ v (165). *On asking questions.*

The venerable Sāriputta said: 'All who question another are in five states (of mind) or one of them. What five?

One being foolish and blind questions another;[2] one filled with evil desires and covetousness; one contemptuously; one seeking knowledge; or one questions another uncertainly,[3] thinking: If questioned by me he explain rightly, it is well; but if questioned by me he explain not rightly, I will explain to him.

Reverend sirs, all who question another are in these five states or in one of them.

Reverend sirs, when I question another, verily I am thus minded: If I question another and he rightly explain, it is well; if not, I will rightly explain to him.'

§ vi (166). *Ending.*

The venerable Sāriputta said: 'Herein, sirs, a monk, who has achieved virtue, achieved concentration, achieved insight, may both completely[4] enter the ending of perception and feeling and may emerge therefrom—this is so: if here among visible things he make[5] not the gain of gnosis, he will surely go beyond the deva-community that feed on[6] solid food and arise in a mind-pictured[7] body, provided he enter and emerge from the ending of perception and feeling—this is so.'

When he had thus spoken, the venerable Udāyin said to the venerable Sāriputta: 'This is not so, venerable Sāriputta,

---

[1] The text repeats in full.

[2] *Cf.* above, § 93.

[3] *Pakuppanto,* from √*kup,* to be agitated; *cf. M.* i, 187, of the elements; *F. Dial. trsl.*, wroth. *Cf.* 1 *Corinthians* ix, 26, but just in the opposite way: 'I therefore so run, not as uncertainly.'

[4] *Sam-.*

[5] *Ārādheti,* caus. of √*rādh*; *cf. S.* v, 285; *K.S.* v, 254.

[6] *Kabaliṅkārâhāra-bhakkha. Comy. kāmâvacara,* as elsewhere.

[7] *Manomayaŋ kāyaŋ.* See above, § 44.

nor happens it, that should a monk enter and emerge from the ending of perception and feeling, he will surely go beyond the deva-community that feed on solid food and arise in a mind-pictured body—it is not so!'

A second time . . . and a third time the venerable Sāriputta (spake in like manner to the monks, and a second and a third time the venerable Udāyin replied as before).[1]

Then thought the venerable Sāriputta: 'Even unto a third time the venerable Udāyin[2] cries against me and no monk supports me; what if I were to go to the Exalted One?' And he went to where the Exalted One was and saluted him and sat down at one side. So seated, the venerable Sāriputta addressed the monks (speaking even as before). . . .

And when he had thus spoken, the venerable Udāyin replied: 'This is not so, venerable Sāriputta, nor does it happen that, if a monk enter and emerge from the ending of perception and feeling, he will surely go beyond the deva-community that feed on solid food and arise in a mind-pictured body[3]—it is not so!'

And a second and a third time they spake (in like manner). . . .

Then thought the venerable Sāriputta: 'Verily, before the face of the Exalted One, even unto a third time the venerable Udāyin cries against me and no monk supports me; I had best be silent.' And so the venerable Sāriputta was silent.

Then the Exalted One addressed the venerable Udāyin and said:

'But who, do you hold,[4] Udāyin, has a mind-pictured body?'

---

[1] The text repeats much in full.

[2] *Comy.* Lāla or foolish Udāyin.

[3] See the *Apaṇṇaka-sutta, M.* i, 140: there are these propositions: there are no formless conditions at all and mind-made devas have form; or, there are formless conditions and perception-made devas are formless. Then there is no ending of becoming entirely and perception-made devas are formless; or, there is ending of becoming entirely and Nibbāna here among these visible conditions (can be won). Our *Comy.* observes that Udāyin hearing 'Mind-pictured' disagreed, thinking 'It ought to be among the formless.'

[4] *Paccesi*; see *Dial.* i, 252 *n.* and above, § 144.

'Those devas, lord, who are formless, perception-made.'

'Why thinkest thou, Udāyin, that the word of a witless fool like thee is just the thing to declare?'

Then the Exalted One addressed the venerable Ānanda thus: 'Is it possible,[1] Ānanda, that you can look on with indifference at an elder monk being vexed? Verily, Ānanda, compassion grows not from (suffering) an elder monk to be vexed.'

Then the Exalted One addressed the monks, saying:

'Herein, monks, a monk who has achieved virtue, achieved concentration, achieved insight, may both completely enter the ending of perception and feeling and may emerge therefrom—this is so: if here among visible things he make not the gain of gnosis, he will verily go beyond the deva-community that feed on solid food and arise in a mind-pictured body, provided he enter and emerge from the ending of perception and feeling—this is so.'

Thus spake the Exalted One; and when he had thus spoken, the Well-Gone arose and entered the dwelling.

Now not long after the departure of the Exalted One, the venerable Ānanda went up to the venerable Upavāna[2] and said to him: 'Just now, venerable Upavāna, some (monks) were vexing the elder monk and we never protested unto them. Therefore wonder not, venerable sir, should the Exalted One, after coming from seclusion, bring[3] the matter up and[4] relate the whole affair to the venerable Upavāna. Already even fearfulness[5] is come upon us.'

And in the evening, after coming from seclusion, the Exalted One went to the service hall, and, when come, he sat down on

---

[1] *Atthi nāma. Comy. amarisan' atthe nipāto. Ayaŋ h' ettha attho; Ānanda, tumhe theraŋ bhikkhuŋ vihesiyamānaŋ ajjhupekkhatha? Na vo 'etaŋ marisāmi,' na 'adhivāsemī'-ti.* (Think not 'I suffer this man,' nor 'I bear with him.') *Marisati* and *a-marisana* are rare words and not in our Pāli Dicts. The *Skt.* root must be √*mrish*. I cannot find any other derivatives used in Pāli.

[2] The B.'s personal attendant; see *K.S.* i, 220; *Brethr.* 140. The *Comy.* observes that the B. addressed Ānanda because he was, as it were, the store-keeper of Dhamma.

[3] *Udāhareyya*, from √*hr*.

[4] *Yathā. Comy. kāraṇa-vacanaŋ.*

[5] *Sārajjaŋ*; see above, § 101.

the seat that was ready. So seated, he said to the venerable Upavāna:

'Having how many qualities, Upavāna, does an elder among his fellows in the godly life become pious, loved, respected and what he ought to become ?'

'Lord, having five[1] qualities, an elder becomes what he ought to become. . . . What five ?

Lord, herein he is virtuous . . .; is learned . . .; has a pleasant voice, a good enunciation . . .; at will . . . attains to the four states of musing . . .; and by destroying the cankers . . . enters and abides in the emancipation of the heart, the emancipation of insight. . . .

Verily, lord, having these five qualities an elder among his fellows in the godly life becomes pious, loved, respected and what he ought to become.'

'Well (said), well (said), Upavāna! It is even (as you say). . . . If these five qualities are not completely found in an elder, will his fellows in the godly life respect, honour, reverence and venerate him for his broken teeth, his grey hairs, his wrinkled skin ?[2] But verily, Upavāna, when these five things are found in an elder, then his fellows in the godly life respect him, honour, reverence and venerate him.'

§ vii (167). *Exhortation.*

Then said the venerable Sāriputta to the monks:

'Reverend sirs, when he that exhorteth[3] wishes to exhort another, let him make five things stand up[4] within him, then let him exhort another. What five ?

I[5] will speak timely, not untimely; I will speak about what has happened,[6] not what has not; I will speak with gentleness,

---

[1] See above, § 87, for details; the text here abbreviates.

[2] *Cf. D.* ii, 305; *M.* i, 49; *S.* ii, 2; *DhS. trsl.* 195 *n.*

[3] *Cf.* St. Paul to the *Romans* (xii, 8) and elsewhere.

[4] The text *upaṭṭhapetvā*, but *S.e. upaṭṭhāpetvā*; see above, § 159 *n.*

[5] *Cf.* the whole sutta with *Vin.* ii, 249 *ff.* (*S.B.E.* xx, 317); the five recur at *D.* iii, 236; *M.* i, 126; *A.* v, 81. *Cf.* below V, § 198.

[6] *Bhūtena*, about what has become. *Comy. tacchena, sabhāvena.*

not harshness; I will speak about the Goal,[1] not about what is not the Goal; I will speak with mind of amity, not of ill-will.

Reverend sirs, when he that exhorteth wishes to exhort another, let him make himself make these five things stand up within him, then let him exhort another.

Maybe,[2] sirs, I see some monk being exhorted untimely, moved[3] not timely; exhorted about what has not happened, moved not about what has happened; exhorted in a harsh way, moved not with gentleness; exhorted about what is not the Goal, not about the Goal; exhorted in ill-will, moved not in amity.

In him not exhorted according to Dhamma, on five scores no remorse ought to be set up;[4] (let him think:) " This venerable sir has exhorted untimely, not timely—'there's no need for remorse in thee'—;[5] has exhorted about what has not happened, not what has . . .; has exhorted harshly, not with gentleness . . .; has exhorted on what is not about the Goal, not on what is about the Goal . . .; has exhorted in ill-will, not in amity—'there's no need for remorse in thee.' "

Reverend sirs, in him not exhorted according to Dhamma, on these five scores no remorse ought to be set up.

Reverend sirs, in him that exhorteth not according to Dhamma, on five scores ought remorse to be set up; (let him think:) Untimely is the good man exhorted by thee—'there is need for remorse in thee'—; he is exhorted by thee about what has not happened, not what has . . .; is harshly exhorted by thee, not gently . . .; is exhorted by thee on what is not about the Goal, not on what is about the Goal . . .; is exhorted by thee in ill-will, not in amity—'there is need for remorse in thee.'

" Reverend sirs, in him that exhorteth not according to

---

[1] *Attha-saṅhitena*, from √*dhā*. *Comy.* glosses: *upetena*. See 'First Utterance,' *Vin.* i, p. 10; Mrs. Rhys Davids' *Manual*, p. 112.

[2] *idha*.

[3] *Kupitaŋ*, as in the *Acts*: 'all the city was moved.'

[4] *Upadahātabbo*, also from √*dhā*, *Comy.* *uppādetabbo*.

[5] *Lit.* 'enough for thee of remorse!' an idiom characteristic of sayings recorded elsewhere as of the Founder.

Dhamma, on these five scores ought remorse to be set up. Wherefore? To the end that no monk should think one ought to be exhorted about what has not happened.

'Or I see, sirs, some monk being timely exhorted, moved not untimely . . . *and so forth.*[1] In him, thus exhorted according to Dhamma, on five scores ought remorse to be set up. (*Repeat the contra.*)[1]

So too, in him that exhorteth according to Dhamma, on five scores no remorse ought to be set up. (*Repeat the contra.*)[1] Wherefore? To the end that a monk should think one ought to be exhorted about what has happened.

There ought to be a support, sirs, in two things for a person exhorted, to wit: in truth and in the immovable.[2]

If others exhort me, whether timely or not; about what has happened or not; gently or harshly; about the Goal or not; in amity or in ill-will, I should find support in two things: in truth and in the immovable. If I know: "It is in me, this Dhamma," thinking: "It is," I should declare it, saying: "Wholly found in me is this Dhamma." But if I know: "It is not in me, this Dhamma," thinking: "It is not," I should declare that, saying: "Wholly not found in me is this Dhamma."'

(*The Exalted One said:*[3]) 'And while you are thus speaking, Sāriputta, I suppose some foolish men have not the talent to grasp[4] the matter?'

'Lord,[5] those persons, unbelievers, who—as a means of living,[6] not of faith—go forth from the home to the homeless life—impostors, frauds, deceivers,[7] who are vainly puffed up,[8]

[1] The text repeats.

[2] This recurs at *Vin.* ii, 251; Rhys Davids' *trsl.*: in truth and in freedom from anger; but see above, § 95 *n.*, and *Tr: P.D. s.v. akuppa.*

[3] This may be inferred from *bhante* in the reply.

[4] *Na padakkhiṇaŋ gaṅhanti*; *cf.* above, § 156.

[5] *Cf.* the whole passage with *M.* iii, 6.

[6] *Jīvik' atthā*; see the use at *UdA.* 205.

[7] *Keṭubhino.* *P.E.D.* observes, deriv. unknown, but I suppose it is connected with the *Sk. kaitava.*

[8] *Unnalā uddhatā*; *cf. Colossians* ii, 18: 'Let no man beguile you . . . vainly puffed up by his fleshly mind.' *Cf.* also *A.* i, 70; *S.* i, 61; v, 269.

shifty praters of loose talk, unguarded as to their sense-doors, eating without moderation, unwatchful, who seek not true recluseship, are without zeal in training, luxurious, lax, the first to move in backsliding,[1] who cast aside the yoke of the secluded life, indolent, low in energy, of mindfulness unforgetful, not self-possessed, with uncomposed and wandering minds, dull lack-wits—they, while I speak in this way, have not the talent to grasp the matter. But those clansmen, lord, who of faith go forth from the home to the homeless life—no impostors, frauds, deceivers, not vainly puffed up, not shifty praters of loose talk, who are guarded as to sense-doors, moderate in eating, watchful, who seek true recluseship, are zealous in training, neither luxurious nor lax, who cast aside the yoke of backsliding, move first to seclusion, with energy bestir themselves, are resolved, stand up in mindfulness, self-possessed, composed, one-pointed, wise, no lack-wits—they, while I speak in this way, have the talent to grasp the matter.'

'Let be those unbelieving . . .[2] foolish lack-wits, Sāriputta; speak thou to them who of faith go forth . . .[2] Admonish thy fellows in the godly life, Sāriputta, instruct them;[3] and think then: When I have stirred them up from what is not Saddhamma, I will make them stand fast in Saddhamma.[4] Verily, Sāriputta, train thyself in this way.'

§ viii (168). *Virtue.*

(*The venerable Sāriputta repeats* § 24 *to the monks.*)[2]

§ ix (169). *Coming to know.*

Now the venerable Ānanda went up to the venerable Sāriputta and greeted him and, after exchanging the words of customary greetings, sat down at one side. So seated, the venerable Ānanda said to the venerable Sāriputta:

'How far, reverend Sāriputta, does a monk come speedily to

---

[1] *Okkamana.*
[2] The text repeats in full.
[3] *Anusāsa.*
[4] *Cf.* above, § 88.

know[1] aptness in things[2] so that his grasp is a good grasp; so that he grasps much and forgets not what he has grasped?'

'I know[3] the venerable Ānanda has heard much; let the venerable Ānanda throw light upon the matter.'

'Well then, reverend Sāriputta, hearken and give heed and I will speak.'

'Very well, reverend sir,' replied the venerable Sāriputta; and the venerable Ānanda said:

'Take the case, reverend Sāriputta, of a monk who is apt at meanings, apt at Dhamma, apt at letters,[4] apt at language,[4] apt at orderly sequence[5]—thus far, reverend Sāriputta, a monk comes speedily to know aptness in things and his grasp is a good grasp, he grasps much and forgets not what he has grasped.'

'It is marvellous, sir, it is wonderful, how well this has been put by the venerable Ānanda! We hold the venerable Ānanda is possessed of these five things: the venerable Ānanda is apt at meanings, apt at Dhamma, apt at letters, apt at language and apt at orderly sequence.'[6]

§ x (170). *Bhaddaji.*

Once, while the venerable Ānanda was dwelling near Kosambī in Ghosita Park, the venerable Bhaddaji[7] came up and greeted him and, after exchanging the words of customary greetings, sat down at one side. So seated, the venerable Ānanda said to the venerable Bhaddaji:

'Good Bhaddaji, what is the best of sights, what the best

---

[1] *Khippa-nisanti. Comy. Khippaŋ nisāmayati, upadhāreti.*

[2] *Kusalesu dhammesu. Dict.* meanings of *kusala* are: fitting, healthy, well, skilful, expert; it is used both adjectivally and as a noun; see Mrs. Rhys Davids' remarks, *DhS. trsl.* lxxxii. *Comy. cheko*; *ad A.* iv, 296, of *dhammesu*: the skandhas, elements, spheres, etc.

[3] *Kho.*

[4] *Vyañjana* and *nirutti.* There is a suggestion in these five terms of literary preoccupation; an attention to the formulated mandates, rather than to their meaning, that argues a later compilation.

[5] *Pubbāpara-. Comy.* of *attha*, of *dhamma*, of *pada*, of *akkhara*, and of *anusandhi.*

[6] Quoted at *UdA.* 11.

[7] See *Brethr.* 129.

of sounds, what the best of joys, what the best of conscious states, and what is the best of becomings?'

'There is Brahmā, sir, who is overcomer, by none overcome,[1] he is the seer of whatever may be, with power and dominion; who sees him of the Brahmās, that is the best of sights.

There are the devas of radiant splendour, in whom joy flows and overflows, who ever and again utter a cry of: "Joy, oh joy!" who hears that sound—it is the best of sounds.

There are the all-lustrous devas, rejoicing just in quiet,[2] who feel joy—that is the best of joys.

There are the devas who go to the sphere of nothingness—theirs is the best of conscious states.

There are the devas who go to the sphere of neither consciousness nor unconsciousness—theirs is the best of becomings' (*i.e. lives, or worlds*).

'This is but the way of the many folk, this (talk) of the venerable Bhaddaji.'

'The venerable Ānanda has heard much; let the venerable Ānanda throw light upon the matter!'

'Very well, reverend Bhaddaji, listen and pay attention and I will speak.'

'Yes, sir,' he replied; and the venerable Ānanda said:

'When,[3] while one looks, the cankers are destroyed—that is the best of sights.

When, while one listens, the cankers are destroyed—that is the best of sounds.

When, while one rejoices, the cankers are destroyed—that is the best of joys.

When, while one is conscious, the cankers are destroyed—that is the best of conscious states.

When, while one has become,[4] the cankers are destroyed—that is the best of becomings.'

---

[1] This is stock; *cf. D.* i, 18; iii, 135; *A.* ii, 24; *It.* 15: *abhibhū anabhibhūto,* sometimes used of the Tathāgata.

[2] *Te santaŋ yeva tusitā. S.e.* reads *te santaññ' eva sukhitā.*

[3] *Anantarā,* no interval, immediately. *Comy. anantarā yeva!*

[4] *Yathā bhūtassa.*

CHAPTER XVIII.—THE LAY-DISCIPLE.

§ i (171). *Fearfulness.*

Once, while the Exalted One dwelt near Sāvatthī in Jeta Grove at Anāthapiṇḍika's Park, he addressed the monks, saying: 'Monks.'

'Yes, lord,' they replied; and the Exalted One said:

'Monks, following five things,[1] fearfulness comes upon a layman. What five?

He takes life, takes what is not given, is given over to lusts of the flesh, lies and takes spirituous liquors that cause indolence.

Monks, following these five things, fearfulness comes upon a layman.'

(*Following the five opposite things, confidence comes.*)[2]

§ ii (172). *Confidence.*

'Monks, following five things, a layman lives the home-life without confidence. What five?' (*Repeat as in* § 171.)

(*Following the five opposite, he lives with confidence.*)[2]

§ iii (173). *Hell.*

'Monks, following five, he is duly thrown into hell. . . .[2]

Following the five opposite, he is duly thrown into heaven. . . .'

§ iv (174). *Hatred.*

Now the householder, Anāthapiṇḍika, visited the Exalted One, saluted him and sat down at one side; and the Exalted One spoke to the householder, thus seated, and said:

'Householder, he who has not got rid of the five dread hatreds is called virtueless and arises in hell. What five?

Taking life, taking what is not given, fleshly lusts, lying and indulgence in spirituous liquor that cause indolence. Verily, these five . . .

But one who has got rid of these . . . is called virtuous and arises in heaven.

---

[1] *Dhammā.*

[2] The text repeats much in full.

When, householder, the taker of life,[1] by reason of his taking life, breeds dread hatred in this world or breeds dread hatred hereafter, he feels in the mind pain and grief; but he who abstains from taking life breeds no dread hatred in this world, nor none hereafter, nor does he feel in his mind pain and grief; thus that dread hatred for him who abstains from taking life is suppressed.

So, too, the dread hatred bred of taking what is not given . . . of fleshly lusts . . . of lying . . . and of indulging in spirituous liquors that cause indolence for him who abstains therefrom . . . is suppressed.

Who[2] in this world brings life to death, speaks lies,
Goes to another's wife, takes things not given,
Who drinks strong drink—these five hate-breeding things
Not giving up—immoral he, 'tis said:
When body fails that fool is born in hell.
But whoso ne'er takes life, nor speaketh lies,
Nor goes to another's wife, takes things not given,
Nor drinks strong drink, is not addict of these
Hate-breeding things—moral is he, 'tis said:
At death that wise man will arise in heaven.'

§ v (175). *The outcast.*[3]

'Monks; pursuing five things, a layman is the outcast of laymen, the dirt of laymen, the offscouring of laymen. What five?

He is without faith, without morals, is a diviner by curious ceremonies,[4] he believes in luck,[5] not deeds, he seeks outside

---

[1] This recurs at *A.* iv, 406; v. 183; with *v.l.* and *S.e.* we should insert *pāṇātipātī*.

[2] The first three lines of our text recur at *Dhp.* 246-7; *S.e.* reads *atipāteti*. *Cf. S.* iv, 343.

[3] *Caṇḍāla.*

[4] *Kotūhala-maṅgalika*; *kotūhala* has been confused with *kolāhala* (and *halāhala*): tumult; see *P.E.D. s.v.*; *Q. of M.* i, 143 (the native gloss is near the meaning); *Maṅgalajātaka*, i, 371 explains the meaning; our *Comy. iminā idaŋ bhavissatī -ti evaŋ pavattattā kotūhala-saṅkhātena diṭṭha-suta-muta-maṅgalena samannāgato* (*cf. J.* i, 374); the *Sk.* is *kautūhala*, curiosity, interest; *kautaka-maṅgala*, a solemn ceremony, a festival, and so, no doubt, noise (*cf. UdA.* 156: *kotūhalahāsa*). See also *M.* i, 265: *vata-kotūhala-maṅgalāni*; below VI, § 93.

[5] *Maṅgalaŋ pacceti no kammaŋ. Comy. maṅgalaŋ oloketi.*

(the Order) for a gift-worthy person and there first offers service.

Monks, pursuing these five things, a layman is the outcast of laymen, the dirt, the offscouring of laymen.

Monks, pursuing five things, a layman is the jewel of laymen, the lily of laymen, the lotus of laymen. What five?

(*Just the opposite five.*)[1]

§ vi (176). *Zest.*[2]

Then the householder, Anāthapiṇḍika, with about five hundred lay-disciples around him, came to the Exalted One, saluted and sat down at one side; and the Exalted One spoke to him, so seated, and said:

'Verily, householder, you have served the Order of monks with gifts of the requisites: the robe, alms, lodging and medicine for sickness—but you must not be satisfied just by the thought: "We have served the Order with gifts of the requisites."

Wherefore, householder, train yourself thus:

Come now,[3] let us, from time to time, enter and abide in the zest that comes of seclusion.

Verily, train yourself thus, householder.'

And when he had thus spoken, the venerable Sāriputta said to the Exalted One: 'It is marvellous, lord, it is wonderful, how well the Exalted One has spoken. . . . Lord, what time the Ariyan disciple enters and abides in the zest that comes of seclusion, for him five things become not: for him in that time the pain and grief that follow lust become not; the pleasure and gratification that follow lust become not; the pain and grief that follow evil become not; the pleasure and gratification that follow evil become not;[4] for him in that time the pain and grief that follow doing good become not. Lord, what time the Ariyan disciple enters and abides in the zest that comes of seclusion, for him these five things become not.'

'Well done, well done, Sāriputta! (It is even as you say.) . . .[1]

---

[1] The text repeats.

[2] *Pīti.*

[3] *kinti.* *Comy.* *kena nāma upāyena.*

[4] *Comy.* observes that he may go forth to shoot a deer or pig and miss, and so become depressed; or he may hit and kill and be glad.

What time, Sāriputta, the Ariyan disciple enters and abides in the zest that comes of seclusion, for him in that time these five things become not.'

§ vii (177). *Trades.*

'Monks, these five trades ought not to be plied by a lay-disciple. What five?

Trade in weapons, trade in human beings, trade in flesh,[1] trade in spirits and trade in poison.

Verily, monks, these five trades ought not to be plied by a lay-disciple.'

§ viii (178). *Rajahs.*

'Now what think you, monks, has this thing been seen and heard of by you: "This man gave up taking life and abstains therefrom; and rajahs, because he abstains from taking life, seize and slay him or put him in fetters or thrust him forth (from the country)[2] or wreak their wrath[3] upon him"?'

'No, indeed, lord, it has not.'

'Well, monks, neither by us has this thing been seen nor heard of. . . .[4]

But if folk give evidence against him of just some evil deed as this: "This man has caused the death of a woman or man," then rajahs, because he has taken life, seize and slay him or put him in fetters or thrust him forth from the country or wreak their wrath upon him—has such a thing been seen and heard of by you?'

'Lord, by us this thing has been both seen and heard of; yea, and we shall hear of it again.'

'. . . monks, have you seen and heard that rajahs seize and slay . . . a man who abstains from taking what is not given?'

'No indeed, lord.'

'But if folk tell of his evil deed, saying: "This man stealthily took from village or forest what was not given

---

[1] *Comy.* he breeds and sells pigs, deer, etc.

[2] So *Comy.*

[3] *Yathāpaccayaŋ vā karoti. Comy. yathâdhippayo yathâjjhasayaŋ karoti.*

[4] The text repeats.

him,"—have you seen and heard that rajahs seize and slay . . . him for that ?'

'Yes, lord. . . .'

'. . . and if a man abstain from the lusts of the flesh ?'

'No, lord.'

'But if folk say of him: "This man had intercourse with others' wives or others' maidens" ?'

'Yes, lord. . . .'

'. . . or if a man abstain from lying ?'

'No, lord.'

'But if folk say of him: "This man by lying has broken up the home[1] of this householder or that householder's son" ?'

'Yes, lord. . . .'[2]

'What think you, monks, has this thing been seen and heard of by you: "This man gave up drinking all spirituous liquors that cause indolence and abstains therefrom; and rajahs, because he does so, seize and slay him or put him in fetters or thrust him forth from the country or wreak their wrath upon him" ?'

'No, indeed, lord, it has not.'

'Well, monks, neither by us has this thing been seen nor heard of. . . .

But if folk give evidence against him of just some evil deed as this: "This man, given over to drinking indolence-causing liquors, has taken the life of some woman or man; . . . has stealthily taken from village or forest what was not given him; . . . has had intercourse with others' wives or others' maidens; . . . has by lying broken up the home of this householder or that householder's son,"—then rajahs, because he is given over to drink, seize and slay him or put him in fetters or thrust him forth from the country or wreak their wrath upon him—has such a thing been seen or heard of by you ?'

'Lord, by us this thing has been both seen and heard of; yea, and we shall hear of it again.'

---

1 *Attha*; *cf*. *S*. iv, 347, where this recurs.

2 The text repeats all in full.

§ ix (179). *The home-man.*

Now the householder Anāthapiṇḍika, surrounded by about five hundred lay-disciples, visited the Exalted One and, after saluting, sat down at one side. Then the Exalted One addressed the venerable Sāriputta and said:

'Sāriputta, any white-frocked home-man[1] you know, who acts controlled[2] in the five steps of the training and obtains at will, easily and without difficulty the four[3] very purposive abodes of ease, here amid things seen, may, should he desire, declare just the (state of) self by the self, saying: "Destroyed is hell for me; destroyed is animal-rebirth; destroyed is the realm of ghosts; destroyed for me is the wayward way, the ill way, the abyss; I am he who has won to the Stream, not subject to any falling away, sure and bound for enlightenment." He acts controlled in what five steps of the training?

Herein, Sāriputta, the Ariyan disciple abstains from taking life, from taking what is not given, from fleshly lusts, from lying and from drinking spirituous liquors that cause indolence.

He acts controlled in these five steps of the training.

What are the four abodes of ease, very purposive, he obtains at will . . . here amid things seen?

Herein, Sāriputta, the Ariyan disciple has unwavering faith in the Buddha: Of a truth he is that, the Exalted One, arahant, fully enlightened, walking in knowledge, well gone, wise in the ways of the worlds, with none greater, tamer of tamable men, teacher of devas and men, Buddha, lord. This is the first very purposive abode of ease, won, here amid things seen, by purifying impure thought, by cleansing unclean thought.

Again, Sāriputta, the Ariyan disciple has unwavering faith in Dhamma: Well declared by the Exalted One is Dhamma, one to be seen here and now, not for other times, bidding one

---

[1] *Gihin* as opposed to the yellow-robed *pabbajita*, one gone forth.

[2] *Saŋvuta-kammanta.* *Comy. pihita-*.

[3] *Cf. A.* iv, 405 *ff.*; *D.* ii, 93; *S.* v, 357; the four are called the mirror of Dhamma. *Cf. Gotama the Man*, pp. 169, 229.

come and see, a guide to be understood by wise men, each for himself. This is the second abode of ease. . . .

He has unwavering faith in the Order: Well trained is the Exalted One's Order of disciples; trained in uprightness is the Exalted One's Order of disciples; trained in method is the Exalted One's Order of disciples; trained in the way of right[1] is the Exalted One's Order of disciples—the four pairs of men, the eight male persons—this is the Exalted One's Order of disciples, worthy of offerings, worthy of oblations, worthy of gifts, meet to be reverently saluted, a field for merit, none greater in the world. This is the third abode of ease. . . .

Moreover, Sāriputta, the Ariyan disciple is possessed of virtues beloved by Ariyans—whole, unbroken, untarnished, without blemish, bringing freedom, praised by wise men, incorrupt, conducive to concentration. This is the fourth very purposive abode of ease, won, here amid things seen, by purifying impure thought, by cleansing unclean thought.

These are the four abodes of ease. . . .

Sāriputta, any white-frocked home-man you know, who acts controlled in these five steps of the training and obtains at will, easily and without difficulty, these four very purposive abodes of ease, here amid things seen, may, should he desire, declare just the (state of) self by the self and say: Destroyed is hell for me; destroyed is animal-rebirth; destroyed is the realm of ghosts; destroyed for me is the wayward way, the ill way, the abyss; I am he who has won to the Stream, not subject to any falling away, sure and bound for enlightenment.

Seeing hell's fearfulness, shun wickedness;
Wise men shun that, firm set in Ariyan Dhamma.
Not harming aught that breathes where progress is ;[2]
Lie not, nor knowingly touch things ungiven;
Live gladly with thine own, leave[3] others' wives;

---

[1] *Sāmīci.* [2] *Vijjamāne parakkame.*

[3] *Ārame*; *S.e.* and *v.l.* *nârame*; at *A.* iv, 137 we have *āramati* in the same sense; *P.E.D.* omits, but see *ārata, ārati*; the root is $\sqrt{}$*ram*, meaning to set at rest, to be at ease, to delight in.

No man should drink strong drink[1] that dulls the thought;
Mind[2] thou the Buddha, think on Dhamma oft;
With fair and harmless thoughts make thyself fit
For heav'n. For him who merit's meed would win,[3]
With gift in Dhamma[4] furnishèd, that gift,
First giv'n to godly men, will richly ripen.
Here I'll make known such men, list Sāriputta!
Mid[5] cows, black, white, red, tawny, dapple, dove,
Is found the well-tamed ox, strong beast of burden,
Gentle and swift to move, on whom they set
The load and yoke whate'er his hue may be:
So among men of noble, brāhman, low,
Or serf breeds, outcasts, aboriginals,
Is found the well-tamed, pious, modest man,
Just,[6] virtuous, truth-speaking, done with birth
And death, accomplished in the godly life,
With load put down, done what was to be done,
Rid of the cankers, yea and gone beyond
All states, not clinging, cool—lo! in that field
Of faultless men a gift will richly ripen.
The witless, loreless[7] fools, all-ignorant,
Give gifts outside that field nor serve good men.
But they, with faith firm rooted in the Well-gone,
Who serve the good—wise men and by wise men
Held wise[8]—go to the deva-realm, or here
Are born within some clan;[9] and as wise men
In gradual course attain Nibbāna's bliss.'

---

[1] *Merayaŋ vāruṇiŋ. Comy. catubbidhaŋ merayaŋ, pañcavidhañ ca suraŋ; vāruṇī* is a *Jātaka* word and does not seem to recur in the four *Nikāyas*; it is odd that the Commentaries do not connect it with Varuṇa's daughter, the Hindu goddess of spirituous liquor; see *J.* i, 251.

[2] *Cf. Romans* viii, 5.

[3] *Jigiŋsato.*

[4] *Deyya-dhamma:* a *Dhamma*-ly gift, but see *P.E.D. s.v.*

[5] From here onwards recurs at *A.* i, 162, see *G.S.* i, 145; *Comy.* refers to *AA.* ii, 258.

[6] This line of the text recurs above, § 42.

[7] *Assutāvino.*

[8] *Sappaññe dhīrasammate.*

[9] In spite of the text above, *Comy.* omits the *śudras* in explaining the clans or families.

§ x (180). *Gavesin, the seeker.*

Once the Exalted One with a great following of monks walked a walk among the Kosalans.

And as the Exalted One went along the highway he saw a place where grew a big grove of sāl trees; and seeing it there, he moved down from the road and went towards it and made his way among the trees; and at a certain place he smiled.[1]

Now the venerable Ānanda thought: 'What cause now, what reason[2] moved the Exalted One to show a smile? Not for nothing do Tathāgatas smile.' And the venerable Ānanda asked him concerning the matter. . . .

(Then said the Exalted One:)

'At this place, Ānanda, in olden times there was a rich and flourishing city thronged with many people; and by the city, Ānanda, there dwelt the Exalted One, Kassapa,[3] arahant, fully enlightened; and Gavesin was a lay-disciple of the Exalted One, Kassapa; but he kept not the moral precepts.

Now because of Gavesin there were about five hundred who testified[4] and were stirred to discipleship, but they kept not the moral precepts. Thought he: "I have greatly served these five hundred lay-disciples, being the first to move and bestir myself; yet I keep not the moral precepts nor do these five hundred others. This is a levelling of levels,[5] leaving no whit of a more. Come now, I'm for something more!" So Gavesin went up to the five hundred and said: "Know, good sirs,[6] from today that I keep the moral precepts."

Then, Ānanda, those five hundred thought to themselves: "Verily, Master Gavesin has greatly served us, being first to move and bestir himself, and this same Master Gavesin will

[1] This setting recurs elsewhere; see *M.* ii, 45, 74; *cf. S.* ii, 254; *Vin.* iii, 105. *Comy.* observes that in smiling the B. merely showed the tips of his teeth and laughed not as ordinary men who smack their bellies and say, Ho ho!

[2] *Hetu paccayo.*

[3] He who immediately preceded Gotama Buddha.

[4] *Paṭidesitāni samādapitāni. Comy. Upasaka-bhāvaŋ paṭidesitāni samādapitāni saraṇesu patiṭṭhāpitāni; cf. A.* iv, 66.

[5] *Icc' etaŋ sama-samaŋ.*

[6] *Āyasmanto.*

now keep the moral precepts—why then not we too?"[1] Then went those five hundred lay-disciples to Gavesin and told him that they too henceforth would keep the moral precepts.

Again . . . thought Gavesin: "This also is a levelling of levels, leaving no whit of a more; I'm for something more!" and went and told them, saying: "Know, sirs, from today I follow the celibate's life, the life remote,[2] giving up sex-life, common among men."[3] Then thought those others . . . "Why not we too?" and did likewise.

Again . . . thought Gavesin: "This is also a levelling of levels, leaving no whit of a more; I'm for something more!" and went and told them, saying: "Know, sirs, from today I am a one-mealer and abstain from night-eating, giving up eating at wrong times." Then thought they . . . "Why not we too?" and did likewise.

Now the lay-disciple Gavesin considered thus: "I have greatly served these five hundred lay-disciples, being the first to move and bestir myself; I have kept the moral precepts, and now they too have done this; I have followed the life remote . . . and now they too have done this; I have become a one-mealer . . . and now they too have done this. This is indeed a levelling of levels, leaving no whit of a more. Come now, I'm for something more."

And, Ānanda, the lay-disciple Gavesin went to the Exalted One, Kassapa, arahant, fully enlightened, and, having come, said to him:

"Lord, grant that I may go forth beside the Exalted One; grant me full acceptance!"[4]—and Gavesin, the lay-disciple, obtained permission to go forth beside Kassapa, the Exalted One, arahant, fully enlightened; he obtained full acceptance.

---

[1] The text reads *kimaṅga pana mayaṃ*, but with *S.e.* and *Comy.* we should read *pana na*.

[2] *Brahmacārī ārācārī*. *Cf. A.* iv, 249; *D.* i, 4; *M.* iii, 33. The text repeats all in full.

[3] *Gāmadhammā*, *lit.* thing of the village, or, in India, where 'village' was more 'urban' than with us, 'thing of communal life.'

[4] *Upasampadā*; see below V, § 251.

Now not long after his acceptance, Ānanda, Gavesin the monk, living alone, withdrawn, zealous, ardent, resolved, entered into and abode in that unsurpassed goal of the godly life, here among visible things, realizing it by his own knowledge—that goal for the good of which clansmen's sons rightly go forth from the home to the homeless life—and he declared: Destroyed is birth, lived is the godly life, done is the task, there is no more this-ness!

Thereafter, Ānanda, the monk Gavesin was numbered among the arahants.

Then thought those five hundred lay-disciples: "Master Gavesin has done us a great service, he is first to move and bestir himself; and now he has had his hair and beard shaved off, donned the yellow robe, and goes forth from the home to the homeless life; why then not we too?" And those five hundred lay-disciples, Ānanda, went and begged the Exalted One, Kassapa, saying: "Grant, lord, that we may go forth beside the Exalted One; grant us full acceptance!"—and those five hundred obtained permission. . . .

Then thought the monk Gavesin: "I, verily, can obtain this unsurpassed bliss of liberation at will, easily, and without difficulty; would that these five hundred monks could obtain this bliss in like manner!"

Ānanda, those five hundred monks abode alone, withdrawn, zealous, ardent, resolved; and, not long after, entered and dwelt in that unsurpassed goal of the godly life, here among visible things, realizing it by their own knowledge—that for which clansmen's sons rightly go forth—and declared: Destroyed is birth, lived is the godly life, done is the task, there is no more this-ness!

Thus verily, Ānanda, those five hundred monks with Gavesin at their head, in striving from higher things to higher, from strength to strength, came to realize a liberation, above which there is no higher.

Wherefore, Ānanda, train yourselves in this way:

From higher to higher, from strength to strength,[1] we will

---

[1] *Uttaruttariŋ paṇītapaṇītaŋ.*

This, monks, is the fourth ancient brāhman thing now seen in dogs, not in brāhmans.

Monks, in former times brāhmans sought food for the evening meal[1] in the evening, for the morning meal in the morning; now, after cramming their bellies to the uttermost, they take away the remainder. Monks, today dogs seek food for the evening meal in the evening, for the morning meal in the morning. This, monks, is the fifth ancient brāhman thing now seen in dogs, not in brāhmans.

Verily, monks, these are the five ancient brāhman things. . . .'

§ ii (192). *Brāhman Doṇa.*

Now brāhman Doṇa[2] visited the Exalted One and greeted him; and after exchanging the customary words of greetings, sat down at one side. So seated, brāhman Doṇa said to the Exalted One:

'I have heard it said, Master Gotama, that Master Gotama does not salute aged, venerable brāhmans, well stricken in years, long on life's road, grown old—nor rise up for them, nor offer them a seat. Master Gotama, it is just so; Master Gotama does none of these things . . . to aged, venerable brāhmans. . . . This is not right, Master Gotama.'[3]

'Do *you* not[4] profess to be a brāhman, Doṇa ?'

'If of anyone, Master Gotama, in speaking rightly it should be said: "The brāhman is well born on both sides, pure in descent as far back as seven generations, both of mother and father, unchallenged and without reproach in point of birth;[5] studious, carrying the mantras in mind, a past master in the three Vedas with the indices and ritual, in phonology too,

---

[1] *Sāya-m-āsa*, a *Jātaka* compound.

[2] This brāhman is presumably the same as at *A.* ii, 37. *Bu.* offers no help; there is also the Doṇa who received the B.'s bowl, *D.* ii, 166: for the Tibetan story known as *Droṇasama*, *cf.* Rockhill's *Life*, and *Chwang*, ii, 43, possibly there a nickname.

[3] This para. recurs at *A.* iv, 173.

[4] '*Tvam pi no paṭijānāsi?*' *Vv.ll.* of *no* are *ne* and *kho.*

[5] *Cf.* above, § 134.

and fifthly in the legends; an expert in verse and grammar, skilled in reading the marks of a great man, in speculation on the universe "[1]—to be sure of me, Master Gotama, in speaking rightly that thing should be said; for I, Master Gotama, am so born . . . so skilled. . . .'

'Doṇa, those brāhman-sages of old, mantra-makers, mantra-sayers, whose ancient collection of mantra verses, hymns and sayings, brāhmans now ever hymn, ever say, ever word the word, ever have the sayings said—to wit: Aṭṭhaka, Vāmaka, Vāmedeva, Vessāmitta, Yamadaggi, Aṅgīrasa, Bhāradvāja, Vāseṭṭha, Kassapa and Bhagu[2]—they these five brāhmans have declared: the Brahma-like,[3] the deva-like, the bounded, the breaker of bounds and, fifthly, the brāhman-outcast. Which of them, Doṇa, are you?'

'*We* know not of these five brāhmans, Master Gotama; yet we know that we *are* brāhmans. It were well for me if Master Gotama would teach me Dhamma so that I may know of these five.'

'Then listen, brāhman, give heed and I will speak!'

'Yes, sir,' replied he; and the Exalted One said:

'And how, Doṇa, becomes a brāhman Brahma-like?

Take the case, Doṇa, of a brāhman who is well born on both sides, pure in descent as far back as seven generations, both of mother and father, unchallenged and without reproach in point of birth—he for eight and forty years[4] leads the Brahma-life of virginity,[5] applying himself to the mantras;[6] then, completing that course, he seeks the teacher's fee for teaching according to Dhamma, not non-Dhamma. And what there is Dhamma, Doṇa? Never as ploughman[7] nor

---

[1] *Cf. G.S.* i, 146; *D.* i, 120; *M.* ii, 147; *Sn.* p. 105; *Mil.* 10. At *A.* i, 163 this section follows the verses given in our § 179.

[2] This is also stock; see *Vin.* i, 245, *D.* i, 104, *M.* ii, 170; *cf. A.* iv, 61. Our *Comy.* repeats *DA.* i, 273.

[3] *Brahma-sama.*

[4] *Cf. Āpastamba*, ii, 12 *f.* (*S.B.E.* ii, 7, also *Manu* referred to there); *A.* iv, 37; *Sn.* 289; *SnA.* 316 *ff.* refers to our text.

[5] *Komāra-brahmacariyaṃ.*

[6] *Comy.* the Vedas.

[7] This list recurs at *M.* i, 85; *A.* iv, 281.

trader nor cowherd nor bowman nor rajah's man nor by any craft (to get his living), but solely by going about for alms, despising not the beggar's bowl.[1] And he hands over the teacher's fee for teaching, has his hair-beard shaved off, dons the yellow robe and goes forth from the home to the homeless life.

And thus gone forth, he abides[2] in mind pervading with amity one world quarter, so a second, a third, a fourth; then above, below, athwart, everywhere, the whole wide world he pervades with thoughts of amity, far-reaching, expansive, measureless, without hatred or ill-will. He abides in mind pervading with pity . . . sympathy . . . poise, one world quarter, so a second, a third, a fourth; then above, below, athwart, everywhere, the whole wide world he pervades with thoughts of pity, sympathy and poise, far-reaching, expansive, measureless, without hatred or ill-will. And having made these four Brahma-abidings[3] become, on the breaking up of the body after death, he arises in the well-faring Brahma-world. Thus, Doṇa, a brāhman becomes Brahma-like.[4]

And how, Doṇa, becomes a brāhman deva-like?

Take the case, Doṇa, of a brāhman of similar birth and conduct. . . .[5] He does not get a living by ploughing and so forth, but by going about for alms. . . . He hands over the teacher's fee for teaching and seeks a wife according to Dhamma, not non-Dhamma. And what there is Dhamma? Not with one bought or sold, but only with a brāhmaṇī on whom water has been poured.[6] And he goes only to a brāhmaṇī, not to the daughter of a noble, low-caste man or serf, nor to the daughter of an outcast, hunter, bamboo-

---

[1] *Comy.* the beggar's portion.

[2] *Cf. D.* iii, 223; *M.* ii, 76; *S.* v, 115; *A.* iv, 390.

[3] *Brahma-vihāre.*

[4] *Brahma-sama*; see *Expos.* i, 262; *Sn.* 508.

[5] The text repeats nearly all in full throughout the sutta.

[6] *Udak' ūpassaṭṭha. Comy.* glosses: *pariccattaṃ*, and explains: after pouring water on her hands they give her to him. *Upa√sṛj* can mean: to cause to flow (water) in *Skt.*; *cf.* the ceremony at *A.* iv, 210; it is now used in Ceylon.

worker, cart-maker, or aboriginal;[1] nor goes to a woman with child, nor to one giving suck, nor to one not in her season. And wherefore, Doṇa, goes not a brāhman to one with child? If he go, the boy or girl will surely be foully born;[2] therefore he goes not. And wherefore goes he not to one giving suck? If he go, the boy or girl will surely be an unclean suckling;[3] therefore he goes not. And wherefore goes he not to one not in her season? If, Doṇa, a brāhman go to one in her season,[4] never for him does the brāhmaṇī become a means for lust, for sport, for pleasure; the brāhmaṇī is for the brāhman just a means to beget offspring. And when in wedlock[5] he has begotten (a child), he has his hair-beard shaved off . . . and goes forth. . . . And being thus gone forth, aloof from sensuous appetites . . . he enters and abides in the first (to the) fourth musing. And having made these four musings become, on the breaking up of the body after death, he arises in the well-faring heaven[6] world Thus, Doṇa, a brāhman becomes deva-like.

And how, Doṇa, becomes a brāhman bounded?[7]

Take the case, Doṇa, of a brāhman of similar birth and conduct . . . who weds in like manner. . . .[8] And when in wedlock he has begotten a child, the fondness for children obsesses him and he settles on the family estate[9] and does not go forth from the home to the homeless life. In the bounds of the brāhmans of old he stays nor transgresses them; and it is said: "Within bounds he keeps and transgresses not." And therefore the brāhman is called bounded. Thus, Doṇa, the brāhman becomes bounded.

---

[1] *Cf. M.* ii, 183.

[2] *Atimīḷhajo. Comy. atimīḷhe mahāgūtharāsimhi jāto; Tr. Dict.* suggests *adhi-* for *ati-*.

[3] *A-suci-paṭipīto, S.e.* so; *P.E.D.* prefers *v.l. piḷita*, but √*pā* connects with *pāyamāna* of the text.

[4] With *S.e.* we should read *utuniŋ* for *an-* of the text.

[5] Text *methunaŋ*, with *v.l. mithunaŋ*; *Comy.* and *S.e.* so; *P.E.D.* does not notice this form, but see *Childers* and *Skt. Dict. s.v. Comy.* observes: *Dhītaraŋ vā puttaŋ vā uppādetvā.* . . .

[6] *Saggaŋ lokaŋ.*

[7] *Mariyāda, SnA.* 318 *ff.*

[8] The text repeats nearly all in full throughout the sutta.

[9] We should read *kuṭumbaŋ* with *Comy.* and *S.e.*

And how, Doṇa, becomes a brāhman a breaker of bounds?[1]

Take the case, Doṇa, of a brāhman of similar birth and conduct. . . . He hands over the teacher's fee and seeks a wife either according to Dhamma or non-Dhamma: one bought or sold or a brāhmaṇī on whom the water-pouring ceremony has been performed. He goes to a brāhmaṇī or to the daughter of a noble or a low-caste man or a serf; to the daughter of an outcast or a hunter or a bamboo-worker or a cart-maker or an aboriginal; he goes to a woman with child, to one giving suck, to one in her season, to one not in her season; and for him the brāhmaṇī becomes just a means for lust, for sport and for pleasure or to beget offspring. And he keeps not within the ancient brāhman bounds, but transgresses them; and it is said: "He keeps not within bounds but transgresses," and therefore he is called a breaker of bounds. Thus, Doṇa, the brāhman becomes a breaker of bounds.

And how, Doṇa, becomes a brāhman a brāhman-outcast?

Take the case, Doṇa, of a brāhman of similar birth . . .; he for eight and forty years leads the Brahma-life of virginity, applying himself to the mantras; then, completing that course, he seeks the teaching fee for teaching; (he gets his living) according to Dhamma or non-Dhamma: as ploughman, trader, cowherd, bowman, rajah's man or by some craft or, despising not the beggar's bowl, just by going about for alms. On handing back the teacher's fee, he seeks a wife according to Dhamma or non-Dhamma: one bought or sold, or a brāhmaṇī on whom water has been poured. He goes to a brāhmaṇī or any other woman . . .; one with child, giving suck and so forth . . .; and she is for him a means for lust . . . or to beget offspring. He leads a life doing all these things. Then the brāhmans say thus of him: "How is it that an honourable brāhman leads this sort of life?" and to this he replies: "Just[2] as fire burns clean things or unclean,

---

[1] *Sambhinna-mariyāda.*

[2] I cannot trace this simile elsewhere, but for the sentiment *cf.* *Sn.* 547, 812; *J.* v, 485.

but not by that is the fire defiled; even so, good sirs, if a brāhman lead a life doing all these things, not by that is a brāhman defiled." And it is said: "He leads a life doing all these things," and therefore he is called a brāhman-outcast. Thus, Doṇa, a brāhman becomes a brāhman-outcast.

Verily, Doṇa, those brāhman-sages of old, mantra-makers, mantra-sayers, whose ancient collection of mantra verses, hymns and sayings, brāhmans now still hymn, say, word each word, and have the sayings said—to wit: Aṭṭhaka and the rest . . .—these five brāhmans declared: the Brahma-like, the deva-like, the bounded, the breaker of bounds and, fifthly, the brāhman-outcast. Which of them, Doṇa, are you?'

'If such there are,[1] Master Gotama, we at least do not fulfil (the ways of) the brāhman-outcast!

But it is marvellous what you say, Master Gotama, . . . let Master Gotama take me as a lay-disciple, gone to his refuge, henceforth as long as life lasts.'

§ iii (193). *Brāhman Sangārava.*[2]

Now brāhman Sangārava[3] visited the Exalted One and greeted him; and after exchanging the customary words of greetings, sat down at one side. So seated, brāhman Sangārava said to the Exalted One:

'What is the cause, Master Gotama, what is the reason, why sometimes[4] even mantras long studied are not clear,[5] not to speak of those not studied; and what is the cause, what the reason, why sometimes even mantras not long studied are clear, not to speak of those studied?'

'When, brāhman, one dwells with heart possessed by lust and passion, overwhelmed by lust and passion, and knows

---

[1] *Evaŋ sante.*

[2] The whole sutta recurs at *S.* v, 121 *ff.* (*K.S.* v, 102), 'At Sāvatthī.'

[3] Discourses with this brāhman occur at *S.* i, 183; *A.* i, 168; v, 232, 252; *cf.* also *M.* ii, 210 (there termed *māṇavo,* young; see *K.S.* i, 231 *n.*).

[4] *Ekadā*; *P.E.D.* does not give this meaning but see *Skt. Dict.* (Macdonell's).

[5] *Na ppaṭibhanti.* *K.S. trsl.* 'do not recur,' from √*bhā,* to shine.

not the escape[1] from the surge thereof, as it really is; then he knows not, sees not the self-goal, as it really is; knows not, sees not another's goal, as it really is; knows not, sees not the goal of both, as it really is; then even the mantras long studied are not clear, not to speak of those not studied.

Suppose, brāhman, a pot of water, mixed with lac, tumeric, blue or yellow dye,[2] and a man with eyes to see were to look there for his own face-reflection—he would not know it, he would not see it, as it really was; even so, brāhman, when one dwells with heart possessed by lust and passion, overwhelmed thereby, and knows not the escape from the surge thereof, as it really is; then he knows not, sees not the self-goal, another's goal, the goal of both, as it really is; then even the mantras long studied are not clear, not to speak of those not studied.

Again, brāhman, when one dwells with heart possessed by ill-will, overwhelmed by ill-will, and knows not the escape from the surge thereof, as it really is; then he knows not, sees not the self-goal, another's goal, the goal of both, as it really is; then even the mantras long studied are not clear, not to speak of those not studied.

Suppose, brāhman, a pot of water, heated on the fire, boiling up and bubbling over, and a man with eyes to see were to look there for his own face-reflection—he would not know it, he would not see it, as it really was; even so, brāhman, when one dwells with heart possessed by ill-will . . .; then even the mantras long studied are not clear. . . .

Again, brāhman, when one dwells with heart possessed by sloth and torpor . . . then even the mantras long studied are not clear. . . .

---

[1] *Nissaraṇa. Comy.* observes that in respect of lust the escape is by elimination, suitable resort and cutting off by means of '*asubha*' musing, insight and the way of arahantship, respectively; of ill-will the first and third, substituting '*mettā*' for '*asubha*' and the way of the Non-returner; of sloth and torpor the same but by means of '*ālokasaññā*' and arahantship; of flurry and worry the same but substituting calm for '*ālokasaññā*'; the escape from doubt is by elimination, by Dhamma-determining (*-vavatthāna*).

[2] For this list see *M.* i, 127; S. ii, 101.

Suppose, brāhman, a pot of water, covered over with slimy moss and water-plants,[1] and a man were to look there for his own face-reflection—. . . he would not see it . . .; even so, brāhman, when one dwells with heart possessed by sloth and torpor . . . the mantras long studied are not clear. . . .

Again, brāhman, when one dwells with heart possessed by flurry and worry . . . then even the mantras long studied are not clear. . . .

Suppose, brāhman, a pot of water were shaken[2] with the wind, so that the water trembled, eddied and rippled, and a man were to look there for his own face-reflection—he would not see it . . .; even so, brāhman, when one dwells with heart possessed by flurry and worry . . . the mantras long studied are not clear. . . .

Again, brāhman, when one dwells with heart possessed by doubt, overwhelmed by doubt, and knows not the escape from the surge thereof, as it really is; then he knows not, sees not the self-goal, another's goal, the goal of both, as it really is; then even the mantras long studied are not clear, not to speak of those not studied.

Suppose, brāhman, a pot of water, stirred[2] up, turbid, made muddy, set in a darkened room,[3] and a man with eyes to see were to look there for his own face-reflection—he would not know it, he would not see it, as it really was; even so, brāhman, when one dwells with heart possessed by doubt, overwhelmed by doubt, and knows not the escape from the surge thereof, as it really is; then he knows not, sees not the self-goal, another's goal, the goal of both, as it really is; then even the mantras long studied are not clear, not to speak of those not studied.

But, brāhman, when one dwells with heart neither possessed nor overwhelmed by lust and passion, ill-will, sloth and torpor, flurry and worry and doubt . . . and knows the escape from the surge thereof, as it really is; then he knows, he sees the

---

[1] *Cf.* above, § 162; here *Comy. Tilabījakâdi-bhedena sevālena vā nīla-maṇḍaka-piṭṭhi-vaṇṇena vā udaka-piṭṭhiŋ chādetvā nibbatta-paṇaka-pariyonaddho.*

[2] *Cf. Mil.* 35, 259-60.

[3] *Comy. Anāloka-ṭṭhāne ṭhapito.*

self-goal, as it really is; knows and sees another's goal, as it really is; knows and sees the goal of both, as it really is; then even the mantras not long studied are clear, not to speak of those studied.

Suppose, brāhman, a pot of water, uncontaminated by dyes[1] . . . unheated, not bubbling over . . . free of moss and water-plants . . . without eddy or ripple . . . clear, limpid, pellucid, set in the open, and a man with eyes to see were to look there for his own face-reflection—he would know it, he would see it, as it really was; even so, brāhman, when one dwells with heart neither possessed nor overwhelmed by lust and passion, ill-will, sloth and torpor, flurry and worry and doubt . . .,[1] and knows the escape from the surge thereof, as it really is; then he knows, he sees the self-goal, another's goal, the goal of both, as it really is; then even the mantras not long studied are clear, not to speak of those studied.

This verily, brāhman, is the cause, the reason, why sometimes even mantras long studied are not clear, not to speak of those not studied; and this is the cause, the reason, why sometimes even mantras not long studied are clear, not to speak of those studied.'

'This is marvellous, Master Gotama, . . . let Master Gotama take me as a lay-disciple, gone to his refuge, henceforth as long as life lasts.'

§ iv (194). *Brāhman Kāraṇapālin.*

The Exalted One was once dwelling near Vesālī, at the Gabled Hall, in Mahāvana. Now at that time brāhman Kāraṇapālin[2] built a building for the Licchavis. And brāhman

---

[1] The text repeats mostly in full in the same sequence as before.

[2] I cannot find mention of this brāhman elsewhere; *Comy.* observes that he built buildings for rajahs' families; getting up early, he was having the unfinished walls of a gateway built; he (also) looked after the feeding of the aged. The text reads '*Licchavīnaŋ kammantaŋ kāreti*'; according to Childers (quoting Senart's *Kaccāyanappakaraṇaŋ*) *kāreti* with *acc.* and *gen.* means: he causes someone (*gen.*) to do something (*acc.*); see his *Dict. s.v.*

Kāraṇapālin saw brāhman Piṅgiyānin[1] some way off, coming along; and on seeing him (approach), he said:

'Pray[2] now, whence comes his honour Piṅgiyānin so early in the day?'

'I am come here, sir, from the presence of the recluse Gotama.'

'Well, what thinks his honour Piṅgiyānin of the recluse Gotama's clarity in wisdom;[3] does he think him a wise man?'[4]

'But who am I [to him], sir; and who am I to judge of his clarity? Is it not one who is like him that can alone judge the recluse Gotama's clarity in wisdom?'

'Lofty indeed is the praise with which his honour Piṅgiyānin praises the recluse Gotama.'

'But who am I [to him], sir; and who am I to praise the recluse Gotama? Verily, praised by the praised[5] is his honour Gotama, chief among devas and men.'

'But what good thing does his honour Piṅgiyānin see to have so great faith in the recluse Gotama?'

'Just,[6] sir, as a man, well satisfied with some choice savour, longs not for other savours that are mean; even so, sir, whenever one hears his honour Gotama's Dhamma, whether in the sayings, the psalms, the catechisms or the marvels—none longs for the talks of others: the many-folk, recluses or brāhmans.

---

[1] Nor can I trace this brāhman elsewhere except in the next sutta; *Comy.* observes that he was established in the fruit of a Non-returner.

[2] All this to the similes recurs at *M.* i, 175; ii, 208 of others. The br. K. addresses br. P. by *bhavaŋ* and after conversion by *bho*, speaking of the B. as *samaṇa* firstly, latterly as *bhavantaŋ* (so *S.e.* but *v.l. bhagavantaŋ*); br. P. addresses br. K. by *bho*, speaking of the B. as *samaṇa* and *bhavaŋ*.

[3] *Paññāveyyattiya.*

[4] Our text, S.*e.* and *M.* ii *maññe-ti*, but *M.* i and our *Comy. maññati*, explaining: '*bhavaŋ P. samaṇaŋ Gotamaŋ paṇḍito ti maññati, udāhu no?*'

[5] *Pasattha-pasattho.* Lord Chalmers: 'praise upon praise is his,' but our *Comy.* instances, among others, Pasenadi, Bimbisāra, Cankī, Visākhā, Sakka, Brahmā, observing: *pasatthehi va pasattho-ti pi, pasatthapasattho.*

[6] *Cf. Psalm* cvii, 9 for a similar sentiment.

Just,[1] sir, as a man, overcome by hunger and weakness, may come upon a honey cake and, whenever he taste, enjoy the sweet, delicious savour; even so, sir, whenever one hears his honour Gotama's Dhamma, whether in the sayings, psalms, catechisms or marvels—he wins elation,[2] wins serenity of mind.

Just, sir, as a man may come upon a stick of sandalwood, yellow or red, and, wherever he smell, at the root, in the middle, at the top—may come upon an exceeding fair, delicious smell: even so, sir, whenever one hears his honour Gotama's Dhamma, whether in the sayings, psalms, catechisms or marvels—he finds joy, finds happiness.

Just,[3] sir, as a clever physician might in a trice take away the sickness of one sick and ailing, grievously ill; even so, sir, whenever one hears his honour Gotama's Dhamma, whether in the sayings, psalms, catechisms or marvels—grief, lamentation, suffering, sorrow and despair vanish away.

Just,[3] sir, as a man, tortured by heat, by heat forspent, wearied, craving and thirsty, might come to a pool, clear, sweet, cool, limpid, a lovely resting-place, and might plunge therein, bathe and drink, and allay all woe, fatigue and fret; even so, sir, whenever one hears his honour Gotama's Dhamma, whether in the sayings, psalms, catechisms or marvels—all woe, fatigue and fret is wholly allayed.'

And when he had thus spoken, brāhman Kāraṇapālin arose from his seat, arranged his upper robe on his shoulder, set his right knee on the ground, and, bending forth his outstretched hands towards the Exalted One, three times uttered this utterance:[4]

'Honour to him, the Exalted One, arahant, fully enlightened.
Honour to him, the Exalted One, arahant, fully enlightened.
Honour to him, the Exalted One, arahant, fully enlightened.'

(Then said he:) 'Wonderful is it, Master Piṅgiyānin,

---

[1] This recurs at *M.* i, 114; *cf. Psalm* xxxiv, 8; our text should read *sādu-rasaŋ* or *sāduŋ* with *M.*

[2] *Attamanatā*, with Bu., but see *P.E.D.*

[3] *Cf.* above, § 162.

[4] *Cf. M.* ii, 209; *D.* ii, 288.

wonderful is it, Master Piṅgiyānin! 'Tis just as if one had set upright a thing toppled over, opened out a covered thing, showed a blind man along the road, brought an oil lamp into the dark, so that those that had eyes could see objects—it is just thus that Dhamma has been blazed[1] abroad by his honour Piṅgiyānin in manifold ways.

'I, too,[2] Master Piṅgiyānin, go to that exalted Gotama for refuge, to Dhamma and to the monk-Order; let his honour Piṅgiyānin look upon me as a lay-disciple, to that refuge gone, henceforth as long as life lasts!'

§ v (195). *Brāhman Piṅgiyānin.*

Once, while the Exalted One was dwelling near Vesālī, at the Gabled Hall in Mahāvana, some five hundred Licchavis had gathered round to honour him. And[3] some were dark, dark-skinned, in dark clothes clad, darkly adorned; and some were fair, fair-skinned, in fair clothes clad, fairly adorned; and some were ruddy, red-skinned, in russet clad, in red adorned; and some were white, pale-skinned, in white clothes clad, in white adorned; but of a truth the Exalted One, in grace and glory, outshone them all.

Now brāhman Piṅgiyānin rose from his seat, girt his upper robe about his shoulder, bent forth his outstretched hands to the Exalted One and said:

'It[4] has been revealed to me, O Blessed One; it has been revealed to me, O Well-gone!'

'Speak thou that thing, Piṅgiyānin,' said the Exalted One.

Then brāhman Piṅgiyānin extolled the Exalted One before his face in this same verse:[5]

> Sweet tho' at dawn red lotus-lilies blow,
> 'Tis sweeter in full bloom their blossoms grow:

---

[1] *Pakāsito.* [2] *Es' ahaṃ.*

[3] This is a stock passage; see *D.* ii, 96; *cf. A.* iv, 263, of fairies.

[4] *Sn.* p. 79; *S.* i, 189.

[5] This verse recurs at *S.* i, 81 (*K.S.* i, 107); *J.* i, 116; *Vism.* 388. *Vism trsl.* misses the point of comparison, but see the story there.

Lo! see Angīrasa,[1] illuminant,
Like as the midday sun, all radiant.'[2]

Then those Licchavis presented brāhman Piṅgiyānin with five hundred upper robes and brāhman Piṅgiyānin presented them to the Exalted One.

Then said the Exalted One to those Licchavis:

'Five,[3] O Licchavis, are the treasures rarely revealed in the world. What five?

The Tathāgata, arahant, fully enlightened,[4] is rarely revealed in the world; rare in the world is one able to teach the Tathāgata-declared Dhamma-discipline; rare is one able to recognize the teaching . . .; rare is one who steps his way in Dhamma by Dhamma, recognizing the teaching of the Tathāgata-declared Dhamma-discipline; rare in the world is a person grateful and thankful.

Verily, O Licchavis, these are the five treasures rarely revealed in the world.'

§ vi (196). *Dreams.*

'Monks, to the Tathāgata, arahant, fully awake to the highest[4]—ere his full awakening,[5] when he was not yet wholly awakened[6] and but a being awakening[7]—there came five great dreams.[8] What five?

Monks, the Tathāgata, arahant, fully awake to the highest

---

[1] That is, the B.; our *Comy. Bhagavato aṅga-m-aṅgehi rasmiyo niccharanti, tasmā angīraso-ti vuccati*; see *Brethr.* 251; *Dial.* iii, 189. Thomas' *Life* observes: 'descendant of Angiras' (p. 22). Rockhill gives the Tibetan version thus: 'and as they (the B.'s miraculously born ancestors) were "born from his loins" (the rishi Gautama's) they were called Angīrasas.' I have taken Bu.'s explanation. *Cf.* above, § 192.

[2] *Cf. Thag.* 426. [3] *Cf.* above, § 143. [4] *Sammā-sambuddha.*

[5] *Sambodha.* [6] *an-abhisambuddha.* [7] *Bodhisatta.*

[8] These five are referred to at *J.* i, 69; see Thomas' *Life*, 70 *n.* Our *Comy.* observes that there are four dream-causes: (1) body-disturbances, due to bile, producing dreams such as falling from a precipice or flying or being chased by a beast or robber; (2) previous happenings; (3) being deva-possessed, and devas bring thoughts both for one's good and otherwise; (4) premonitions; this last is the Bodhisat's. *Cf. Milinda*, Dilemma 75 (p. 297).

—ere his full awakening, when he was not yet wholly awakened and but a being awakening—(dreamed that) this mighty world was his bed of state; the mountain-king, Himālaya, his pillow; that his left hand rested[1] on the eastern sea; his right on the western sea; and that both his feet rested on the southern sea. Monks, to the Tathāgata, arahant, fully awake to the highest—ere his full awakening, when he was not yet wholly awakened and but a being awakening—this first great dream came.

Again, . . . he dreamed that there went out from his navel[2] Tiriyā[3] grass and it stopped not, until it touched the clouds. Monks, to the Tathāgata . . . ere his full awakening . . . this second dream came.

Again, . . . he dreamed that white worms with black heads crept up over his feet as far as his knees and covered them. Monks, . . . to him this third dream came.

Again, . . . he dreamed that there came four birds of varied hues from the four quarters of the world and they fell at his feet and became all white. Monks, . . . to him this fourth dream came.

Again, . . . he dreamed that he walked to and fro on a great mountain of dung, but was unbesmeared with dung. Monks, . . . to him this fifth dream came.

Monks, when indeed to the Tathāgata, arahant, fully awake to the highest—ere his full awakening, when he was not yet fully awakened and but a being awakening—there came the dream that this great world was his bed of state . . .; monks, by the Tathāgata, arahant, fully awake to the highest, the unsurpassed, full awakening to the highest[4] was wholly awakened[5] (within him). To him, wholly awakening,[6] this first dream came.[7]

When to him . . . there came the dream that grass went

---

[1] *Ohita* (Thomas *loc. cit.*), 'plunged,' but *Comy. na udakasmiŋ.*

[2] Thomas, 'hand,' but the Pāli is *nābhi.*

[3] *Comy. dabbha,* kusa grass.

[4] *Sammā-sambodhi.*

[5] *Abhisambuddha.*

[6] *Abhisambodha.*

[7] I give a literal trsl. of the five; the meaning no doubt is that the Bodhisat so interpreted the dreams.

out from his navel; monks, by the Tathāgata . . . the Ariyan eightfold Way was wholly awakened (within him) and well proclaimed as far as devas and men (exist).[1] To him, wholly awakening, this second dream came.

When to him there came the dream that white worms with black heads crept up to his knees; monks, many white-robed householders found lifelong refuge in the Tathāgata. To him, wholly awakening, this third dream came.

When to him there came the dream that the four birds of the four quarters fell white at his feet; monks, these four castes—noble, brāhman, low and serf—went forth from the home to the homeless life into that Dhamma-discipline taught by the Tathāgata and realized unsurpassed liberation. To him, wholly awakening, this fourth dream came.

When he dreamed that he walked on the mountain of dung; monks, the Tathāgata received the requisites:—robe, alms, lodging and medicaments for sickness—and in them the Tathāgata found enjoyment, yet was not tied, trussed nor attached[2] thereto, seeing the danger, wise as to the escape therefrom. To him, wholly awakening, this fifth dream came.

Monks, to the Tathāgata, arahant, fully awake to the highest —ere his full awakening, when he was not yet fully awakened and but a being awakening—there came these five great dreams.'

§ vii (197). *The rains.*

'Monks, there are these five stays[3] to rain, and seers know not the signs thereof, nor can their eyes penetrate there. What five?

Monks, when above in the sky the fiery element rages, the pent up storm clouds part their ways—this, monks, is the first stay to rain, and seers know not the sign thereof, nor can their eyes penetrate there.

Again, when above in the sky the windy element rages,

---

[1] *Yāva devamanussehi suppakāsito*; see the discussion on this at *Dial.* ii, 236 and *P.E.D. s.v. yāva.*

[2] *Cf. D.* i, 245; *M.* i, 173; *S.* ii, 270.

[3] *Cf. Job* xxxviii, 37: 'Who can stay the bottles of heaven?'

GS

the pent up storm clouds part their ways—this, monks, is the second stay to rain. . . .

Again, when Rāhu,[1] the asura king, gathers water with his hand and spills it into the mighty ocean—this, monks, is the third stay to rain. . . .

Again, when the rain-cloud devas are indolent—this, monks, is the fourth stay to rain. . . .

Again, monks, when men are not Dhamma-doers—this is the fifth stay to rain. . . .

Verily, monks, these are the five stays to rain, and seers know not the signs thereof, nor can their eyes penetrate there.'

§ viii (198). *The word.*[2]

'Monks, if a word have five marks, it is well spoken, not ill spoken, nor is it blameworthy nor blameable by the wise.

It is spoken in season,[3] it is spoken in truth, it is spoken softly,[4] it is spoken about the goal, it is spoken in amity.

Verily, monks, if a word have these five marks, it is well spoken, not ill spoken, nor is it blameworthy nor blameable by the wise.'

§ ix (199). *The family.*

'Monks, when virtuous world-forsakers approach a family, men there in five ways beget much merit. In what five?

Monks, when virtuous world-forsakers approach, men, seeing them, make calm their hearts; monks, that leads heavenward and the family then has stepped a step along the way.[5]

Or when they approach, men stand up, salute and offer a seat; monks, that leads to birth in higher rank and the family then has stepped a step along the way.

Or they rid themselves of all stain of meanness; monks, that leads to great power and the family then has stepped a step along the way.

---

1 Who at eclipses swallows the moon.

2 *Cf.* above, § 167, also *Sn.* p. 78; *S.* i, 188.

3 *Cf. Proverbs* xv, 23: 'A word spoken in due season, how good it is!'

4 *Job* xli, 3; *Proverbs* xv, 1.

5 *Paṭipadaŋ paṭipannaŋ hoti.*

Or they share (their food) as means and power allow; monks, that leads to great wealth and the family then has stepped a step along the way.

Or when virtuous world-forsakers approach, men ask, make question about and listen to Dhamma; monks, that leads to great wisdom and the family then has stepped a step along the way.

Monks, when virtuous world-forsakers approach a family, men there in these five ways beget much merit.'

§ x (200). *The escape.*

'Monks, there are these five elements of escape. What five?

Monks,[1] take the case of a monk who thinks on lust and whose heart leaps[2] not up at lustful thoughts, yet becomes not calm, nor firm, nor inclined[3] thereunto; but whose heart at the thought of giving up all leaps up, becomes calm,[4] becomes firm and inclined thereunto—that heart of his is well gone,[5] well become, well lifted up, well unyoked from lustful thoughts; and he is freed from the cankers that surge—lust-caused, painful and burning—nor feels he that feeling. This is declared to be the escape from lusts.

Again, monks, take the case of a monk who thinks on ill-will . . . on hurt . . . on form . . . but whose heart leaps not up at these thoughts . . .; but (at the thought of the opposites) . . . becomes inclined thereunto—that heart of his is well gone . . . and he is freed from the cankers that surge . . . nor feels he those feelings. Such is declared to be the escape from those thoughts. . . .

Again, monks, take the case of a monk who thinks on his bundle of life[6] and whose heart leaps not up at that thought; yet becomes not calm, nor firm, nor inclined thereunto;

---

[1] *Cf.* the whole sutta with *D.* iii, 239; below VI, § 13.

[2] This is stock; *M.* i, 186; *S.* iii, 134; *It.* 43, etc.

[3] *Na vimuccati. Comy. nâdhimuccati.*

[4] We find this traditional phrase used in *Mil.* p. 325 *f.*

[5] *S.e.* and *Comy.* with *v.l. sugataṃ.*

[6] *Sakkāya*; *cf.* 1 *Samuel* xxv, 29; from $\sqrt{ci}$, to heap (? the *khandhas*).

but whose heart at the thought of the ending of his bundle of life leaps up, becomes calm, becomes firm, and inclined thereunto—that heart of his is well gone, well become, well lifted up, well unyoked from the thought of his bundle of life; and he is freed from the cankers that surge—caused by the bundle of life, painful and burning—nor feels he that feeling. This is declared to be the escape from one's bundle of life.

Lust-delights obsess[1] him not, delight in thoughts of ill-will . . . hurt . . . form . . . in his bundle of life obsess him not; he is free of all those obsessions . . . and, monks, this monk is said to be obsession-free; he has cut off craving, rolled back the bolts, and, mastering pride completely, has made an end of Ill.[2]

Verily, monks, these are the five elements of escape.'

CHAPTER XXI.—KIMBILA.

§ i (201). *Kimbila.*

Once,[3] when the Exalted One was dwelling near Kimbilā in the Bamboo[4] Grove, the venerable Kimbila visited him and, after saluting, sat down at one side. So seated, he spoke thus to the Exalted One:

'Lord, what is the cause, what is the reason, whereby, when the Exalted One has passed away completely, Saddhamma does not become long-lasting?'

'Suppose, Kimbila, after the Tathāgata has passed away completely, the monks and the nuns, the lay-disciples both men and women, live without[5] reverence, without heed,

---

[1] *Nânuseti. Comy. na nibbattati.*

[2] *Cf. M.* i, 122; *It.* 47; *A.* iv, 8.

[3] *Cf. A.* iv, 84, where this sutta recurs of 'seven'; also *K.S.* ii, 152; v, 151.

[4] *Comy.* observes that he was a 'chetty's' (*seṭṭhi*, banker) son in that city. *S.e.* and *Comy.* read *Nicelu-vane* for our *Veḷu-vane*, explaining: *Mucalinda-*; see *UdA.* 100. *Cf. Vin. T.* ii, 309; *M.* i, 205, etc.

[5] *Comy.* says they will go to a shrine with umbrellas up, sandals on, chattering; they will sleep or talk when there is preaching; they will gesticulate in the midst of the Order; they will not fulfil the training; they will fight and quarrel with one another.

for the Teacher; without reverence, without heed for Dhamma . . . for the Order. . . for the training; without reverence, without heed for one another—this is the cause, this is the reason, whereby, when the Tathāgata has passed away completely, Saddhamma does not become long-lasting.'

'And what, lord, is the cause, the reason, whereby, after the Tathāgata has passed away, Saddhamma becomes long-lasting?'

'Suppose, Kimbila, monks, nuns and lay-disciples revere and give heed to the Teacher, Dhamma, the Order, the training; revere and give heed to one another—this is the cause, the reason, whereby, when the Tathāgata has passed away, Saddhamma becomes long-lasting.'

§ ii (202). *On hearing Dhamma.*

'Monks, there are these five advantages from hearing Dhamma. What five?

He hears things not heard; purges things heard; dispels doubt; makes straight[1] his view; and his heart becomes calm.

Verily, monks, these are the five advantages from hearing Dhamma.'

§ iii (203). *The thoroughbred.*[2]

'Monks, if a rajah's fine thoroughbred have five points, it is of worth to the rajah, valuable to the rajah, and is reckoned a rajah's asset. What five?

Straightness,[3] swiftness, gentleness,[4] patience and restraint.

Verily, monks, if a rajah's thoroughbred have these five points, it is reckoned a rajah's asset. . . .

Even so, monks, if a monk have five things,[5] he is worthy of offerings, worthy of gifts, worthy of oblations, meet to be reverently saluted, the world's peerless field for merit. What five?

---

[1] *Ujuŋ karoti.*

[2] *Ājāniyo.* This is a common simile; see *J.P.T.S.*, 1906, p. 64.

[3] *Ajjavena. Comy. uju-bhāvena, avaṅka-gamanena. Cf. DhS. trsl.* 348 *n*.

[4] *Maddavena. Comy. sarīra-mudutāya* (? 'tender hide').

[5] *Cf. Sn.* 292; *J.* iii, 274; *D.* iii, 213.

Straightness,[1] swiftness,[2] gentleness, patience and restraint.

Verily, monks, if a monk have these five things, he is worthy of offerings . . . the world's peerless field for merit.'

§ iv (204). *The powers.*[3]

'Monks, there are these five powers. What five?

The power of faith, conscientiousness, fear of blame, energy and insight.

Verily, monks, these are the five powers.'

§ v (205) *Mental barrenness.*[4]

'Monks, there are these five forms of mental barrenness. What five?

Monks, suppose a monk has doubts and is perplexed[5] about the Teacher, is not certain nor sure in him; monks, whoso thus doubts . . . his heart inclines not to ardour, devotion, perseverance, exertion. Where the heart does not so incline, it is the first form of mental barrenness.

Again, suppose a monk has doubts and is perplexed about Dhamma . . . the Order . . . the training . . .; becomes angry with his fellows in the godly life, displeased with them, upset about them, becomes as a barren waste for them; monks, whoso becomes thus . . . his heart inclines not to ardour, devotion, perseverance, exertion. Where the heart does not so incline, it is the fifth form of mental barrenness.

Verily, monks, these are the five forms of mental barrenness.'

§ vi (206). *Mental bondage.*[6]

'Monks, there are these five forms of mental bondage. What five?

---

[1] *Comy. Ñāṇassa ujuka-gamanaŋ.*

[2] *Comy. Sūrassa hutvā, ñāṇassa vahana-bhāvo.*

[3] Above, § 1.

[4] *Cf. D.* iii, 237; *M.* i, 101; *A.* iv, 460; *Comy.* observes that it is a stubbornness of heart; dust (in the eyes), *kacavara-bhāva*; a stumbling, *khāṇuka-bhāva.*

[5] *Vicikicchati. Comy. vicinanto kicchati, dukkhaŋ āpajjati, vinicchituŋ na sakkoti.*

[6] The references for § 205 apply here.

Monks, suppose a monk is not wholly free of passion as regards the lusts, nor free of desire, nor free of fondness, nor free of thirst, nor free of fever, nor free of craving; monks, whoso is not wholly free . . . his heart inclines not to ardour, devotion, perseverance, exertion. Where the heart does not so incline, it is the first form of mental bondage.

Again, suppose he is not wholly free of passion and so forth as regards the body . . . form[1] . . .; or, after eating as much as his belly will hold, gives himself over to the ease of bed, of lying on his back, of slumber . . .; or, he lives the godly life set on gaining some deva-body, thinking: "By this virtue, practice, austerity, or godly living I shall become a deva or one of a deva's retinue"; monks, whoso is not wholly free from all such . . . his heart inclines not to ardour, devotion, perseverance, exertion. Where the heart does not so incline, it is the fifth form of mental bondage.

Verily, monks, these are the five forms of mental bondage.'

§ vii (207). *Gruel.*

'Monks, there are these five advantages from gruel. What five?

It checks hunger, keeps off thirst, regulates wind, cleanses the bladder[2] and digests raw remnants of food.

Verily, monks, these are the five advantages of gruel.'

§ viii (208). *The tooth-stick.*[3]

'Monks, there are these five disadvantages from not chewing a tooth-stick. What five?

The eyes become affected;[4] the mouth becomes bad-smelling; the channels of taste[5] are not purified; phlegm and mucus[6] get on food; and one does not enjoy food.

---

[1] *Comy.* his own body, but outside forms.

[2] *Vatthi. Comy. dhamaniyo.*

[3] See *Vin* ii, 137 (*S.B.E.* xx, 147), where this recurs.

[4] *Acakkhussaŋ. Comy. na cakkhūnaŋ hitaŋ; cakkhuŋ visuddhaŋ na karoti. Cf.* Rhys Davids' note at *S.B.E. loc. cit.*

[5] *Rasa-haraṇiyo.*

[6] *Pittaŋ semhaŋ.*

Verily, monks, these are the five disadvantages from not chewing a tooth-stick.'

(*The opposite are the advantages from the use of a tooth-stick.*)

§ ix (209). *The plain-song.*[1]

'Monks, there are these five disadvantages to one preaching Dhamma in a long-drawn,[2] plain-song voice. What five?

He is either carried away himself[3] by the sound; or others are carried away thereby; or householders are offended and say: "Just as we sing, for sure, these recluse Sakya sons sing!"; or as he strives after purity of sound, there is a break in concentration; and folk coming after fall into the way of (wrong) views.[4]

Verily, monks, these are the five disadvantages to one preaching Dhamma in a long-drawn, plain-song voice.'

§ x (210). *Forgetful in mindfulness.*

'Monks, there are these five disadvantages to one who, forgetful in mindfulness, not self-possessed, falls asleep. What five?

Badly[5] he sleeps, badly he wakes, he sees evil visions, devas guard him not, and impurity[6] is emitted.

Verily, monks, these are the five disadvantages to one falling asleep, forgetful in mindfulness, not self-possessed.'

(*But*[7] *the opposite are the advantages to one falling asleep set in mindfulness.*)

Chapter XXII.—The Abuser.

§ i (211). *Abuse.*

'Monks, that monk who abuses and reviles men that lead the godly life; who rails at Ariyans[8]—five disadvantages may be expected for him. What five?

---

[1] This recurs at *Vin.* ii, 108 (*S.B.E.* xx, 72): *gītā.*

[2] *Āyatakena. Comy. dīghena . . .*

[3] *Attanā pi sārajjati, v.l. attā.*

[4] *Cf.* above, § 79; below V, § 218.

[5] *Cf. A.* iv, 150; v, 342; *J.* ii, 61; *Mil.* 198; *Vism.* 311.

[6] *Asuci*; Childers, quoting *Abhidhāna-ppadīpikā*, 'semen virile.'

[7] The text repeats in full.

[8] *Cf. A.* v, 169.

Either he merits expulsion, a definite hindrance;[1] or he commits a foul offence;[2] or he is stricken by a grievous[3] disease or illness; or he dies muddled (in thought);[4] and on the breaking up of the body after death he arises in the wayward way, the ill way, the abyss, hell.

Monks, that monk who abuses and reviles men that lead the godly life; who rails at Ariyans—these five disadvantages may be expected for him.'

§ ii (212). *Strife.*

'Monks, that monk who is a maker of strife, a maker of quarrels, a maker of contention, a maker of brawls, a maker of disputes[5]—five disadvantages may be expected for him. What five?

He[6] reaches not the unreached (state); he falls away from the reached; an evil rumour of his worth spreads abroad; he dies muddled (in thought); and after death he arises . . . in hell.

Monks, that monk who is a maker of strife . . . a maker of disputes—these five disadvantages may be expected for him.'

§ iii (213). *Morals.*

'Monks,[7] there are these five disadvantages to one wanting morals, failing in morals. What five?

Consider,[8] monks, the man without morals, failing in morals—he comes to suffer much loss in wealth through neglect. This, monks, is the first disadvantage to one wanting morals, failing in morals.[9]

---

[1] *Chinna-paripantho*, a 'cut,' precise hindrance; *cf. paricchindati. Comy. lok' uttara-paripanthassa chinnattā.* The compound is unusual; *chinna-* generally means 'without.'

[2] *Cf. S.* ii, 271; *A.* v, 169.

[3] Our text with *S.e.* reads *bāḷha*; *A.* ii, 174 and v, 169 *gāḷha*; but *cf. D.* i, 72.

[4] Nyāṇatiloka has a restless death, which is hardly accurate.

[5] *Cf. Vin.* i, 328; ii, 1.

[6] *Cf. A.* v, 169, 317.

[7] This sutta recurs at *D.* ii, 85-6; iii, 236; *Vin.* i, 227-8; *Ud.* 86; it is noticed at *Vism.* 54.

[8] *Idha.*

[9] *Sīla-*, elsewhere generally trsld. 'virtue.'

Or an evil rumour spreads about him. This is the second disadvantage. . . .

Or whatever group he approach, whether nobles or brāhmans, householders or recluses, he does so without confidence and confused. This is the third . . .

Or he dies muddled (in thought).[1] This is the fourth . . .

Or on the breaking up of the body after death he arises in the wayward way, the ill way, the abyss, hell. This is the fifth . . .

Verily, monks, these are the five disadvantages to one wanting morals, failing in morals.

Monks, there are these five advantages to the moral, perfect in morals. What five ?'

(*Just the converse of the foregoing.*)

§ iv (214). *A man full of talk.*

'Monks, there are these five disadvantages to a person full of talk. What five ?

He talks falsely, he talks maliciously, talks roughly, talks as a vain babbler[2] and arises, after death, . . . in hell.

Monks, these are the five disadvantages to a person full of talk.

Monks, there are these five advantages to a person discreet[3] in talk. What five ?'

(*The opposite.*)

§ v (215). *Impatience (a).*

'Monks, there are these five disadvantages from being impatient. What five ?

Not to many folk is he dear or pleasing; he is hated much; is avoided by many; dies muddled in thought and rises in . . . hell.

---

[1] *Sammūḷha*, as before, but here *Comy.* observes: lying on his death-bed he sees his wicked deeds revolve before him.

[2] *Samphappalāpa*; *cf.* 2 *Timothy* ii, 16: 'Shun profane and vain babblings, for they will increase unto more ungodliness.'

[3] *S.e.* with text *manta-*, *Comy.* observing: *mantā vuccati paññā, tāya paricchinditvā bhaṇante*; *cf. SnA.* 204. Our *Comy.* notes: *matta-bhāṇismim-ti mattā vuccati paññā; iti kesuci.*

Monks, these are the five disadvantages from being impatient.'

(*The opposite are the five advantages from being patient.*)

§ vi (216). *The same* (*b*).

(*Substitute* 'harsh'[1] *and* 'remorseful' *for the second and third clauses.*)

§ vii (217). *The troubled mind* (*a*).

'Monks, there are these five disadvantages to one of troubled mind. What five ?

The self upbraids the self; from knowledge[2] the wise dispraise him; an evil rumour of his worth goes abroad; he dies muddled in thought. . . .

Monks, these are the five disadvantages to one of troubled mind.'

(*But the opposite are the advantages of an untroubled mind.*)

§ viii (218). *The same* (*b*).

'There are these (other) five . . .

Wild[3] (thoughts) are not calmed; and some of those that are calmed become otherwise; the Teacher's behest is left undone; folk coming after fall into the ways of wrong views; and one's heart wins not to peace.

Verily, monks, these are the five . . .

Monks, there are these (other) five advantages to one of untroubled mind. What five ?

Wild thoughts are calmed; and those that are, become much more so; the teacher's behest is done; after-folk get right views; and one's heart wins to peace.

Verily, monks, these are the five advantages of the untroubled mind.'

§ ix (219). *Fire.*

'Monks, there are these five disadvantages from fire. What five ?

---

[1] The text reads *luddho, v.l. kuddho,* but *S.e.* and *Comy. luddo,* the latter glossing: *dāruṇo, kakkhaḷo.*

[2] *Anuvicca.*

[3] *Appasannā na ppasīdanti.*

It is bad for the eyes;[1] causes ugliness;[2] causes weakness; (folk-)gatherings grow; and tales of animals are told because of it.

Verily, monks, these are the five disadvantages from fire.'

§ x (220). *In Madhurā.*[3]

'Monks, there are these five disadvantages in Madhura. What five?

(The ground) is uneven; there is much dust; there are fierce dogs; bestial yakkhas; and alms are got with difficulty.

Monks, these are the five disadvantages in Madhurā.'

Chapter XXIII.—Wandering Afield.

§ i (221). *Wandering afield* (*a.*)

'Monks, there are these five disadvantages to one who spends his days wandering afield, wandering aimlessly. What five?

One[4] does not hear the not-heard; one does not purge things heard; one is not reassured by what one hears; one is stricken by some grievous disease or illness; and one is friendless.[5]

Monks, these are the five disadvantages to one who spends his days wandering afield, wandering aimlessly.'

(*Monks, the opposite five are the advantages of wandering with an aim.*)

---

[1] *Acakkhusso*; see above, § 208.

[2] *Dubbaṇṇakaraṇo.*

[3] This no doubt is Madhurā or Mathurā on the Jumna; see Rhys Davids, *Buddh. India*, 36. *Comy.* tells of how the B. met a yakkhinī there who put out her tongue at him. M. is not mentioned in *D.*, only in one sutta in *M.*, never in *S.*, and thrice in *A.* Later than the Buddha it became a Jain centre, 300 B.C., see *C.H.I.* i, 167. However, when the Chinese pilgrims Fa Hsien and Yuan Chwang visited it, Buddhism flourished there (Watters, p. 301). Quoting the *Mūla-sarvāstivāda-nikāya-vinaya*, he gives the following five 'defects': 'the ground was uneven, it was covered with stones and brickbats, it abounded in prickly shrubs, the people took solitary meals, and there were too many women' (p. 312, vol. i).

[4] *Cf.* above, § 202. Here text reads *gāḷhaṃ*, and so *S.e.*

[5] *Na mittavā*, not noticed by *P.E.D.*, but see *Childers*.

§ ii (222). *The same* (*b*).

(*For the first three substitute* 'reaches not the unreached; falls from the reached; is not reassured by the (state) reached,' *and the converse.*)

§ iii (223). *Staying too long*[1] (*a*).

'Monks, there are these five disadvantages from staying too long in a place. What five?

Many belongings and their massing; much medicine and its massing; many duties[2] and things to be done and their concern;[3] one lives with householders and wanderers, mixing with them, not averse from laymen's company; when one leaves that place, one leaves it with regret.

Monks, these are the five disadvantages. . . .

Monks, there are these five advantages from staying for equal periods at places. What five?'

(*The opposite.*)

§ iv (224). *The same* (*b*).

'Monks, there are these five disadvantages from staying too long in a place. What five?

One[4] grudges (sharing) one's lodging, or the families (who provide alms), or one's possessions, or fame;[5] one grudges (sharing) Dhamma.

Monks, these are the five . . .'

(*The opposite are advantages to one who stays equal periods at places.*)

§ v (225). *The visitor of families* (*a*).

'Monks, there are these five disadvantages to the visitor of families. What five?

---

[1] *Ati-nivāsa* and *sama-vattha-vāsa.*

[2] *Cf.* § 90.

[3] Text reads *a-vyatto* (inept); *v.l.*, *S.c.* and *Comy. vyatto-ti vyāsatto.*

[4] See *DhS. trsl.* 299; *Expos.* 480; *D.* iii, 234; *A.* iv, 459.

[5] *Vaṇṇa. Comy. guṇa*, grace.

In going uninvited he offends;[1] by sitting in solitude he offends; in using an obscure seat he offends; in teaching Dhamma to women in more than five or six words he offends; he lives engrossed in thoughts of lust.

Monks, these are the five disadvantages. . . .'

§ vi (226) *The same* (*b*).

'Monks, there are these five disadvantages to a monk, who visits families and lives in their company too much. What five ?

He[2] often sees women-folk; from seeing them, companionship comes; from companionship, intimacy; from intimacy, amorousness; when the heart is inflamed, this may be expected: either joyless he will live the godly life or he will commit some foul offence or he will give up the training and return to the lower life.

Verily, monks, these are the five disadvantages. . . .'

§ vii (227). *Riches.*

'Monks,[3] there are these five disadvantages in riches. What five ?

Riches are in danger of fire, in danger of floods, in danger of rajahs, in danger of robbers, in danger of unloved heirs.[4]

Verily, monks, these are the five . . .

Monks, there are these five advantages in riches. What five ?

With the help of riches, one makes oneself happy, glad, and keeps that great happiness; one makes one's parents . . .

---

[1] *Anāmantacāra.* *Comy.* observes that on being invited to a meal, from not asking a good monk, he calls on families either before the meal or after—so in respect of the training, it is said he commits a fault. At *Vin.* i, 255 this word recurs with the fault *a-samādāna-cāra*, going for alms without taking all one's robes; possibly Bu. has made an ecclesiastical offence of it, when it really means the family visited is offended, as must be in the second and third clauses.

[2] *Cf.* above, § 55.

[3] *Cf.* above, § 41.

[4] *A-ppiyehi dāyādehi.*

wife, children, slaves, work-folk, men . . . friends and companions happy, glad, and keeps them so; for recluse and brāhman one institutes offerings of lofty aim, connected with a happy hereafter, ripening to happiness, leading heavenward. Verily, monks, these are the five . . .'

§ viii (228). *The meal.*

'Monks, there are these five disadvantages in a family who eat when the sun is right up.[1] What five?

Their honoured visitors they honour not in time; the devas who receive oblations they honour not in time; recluses and brāhmans who have but one meal a day abstain from eating at night, eating at wrong times, they honour not in time; their slaves, work-folk and men work as men averse[2] from work; moreover as long as food is eaten unseasonably it lacks strengthening[3] qualities.

Monks, these are the five . . .'

(*The opposite are the advantages in a family who eat in season.*)

§ ix (229). *The snake* (*a*).

'Monks, there are these five disadvantages in a black snake.[4] What five?

It is unclean, evil-smelling, timid,[5] fearful and betrays friends.

These, monks, are the five . . .

Even so, monks, there are these five disadvantages in a woman. What five?

She is unclean, evil-smelling, timid, fearful and betrays friends.

Verily, monks, these are the five . . .'

---

[1] *Ussūra. Comy. atidivā.*

[2] *Vimukha. Comy.* observes: they give up and sit down.

[3] *Anojavanta. Comy. ojaŋ pharituŋ na sakkoti.*

[4] *Cf. Vism. trsl.* 797, where a water snake simile is given and is called *kaṅha-sappa* at 812.

[5] *Sabhīru. Comy.* '*saniddo mahāniddaŋ niddāyati.*' It is not clear how such an explanation arose.

§ x (230). *The same (b).*

'There are these five disadvantages in a black snake.

It is full of anger, ill-will, it is deadly poisonous,[1] forked tongued and betrays friends.[2]

These, monks, are the five . . . And even so, monks, these same five . . . are in a woman.

Now the deadly poison of a woman is this: she is almost always very passionate. The forked tongue is this: she is almost always slanderous in speech. And the betrayal of friends is this; she almost always commits adultery.

Verily, monks, these are the five disadvantages in a woman.'

Chapter XXIV.—In Residence.

§ i (231). *In residence.*

'Monks, if a monk in residence follow the course of five things, he becomes not what he ought to become.[3] What five?

He becomes accomplished neither in manner nor in service;[4] becomes neither one who has heard much nor one who bears much in mind; nor a marker of his ways[5] nor fond of solitude; his words are not lovely nor lovely is their making; he becomes a dullard and witless.

Verily, monks, if a monk in residence follow the course of these five things, he becomes not what he ought to become.'

(But following the course of the opposite five, he becomes what he ought to become.)

§ ii (232). *The pious.*[6]

'Monks, if a monk in residence follow the course of five things, he becomes among his fellows in the godly life pious

---

[1] *Ghora-visatā. P.E.D.* omits this derivative of *visa.*

[2] At J. v, 447 these five are given in *Comy.* in explanation of '*kaṇha-sappasirūpama*'; and the sub-comment on the three last terms is the same as given here; for this simile *cf.* above, § 76.

[3] *A-bhāvanīyo hoti. Comy.* on the positive: *vaḍḍhanīyo hoti.*

[4] *Ākappa-* and *vatta-.*

[5] *Paṭisallekhitar*; *cf.* above, § 181; *P.E.D.* omits.

[6] *Piyo.*

and pleasing, respected and what he ought to become. What five?

He becomes virtuous[1] . . .; becomes one who has heard much . . .; his words are lovely . . .; he attains to the four states of musing . . .; and he enters and abides in mind-emancipation, insight-emancipation. . . .

Verily, monks, . . . he becomes what he ought to become.'

§ iii (233). *Grace.*[2]

'Monks, if a monk in residence follow the course of five things, he graces his residence. What five?

He becomes virtuous[3] . . .; he is able to teach, incite, rouse and satisfy with Dhamma talk those who visit him; and he attains to the four states of musing. . . .

Verily, monks, . . . he graces his residence.'

§ iv (234). *Of great service.*

'Monks, if a monk in residence follow the course of five things, he becomes of great service to his residence. What five?

He becomes virtuous[3] . . .; he repairs things broken and dilapidated; and when many monks of the Order have come, monks from various parts of the country, he speaks to the householders who approach, saying: "See, good sirs, many monks from various parts of the country have arrived; do good; now's the time to make merit!" and he attains to the four states of musing. . . .

Verily, monks, . . . he becomes of great service to his residence.'

§ v (235). *Taking pity.*

'Monks, if a monk in residence follow the course of five things, he takes pity on householders. What five?

He incites them to greater virtue;[4] he makes them live in the mirror of Dhamma;[5] when visiting the sick, he stirs up mindfulness, saying: "Let the venerable ones set up mind-

---

[1] See above, § 87, for full details.
[2] *Sobhanā.*
[3] Repeat the first three of § 232.
[4] *Adhisīla. Comy. pañca-sīla.*
[5] See above, § 179, *n.* 3.

fulness, that thing most worth while !";[1] when many monks of the Order have come, he urges the householders to do good . . .; and when they give him food, whether mean or choice, he enjoys it by himself, nor frustrates (the effect of that) gift of faith.[2]

Verily, monks, . . . he takes pity on householders.'

§ vi (236). *The reward of dispraise.*

'Monks, if a monk in residence follow the course of five things, as his reward he is surely cast into hell. What five ?'

(*Repeat* § 116 *above, with changes.*)

§ vii (237). *Stinginess* (*a*).

'Monks, if a monk in residence follow the course of five things, as his reward he will surely be cast into hell. What five ?

Without testing or plumbing the matter, he speaks in praise of the unpraiseworthy; speaks in dispraise of the praiseworthy; is stingy over (sharing) his lodging, greedy[3] as to it; stingy as to the family (who provides), greedy as to it; and he frustrates the gift of faith.

Monks, . . . his reward is being cast into hell.'

(*But the course of the five opposite things brings him to heaven.*)

§ viii (238). *The same* (*b*).

(*Repeat the foregoing, omitting greediness and changing the last clause to:* he is stingy as to gains.)

§ ix (239). *The same* (*c*).

(*Omit the first two clauses, add:* he is stingy as to praise and he frustrates the gift of faith.)

§ x (240). *The same* (*d*).

(*Repeat* § 239, *changing the last clause to:* he is stingy of Dhamma.)[4]

---

[1] *Araha-ggata. Comy. sabba-sakkāranaŋ arahe ratana-ttay' eva gataŋ.*

[2] *Cf.* above, § 116, also *Vin.* i, 298.

[3] *Āvāsa-paligedhī. Comy. āvāsaŋ balava-giddhi-vasena gilitvā viya ṭhito* (*gijjha, Skt. gṛdhra,* is a vulture).

[4] The text repeats all in full.

Chapter XXV.—Walking in Evil.

§ i (241). *One who has walked in evil.*

'Monks, there are five disadvantages to one who has walked in evil. What five?

The self upbraids the self;[1] with knowledge the wise dispraise him; an evil rumour of his worth goes about; he dies a lunatic; and on the breaking up of the body after death, he arises in the wayward way, the ill way, the abyss, hell.

Verily, monks, these are the five disadvantages to one who has walked in evil.'

(*But the opposite five are the advantages to one who has walked in good.*)[2]

§§ ii-iv (242-244). *The same.*

'Monks, there are these five disadvantages to one who in deed . . . in word . . . and in thought has walked in evil.'

(*Repeat* § 241 *and the converse.*)[3]

§§ v-viii (245-248). *The same.*

(*Repeat the foregoing, changing the last two clauses to:* he turns from Saddhamma;[4] he is not set in Saddhamma.)[3]

§ ix (249). *The cemetery.*

'Monks, there are these five disadvantages in a cemetery. What five?

It is unclean, evil-smelling, fearful, the haunt of bestial non-humans,[5] and is the cause of many folk wailing.[6]

Verily, monks, these are the five disadvantages.

Even so, monks, there are these five disadvantages in a cemetery-like person. What five?

Consider, monks, some person who follows the course of unclean action in deed, word and thought—I declare this to be his uncleanness. Monks, just as that cemetery is unclean, thus-like I declare this person to be.

---

[1] *Cf.* above, § 217.

[2] The text repeats.

[3] The text does not repeat in full.

[4] *Cf.* above, § 88.

[5] As at § 77 above, see note.

[6] *Ārodana*, causative of $\sqrt{rud}$.

Whoso follows such a course, an evil rumour of his worth goes about—I declare this to be his evil smell. Monks, just as that cemetery is evil-smelling, thus-like I declare this person to be.

At once his course is such, his pious[1] fellows in the godly life turn themselves from him and keep far away—I declare this to be his fearfulness. Monks, just as that cemetery is fearful, thus-like I declare this person to be.

As he follows that unclean course, he lives with others, sharing their ways—I declare this to be his bestial haunting.[2] Monks, just as that cemetery is the haunt of bestial non-humans, thus-like I declare this person to be.

Seeing him thus following this course of unclean action in deed, word and thought, his pious fellows in the godly life become vexed and say: "Alas! this is an ill thing for us, who have to live with such a person!"—I declare this to be his making others wail. Monks, just as that cemetery is the cause of many folk wailing, thus-like I declare this person to be.

Verily, monks, there are these five disadvantages in a cemetery-like person.'

§ x (250). *Devotion*[3] *to one person.*

'Monks, there are these five disadvantages of devotion to one person. What five?

Monks, when a person becomes very devoted to a person and that person falls into an error such that the Order suspend him, then he will think: "The Order has suspended him who is dear and lovely to me!' And he will be no more full of devotion for the monks, and from being without that devotion he will not follow other monks, and from not following other monks he will not hear Saddhamma, and from not hearing Saddhamma he will fall away from Saddhamma. This, monks, is the first disadvantage of devotion to one person.

Or that person falls into an error such that the Order make him sit on the outskirts (of a gathering). . . .

---

1 *Pesala*, following the traditional explanation: *piya-sīla*.

2 *Vāḷâvasatha*.

3 *Pasāda*, more lit. satisfaction, or faith.

Or when a person becomes very devoted to a person and that person is gone to a distant place . . . or wanders[1] (in mind) . . . or is dead, then he will think: "He is dead, he who was dear and lovely to me!" And he will not follow other monks, and from not following other monks he will not hear Saddhamma, and from not hearing Saddhamma he will fall away from Saddhamma. This, monks, is the fifth disadvantage of devotion to one person.

Verily, monks, these are the five disadvantages of devotion to one person.'

Chapter XXVI.—Acceptance.

§ 251. *Acceptance.*

'Monks, acceptance[2] ought to be granted by a monk endowed with these five things. What five?

Herein, monks, the monk is endowed with the whole body of virtue . . . the whole body of concentration . . . the whole body of insight . . . the whole body of emancipation . . . is endowed with the whole body of knowledge and vision of emancipation with no need to train.[3]

Monks, acceptance ought to be granted by a monk so endowed.'

§§ 252-253. *Protection and service.*

'Monks, protection ought to be given by a monk endowed with these five things. A novice ought to serve a monk endowed with these five things. What five?' (*Repeat as before.*)

§ 254. *Stinginess.*

'Monks, there are these five forms of stinginess.[4] What five?

Stinginess as to one's lodging, family, gains, fame and Dhamma.

---

[1] *Vibbhanto.*

[2] *Upasampādetabbaṃ*: this is the second stage of monkhood; there is first the *pabbajjā*, the going forth, then the *upasampadā*, the acceptance or 'full orders' (both by and of the monk).

[3] *Cf. Vin.* i, 62 *ff.*; above, § 108.

[4] *Cf.* above, § 237.

Verily, monks, there are these five; now the meanest of these five, monks, is this: stinginess as to Dhamma.'

§ 255. *The godly life.*

'Monks, one lives the godly life by abandoning, cutting off these five forms of stinginess. What five?' (*Repeat as before.*)

§ 256. *Musing.*

'Monks, if one abandon not these five things, one cannot enter and abide in the first musing.[1] What five?' (*Repeat as before. The converse also obtains.*)

§§ 257-263.

'Monks, unless one abandon these five things, one cannot enter and abide in the second musing . . . the third . . . the fourth . . . one cannot realize the fruit of Streamwinning . . . of Once-returning . . . of Non-returning . . . of arahantship. What five?' (*Repeat as before, with the opposite.*)

§§ 264-271.

(*Repeat the foregoing, changing the fifth clause to* 'ingratitude and benefits forgot.')

§ 272. *The food-steward.*

'Monks, if a monk follow the course of five things, he ought not to be selected as a food-steward. What five?

He[2] goes astray from wish, from hatred, from confusion, from fear, and knows not a ration from what is not.

Monks, if a monk follow the course of these five things . . .' (*But let him be selected if he follow the opposite course.*)

§§ 273-277. *The same.*

'(Similarly) if selected, he ought not to be sent . . .; he ought to be known as a fool . . .; as one who goes about to hurt and injure himself . . .; as one whose reward will be hell. . . .' (*But in each case the opposite obtains.*)

---

[1] *Jhāna.*

[2] See *S.B.E.* xx, 25 (*Vin. Texts.* iii); *Vin.* ii, 176; *D.* iii, 228; *A.* iv, 370.

§§ 278-342. *Of others.*

'(Similarly)[1] of him who allots quarters . . . and knows ~~not~~ an allotment from what is not . . .; the quarters-receiver[2] . . . ; the stores-keeper . . . who knows not what is guarded from what is not . . .; the robe-receiver . . . who knows not what is taken from what is not . . .; of him who metes out robes . . .; gruel . . .; fruit . . .; food . . .; small things[3] . . .; the receiver of undergarments . . .; bowls . . .; of him who looks after the park-keepers . . .; the novices . . .' (*and in each case the opposite*).

§ 343. *The fivefold.*

'Monks, if a monk follow the course of five things, he will be cast into hell. What five?

He takes life, takes what is not given. . . .'[4] (*But the converse holds.*)

§§ 344-350. *The same.*

'So, too, of a nun . . . those in training . . . novices, male and female . . . lay-disciples, man and woman.'[5] (*And the converse holds.*)

§ 351-360. *The same.*

'So,[6] too, of the ascetic[7] . . . the Jain[8] . . . the shaveling[9] . . . him with braided hair[10] . . . the wanderer[11] . . . the

---

1 The text is much abbreviated; suttas 272-277 are applied here in each instance, except that the last item of the 'five things' varies with the monk's job.

2 *S.e.* includes this with *v.l.* of text.

3 That is, needles, scissors, sandles, girdles, braces, etc.; see *S.B.E.* xx, 222.

4 Above, § 145.

5 *S.e.* with *v.l.* so.

6 See *Dial.* i, 200 *ff.*; Thomas' *Life*, 137; Mrs. Rhys Davids' *Gotama*, 193.

7 *Comy. nagga-pabbajito.*

8 *Comy. purima-bhāga-paṭicchanno.*

9 *S.e.* and *Comy. buddha-* for text *muṇḍa-*; *Comy.* explains: *nigaṇṭha-sāvako.*

10 *Comy. tāpaso.*

11 *Comy. channa-paribbājako.*

follower of Magaṇḍa[1] . . . the follower of the sect of the triple staff . . . the follower of the unobstructed . . . the follower of the sect of Gotama . . . the follower of deva rites.[2] . . .'

§ 361. *Passion.*

'Monks, for the full understanding of passion five things ought to be made to become. What five?

The thought of the unattractive, of death, of perils, of the cloying of food, of there being no real joy in the whole world.

Verily, monks, for the full understanding of passion these five things ought to be made to become.'

§§ 362-363. *The same.*

'The thought of impermanence, of no-self, of death. . . .

Of impermanence, of ill in impermanence, of there being no-self in ill, of renunciation, of dispassion. . . .'

§§ 364-365. *The same.*

'. . . These five ought to be made to become. What five?

The governance[3] by faith, energy, mindfulness, concentration and insight. . . .

The power of faith, energy, mindfulness, concentration and insight.

Verily, monks, for the full understanding of passion these five things ought to be made to become.'

§§ 366-400. *Of passion.*

'Monks, for the comprehension . . . the exhaustion . . . the abandoning . . . the destruction . . . the decay of . . . the freedom from passion for . . . the ending . . . the quittance . . . the renunciation of passion these (*five sets of five things*, §§ 361-365) ought to be made to become. . . .'

---

[1] Of the others *Comy.* remarks: *titthiyā eva.* Our text reads *magaṇḍiko,* but *S.e.* and *Comy. magandiko*; *maganda* in *Skt.* means a usurer.

[2] *Deva-dhammiko,* or it may mean fatalist, a believer in luck (?).

[3] *Indriya:—saddhindriya,* etc.

§§ 401-1,200. *Of other conditions.*

'Of hatred . . . illusion . . . anger . . . enmity . . . hypocrisy . . . malice . . . envy . . . avarice . . . deceit . . . craftiness . . . obstinacy . . . impetuosity . . . pride . . . arrogance . . . intoxication . . . indolence . . .'[1]

The table of contents.

A learner's powers, the powers and then *the fivefold,*
And *Sumanā* with *rajah Muṇḍa*, fifth,
The hindrances, thoughts, with *the warrior*, eighth,
The elder, Kakudha, th' abodes of comfort,
And *Andhakavinda*, the chapter twelve,
The sick, the rajah, Three-thorn grove, Saddhamma,
Malice, the lay-disciple and *the forest,*
The brāhman, Kimbila, the twenty-first,
The abuser then, then *wandering afield,*
In residence, the chapter twenty-four,
Walking in evil, and *acceptance* last.

THE BOOK OF THE FIVES IS ENDED.

---

[1] This formula recurs at *A.* i, 100, 299; ii, 257; iii, 278, 452; iv, 148, 349, 456; v, 310, 361, in respect of 'two' *dhammā*: things, conditions or qualities and so forth to 'eleven.' Sometimes the editors of the *roman* texts show the formula as though one sutta were intended—*e.g.*, *A.* i, 100 —and sometimes as above with the abbreviation mark. I venture to suggest that there are 4,250 suttas intended with this formula, thus: (17 × 10) × 1, 1, 3, 5, 3, 3, 3, 2, 3, and 1 respectively, and that the statement at the end of *A.* v, p. 361, that the *Anguttara Nikāya* contains 9,557—and this is confirmed in the *Comys. AA.* i, 3 and *DA.* i, 23, also *Exp.* i, 32—is not far short of the mark, *pace* Hardy, *A.* v, p. vi.

THE BOOK OF THE SIXES

(*CHAKKA-NIPĀTA*)

CHAPTER I.—THE WORTHY.

§ i (1). *Worthy of offerings* (*a*).

THUS have I heard: Once, while he dwelt near Sāvatthī at Jeta Grove in Anāthapiṇḍika's Park, the Exalted One addressed the monks, saying: 'Monks.'

'Lord,' they replied; and the Exalted One said:

'Monks, a monk who follows six things is worthy of offerings, worthy of gifts, worthy of oblations, meet to be reverently saluted, the world's peerless field for merit. What six?

Monks,[1] herein a monk on seeing a form with the eye is neither elated nor depressed, but abides in poise,[2] mindful and self-possessed; on hearing a sound with the ear . . .; on smelling a smell with the nose . . .; on tasting a taste with the tongue . . .; on touching a touchable with the body . . .; on becoming aware of an idea with the mind he is neither elated nor depressed, but abides in poise, mindful and self-possessed.

Verily, monks, a monk who follows these six things is worthy of offerings, worthy of gifts, worthy of oblations, meet to be reverently saluted, the world's peerless field for merit.'

Thus spake the Exalted One; and with their hearts lifted up those monks rejoiced exceedingly in the word of the Exalted One.

§ ii (2). *The same* (*b*).

'Monks, a monk who follows these six things is also worthy . . . What six?

Monks, herein a monk experiences psychic power in manifold

---

[1] *Cf. D.* iii, 281; *M.* iii, 240; *A.* v, 30; ii, 198

[2] *Comy.* observes that this state is not from want of noticing the object nor from not knowing about it, but from composure.

modes . . .; with the deva-ear hears sounds . . .; by mind compassing mind[1] knows others' thoughts . . .; remembers previous lives[2] . . .; with the deva-eye sees beings faring on according to their deeds . . .; by destroying the cankers enters and abides in the canker-free mind-emancipation, insight-emancipation, realizing this here and now entirely by his own knowledge.[3]

Monks, a monk who follows these six things is worthy. . . .'

§ iii (3). *Faculties.*

'. . . These six also. . . .

The faculties[4] of faith, energy, mindfulness, concentration, and insight; destroying the cankers, he enters and abides in the canker-free mind-emancipation, insight-emancipation. . . .

. . . These are the six . . .'

§ iv (4). *Powers.*

'. . . These six also. . . .

The power of faith, energy, mindfulness, concentration, insight; destroying the cankers. . . .'

§ v (5). *The thoroughbred* (*a*).

'Monks,[5] a rajah's goodly thoroughbred endowed with six points is fit for a rajah, is a rajah's asset, is reckoned a rajah's portion. What six?

Herein, monks, the goodly thoroughbred endures forms, sounds, smells, tastes, touches, and has beauty.

Monks, a rajah's thoroughbred with these six points is fit for a rajah. . . . Even so, monks, a monk with six qualities is worthy of offerings . . . the world's peerless field for merit. What six?

---

[1] *Cetasā ceto paricca.*

[2] Literally previous dwellings ('Life' in Pali has no plural).

[3] The text abbreviates to some extent; see above V, § 23.

[4] *Indriya*, or 'governance,' p. 200; see *D.* iii, 239 for the five.

[5] *Cf.* above V, § 139.

Herein, monks, a monk endures[1] forms, sounds, smells, tastes, touches and things of the mind.

Verily, monks, a monk with these six qualities is worthy of offerings. . . .'

§§ vi-vii (6-7). *The same* (*b-c*).

(*Repeat* § 5, *changing* 'beauty' *to* 'strength' *and* 'speed.')[2]

§ viii (8). *Above all.*

'Monks, these six are above all.[3] What six?

The sight above all; the sound above all; the gain above all; the training above all; the service above all; the ever minding above all.

Verily, monks, these six are above all.'

§ ix (9). *Ever minding.*[4]

'Monks, there are these six states of ever minding. What six?

The ever minding of the Buddha; the ever minding of Dhamma; the ever minding of the Order; the ever minding of virtue; the ever minding of liberality; the ever minding of the devas.

Monks, these are the six states of ever minding.'

§ x (10). *Mahānāma.*

Once, while the Exalted One was dwelling near Kapilavatthu in Banyan Tree Park, there came to him Mahānāma,[5] the Sakya, who saluted and sat down at one side. So seated, Mahānāma, the Sakya, said this to the Exalted One:

---

[1] *Cf.* above V, § 85.

[2] The text repeats almost in full.

[3] *Anuttariyāni*, no higher states; see below, § 30, for details; *D.* iii, 250, 281; below, § 121; *cf. M.* i, 235; *D.* iii, 219.

[4] *Anu-ssati*, *Vism.* ch. vii, 'Recollections'; below, § 25; *D.* iii, 250; *A.* i, 207 (*G.S.* i, 187 *ff.*); *A.* v, 329 *ff.*

[5] *Comy.* the B.'s first cousin; see *Vin. Texts* iii, 224 (*S.B.E.* xx).

'Lord,[1] the Ariyan disciple who has won the fruit,[2] grasped the message, what life lives he in abundance?'

'Mahānāma,[3] the Ariyan disciple who has won the fruit, grasped the message, lives this life in abundance:

The Ariyan disciple, Mahānāma, is ever minding the Tathāgata: "He is the Exalted One, arahant, fully enlightened, perfected in knowledge and way of life, one well-gone, a knower of the worlds, none higher, a tamer of tamable men, a teacher, the awake among devas and men, the Exalted One!" Mahānāma, what time the Ariyan disciple minds the Tathāgata, his heart is never overwhelmed[4] by passion, never overwhelmed by hatred, never overwhelmed by infatuation; then, verily, is the way of his heart made straight because of the Tathāgata. And with his heart's ways straightened, Mahānāma, the Ariyan disciple becomes zealous[5] of the goal, zealous of Dhamma, wins the joy that is linked to Dhamma; and of his joy zest is born; when his mind is rapt in zest, his whole[6] being becomes calm; calm in being, he experiences ease; and of him that dwelleth at ease the heart is composed.

Mahānāma, of this Ariyan disciple it is said: Among uneven folk he lives evenly;[7] among troubled folk he lives untroubled;

---

[1] See the references to this sutta at *Vism. trsl.* 257 *ff.* The items in the discourse closely follow those in the talk with Visākhā, *G.S.* i, pp. 185-195, the three sorts of feast-day keeping there replaced here by the six *Anussatis* only.

[2] *Āgata-phalo viññāta-sāsano.* I cannot trace these compounds elsewhere in the four *Nikāyas*. Our *Comy.* observes: *Ariya-phalaŋ assa āgatan-ti* and *Sikkhā-ttaya-sāsanaŋ etena viññātan-ti.* They recur, however, at *Mhvs.* xiv, 27 (*trsl.* p. 93), and the *ṭīkā* thereon (*Colombo ed.*, 1895, p. 233) observes: *Ettha tatiya-phale ṭhitattā ariya-maggena āgata-anāgāmi-phalo-ti*, and *Ariya-maggen' eva suṭṭhu vijānita-sambuddha-sāsano.*

[3] According to our *Comy.* and *Vism.* M. was a Streamwinner.

[4] *Pariyuṭṭhita.*

[5] *Attha-vedaŋ, dhamma-vedaŋ. Comy.* says *veda* is the *pīti-pāmojjan* that arises in respect of *aṭṭha-kathā* and *Pāḷi*. See *Vism. trsl.* 261. We see this late scholastic interpretation in Nyanatiloka's rendering: 'understanding of exposition and of law.'

[6] *Kāya. Comy. nāma- ca karaja- ca.*

[7] With *Comy.*, *S.e.* and *v.l.* we should read *sama-ppatto*; the former explains: *samaŋ upasamaŋ patto hutvā.*

with the ear for Dhamma won, he makes become the ever minding of the Buddha.

Again, Mahānāma, the Ariyan disciple is ever minding Dhamma: "Well declared by the Exalted One is Dhamma, a view for this life, nor for this only,[1] bidding come and see, a guide, to be known by the wise each for himself." Mahānāma, what time the Ariyan disciple minds Dhamma, his heart is never overwhelmed by passion, hatred, infatuation; then, verily, is the way of his heart made straight because of Dhamma. And with his heart's ways straightened, he becomes zealous of the goal . . . experiences ease . . . and at ease the heart is composed.

Of him it is said: Among uneven folk he lives evenly . . . and makes become the ever minding of Dhamma.

Again, Mahānāma, the Ariyan disciple is ever minding the Order: "The Exalted One's Order of disciples has rightly stepped the way, has straightly stepped the way, has fitly stepped the way, has wholly stepped the way, that is: the four pairs among men, the eight persons among mankind; and this Order of disciples of the Exalted One is worthy of offerings, worthy of gifts, worthy of oblations, meet to be reverently saluted, the world's peerless field for merit." Mahānāma, what time the Ariyan disciple minds the Order . . . he becomes zealous of the goal . . . and is composed.

Of him it is said: Among uneven folk he lives evenly . . . and makes become the ever minding of the Order.

Again, Mahānāma, the Ariyan disciple is ever minding the virtues in the self: "They are unbroken, without a flaw, spotless, without blemish; they bring freedom and are praised by wise men; they are incorruptible and lead to concentration."[2] Mahānāma, what time the Ariyan disciple minds virtue in the self . . . he becomes zealous of the goal . . . and is composed.

---

[1] *Sanditthiko akāliko*, etc.; *cf.* 'Everyman, I will go with thee,' etc. *Cf.* below, § 47. *Akāliko*, lit. 'not-time-ish,' means for life in other worlds reckoned by *kalpa*, not *kāla*. *Cf. Sakya*, p. 413.

[2] *S.e.* reads *samādhi-saŋvattanikāṇî-ti*.

Of him it is said: Among uneven folk he lives evenly . . . and makes become the ever minding of virtue.

Again, Mahānāma, the Ariyan disciple is ever minding liberality in the self: "It is indeed a gain for me, indeed I have greatly gained, I who among folk, overwhelmed by the taint of stinginess, live the home-life heart-free of the stingy taint, giving freely, open-handed, loving bounty, within reach of all, finding joy in alms-distribution." Mahānāma, what time the Ariyan disciple minds liberality in the self . . . he becomes zealous of the goal . . . and is composed.

Of him it is said: Among uneven folk he lives evenly . . . and makes become the ever minding of liberality.

Then, Mahānāma, the Ariyan disciple makes become the ever minding of the devas: "There are the Four Royal devas, there are the devas of the Thirty, the Yāma devas, the Tusita devas, the devas who delight in creating, the devas who have power over others' creations, the Brahma-world devas,[1] and there are the devas beyond that; because their faith was such, those devas fared hence and arose there, I also have such faith; because their virtue . . . learning . . . liberality . . . and wisdom was such, they fared hence and arose there, all these qualities are mine also." Mahānāma, what time the Ariyan disciple minds both in himself and in those devas faith, virtue, learning, liberality and wisdom, his heart is never overwhelmed by passion, never overwhelmed by hatred, never overwhelmed by infatuation; then, verily, is the way of his heart made straight because of the devas. And with his heart's ways straightened, the Ariyan disciple becomes zealous of the goal, zealous of Dhamma, wins the joy that is linked to Dhamma; and of his joy zest is born; when his mind is rapt in zest, his whole being becomes calm; calm in being, he experiences ease; and of him that dwelleth at ease the heart is composed.

Mahānāma, of this Ariyan disciple it is said: Among uneven folk he lives evenly; among troubled folk he lives untroubled;

---

[1] *Devā Brahma-kāyikā.*

with the ear for Dhamma won, he makes become the ever minding of the devas.

Mahānāma, the Ariyan disciple who has won the fruit, grasped the message, lives this life in abundance.'

Chapter II.—Be Considerate.

§ i (11). *On being considerate* (*a*).

'Monks, there are six ways of being considerate.[1] What six? Herein, monks, a monk's part is amity in deed towards his fellows in the godly life,[2] openly and in private; verily, this is a way of being considerate.

Again, his part is amity in word, . . . amity in thought towards his fellows in the godly life, openly and in private; this also is a way of being considerate.

Then, those proper gains, gotten according to rule—be they but bowl-scraps—he loves to share them impartially,[3] to have them in common with his virtuous fellows in the godly life; this also is a way of being considerate.

And those virtues that are unbroken, without flaw, spotless, without blemish, bringing freedom, praised by wise men, incorruptible, leading to concentration—he dwells one in virtue with them among his fellows in the godly life, openly and in private; this also is a way of being considerate.

And that Ariyan view, saving, leading him who acts accordantly to the utter destruction of Ill—he dwells one in view with that among his fellows in the godly life, openly and in private; this also is a way of being considerate.

Verily, monks, these are the six ways of being considerate.'

§ ii (12). *The same* (*b*).

'Monks, there are these six ways of being considerate, which endear, bring honour, lead to concord, banish contention, lead to unity, lead to singleness of heart. What six?' (*Repeat as before.*)

---

[1] *Sārāṇīyā*, lit. 'that ought to be remembered.' *Comy. sāritabba-yuttakā*, as at *J.* iv, 99; see *D.* ii, 80; iii, 245; *M.* i, 322.

[2] *Brahma-cārīsu.*

[3] *Appaṭivibhatta-bhogī. Comy. āmisa-, pugggala-paṭivibhattañ ca.*

§ iii (13). *Amity.*

'Monks, there are these six factors whereby should be escape.[1] What six?

Monks, suppose a monk were to say this: "Of a truth, I have made mind-emancipation become by amity, made an increase of it, made a vehicle of it, made a home of it, dwelt with it, gathered it together, set it well going: yet ill-will invades my heart and stays!" Speak to him and say: "Go to now, speak not so, reverend sir, distort not the word of the Exalted One! Ill it is to distort his word thus.[2] Verily, the Exalted One would never speak so; it is not possible, sir, nor could it happen, that when mind-emancipation is made become by amity, made an increase of, made a vehicle of, made a home of, dwelt with, gathered together and set well going, ill-will can invade one's heart and stay. It is not possible. Indeed, sir,[3] this is just the escape from ill-will, I mean, mind-emancipation by amity."

Or suppose a monk were to say this: "Of a truth, I have made mind-emancipation become by pity . . .; yet fell thoughts invade my heart and stay!" Speak to him in like manner . . . for this is just the escape from fell thoughts, I mean, mind-emancipation by pity.

Or suppose he were to say: "I have made mind-emancipation become by (kindly) joy . . .; yet enmity invades my heart and stays!" Speak to him in like manner . . . for this is just the escape from enmity, I mean, mind-emancipation by (kindly) joy.

Or suppose he say: "I have made mind-emancipation become by poise . . .; yet passion invades my heart and stays!" Speak to him likewise . . . for this is just the escape from passion, I mean, mind-emancipation by poise.

Or suppose he say: "I have made mind-emancipation become by the signless[4] . . .; yet my thoughts run after

[1] *Cf. D.* iii, 247 for all this; *Expos.* 259.

[2] This passage is stock; *cf. M.* i, 130; iii, 207.

[3] *Āvuso*; so the monk is still addressing his fellow-monk, though *-ti* is omitted. However, *D.* iii reads *āvuso* throughout for our *bhikkhave*.

[4] *A-nimitta.* *Comy.* it is so called because the passion, form and permanence signs become not; see *K.S.* i, 239 *n.*; *Cpd.* 211, *n.*

signs!"[1] Speak to him likewise[2] . . . for this is just the escape from all signs, I mean, mind-emancipation by the signless.

Or suppose, monks, a monk were to say this: "I am free[3] of the thought 'I am,' nor do I perceive within me the thought 'This I am,' yet the dart[4] of doubt and questioning 'How, how?' invades my heart and stays!" Speak to him and say: "Go to now, speak not so, reverend sir, distort not the word of the Exalted One! Ill it is to distort his word thus. Verily, the Exalted One would never speak so; it is not possible, sir, nor could it happen, that when one is free of the thought 'I am' and sees not within one the thought 'This I am,' the dart of doubt and questioning 'How, how?' can invade the heart and stay. It is not possible. Indeed, sir, this is just the escape from the dart of doubt and questioning, I mean, the complete rooting out of the conceit 'I am.'"

Verily, monks, these are the six factors whereby should be escape.'

§ iv (14). *The lucky fate.*

Now the venerable Sāriputta addressed the monks, saying: 'Monks, reverend sirs!' and they replied: 'Reverend sir.'

Then said the venerable Sāriputta: 'The more, reverend sirs, a monk thus fashions his life, the more he fashions it to a luckless death,[5] a luckless fate.[6] And how, reverend sirs, does a monk fashion his life to a luckless death, a luckless fate?

Consider, reverend sirs, the monk who,[7] finding delight in worldly activity,[8] is delighted with worldly activity, gets engrossed in the delight of worldly activity; so too of talk, sleep, company, companionship and vain fancies[9]—finding delight

---

[1] *Me nimittânusāri viññāṇaŋ hoti.*

[2] The text repeats all in full.

[3] *S.e.* and *Comy.* read with the text *vigataŋ*; *D.* iii, *vighātaŋ*.

[4] *Dial,* iii, 233 accepts the variant *sallāpaŋ*, debating; but all our readings are *sallaŋ*; *cf.* also *D.* ii, 283.

[5] *Na bhaddakaŋ. Comy. na laddhakaŋ.*

[6] *Kāla-kiriyā*; *cf. A.* i, 261 (*G.S.* i, 240).

[7] *Cf.* above V, § 89; *A.* iv, 331.

[8] *Kamma.*

[9] *Papañca*, or obsessions, or diffuseness. See *Brethr.* 343 *n.*

in each, he is delighted with each and gets engrossed in the delight of each; and thus, reverend sirs, the more he so fashions his life, the more he fashions it to a luckless death, a luckless fate; and of this monk it is said: With his bundle of life[1] he is greatly delighted; he has not got rid of his bundle for the utter ending of Ill.

But the more, reverend sirs, a monk fashions his life in this manner, the more he fashions it to a lucky death, a lucky fate. And how does he so fashion it . . .?

Consider the monk who, finding no delight in worldly activity, is not delighted therewith, gets not engrossed in the delight thereof; nor in talk, sleep, company, companionship, or vain fancies; and thus the more he so fashions his life, the more he fashions it to a lucky[2] death, a lucky fate; and of him it is said: With Nibbāna he is greatly delighted; he has got rid of his bundle of life for the utter ending of Ill.

> Fancy[3]-ensnarled, fawn-like[4] too fancy-fond,
> Ne'er wins he blest Nibbāna's boundless peace:[5]
> But fancy-rid, intent on freedom's way,
> He wins to blest Nibbāna's boundless peace.'

§ v (15). *Without remorse.*

And the venerable Sāriputta said also:

'The more, reverend sirs, a monk thus fashions his life, the more he fashions it to a remorseful fate. And how does he so fashion it . . .?' (*Repeat* § 14.)[6]

§ vi (16). *Nakula's parents.*

Once, while the Exalted One was dwelling among the Bhaggis on Crocodile Hill in the Deer Park at Bhesakaḷā

---

[1] *Sa-kkāyâbhirato*; *kāya* is from $\sqrt{ci}$, a heap or collection; *Comy.* says *te-bhūmaka-vaṭṭaŋ*. (*Cf.* the Biblical use of 'the bundle of life' at 1 *Samuel* xxv, 29.) The *sa-* stresses the *kāya* of things material.

[2] *Bhaddaka.*

[3] These verses recur at *Thag.* 989-90 (*Brethr.* 343) as part of Sāriputta's *aññā* declaration.

[4] *Mago.*

[5] *Yoga-kkhema*, rest from labour; *cf. kshema-yoga.*

[6] The text repeats much in full.

Grove, the goodman of the house, Nakula's father,[1] lay sick and ailing, grievously ill.

Now his dame, Nakula's mother,[2] spoke thus to him:

'I prithee, goodman, die not fretfully;[3] ill is the fate of the fretful; decried by the Exalted One is the fate of the fretful.

Maybe, goodman, you think: "Alas, when I am gone, the goodwife, Nakula's mother, will not be able[4] to support the children, nor keep the household together!"[5] But think not so, goodman; for I am deft at spinning cotton, at carding[6] the matted wool; and I can support the children, keep the household, after you have gone. Wherefore, goodman, die not fretfully; ill is the fate of the fretful; decried by the Exalted One is the fate of the fretful.

Or maybe you think: "The goodwife, when I am gone, will go to another man!"[7] But think not so, goodman; for you and I know how for sixteen years we have lived, as housefolk, the godly life.[8] Wherefore, goodman, die not fretfully. . . .

Or maybe you think: "The goodwife, after I am gone, will have no desire to see the Exalted One, no desire to see the monks of the Order!" But think not so, goodman; for, verily, when you are gone, greater shall be my desire to see the Exalted One, greater shall be my desire to see the Order.[9] Wherefore, goodman, die not fretfully. . . .

Or maybe you think: "The goodwife, after I am gone, will not keep the virtues in full!" But think not so, goodman;

---

[1] *Cf. K.S.* iii, 1; *G.S.* i, 24; *AA.* i, 400.

[2] *G.S.* i, 25; *AA.* i, 457; *A.* iv, 268.

[3] *Sâpekho. Comy. sa-taṇho.*

[4] *Comy.* reads *sakkhati, S.e. -issati.*

[5] *Santharituŋ*, to spread; but here the *Comy. nicchiddaŋ kātuŋ, saṇṭhapetuŋ, pavattetun-ti attho. P.E.D.* omits *nicchiddaŋ.*

[6] *Veṇiŋ olikhituŋ. Comy. eḷaka-lomāni kappetvā, vijaṭetvā, veṇiŋ kātuŋ.*

[7] The text reads *gharaŋ*, but we should read, with *v.l., S.e.* and *Comy., vīraŋ.*

[8] *Brahma-cariya. Cf.* above, p. 159, *n.* 2.

[9] *Comy.* observes that with these three items 'she roared her lion-roar'; but as to the last three she called the B. to witness.

for so long as the Exalted One shall have white-robed women lay-disciples, folk with homes, who keep the virtues in full, I shall be one of them; and if any shall doubt or deny it, let him go and ask the Exalted One, that Exalted One, arahant, fully enlightened, who dwells here among the Bhaggis on Crocodile Hill in the Deer Park at Bhesakaḷā Grove. Wherefore, goodman, die not fretfully. . . .

Or maybe you think: " The goodwife will not gain the calm of heart within herself!" But think not so, goodman; for so long as the Exalted One shall have white-robed women lay-disciples . . ., who gain that state, I shall be one of them; and if any shall doubt or deny it, let him go and ask the Exalted One. . . . Wherefore, goodman, die not fretfully. . . .

Maybe, goodman, you think: " The goodwife, Nakula's mother, will not, in this Dhamma and discipline, win to the firm ground,[1] win a firm foothold,[2] win comfort, dissolve doubt, be freed of uncertainty, win confidence, become self-reliant,[3] live in the Teacher's word!" But think not so, goodman; for so long as the Exalted One shall have white-robed women lay-disciples, folk with homes, who, in this Dhamma and discipline, win to the firm ground, win a firm foothold, win comfort, dissolve doubt, become freed of uncertainty, win confidence, become self-reliant and live in the Teacher's word, I shall be one of them; and if any shall doubt or deny it, let him go and ask the Exalted One, that Exalted One, arahant, fully enlightened, who dwells here among the Bhaggis on Crocodile Hill in the Deer Park at Bhesakaḷā Grove. Wherefore, goodman, die not fretfully; ill is the fate of the fretful; decried by the Exalted One is the fate of the fretful.'

Now while the goodman was being counselled with this counsel by Nakula's mother, even as he lay there,[4] his sickness subsided; and Nakula's father arose from that sickness. And thus that sickness was laid aside by the goodman of the house.

---

[1] *Ogādha-ppattā. Comy. ogādhaṃ anupavesaṃ pattā; cf. UdA.* 345.

[2] *Paṭigādha-. Comy. . . . patiṭṭhaṃ pattā.*

[3] This is stock; *D.* i, 110; *Vin.* i, 12; *Ud.* 49.

[4] *Ṭhānaso.*

Now, not long after he had got up, Nakula's father, leaning on a stick, visited the Exalted One, saluted him, and sat down at one side. And to him, thus seated, the Exalted One said this:

'It has been to your gain, goodman, you have greatly gained, goodman, in having had the goodwife, Nakula's mother, full of compassion, and desiring (your) weal, as a counsellor, as a teacher.

Verily, so long as I have white-robed women lay-disciples, folk with homes, who keep the virtues in full, the goodwife, Nakula's mother, will be one of them; so long as I have lay-disciples . . . who gain the calm of heart within the self, she will be one of them; so long as I have lay-disciples . . . who, in this Dhamma and discipline, win to the firm ground . . . and live in the Teacher's word, the goodwife will be one of them.

It has been to your gain, goodman, you have greatly gained, goodman, in having had the goodwife, Nakula's mother, full of compassion and desire for (your) weal, as a counsellor, as a teacher.'

§ vii (17). *Right things.*[1]

On one occasion, while he dwelt near Sāvatthī at Jeta Grove in Anāthapiṇḍika's Park, the Exalted One, rising from solitude at eventide, approached the service hall;[2] and, on arriving, sat down on the seat ready there.

Then, too, the venerable Sāriputta, rising from solitude at eventide, went to the service hall, saluted the Exalted One, and sat down at one side. So, likewise, came the venerable Mahā Moggallāna, the venerable Mahā Kassapa, the venerable Mahā Kaccāna, the venerable Mahā Koṭṭhita, the venerable Mahā Cunda, the venerable Mahā Kappina, the venerable Anuruddha, the venerable Revata, and the venerable Ānanda[3] . . . and sat down at one side.

---

[1] The text of the *uddāna* for both §§ 16 and 17 reads *Nakula maccha* . . . ; *S.e. Nakula-kusalā macchaŋ* . . .

[2] *Upaṭṭhāna-sālā*, lit. attendance-hall.

[3] For all these, except Mahā Cunda, see *G.S.* i, 16 and ref. there; for Mahā Cunda see below, § 46.

Now, after passing much of the night thus seated, the Exalted One rose and entered the dwelling.

And soon after he had gone, the venerable monks also rose and went, each to his dwelling; but the novices, not long gone forth, newly come to this Dhamma-discipline, went on snoring[1] and sleeping there, even till sunrise.

And the Exalted One, seeing with the deva eye, surpassing the purity of man's, those monks snoring and sleeping till sunrise, went to the service hall and sat down; and being seated, addressed them, saying:

'Monks, where is Sāriputta; where is Mahā Moggallāna; where is Mahā Kassapa, Mahā Kaccāna, Mahā Koṭṭhita, Mahā Cunda, Mahā Kappina, Anuruddha, Revata, Ānanda? Where have these elder-disciples gone, monks?'

'Lord, they, too, soon after the Exalted One's departure, rose and went, each to his dwelling.'

'Monks, then are you now elders, yet novice-like you sleep and snore till sunrise!

'What think you, monks, have you either seen or heard of a warrior rajah, crowned and anointed, living a life of indulgence, given over to the pleasures bed, indolence and sloth to his heart's content; and ruling all his life, the darling and favourite of the country-folk?'

'No, indeed, lord.'

'Well, monks, neither have I . . .

And have you seen or heard of a farmer,[2] a land-owner's son, a general, a village headman,[3] a guildmaster, each living a life of indulgence . . .; and each managing his affairs all his life, the darling and favourite of his underlings?'

'No, indeed, lord.'

'Well, monks, neither have I . . .

Then have you seen or heard of a recluse or godly man[4] indulging himself to his heart's content in the pleasures of

---

[1] *Kākacchamānā. Comy. kāka-saddaṃ karontā, dante khadantā* (gnashing teeth, as a sleeping infant often does).

[2] *Cf.* above V, § 58. *Comy.* here: *yo raṭṭhaṃ bhuñjati.*

[3] *Gāma-gāmiko. Comy. gāma-bhojako,* landlord.

[4] *Brāhmaṇa.*

bed, indolence and sloth, with sense-doors unguarded, knowing no moderation in eating, not practising vigilance, no seer of right things, nor practising the practice—day in day out—of making become things that wing to his awakening;[1] yet, having destroyed the cankers and being canker-free, entering and abiding in mind-emancipation, in insight-emancipation and realizing it, here now, by his own knowledge?'

'No, indeed, lord.'

'Well, monks, neither have I . . .

Wherefore, monks, train yourselves thus:

We will become guarded as to the sense-doors, know moderation in eating, be practised in vigilance, seers of right things, and dwell—day in day out—practising the practice of making become things that wing to our awakening.[2]

Verily, monks, train yourselves thus.'

§ viii (18). *The fish.*[3]

Once, when the Exalted One with a great company of monks walked a walk among the Kosalese, he saw, as he went along the highway, a fisherman, who had caught a haul of fish and was selling them as a fishmonger; and the Exalted One at the sight stepped off the road and sat down at the foot of a tree on a seat made ready for him. And, sitting there, he said to the monks:

'Monks, see you that fisherman selling fish as a fishmonger . . .?'

'Yes, lord.'

'Then what think you, monks, have you either seen or heard of a fisherman fishmonger slaughtering and selling fish; and as a result of such deeds, of that way of living, going about on an elephant[4] or on horseback or in a chariot or carriage

---

[1] *Cf.* above V, § 56.

[2] *Comy.* the thirty-seven; see *Buddhist Suttas*, p. 62, *Vism. trsl.* 832, and elsewhere. Originally, most likely thirty. *Cf. K.S.* v, Contents and Introduction.

[3] This and the following suttas are omitted in Nyāṇatiloka's translation.

[4] *Hatthi-yāyī. Comy. hatthinā yānī.* The higher estate is in each case presumably that of an after-life.

or feasting at feasts[1] or living in the abundance of great wealth ?'

'No, indeed, lord.'

'Well, monks, neither have I . . . And why is that ? Verily, monks, evilly minded he gloats on fish being slaughtered, being brought to the slaughter; and because of that he goes not about on an elephant nor on horseback nor in a chariot nor carriage nor feasts at feasts nor lives in the abundance of great wealth.

What think you, monks, have you either seen or heard of a butcher slaughtering and selling cattle . . . rams . . . pigs . . . or beasts of the forest[2] . . . and living in the abundance of great wealth ?'

'No, indeed, lord.'

'Well, monks, neither have I . . . And why is that ? Verily, monks, it is because he gloats evilly on their being slaughtered, being brought to the slaughter. . . . Indeed, monks, he who gloats evilly on creatures being slaughtered, being brought to the slaughter, shall not go about on elephants nor on horseback nor in chariots nor in carriages nor feast at feasts nor live in the abundance of great wealth.

But what shall be said of him who gloats evilly on human beings being slaughtered, being brought to the slaughter ? Verily, monks, it shall be to his harm and hurt for many a day; for, on the breaking up of the body after death, he shall arise in the wayward way, the ill way, the abyss, hell.'

§ ix (19). *Mindfulness of death*[3] (*a*).

Once, when the Exalted One was staying in the Brick Hall at Nādika,[4] he addressed the monks, saying: 'Monks.'

'Lord,' they replied; and the Exalted One said:

'Monks, mindfulness of death, when made become, made

---

[1] *Bhogabhogī*.

[2] For this set see *M*. i, 342; *A*. ii, 207; *J*. v, 270; below, § 57.

[3] *Cf*. *A*. iv, 316.

[4] So our text, *S.e.* and *Comy.*; see *K.S.* ii, 51 for variants; Watters' *Chwang*, ii, 86, '*Nataka*' on the Ganges between Vesālī and Patna; possibly, therefore, the name is connected with *nadī*.

to increase, is very fruitful, great in weal, merging in the deathless, having the deathless as consummation.[1] Monks, make mindfulness of death become more!'

And when he had spoken thus, a monk said to him: 'I, lord, make mindfulness of death become.'

'How so, monk?'

'Herein, lord, such is my thought: Were I day and night to abide mindful of the Exalted One's word, much would be done by me—thus, lord, I make mindfulness of death become.'

And another said: 'I too, lord, make mindfulness become.'

'How so, monk?'

'Herein, lord, such is my thought: Were I day-long to abide mindful of the Exalted One's word, much would be done by me. . . .'

And another said: 'Such is my thought: Were I to abide mindful just so long as I eat an alms-meal . . .' And another: 'As I munch and swallow four or five morsels . . .' And another: 'As I munch and swallow only one morsel . . .'

And another said: 'I too, lord, make mindfulness of death become.'

'How so, monk?'

'Lord, such is my thought: Were I to abide just so long as I breathe in and out or breathe out and in, mindful of the Exalted One's word, much would be done by me—thus, lord, I make mindfulness of death become.'

And when he had thus spoken, the Exalted One said to the monks:

'Monks, the monk who makes mindfulness of death become thus: "Were I day and night to abide mindful . . ." or he who thinks thus: "Were I day-long to abide so . . ." or thinks: "As I eat an alms-meal . . ." or "Munch and swallow four or five morsels . . ., mindful of the Exalted One's word, much would be done by me"—those monks are said to live indolently; slackly they make mindfulness of death become for the destruction of the cankers.

---

[1] *Pariyosānā.*

But the monk who makes mindfulness of death become thus: "Were I to abide mindful as I munch and swallow one morsel . . ."; and he who thinks thus: "Were I to abide mindful of the Exalted One's word as I breathe in and out or out and in, much would be done by me"—those monks are said to live earnestly; keenly they make mindfulness of death become for the destruction of the cankers.

Wherefore, monks, train yourselves thus:

We will live earnestly;[1] keenly will we make mindfulness of death become for the destruction of the cankers.

Train yourselves thus, monks.'

§ x (20). *The same*[2] (*b*).

Once, at Nādika in the Brick Hall, the Exalted One addressed the monks, saying:

'Monks, mindfulness of death, when made become, increased, is very fruitful, great in weal, merging in the deathless, having the deathless as consummation. How so, monks . . . ?

Consider the monk who, when day declines and night sets in, reflects thus: "The chances of death for me are many. Snake, scorpion, or centipede may bite me and bring death and hinder[3] me; I may stumble and fall, the food I have eaten may make me ill, bile may convulse me, phlegm choke me, cutting winds within rack me and bring death and hinder me."[4] Monks, let that monk reflect thus: "Have I given up every evil and wicked thing which, were I to die to-night, would hinder me?" Monks, if, on reflection, he know that he has not, let an urge in great measure be made by that monk, an effort, an endeavour, an exertion, a struggle, let him get mindfulness and self-possession.

Monks, just as were his cloth and hair on fire he would make an urge in great measure, an effort, an endeavour, an

---

[1] *Cf.* the dying instruction: 'Earnestly achieve.' See above, p. 92.

[2] *Cf. A.* iv, 320.

[3] *Comy.* death is a hindrance to life, to a recluse's duties, to the ordinary man working for heaven or to one on the Way.

[4] *Cf.* above V, § 77.

exertion, a struggle, would get mindfulness and self-possession, to put out the fire thereof; even so let an urge in great measure be made by him, an effort, an endeavour, an exertion, a struggle, let him get mindfulness and self-possession, to give up every evil and wicked thing.

But if, monks, on reflection he knows there is no evil or wickedness that has not been given up by him, which, were he to die that night, would hinder him, let him live with zest and delight, training himself day and night in the ways of right.

And let him act likewise, monks, when night is spent and day breaks. . . .

Monks, mindfulness of death, when made thus become, made to increase, is very fruitful, great in profit, merging in the deathless, having the deathless as consummation.'

CHAPTER III.—ABOVE ALL.

§ i (21) *At Sāmagāma.*[1]

The Exalted One once dwelt among the Sakkas at Sāmagāma[2] near the lotus-pond.

Now, when the night was far spent, a deva of exceeding loveliness, lighting up the whole lotus-pond, approached him, saluted and stood at one side. Thus standing, the deva said to the Exalted One:

'Lord, these three things lead to a monk's failure. What three? Delight[3] in worldly activity,[4] delight in talk, delight in sleep. Lord, these three things lead to the falling away of a monk.' Thus spake that deva and the Master approved. Then thought the deva: 'The Master is one in thought with me,' and, saluting the Exalted One, keeping him on his right, vanished thence.

And when that night was over, the Exalted One addressed

---

[1] In the *Uddāna*: *Sāmako. S.e. Samako.*

[2] *Sāmagāmake. Comy. Sāmakānaŋ ussannattā evaŋ laddha-nāme gāmake*; the name recurs at *M.* ii, 243 as *Sāmagāma*; *MA.* (*Aluvihāra ed.*, p. 829) merely repeats our comment.

[3] *Cf.* above VI, § 14; *It.* 71; below, §§ 31 and 69

[4] *Kamma.*

the monks and told them all that had occurred[1] . . . and said:

'Monks, it is to the discredit of each one of you, it is to the loss of each one of you,[2] that even devas know the things that lead to your failing in righteousness.

Monks, other three things that lead to failure I will also teach you; listen, pay heed and I will speak.'

'Yes, lord,' rejoined those monks; and the Exalted One said:

'And what, monks, are the three? Delight in company, evil speaking and friendship with bad men. Verily, monks, these are the three things that lead to failure.

Monks, all those who in the long road of the past have failed in righteousness, have failed in righteousness just because of these six things; all those who in the long road of the future shall fail in righteousness, shall do so because of these six things; yea, monks, all who now fail in righteousness, fail therein just because of these six things.'

§ ii (22). *The unfailing.*

'Monks, six are these things that fail not I will teach you; listen, pay heed. . . .

And what, monks, are these six?

Delighting not in worldly activity,[3] in talk, in sleep, in company; fair speech and friendship with good men.

Verily, monks, these are the six . . .

Monks, all those who in the long road of the past . . . the long road of the future . . . yea, all those who now fail not in righteousness, fail not therein just because of these six things.'

§ iii (23). *Fear.*[4]

'Monks, "fear" is a name for sense-desires; "pain" is a name for sense-desires; "disease" is a name for sense-desires; "blain" is a name for sense-desires; "bondage" is a name for sense-desires; "bog" is a name for sense-desires.

---

[1] The text repeats.

[2] *S.e.* reads *tesaŋ vo dulladdhā.*

[3] *Kamma.*

[4] *Cf. A.* iv, 289 for eight; also *Sn.* 51; *SnA.* 100.

And wherefore, monks, is fear a name for sense-desires? Monks, impassioned by sensuous passions, bound by passionate desire, neither in this world is one free from fear, nor in the next world is one free from fear. Therefore "fear" is a name for sense-desires.

So too, monks, of "pain," "disease," "blain," "bondage," "bog," impassioned by sensuous passions, bound by passionate desire, neither in this world nor in the next is one free from any of these things. Therefore, monks, they are names for sense-desires.

> Fear,[1] pain, disease, blain, bondage, bog are names
> For sense-desires to which the worldlings cling.
> They who see fear in grasping[2]—source of birth
> And death—grasp not and, ending both, are freed;
> Won is the peace, blissful in perfect cool[3]
> They dwell here now, all fear and hate long gone,
> All Ill surpassed.'

§ iv (24). *Himālaya.*

'Monks, with six things endowed, a monk may cleave the mountain-king, Himālaya, but who shall say it of rude ignorance? What six?

Herein,[4] monks, a monk is skilled in the attainment of concentration, skilled in maintaining concentration, skilled in emerging from concentration, skilled in the weal[5] of concentration, skilled in the range of concentration, skilled in the resolve for concentration.

Verily, monks, with these six things endowed, a monk may cleave the mountain-king Himālaya, but who shall say it of rude[6] ignorance?'

---

1 For the first two lines of the text *cf. A.* iv, 290; for the second *pāda* of the second line see *J.P.T.S.*, 1909, 342; the last four lines (text) recur at *M.* iii, 187; *A.* i, 142; with the last *pāda cf. It.* 4.

2 *Upādāne. Comy.* the fourfold—*i.e., kāma, diṭṭhi, sīlabbata, attavāda.*

3 *Abhinibbutā.*

4 *Cf. A.* iv, 34; *S.* iii, 263 *ff.*

5 *Kallita-.*

6 *Chava. Comy. lāmika.*

§ v (25). *Ever minding.*

'Monks, there are these six states of ever minding.[1] What six?

Herein, monks, the Ariyan disciple ever minds the Tathāgata: "He is the Exalted One. . . ." Monks, what time the Ariyan disciple minds the Tathāgata, his heart is not lust-obsessed, nor hate-obsessed, nor obsessed by infatuation; upright in heart is he at that time, moved, freed, raised from greed; and this greed, monks, is a name for the fivefold sensuous pleasures. Verily, monks, by making this thought their object,[2] some men thereby are purged.[3]

Again, the Ariyan disciple ever minds Dhamma: "Well declared by the Exalted One is Dhamma . . ." . . . some men thereby are purged.

. . . ever minds the Order: "The Exalted One's Order of disciples has rightly stepped the way. . . ."

. . . ever minds the virtues in himself: "They are unbroken, without flaw, spotless. . . ."

. . . ever minds liberality in himself: "'Tis indeed a gain to me, indeed I have greatly gained, I who live heart-free of the stingy taint. . . ."

Or the Ariyan disciple ever minds the devas: "There are the Four Royal Devas, the Thirty and so forth; who because of their faith, virtue, learning, liberality, wisdom, have become so; mine also are these qualities." Monks, what time the Ariyan disciple minds the faith, virtue, learning, liberality, wisdom, both in himself and in those devas, his heart is not lust-obsessed, nor hate-obsessed, nor obsessed by infatuation; upright in heart is he at that time, moved, freed, raised from greed; and this greed, monks, is a name for the fivefold sensuous pleasures. Verily, monks, by making this thought their object, some men thereby are purged.

Monks, these are the six states of ever minding.'

---

[1] *Cf.* above VI, §§ 9 and 10; the text is mostly in full; *Vism.* 226.

[2] *Ārammaṇaŋ karitvā. Comy. idaŋ Buddhânussati-kammaṭṭhānaŋ.*

[3] *Comy.* they attain Nibbāna.

§ vi (26). *Kaccāna.*[1]

Then said the venerable Mahā Kaccāna to the monks: 'Monks, reverend sirs!' 'Reverend sir,' they rejoined; and the venerable one said:

'It[2] is wonderful, reverend sirs; it is amazing how this escape from the noose[3] was conceived by that Exalted One, knower, seer, arahant, fully awake—to purge man, overcome grief and woe, clear away pain and distress, win truth,[4] realize Nibbāna—I mean the six states of ever minding. What six?

Consider, reverend sirs, the Ariyan disciple who is ever minding the Tathāgata: "He is the Exalted One. . . ." When he so minds him, his heart is not lust-obsessed . . ., but made upright, moved, freed, raised from greed; . . . and, sirs, that Ariyan disciple lives at all times with heart spacious, large, lofty, boundless, free of hatred and ill-will. Verily, reverend sirs, by making this thought their object, some men thereby become pure in nature.

And so, too, of the Ariyan disciple who ever minds Dhamma . . . the Order . . . the virtues in himself . . . liberality in himself . . . the devas[5] . . ., that Ariyan disciple lives at all times with heart spacious, large, lofty, boundless, free of hatred and ill-will. Verily, reverend sirs, by making such thoughts their object, some men thereby become pure in nature.

It is wonderful, amazing, sirs, how this escape from the noose was conceived by the Exalted One, to purge man, overcome grief and woe, clear away pain and distress, win truth, realize Nibbāna—I mean these six states of ever minding.'

§ vii (27). *The times (a).*

Now a certain monk visited the Exalted One, saluted him and sat down at one side; and so seated, he said to the Exalted

---

[1] See above VI, § 17.

[2] This is a stock para.; see *A.* iv, 426, where Ānanda uses it. Our *Comy.* is much the same as on *A.* iv.

[3] *Sambādha.*

[4] *Ñāya.*

[5] The text repeats nearly all in full.

One: 'Lord, how often should one go and see a monk who is a student of mind?'[1]

'Monk, these six times. . . . What six?

Herein, monk, when a monk is obsessed in heart by passionate lust, overwhelmed by passionate lust and knows no refuge, as there really is, from the surge of passionate lust; then let him visit a monk, who has made a study of mind, and say this to him: "Good sir, I am indeed obsessed in heart by passionate lust, overwhelmed thereby, nor know I any refuge from the surge thereof. Well were it for me, if the venerable one would teach me Dhamma to rid me of this lusting." Then the monk will teach him Dhamma to rid him of that lust. This, monk, is the first time to go and see a monk who has made a study of mind.

Again, when in heart he is obsessed by ill-will[2] . . . sloth and torpor . . . flurry and worry . . . or by doubt, is overwhelmed thereby, nor knows a refuge from the surge thereof; then let him visit a monk, who has made a study of mind, and say: "Good sir, I am obsessed in heart by this and that . . . nor know I any refuge from the surge thereof . . . let the venerable one teach me Dhamma!"—and he does so. This, monk, is the second . . . the fifth time to go and see a monk. . . .

Moreover, monk, when from some image,[3] as he concentrates thereon, there comes not to him at intervals canker-destruction, nor knows he that image nor realizes it; then let him visit a monk, who has made a study of mind, and say: "Good sir, from this image, as I concentrate thereon, there comes not to me at intervals canker-destruction, nor know I this image nor realize it. Well were it for me, if the venerable

---

[1] *Mano-bhāvanīya. Comy. ettha manaŋ vaḍḍheti. K.S.* iii, 1 and v, 320: 'worshipful'; *F. Dial.* ii, 304: 'of great intellect.' *Cf. Gotama the Man*, p. 153; *Sakya*, p. 245; *Manual*, p. 223.

[2] *Comy.* explains Dhamma in the first five as (1) *asubha-kammaṭṭhāna*; (2) *metta-*; (3) *thīna-middha-vinodana-* or *āloka-saññā* or *viriyârambha-vatthu*; (4) *samatha-kammaṭṭhāna*; (5) *tiṇṇaŋ ratanānaŋ guṇakathaŋ kathento.*

[3] *Nimitta*, mental reflex.

one would teach me Dhamma to the end that I may destroy the cankers.'' Then the monk will teach him Dhamma to destroy the cankers. This, monk, is the sixth time to go and see a monk who has made a study of mind.'

§ viii (28). *The same* (*b*).

Once, when many elders dwelt at the Deer Park in Isipatana, near Benares, there arose by chance this talk among them, as they sat assembled in the round hall,[1] after breakfast, on their return from alms-collecting: 'What's the proper time, reverend sirs, to go and see a monk who is a student of mind?'

Now having stated this, a certain monk said to the elders: 'When, reverend sirs, a monk, a student of mind, has returned from alms-collecting, breakfasted, washed his feet, seated himself, crossed his legs, straightened his body and made mindfulness stand up, as it were, before him; then is the time to go and see that monk.'

And after he had thus spoken, another said: 'Nay, reverend sirs, that is not the time . . .; for when he has returned, breakfasted and so forth . . ., he is languid from his walk and is not then completely at ease; or he is languid after his meal and is not then completely at ease. Wherefore that is not the time to go and see that monk. But when, sirs, in the evening he has risen from seclusion and is seated in the shade of his lodging, cross-legged, with body erect, with mindfulness set before him; then is the time to go and see that monk.'

Then said another: 'Nay, verily, that is not the time . . .; for when, reverend sirs, in the evening he has risen from seclusion and is seated in the shade . . ., whatsoever concentration-image he has by day concentrated on, just that will then beset him. Wherefore that is not the time to go and see that monk. But when, sirs, night recedes and day dawns and he is seated cross-legged with body erect with mindfulness set before him; then is the time to go and see that monk.'

But another monk said: 'Indeed, neither is that the time . . .; for when day dawns and the monk is seated cross-legged

---

[1] *Maṇḍala-māḷe. Comy. bhojana-sālāya.*

. . . with mindfulness before him, then is his body endued with strength[1] and he finds comfort in pondering on the teaching of the Buddhas. Wherefore that is not the time to go and see that monk.'

And when he had thus spoken, the venerable Mahā Kaccāna said this to the elders:

'From the mouth of the Exalted One, reverend sirs, have I heard this; from his own mouth have I received this: There are these six times for a monk to go and see a monk who is a student of mind. What six?' (*Mahā Kaccāna repeats* § 27.)[2]

'From the mouth of the Exalted One have I heard this; from his very mouth have I received this.'

§ ix (29). *Udāyin.*[3]

And the Exalted One addressed the venerable Udāyin, saying: 'How many states are there, Udāyin, of ever minding?' Now when he had thus spoken, the venerable Udāyin was silent. And a second and a third time the Exalted One spoke in like manner, but the venerable Udāyin remained silent.

Then said the venerable Ānanda to the venerable Udāyin: 'Udāyin, reverend sir, the Master addresses you.'

'I am listening to the Exalted One, Ānanda, reverend sir! Lord, a monk remembers[4] many previous existences, that is to say: one birth, two births and so on; he remembers many previous existences in all their modes, in all their detail. This, lord, is a state of ever minding.'[4]

Then said the Exalted One: 'I knew, Ānanda, this foolish fellow, Udāyin, did not live intent on higher thought.[5] How many states of ever minding are there, Ānanda?'

'Lord, there are five states. What five?

Herein, lord, a monk, aloof from sensuous desires, . . . enters and abides in the first musing . . . the second . . . in

---

1 *Oja-ṭṭhāyi.* *Comy. ojāya ṭhito, patiṭṭhito.*

2 The text abbreviates.

3 *Comy. Lāḷ 'Udāyin,* foolish Udāyin; see *Vin.* i, 115; *Dial* iii, 109.

4 *Anussarati* and *anussati*, both from $\sqrt{smṛ}$.

5 *Adhicitta.* *Comy. samādhi-vipassanā-citta.*

the third musing.[1] This state of ever minding, lord, thus made become, thus made to increase, leads to dwelling at ease here now.

Again, lord, he concentrates on the thought of light,[2] fixes his mind on the thought of day—as by day, so by night; as by night, so by day—thus with mind neither hampered nor hindered, he makes his thought become radiant.[3] This state of ever minding, lord, thus made become, thus made to increase, leads to the gain of knowledge and insight.

Again, lord, he considers this body, upwards from the soles of his feet, downwards from the hair of his head, as skin-bound, as full of diverse impurities: There is in this body the hair of the head, the hair of the body, nails, teeth, skin, flesh, sinews, bones, marrow, kidneys, heart, liver, pleura, spleen, lungs, intestines, mesentery, belly, dung, bile, phlegm, pus, blood, sweat, fat, tears, lymph, spittle, snot, synovia, urine.[4] This state of ever minding, lord, thus made become, thus made to increase, leads to the riddance of passionate lust.

Again, lord, suppose he see a body cast away in a cemetery, one day dead, two days dead or three days dead, bloated, blue-black, a mass of pus;[5] he compares his own body thus: This body too is subject thus; thus it will come to be; this is not passed.[6] Or suppose he see such a body being eaten by crows,[7] ravens, vultures, dogs, jackals, vermin; he compares

---

[1] The fourth is not included, being beyond '*sukha*.'

[2] *D.* iii, 223; *A.* ii, 45; iv, 86; *S.* v, 279.

[3] *Comy.* *Dibba-cakkhu-ñāṇ' aṭṭhāya sah' obhāsakaŋ cittaŋ brūheti, vaḍḍheti.*

[4] This list recurs at *D.* ii, 293; *M.* i, 57; *A.* v, 109; *S.* v. 278 (*trsl.* gives thirty-two parts in error, though at *Kh.* 2 there are thirty-two); see *Vism.* 285-303, to which our *Comy.* refers.

[5] *M.* and *D. loc. cit.*; *M.* iii, 91. *Comy.* observes: swollen like a goat-skin blown up; puffy, loathsome in repulsiveness; mottled, purplish; red where the flesh runs, white where the pus collects, but mostly blue (as if clad in blue robes !); and pus trickles from the broken places and from the nine orifices.

[6] With *Comy.*, *S.e.* and other passages reading *etaŋ.*

[7] *Comy.* perched on the belly, tearing at the belly-flesh, the cheeks, the eyes.

his own body in like manner. So too, a body that is a chain of bones, with flesh and blood, sinew-bound; or fleshless but blood-bespattered, sinew-bound; or without flesh or blood, sinew-bound; or but bones scattered here and there: here a hand-bone,[1] there a foot-bone, there a leg-bone, here a thigh-bone, here a hip-bone, there a back-bone, here a skull. . . . Should he see a body, cast away in a cemetery, the bones of which are white as a sea-shell, a heap of bones, a rotting, powdering mass, years old; he compares his own body thus: This body too is subject thus; thus it will come to be; this is not passed. This state of ever minding, lord, thus made become, thus made to increase, leads to the rooting out of the conceit "I am."

Then, lord, putting by ease, . . . a monk enters and abides in the fourth musing. This state of ever minding, lord, thus made become, thus made to increase, leads to the complete penetration of the countless elements.[2]

Lord, there are these five states of ever minding.'

'Well done, well done, Ānanda; and hold, too, this sixth to be a state of ever minding: Herein, Ānanda, a monk goes out mindful, comes in mindful, stands mindful, sits mindful, lies down mindful and is mindful in performing action.[3] This state of ever minding, Ānanda, thus made become, thus made to increase, leads to mindfulness and self-possession.'

§ x (30). *Above all.*

'Monks, these six are above all.[4] What six?

The sight above all; the sound above all; the gain above all; the training above all; the service above all; the ever minding above all.

And what, monks, is the sight above all?

Herein, monks, some go to see the treasures:[5] the elephant, the horse, the gem; to see divers things; to see some recluse

---

[1] *Comy.* the bones of the hand consist of sixty-four pieces.

[2] *Dhātu.*

[3] *Kammaŋ adhiṭṭhāti. S.e.* so, but *v.l. caŋkamaŋ*, which is probably correct; *cf. S.* ii, 282; *UdA.* 231; *Nidd.* i, 26.

[4] See above VI, § 8.

[5] *Dial.* ii, 204 *ff.*

or godly man, wrong in view, treading the wrong path. And is that the sight, monks? No, I say it is not; it is indeed a mean sight, common, vulgar, un-Ariyan, not well-found, leading not to world-weariness, dispassion, ending, calm, knowledge, awakening, Nibbāna.[1] But some, endued with faith and piety, sure in trust,[2] go to see the Tathāgata or the Tathāgata's disciple. That, monks, is the sight above all sights for purging man, overcoming grief and woe, clearing away ill and pain, winning truth, and realizing Nibbāna; I mean, going to see the Tathāgata or his disciple, endued with faith and piety, sure in trust. This, monks, is called the sight above all. Herein is the sight above all.

And what, monks, is the sound above all?

Herein, monks, some go to hear the sound of the drum, the lute, the sound of song; to hear divers things; to hear the Dhamma of some recluse or godly man, wrong in view, treading the wrong path. And is that the sound, monks? No, I say it is not; it is indeed a mean sound. . . . But some, endued with faith and piety, sure in trust, go to hear the Tathāgata's Dhamma or his disciple's. That, monks, is the sound above all sounds for purging man . . .; I mean, going to hear the Tathāgata's Dhamma. . . . This, monks, is called the sound above all. Herein is the sight and sound above all.

And what, monks, is the gain above all?

Herein, monks, some gain the gain of a son or a wife or wealth; gain divers things; gain faith in some recluse or godly man, wrong in view, treading the wrong path. And is that the gain, monks? No, I say it is not; it is indeed a mean gain. . . . But some, endued with faith and piety, sure in trust, gain faith in the Tathāgata or his disciple. That, monks, is the gain above all gains for purging man . . .; I mean, gaining faith in the Tathāgata. . . . This, monks, is called the gain above all. Herein is the sight, sound and gain above all.

---

[1] Clause borrowed from the First Utterance.

[2] *Niviṭṭha-saddho, niviṭṭha-pemo* (from √*prī*), *ekantagato abhippasanno.*

And what, monks, is the training above all?

Herein, monks, some train in elephant-lore, in horsemanship, in the use of the chariot, the bow, the sword;[1] train in divers ways; train after the way of some recluse or godly man, wrong in view, treading the wrong path. And is that the training, monks? No, I say it is not; it is indeed a mean training. . . . But some, endued with faith and piety, sure in trust, train in the onward course of virtue, thought and insight[2] according to the Dhamma-discipline declared by the Tathāgata. That, monks, is the training above all training for purging man . . .; I mean, training in the onward course. . . . This, monks, is called the training above all. Herein is the sight, sound, gain and training above all.

And what, monks, is the service above all?

Herein, monks, some serve a warrior, a brāhman, a householder; serve divers folk; serve some recluse or godly man, wrong in view, treading the wrong path. And is that the service, monks? No, I say it is not; it is indeed a mean service. . . . But some, endued with faith and piety, sure in trust, serve the Tathāgata or his disciple. That, monks, is the service above all services for purging man . . .; I mean, serving the Tathāgata or his disciple. . . . This, monks, is called the service above all. Herein is the sight, sound, gain, training and service above all.

And what, monks, is the ever minding above all?

Herein, monks, some ever mind the gain of a son or a wife or wealth; ever mind divers gains; ever mind some recluse or godly man, wrong in view, treading the wrong path. And is that the ever minding, monks? No, I say it is not; it is indeed a mean ever minding, common, vulgar, un-Ariyan, not well-found, leading not to world-weariness, dispassion, ending, calm, knowledge, awakening, Nibbāna. But some, endued with faith and piety, sure in trust, ever mind the Tathāgata or the Tathāgata's disciple. That, monks, is the ever minding above all ever minding for purging man, over-

---

[1] *Cf. Vin.* ii, 10; *Mil.* 66.

[2] *Adhisīla, adhicitta, adhipaññā.*

coming grief and woe, clearing away ill and pain, winning truth, and realizing Nibbāna; I mean, ever minding the Tathāgata or his disciple, endued with faith and piety, sure in trust. This, monks, is called the ever minding above all.

Verily, monks, these are the six above all.

They who have found the noblest sight, the sound
Above all sounds, the gain of gains; have found
Joy in the training, are on service set,
Who make the ever minding more-become:
They who have found, linked to right loneliness,
The deathless way to peace[1]—joyous in zeal,
Restrained by virtue, wise, they verily
Shall in due time know where all Ill doth end.'

Chapter IV.—The Devas.

§ i (31). *In training.*

'Monks, these six things lead to failure for a monk in training. What six?

Delight[2] in worldly activity,[3] in talk, in sleep, in company, being unguarded as to the doors of the senses and immoderate in eating.

Monks, these are the six . . .' (*The opposite lead not so.*)

§ ii (32). *They fail not* (*a*).

Now, when night was far spent, a deva of exceeding loveliness, lighting up the whole of Jeta Grove, approached the Exalted One, saluted and stood at one side. Thus standing, the deva said: 'Lord, these six things lead not to a monk's failure. What six? Reverence for the Master, for Dhamma, for the Order, the training, earnestness and for good-will.[4]

---

[1] *Viveka-paṭisaŋyuttaŋ khemam amata-gāminaŋ*; for the first compound see *Thag.* 589; the second half of the line recurs at *M.* i, 508 (see *Tr.'s n.* at 571); there the reading is *-gāminaŋ*, with our *v.l.* and *S.e.* Our *Comy.* is silent.

[2] *Cf.* above VI, § 22.

[3] *Kamma.*

[4] Above VI, § 21; below, § 79; *A.* iv, 28, where the *gāthā* is almost the same.

Verily, lord, these six things lead not to a monk's failure.' Thus spoke the deva and the Master approved; and seeing this, he saluted the Exalted One and passed out on the right.

And when the night was over, the Exalted One addressed the monks and told them all that had taken place. . . .[1]

'Deep reverence for the Master, Dhamma, Order,
Reverence for earnestness and for good-will:
Not thuswise fails a monk; he's nigh Nibbāna.'

§ iii (33). *The same* (*b*).

'Monks, this night a deva . . . came and said to me: "These six things lead not to a monk's failure. What six? Reverence for the Master, Dhamma, Order, training, modesty and fear of blame. . . ." And when he had said this, he passed out on the right.

Deep reverence for the Master, Dhamma, Order,
Esteem for modesty and fear of blame:
Not thuswise fails a monk; he's nigh Nibbāna.'

§ iv (34). *Mahā Moggallāna.*

Once, when the Exalted One dwelt near Sāvatthī, at Jeta Grove in Anāthapiṇḍika's Park, this thought came to the venerable Mahā Moggallāna, gone apart for solitude: 'To how many devas is there this knowledge: We have won to the Stream; are no more for the abyss; in sureness we make for the awakening beyond?'[2]

Now[3] at that time a monk named Tissa had just died and was reborn in one of the Brahmā worlds, and they knew him even there as Tissa the mighty, Tissa the powerful. Then the venerable Mahā Moggallāna—as a strong man might stretch out his bent arm, might bend his stretched arm—vanished from Jeta Grove and appeared in that Brahma-world. And deva Tissa saw the venerable one from afar, coming along, and on

---

[1] The text repeats in full.

[2] *Sambodhi-pārāyanā.*

[3] *Cf. A.* iv, 74, where all this recurs at Rājagaha of *upādiseso* and *an°*-. *Comy.* observes that Tissa was a pupil of M.'s.

seeing him said: 'Come, worthy[1] Moggallāna; welcome, worthy Moggallāna! 'Tis long since you made this round,[2] I mean, came here. Pray be seated, good sir, here is the seat ready.' And the venerable Mahā Moggallāna sat down; and deva Tissa, after saluting, sat down also, at one side.

Then said the venerable Mahā Moggallāna to deva Tissa, so seated: 'To how many devas, Tissa, is there this knowledge: We have won to the Stream; are no more for the abyss; in sureness we make for the awakening beyond?'

'The Four Royal Devas, worthy sir, have this knowledge.'

'What, have they all this knowledge . . .?'

'No, worthy sir, not all. . . . Those Four Royal Devas who possess not perfect[3] faith in the Buddha, Dhamma and Order, possess not perfect faith in the virtues, beloved by Ariyans, they know not that . . .; but those who possess such faith . . . they know: We have won to the Stream, are no more for the abyss; in sureness we make for the awakening beyond.'

'And is it just the Four Royal Devas who have this knowledge, or do the devas of the Thirty . . .; Yāma's devas . . .; the devas of Tusita . . .; the devas who delight in creating . . . and the devas who have power over others' creations also have this knowledge?'

'They also, worthy sir, have this knowledge. . . .

'What, all of them . . .?'

'No, not those who possess not perfect faith in the Buddha, Dhamma, the Order and the virtues . . .; but those who have such faith, they know it. . . .'

And the venerable Mahā Moggallāna approved and commended Brahmā Tissa's words; and, as a strong man might stretch and bend his arm, he vanished from the Brahmā world and appeared at Jeta Grove.

---

1 *Mārisa. Comy.* in that world it is the common form of friendly greeting; but folk here say: 'Whence come you, sir? (*bhavaŋ*). 'Tis long since you came! How did you know the way here? What, did you go astray?'—and the like.

2 *Pariyāyaŋ. Comy. vāraŋ*, choice, or turn; see *Dial* i, 245 *n.*; *K.S.* i, 180.

3 *Cf. S.* v, 394; *D.* ii, 93 (as *Dhammādāsa*); *M.* ii, 51; *A.* ii, 56.

§ v (35). *Parts of wisdom.*

'Monks, these six things are parts of wisdom. What six? The[1] idea of impermanence, the idea of the ill in impermanence, the idea of not-self in ill, the idea of renunciation, of dispassion, of ending.

Monks, these six things are parts of wisdom.'

§ vi (36). *The roots of contention.*

'Monks, these six are the roots of contention.[2] What six?

Monks, suppose a monk be angry, scornful. An he be so, he lives without reverence, respect for the Master, Dhamma or the Order; he fulfils not the training. And he who lives thus, causes contention in the Order, and that is to the hurt and sorrow of many folk, to the harm of many folk, to the hurt and ill of devas[3] and men. Monks, if you see this root of contention among you or among others, strive to rid yourselves of this evil thing; and if you see it not, step the way to stop its future cankering.[4] Thus is this evil root of contention rid; and thus shall there be no future cankering.

Again, monks, suppose a monk be a hypocrite, malicious . . .; envious, mean . . .; deceitful, crafty . . .; evil-minded, wrong in view . . .; view-bound, tenacious, stubborn.[5] An he be any of these things, he lives without reverence, respect for the Master, Dhamma, Order, nor fulfils the training. And he who lives thus, causes contention in the Order . . . to the hurt and ill of devas and men. Monks, if you see these roots of contention, strive to be rid of these evil things; and if

---

[1] *Cf. D.* iii, 283; *A.* iv, 24; on *vijjā-bhāgiyā* see *DhS. trsl.* 338 *n.*

[2] This recurs at *D.* iii, 246; *M.* ii, 245; *Vin.* ii, 89. *Cf. Proverbs* xxii, 10: 'Cast out the scorner, and contention shall go out.'

[3] *Comy.* refers us to *Vin.* i, 252 as to how quarrelling among monks affects devas.

[4] *An-avassavāya paṭipajjeyyātha*, √*sru* and √*pad.*

[5] *Sandiṭṭhi-parāmāsī ādhāna-gāhī duppaṭinissaggī*; *cf. M.* i, 42; *D.* iii, 46; *A.* v, 150. All read *ādhāna-*, with *S.e.* and *Comy.*, but *A.* has *v.l. ādāna*. *Ādāna-gāhī* is 'grasping-seizing' (*cf. ādāna-paṭinissagga* at *Dhp.* 89; *S.* i, 236; v, 24: 'grasping-foregoing'), and our *Comy.* glosses: *daḷha-gāhī.*

you see them not, step the way to stop their future cankering. Thus are these evil roots rid; and thus there shall be no future cankering.

Verily, monks, these six are the roots of contention.'

§ vii (37). *Alms.*

Once, when the Exalted One dwelt near Sāvatthī, at Jeta Grove in Anāthapiṇḍika's Park, Nanda's mother, the Veḷukaṇḍakan[1] lay-disciple, founded an offering, sixfold-endowed, for the Order of monks with Sāriputta and Mahā Moggallāna at the head.

Now the Exalted One, with the deva-eye, surpassing in clarity the eye of man, saw this thing . . ., and addressed the monks thus:

'Monks, this lay-disciple of Veḷukaṇḍaka, Nanda's mother, has founded an offering, sixfold-endowed, for the Order . . . And how, monks, is the offering[2] sixfold-endowed?

Monks, the giver's part is threefold and the receivers' part is threefold.

And what is the giver's threefold part?

Herein, monks, before the gift[3] he is glad at heart;[4] in giving the heart[4] is satisfied; and uplifted is the heart when he has given. This is the giver's threefold part.

And what is the receivers' threefold part?

Herein, monks, they are lust-freed or stepping to cast lust out; are hate-freed or stepping to cast hate out; are delusion-freed or stepping to become so. This is the receivers' threefold part.

Thus the giver's part is threefold and the receivers' part is threefold; thus verily, monks, the offering is sixfold-endowed.

Monks, not easy is it to grasp the measure of merit of such a sixfold-endowed offering, and to say: "Thus much is the yield in merit, the yield in goodliness, making for a lucky hereafter, ripening to happiness, leading heavenward, leading

---

[1] See *G.S.* i, 24; *Brethr.* 41; *A.* iv, 63; *K.S.* ii, 160 (there *-kaṇṭakī*).

[2] *Dakkhiṇā.*

[3] *Dāna.*

[4] *Mano,* then *cittaŋ.*

to weal and happiness, longed for, loved and lovely." Verily, the great mass of merit is reckoned just unreckonable, immeasurable.

Monks, just[1] as it is not easy to grasp the measure of water in the great ocean, and to say: "There are so many pailfuls, so many hundreds of pailfuls, so many thousands of pailfuls, so many hundreds of thousands of pailfuls"—for that great mass of water is reckoned unreckonable, immeasurable; even so, monks, it is not easy to grasp the measure of merit in a sixfold-endowed offering. . . . Verily, the great mass of merit is reckoned unreckonable, immeasurable.

Gladsome before the gift, giving satisfied,
Uplifted having given—that's bounty's[2] fulness.[3]
Lust-freed, hate-freed, delusion-freed, stainless,
Controlled Brahma-wayfarers[4]—that's the best field for bounty.

If one but cleanse[5] himself and give by hand,
For self hereafter, [6]too, great is the fruit.
So giving—faithful, wise, heart-free, discreet—
In the sorrowless, happy world he'll rise.'[7]

§ viii (38). *Self-acting.*

Now a certain brāhman visited the Exalted One, greeted him and, after exchanging the usual polite talk, sat down at one side. So seated, he said to the Exalted One: 'This, Master Gotama, is my avowal, this my view: There is no self-agency; no other-agency.'[8]

---

[1] See above, p. 43, *n*. 2.

[2] *Yañña*.

[3] *Sampadā*. *Comy*. *paripuṇṇatā*, fulfilment.

[4] *Saññatā brahmacārayo*, restrained god-way-ers.

[5] The *Comy*. takes this literally: washing his feet and hands, rinsing his mouth.

[6] *Parato ca*. *Comy*. is silent.

[7] The last line of the text recurs at *It*. 16 and 52.

[8] This is Makkhali Gosala's heresy; see *Dial*. i, 71; *K.S*. iii, 169; *P.E.D*. *s.v*. *atta* and *para* seems to interpret *atta-kāra*, *para-* wrongly; see *DA*. i, 160. *Crit*. *Pāli Dict*. has 'own act'; so Nyāṇatiloka.

'Never, brāhman, have I seen or heard of such an avowal, such a view. Pray, how can one[1] step onwards, how can one step back, yet say: There is no self-agency; there is no other-agency?

What think you, brāhman, is there such a thing as initiative?'[2]

'Yes, sir.'

'That being so, are men known to initiate?'

'Yes, sir.'

'Well, brāhman, since there is initiative and men are known to initiate, this is among men the self-agency, this is the other-agency.

What think you, brāhman, is there such a thing as stepping[1] away . . . stepping forth . . . halting[3] . . . standing . . . and stepping towards anything?'

'Yes, sir.'

'That being so, are men known to do all these things?'

'Yes, sir.'

'Well, brāhman, since there are such things as stepping away, stepping forth and the rest, and men are known to do these things, this is among men the self-agency, this is the other-agency. Never, brāhman, have I seen or heard of such an avowal, such a view as yours. Pray, how can one step onwards,[4] step back and say: There is no self-agency, there is no other-agency?'

'This, indeed, is wonderful,[4] Master Gotama . . .! And henceforth, till life ends, I will go to Master Gotama for help.'

---

[1] √*kram*, to walk, with the prefixes *abhi*, *paṭi*, *nis*, *parā* and *upa*.

[2] *Ārabbhadhātu: ārabbha*, gerund of *ārādheti*, to set on foot; *dhātu*, element, property, condition. *Comy. sabhāva*, 'essence.'

[3] *Thāma* and *ṭhiti*, both from √*sthā*; the former is, I suppose, a causative formation.

[4] *Abhikkamanto* and *abhikkantaŋ*, respectively. Were the latter not 'stock,' we might see a pun here in *abhikkantaŋ*, which means equally 'going forward' (*kram*) and 'very charming' (*kānta*).

§ ix (39). *The means.*[1]

'Monks, there are these three means to heap up[2] deeds. What three ?

Greed is a means to heap up deeds; hate is a means to heap up deeds; delusion is a means to heap up deeds.

Monks, not from greed does not-greed heap up, but from greed surely greed heaps up; not[3] from hate does not-hate heap up, but from hate surely hate heaps up; not from delusion does non-delusion heap up, but from delusion surely delusion heaps up.

Monks, not of deeds, greed-born, hate-born, delusion-born, are devas, are men, nor they who fare along the happy way; monks, of deeds born of greed, hate, delusion, hell is, brute-birth is, the ghost-realm is, and they who fare along the evil way.

Verily, monks, these are the three means to heap up deeds.

Monks, there are these three means to heap up deeds. What three ?

Not-greed is a means to heap up deeds; not-hate is a means to heap up deeds; non-delusion is a means to heap up deeds.

Monks, not from not-greed does greed heap up, but from not-greed surely not-greed heaps up; not from not-hate does hate heap up, but from not-hate surely not-hate heaps up; not from non-delusion does delusion heap up, but from non-delusion surely non-delusion heaps up.

Monks, not of deeds, born of not-greed, not-hate, non-delusion, is hell, brute-birth, the ghost-realm, nor they who fare along the evil way; monks, of deeds, born of not-greed, not-hate, non-delusion, devas are, men are, and they who fare along the happy way.

Verily, monks, these are the three means to heap up deeds.'

§ x (40). *The venerable Kimbila.*

Thus have I said: Once, when the Exalted One dwelt at Kimbilā in Bamboo Grove,[4] the venerable Kimbila visited

---

[1] *Nidāna*, binding on to, $\sqrt{d\bar{a}}$, cause.

[2] *Samudaya.* *Comy.* *piṇḍa-karaṇ' atthāya* (snow)-ball-like. *Cf.* *Ecclesiastes* ii, 26.

[3] *Dhp.* 5 of *vera.*

[4] So text; *Comy.* and *S.e.* *Nicula*; *cf.* *S.* v, 322.

him and, after saluting, sat down at one side. So seated, the venerable Kimbila[1] said to the Exalted One:

'Lord, what reason is there, what cause, whereby, when the Tathāgata has passed away, Saddhamma shall not endure ?'

'Consider, Kimbila, monk, nun and lay-disciple, man and woman, how, when the Tathāgata has passed away, they may dwell without reverence, without respect for the Master; without reverence, without respect for Dhamma; without reverence, without respect for the Order; without reverence, without respect for the training; without reverence, without respect for zeal; without reverence, without respect for good-will. This, Kimbila, is a reason, this a cause, whereby, when the Tathāgata has passed away, Saddhamma shall not endure.'

'But what reason is there, lord, what cause, whereby, when the Tathāgata has passed away, Saddhamma shall endure ?'

'Kimbila, let monk and nun, lay-disciple, man and woman, live with reverence and respect for the Master, Dhamma, Order, training, zeal and good-will; and it shall be a reason, a cause, whereby, when the Tathāgata has passed away, Saddhamma shall endure.'

§ xi (41). *The log of wood.*

Thus have I heard: Once, when the venerable Sāriputta dwelt on Mount Vulture Peak near Rājagaha, he robed early and, taking bowl and cloak, descended the hill with many monks in company.

Now at a certain spot the venerable Sāriputta saw a large log of wood; and there he addressed the monks and said:

'See you, reverend sirs, that large log of wood ?'

'Yes, sir,' they replied.

'An adept[2] monk, reverend sirs, won to mind-control, can, if he wish, view[3] it as earth. Wherefore ? There is, sirs,

---

[1] A Sakyan who joined the Order with Ānanda (*Vin.* ii, 182); he was presumably much exercised over this matter, for *cf.* V, § 201 (*A.* iii, 247) and *A.* iv, 84. *Cf.* also *K.S.* ii, 152; v, 151.

[2] *Iddhimā.*

[3] *Adhimucceyya. Comy. sallakkheyya,* ? trace therein.

in that log of wood the earth element; hence an adept can view it as earth.

He can, if he wish, view it as water . . . as fire . . . as air . . . as beautiful . . . as ugly. Wherefore? There are, reverend sirs, the elements of all these things in that log of wood, whence an adept, won to mind-control, can view that log in such ways.'

§ xii (42). *The venerable Nāgita.*

Thus have I said: Once[1] the Exalted One walked a walk with a great company of monks among the Kosalese and came to a Kosalan brāhman village called Icchānangala. And there in the Icchānangala grove the Exalted One dwelt.

Now the brāhman householders of that place heard: 'The recluse, Master Gotama, the Sakya, gone forth from the Sakya clan, has arrived at Icchānangala and stays in the grove hard by; and of that same Master Gotama this fair report is noised abroad: "He is the Exalted One, arahant, fully enlightened, perfected in knowledge and way . . . awake, exalted. . . ." 'Tis good indeed to see such arahants!'

Then at dawn those brāhman householders went to the grove, taking with them much hard and soft food; and they stood at the gateway making a great tumult.

Now at that time the venerable Nāgita served the Exalted One.

Then said the Exalted One to the venerable Nāgita: 'What is this great tumult, Nāgita? 'Tis as though fisher-folk had caught a great haul!'

'These, lord, are the Icchānangala brāhman householders, who have brought much hard and soft food for the Exalted One and the monks; and they now stand without.'

'*I* have naught to do with homage, Nāgita, nor need I homage. Whosoever cannot obtain at will, freely, readily, the ease of renunciation, the ease of seclusion, the ease of calm, the ease of enlightenment, as I can, let him wallow[2]

---

[1] This sutta with two more items and some variation recurs at *A.* iv, 340; see above, *Fives*, § 30.

[2] *Sādiyeyya*, no doubt from $\sqrt{svad}$, but possibly from $\sqrt{sad}$.

in that dung-like[1] ease, that clog[2] of ease, that ease gotten of gains, favours and flattery.'

'Lord, let the Exalted One accept their offering now; let the Well-gone accept! Lord, now is the time to accept; for whithersoever the Exalted One shall henceforth go, the brāhman householders of town and countryside shall be so inclined. Lord, just as when the rain-deva rains abundantly, the waters flow with the incline; even so, lord, whithersoever the Exalted One shall go the brāhman householders shall be so inclined. And why? So great, lord, is the Exalted One's virtue and wisdom.'

'*I* have naught to do with homage, Nāgita, nor need I homage; but whosoever cannot obtain at will, freely, readily, the ease of renunciation, seclusion, calm, enlightenment, as I can, let him wallow in that dung-like ease, that clog of ease, that ease gotten of gains, favours and flattery.

Suppose, Nāgita, I see a monk seated, rapt, on the outskirts of some village; then I think: "Presently a park-man or a novice will disturb the reverend sir and will oust him from that concentration." So, Nāgita, I am not pleased with that monk's abode.

Or I see one forest-gone, seated nodding in the forest; then I think: "Presently he will dispel sleep and fatigue, attend to the forest-sense[3] and solitude." So, Nāgita, I am pleased with his forest-abiding.

Or I see one forest-gone, seated, rapt; then I think: "Presently he will compose the uncomposed mind or will continue to ward the freed mind." So, Nāgita, I am pleased with his forest-abiding.

Or I see one living on a village outskirts, getting the requisites: robe, alms, bed and medicaments; and, delighting in those gains, favours and flattery, he neglects to go apart, neglects the forest, the woodland ways, the lonely lodgings; he gets his living by visiting village, town and capital. So, Nāgita, I am not pleased with his abiding.

Or I see a monk, forest-gone, getting the requisites, but staving off gains, favours and flattery, neglecting not to go

---

[1] *Miḷha-*. [2] *Middha-*. [3] *Arañña-saññaṃ*. *Cf. Th.* I, *ver.* 110.

apart, neglecting not the woodland ways, the lonely lodgings. So, Nāgita, I am pleased with that monk's forest-abiding.

But when walking along the highway, Nāgita, I see nothing whatever in front nor behind, it suits[1] me, even over the calls of nature.'

CHAPTER V.—DHAMMIKA.

§ i (43). *The elephant.*[2]

Once, when the Exalted One dwelt near Sāvatthī at Jeta Grove in Anāthapiṇḍika's Park, he robed early and, with cloak and bowl, entered Sāvatthī for alms. And having gone his round in Sāvatthī, on his return, after his meal, he said to the venerable Ānanda:

'Let us go, Ānanda, to Migāra's mother's terraced house in East Park, where, when we are come, we will spend the noon-tide.'

'Yes, lord,' replied the venerable Ānanda; and the Exalted One went there with him.

Then in the evening the Exalted One, risen from solitude, said to him: 'Come, Ānanda, we will go to the bathing-place[3] and bathe our limbs.'

'Yes, lord,' he replied; and they went there together. And when he had bathed and come out, the Exalted One stood in a single garment, drying himself.[4]

Now at that time Seta, an elephant of rajah Pasenadi of Kosala, came out of the bathing-place to the sound of many drums and all kinds of music; and folk about, marvelling[5] at the sight, said:

'What a beauty, sirs, is the rajah's elephant; what a picture; what a treat for the eye; what a body he has! The elephant, sirs, is indeed an elephant!'[6]

---

[1] *Phāsu me*; one wonders what he would have thought modern highways suitable for!

[2] *Nāgo*, elephant, serpent and fairy-demon; a phenomenon, prodigy.

[3] *Pubbakoṭṭhaka*; see *n.* at *K.S.* v, 195; but it can hardly refer to a gateway here, but simply an enclosure (*precinct*).

[4] All this recurs at *M.* i, 161; *cf.* also *S.* i, 8; below, § 62.

[5] *Api 'ssu.*

[6] *Nāgo vata bho nāgo.*

And when this had been said, the venerable Udāyin[1] spoke thus to the Exalted One: 'Lord, do folk say: The elephant is indeed an elephant, only on seeing the huge, gross bulk of an elephant, or do they say it on seeing other gross, bulky things ?'

'Folk say it, Udāyin, when they see the huge, gross bulk of an elephant; they say it, too, when they see a huge horse or a bull or a snake or a tree; they say: "The nāga indeed is a nāga !" even when they see a huge man with a gross, fat body. But I declare, Udāyin, that in the deva-world with its Māras and Brahmās, and on earth with its recluses, godly men, devas and men—he who commits no enormity[2] in deed, word or thought, he is a nāga.'

'It is marvellous and amazing, lord—I mean these noble words of the Exalted One: "I declare that in the deva-world or on earth he who commits no enormity in deed, word or thought, he is a nāga.' And now, lord, I will give thanks in verse for the Exalted One's noble words:

> A man and very[3] Buddha he, self-tamed,
> Composed, who treads the deathless path, serene
> In joy, transcending all; whom men adore,
> Whom devas laud—thus have I heard of him,
> The Arahant.[4] All fetters he hath left,
> From jungle to Nibbāna[5] come, his joy
> Lives in renouncing worldly lusts; as gold
> From quarried quartz, that nāga outshines all;
> As Himalay[6] o'er other crags—whose name
> Is Truth o'ertops all nāgas so yclept.

---

[1] *Comy.* Kāḷ' Udāyin; see *Brethr.* 287 (the verses recur there, *Thag.* 689-704); *G.S.* i, 20. *Comy.* explains that 500 monks accompanied the Buddha.

[2] *Āguŋ na karoti, taŋ nāgo.* The poet is less crude in *Th.* 693; *na hi āguŋ karoti so. Cf. Sn. ver.* 522.

[3] *Sam-buddha.*

[4] *Arahato. Brethr.* 'I, an arahant.'

[5] *S.e.* and *Thag. vanā nibbanaŋ āgataŋ.*

[6] Text *himavā 'ññe, S.e. maññe, Comy.* so, with *v.l.* *'v' aññe* with *Thag.*, which is no doubt correct; in Sinhalese script *v*, *c* and *m* are somewhat similar.

Lo! I will limn this nāga-elephant,
Who no enormity commits: Mildness
And harmlessness his forefeet are, his hinder
Austerity and godly life; be-trunked
With faith, white-tusked with equanimity,
His neck is mindfulness, his head is insight;
Each Dhamma-thought's a test;[1] and Dhamma's garner[2]
His belly is, his tail is solitude.
Rapt muser, calm, well self-composed, whose breath
Is zest[3]—that nāga walks composed, composed
He stands, composed he lies, composed he sits,
A nāga e'er controlled—for he is perfect.
Blameless he feeds, nor feeds on foolishness;
Ration and robe he gets and shuns the hoard;
He snappeth every tie, bonds fine and coarse;
He goes where'er he will, he goes care-free.
See how the lovely lotus, water-born,
Sweet-scented, ne'er by water is defiled:[4]
The Buddha, born as very[5] man, puts by
The world and by the world is undefiled,
As lily by the water of the lake.
As blazing fire goes out thro' want of fuel,
And men, of ashes,[6] say: " The fire's gone out!"—
This is a parable of rare presage,[7]

---

[1] *Vīmaŋsā dhamma-cintanā. Comy.* likens this to the elephant feeling with his trunk; *vīmaŋsā*, investigation, is one of the four *Iddhipādas*; see V, § 67.

[2] Text reads *samātapo, v.l. samācāpo*; but *Comy.* and *S.e. samāvāpo*, explaining: *kucchi yeva samāvāpo, samāvāpo nāma samāvāpana-ṭṭhānaŋ. P.E.D.* omits, but the compound seems to occur in *Skt.*; see Macdonell's Dict. *s.v.* $\sqrt{vap}$. At *M.* i, 451 we have *samavāpaka*, a store-room; *Thag.* reads *samāvāso*.

[3] *Assāsa-rato. Comy.* refers this to the *assāsa-passāsa* exercises; see *K.S.* v, 257 *ff.*

[4] *Cf. Sn.* 547; *A.* ii, 39; *Chān. Up. S.B.E.* i, 67; *Bhag. Gītā*, 5, 10.

[5] *Su-jāto*; see *P.E.D. s.v. su* as to its use as *sam-*.

[6] Text and *S.e. sankhāresûpasantesu*, but *Thag.* with our *v.l. angāresu ca santesu*, which I follow.

[7] The text reads *atth' assâyaŋ viññāpanī* for *atthassâyaŋ*; *cf. D.* i, 114; *M.* ii, 260.

Taught by wise men—great nāgas by a nāga
Are recognized when by a nāga[1] taught—
Lust-freed, hate-freed, delusion-freed, stainless,[2]
This nāga, body-freed, shall " go out "[3] freed.'

§ ii (44). *Migasālā.*[4]

One morning the venerable Ānanda, robing early, took bowl and cloak and went to the house of the lay-disciple, Migasālā, and there sat down on seat made ready. And Migasālā came and saluted him and sat down at one side.

So seated, she said to the venerable Ānanda:

'Pray, reverend sir, how ought one to understand this Dhamma taught by the Exalted One: that both he who lives the godly life and he who does not shall become like-wayfarers in the world to come ?

My father, sir, Purāṇa,[5] lived the godly life, dwelling apart, abstaining from common, carnal things; and when he died, the Exalted One explained: He's a Once-returner, dwelling in Tusita.

My uncle,[6] sir, Isidatta, did not live the godly life but rejoiced with a wife; and of him also, when dead, the Exalted One said: He's a Once-returner, dwelling in Tusita.

Reverend Ānanda, how ought one to understand this Dhamma . . . ?'

'Even, sister, as the Exalted One has said.'[7] And when the venerable Ānanda had received alms in Migasālā's house, he rose from his seat and departed.

Now on his return from alms-gathering, after his meal, the venerable Ānanda visited the Exalted One, saluted him

---

[1] Text misprints *nāyena* for *nāgena*. [2] *Cf.* above VI, § 37.

[3] *Comy.*, *S.e.* and *Thag. parinibbissati.* The *thera* is here no doubt prophesying, so above I take *attha* as presage.

[4] *Cf.* the whole sutta with *A.* v, 137 *ff.*

[5] These two brothers were the rajah Pasenadi's chamberlains or chariot makers; see *K.S.* v, 303 *ff.*

[6] Text *petteyyo piyo* with *S.e.*, see *Childers*; but at *A.* v, *pettāpiyo* with *Tr. P.M.* 62, 16.

[7] *Comy.* observes that Ānanda did not know the answer.

and sat down at one side; and so seated, he told the Exalted One all that had occurred . . .[1] adding: 'I told her, lord, to understand the matter even as the Exalted One had explained.'

'But, Ānanda, who is the lay-disciple, Migasālā—a foolish, frail, motherly body with but mother-wit—to understand the diversity in the person of man ?[2]

These six persons, Ānanda, are found in the world. What six ?

Consider, Ānanda, one well restrained, a comely person, in whose company his fellows in the godly life take pleasure; yet in whom hearing (Dhamma) is of none effect, much learning is of none effect,[3] in whom there is no view-penetration, who wins not temporary release[4]—he, on the breaking up of the body after death, sets out to fall, not to excel; fares to a fall, fares not to excellence.

Consider another well restrained likewise . . .; but in whom hearing (Dhamma) has effect, much learning has effect, in whom there is view-penetration, who wins temporary release—he, after death, sets out to excel, not to fall; fares to excellence, not to a fall.

And the measurers measure them, saying: "His stature[5] is just this, the other's just that; in what way is[6] one wanting, one exalted ?" And that measuring, Ānanda, is to the measurers' harm and hurt for many a day.

Now the one . . . in whom listening has effect . . . who wins temporary release—that person, Ānanda, has marched further forward, is more exalted than the former. And why

---

[1] The text repeats in full.

[2] The construction is peculiar (*cf. A.* iii, 237): *Kā ca Migasālā . . . ambakā, ambakapaññā* (*Comy., S.e.* and *A.* v, so for *saññā*) *ke ca purisapuggala-paropariyañāṇe.* (*Cf. K.S.* v, 270, § 10.) *Purisa-puggala* is possibly a transition from the more honourable *purisa* to the *puggala*, male, adopted by the Sangha when 'the man' concept was worsening.

[3] *Comy. ettha bāhusaccaŋ vuccati viriyaŋ viriyena kattabba-yuttakaŋ akataŋ hoti.* (*Cf.* Locke's definition of 'effect': the substance produced into any subject by the exerting of power.—*Webster's Eng. Dict.*)

[4] *Cf.* above, p. 131, *n.* 1.

[5] *Dhammā.* [6] *Kasmā.*

is that? The stream of Dhamma carries him forward,[1] Ānanda. But who save the Tathāgata can judge that difference?[2] Wherefore, Ānanda, be no measurer of persons; measure not the measure of persons; verily, Ānanda, he digs[3] a pit for himself who measures the measure of persons. I alone, Ānanda, can measure their measure—or one like me.

Consider, Ānanda, a person in whom wrath and pride are conquered, but in whom greed from time to time surges; in whom hearing (Dhamma) is of none effect . . .: and another . . . in whom hearing has effect . . .—he, after death, sets out to excel, not to fall; fares to excellence, not to a fall. . . . That person has marched further forward, is more exalted than the former. . . . I alone, Ānanda, can measure their measure. . . .

Consider one in whom wrath and pride are conquered, but in whom the whirl[4] of words from time to time surges; in whom hearing (Dhamma) and learning are of none effect, in whom there is no view-penetration, who wins not temporary release—he, after death, sets out to fall, not to excel; fares to a fall, fares not to excellence: and another, likewise, but in whom hearing (Dhamma) and learning have effect, in whom there is view-penetration, who wins temporary release—he, after death, sets out to excel, not to fall; fares to excellence, not to a fall.

And the measurers measure them likewise, and it is to their harm and hurt for many a day.

And in whom hearing (Dhamma) and learning have effect . . . that one has marched further forward, is more exalted than the former. And why? The Dhamma-stream carries him forward. But who save the Tathāgata can judge this difference? Wherefore, Ānanda, be no measurer of persons; measure not the measure of persons. Verily, Ānanda, he digs a pit for himself who measures the measure of persons.

---

[1] *Dhamma-soto nibbahati. Comy. Sūraŋ hutvā pavattamānaŋ vipassanāñāṇaŋ nibbahati, ariya-bhūmiŋ sampāpeti. Nibbahati* is either from √*barh*, to increase, or √*vah*, to carry, with *nis*, 'out,' 'to completion.'

[2] Reading *tadantaraŋ*, with *S.e.* and *Comy. taŋ antaraŋ, taŋ kāraṇaŋ*.

[3] *Khaññati. Comy. guṇa-khaṇanaŋ pāpuṇāti.*

[4] *Vacī-sankhārā*, speech activities; see *Vism.* 531, *trsl.* 633.

I alone, Ānanda, can measure their measure—or one like me.

And who is the lay-disciple, Migasālā—a foolish, frail, motherly body with but mother-wit—to understand the diversity in the person of man? Verily, Ānanda, these six persons are found in the world.

Ānanda, with such virtue as Purāṇa was endowed, Isidatta may become endowed; herein Purāṇa fares not Isidatta's way but another's: with such insight as Isidatta was endowed, Purāṇa may become endowed; herein Isidatta fares not Purāṇa's way but another's.

Thus verily, Ānanda, both these men are wanting in one thing.'

§ iii (45). *The debt.*

'Monks, is poverty a woeful thing for a worldly wanton?'

'Surely, lord.'

'And when a man is poor, needy, in straits,[1] he gets into debt; and is that woeful too?'

'Surely, lord.'

'And when he gets into debt, he borrows;[2] and is that woeful too?'

'Surely, lord.'

'And when the bill falls due,[3] he pays not and they press[4] him; is that woeful too?'

'Surely, lord.'

'And when pressed, he pays not and they beset[5] him; is that woeful too?'

'Surely, lord.'

'And when beset, he pays not and they bind him; is that woeful too?'

'Surely, lord.'

---

[1] *S.e.* with text *anāḷiko, Comy. anāḷhiyo*; see *P.E.D. s.v.*

[2] *Vaḍḍhiŋ paṭisuṇāti.*

[3] *Kālâbhataŋ vaḍḍhiŋ. P.E.D.* omits.

[4] *Codenti,* √*cud,* to urge; *cf. Sn.* 120.

[5] *Anucaranti pi naŋ. Comy.* they dog his footsteps and vex him, throwing mud at him in public or in a crowd, and do like things that cause pain (*ātapa-ṭṭhapana-*).

'Thus, monks, poverty, debt, borrowing, being pressed, beset and bound are all woes for the worldly wanton.

Monks, it is just the same for anyone who has no faith in right things, is not conscientious about right things, has no fear of blame about right things, no energy for right things, no insight into right things; he is said to be poor, needy, in straits, in the Ariyan discipline.

Now that very man—poor, needy, in straits, wanting in faith, conscientiousness, fear of blame, energy and insight concerning right things—works evilly in deed, word and thought. I call that his getting into debt. And to cloak[1] his evil deeds, he lays hold upon false hope:[2] "Let none know[3] this of me" he hopes; "Let none know this of me" he resolves; "Let none know this of me" he says; "Let none know this of me" he strives in act. So likewise to cloak his evil words . . . his evil thoughts. I call that his borrowing. Then his pious fellows in the godly life say thus: "This venerable sir acts in this sort, carries on in this way." I call that his being pressed. Then, gone to forest, tree-root or lonely place, evil, unrighteous thoughts and attendant remorse pursue him. I call that his being beset.

And that man, monks—poor, needy, in straits—having worked evilly in deed, word and thought, on the breaking up of the body after death, is bound in hell's bonds or the bonds of some beast's womb; and I see no other single bondage, monks,[4] so harsh, so bitter, such a bar to winning the unsurpassed peace from effort—I mean, hell's bonds or the bonds of a beast's womb.

Woeful i' the world is poverty and debt
'Tis said. See[5] how the poor wanton, plunged in debt,
Suffers, is then beset, e'en bound with bonds—
A woe indeed for one who pleasure craves!
So in the Ariyan discipline, who lives
Sans faith, sans shame, sans fear of blame, fashions[6]

---

[1] *Paṭicchādana-hetu.*

[2] *Pāpikaŋ icchaŋ paṇidahati*; *cf. Hebrews* vi, 18.

[3] With *Comy.* and *S.e. jaññā*; see *Sn. loc. cit.*

[4] *Cf. S.* ii, 226 *ff.*

[5] *Cf. Proverbs* xxi, 25-26.

[6] *Vinicchayo. Comy. vaḍḍhako.*

Ill deeds and, working evilly in deed,
In word and thought, hopes none shall know of it.
Wavering[1] in deed, in word, in thought, he breeds[2]
A brood of evil deeds, here, there, again—
Fool, evil-doer, who knows his own misdeeds,
He suffers as the wanton, plunged in debt!
Longings and evil thoughts in forest, town,
Beset him then, with black remorse's horde[3]—
Fool, evil-doer, who knows his own misdeeds,
For him a beast's womb waits or bonds in hell;
Those woeful bonds from which the sage is freed.

Who, gladdening, gives from plenty, justly won,
Casting a win both ways[4]—believing man,
Seeker of homely joys—for him here's weal,
Hereafter, bliss. Such is the goodman's standard,
For merit grows by generosity.[5]
So in the Ariyan discipline, who's set
In faith, wise, modest and by virtue ruled,
Is called "blythe dweller" in that discipline.
Erstwhile unsullied bliss he wins, then poise
Preserves;[6] the five bars[7] passed, with ardent zeal,
The musings enters, watchful, apt, intent;
Breaks all the bonds and knows reality;
And grasping naught, wholly his heart's released.
If in that high release, where life's[8] bonds break,
This gnosis comes: "Immutable's release!"
Then is that gnosis final, unsurpassed
That bliss, a griefless state of passionless peace—
That (for the saint) is debtlessness supreme.'

---

[1] *Saŋsappati. Comy. paripphandati*; *cf. A.* v, 289; *James* i, 6.

[2] *Pāpakammaŋ pavaḍḍhento.*

[3] *Yassa vippaṭisāra-jā. Comy. ye assa vippaṭisārato jātā.*

[4] *Ubhayattha kaṭa-ggāha*; *cf. Thag.* 462; *S.* iv, 352; *J.* iv, 322: referring to throwing dice.

[5] The two lines of the text recur at *A.* iv, 285; *cf.* also *J.P.T.S.*, 1909, 336.

[6] *Comy.* observes that these two refer to the third and fourth musings.

[7] Viz. lust, ill-will, torpor, worry and doubt. [8] *Bhava*, becoming.

§ iv (46). *Mahā Cunda.*

Thus have I heard: Once the venerable Mahā Cunda[1] lived among the Cetis[2] at Sahajātī;[3] and there he spoke to the monks, saying:

'Monks, reverend sirs!'

'Reverend sir,' they rejoined; and the venerable Mahā Cunda said:

'There are some monks, Dhamma-zealots,[4] who blame musers, saying: "These fellows say: 'We are musers, we are musers!' They muse and are bemused![5] And what do they muse about; what good's their musing; how muse they?" Thereat neither the Dhamma-zealots nor the musers are pleased; nor have they fared onwards for the weal of many folk, for their happiness, their good, nor for the weal and happiness of devas and men.

And there are some monks, musers, who blame Dhamma-zealots, saying: "These fellows say: 'We are Dhamma-zealots, we are Dhamma-zealots!' They are puffed up, proud, excitable fellows, mouthy speechifiers, forgetful of mindfulness, lacking self-possession and composure, with their thoughts a-wander and their sense-governance rude.[6] And what is their Dhamma zeal; what good's their Dhamma zeal; how are they zealous in Dhamma?" There, too, neither the musers nor the Dhamma-zealots are pleased; nor have they fared onwards for the weal of many folk. . . .

And there are some Dhamma-zealots who just praise Dhamma-zealots; who praise not musers. There, too, neither Dhamma-zealots nor musers are pleased. . . .

And so . . . neither are pleased; nor have they fared

---

[1] Sāriputta's younger brother; see *Brethr.* 119; above IV, § 17.

[2] *Buddh. India*, 26. Pronounced Ché-ti (Chay-tee).

[3] *Comy.* simply *nigame*; it was on the Ganges and was where Revata met the elders concerning the ten Vajjian heresies, *Vin* ii, 300 (*Vin. Texts*, iii, 396); *Mvaṃsa trsl.* 22; *C.H.I.* i, 214. *Cf. A.* v, 41 for another talk by Mahā Cunda there.

[4] *Dhamma-yogā bhikkhū.*

[5] *Jhāyanti pajjhāyanti. Comy. Upasagga-vasena vaḍḍhitāni.*

[6] *Pākaṭ' indriyā.*

onwards for the weal of many folk, for their happiness, their good, nor for the weal and happiness of devas and men.

Wherefore, sirs, you should train yourselves thus: Being Dhamma-zealots, we will praise musers. Thus should you train yourselves, reverend sirs. And why? Verily, sirs, these wondrous persons are hardly found in the world—they who live with their whole being in tune with the deathless.[1]

And you should train yourselves thus, reverend sirs: Being musers, we will praise Dhamma-zealots. Thus should you train yourselves, reverend sirs. And why? Verily, sirs, these wondrous persons are hardly found in the world—they who with insight penetrate and see the deep way of the goal.'[2]

§ v (47). *For this life* (*a*).

Now Sīvaka of the Top-knot,[3] a wanderer, visited the Exalted One, greeted him and, after exchanging the usual compliments, sat down at one side. So seated, he said to the Exalted One:

'They say, sir,[4] "Dhamma's for this life,[5] Dhamma's for this life!" But how, sir, is Dhamma for this life, for other worlds,[6] bidding "Come see," leading onwards, knowable to the wise by its relation to self?'[7]

'Come, Sīvaka, I will just question you in turn about this; answer as you please.

Now what think you, Sīvaka, suppose there's greed here in the self,[8] would you know: "There's greed here in myself"—or suppose there's no greed, would you know there was none?'

'Surely, sir.'

'Well, when you know there's either greed or none, thus is

---

[1] *Ye amataŋ dhātuŋ kāyena phusitvā viharanti.* Lit. 'live having touched with the body (or by act) the deathless conditions.'

[2] *Ye gambhīraŋ attha-padaŋ paññāya ativijjha passanti. Cf. A.* iv, 362. *Comy.* of course explains: *Gūḷhaŋ paṭicchannaŋ khandha-dhātu-āyatanâdi-atthaŋ.*

[3] *Moliya-sīvaka*; *cf. S.* iv, 230.

[4] *Bhante.*

[5] *Saŋ-* (*sa-* or *sayan* ?) *diṭṭhi-ka*. *Cf.* above VI, § 10.

[6] *Akāliko*, not of earthly time-measure.

[7] *Pacc-attaŋ.*

[8] *Ajjh-attaŋ. Comy. Niyakajjhatte.*

Dhamma for this life, for other worlds, bidding "Come see," leading onwards, knowable to the wise by its relation to self.

Then again, suppose there's hatred, infatuation . . . or otherwise . . .; suppose these three have some hold[1] . . . or otherwise . . . would you know in each case that that was so ?'

'Surely, sir.'

'Well, when you know it, thus is Dhamma for this life, for other worlds, bidding "Come see," leading onwards, knowable to the wise by its relation to self.'

'This is indeed wonderful, sir ! . . . Henceforth, till life ends, I will go to the Exalted One for help.'

§ vi (48). *The same* (*b*).

Then a brāhman approached the Exalted One, greeted him in like manner, sat down and[2] . . . asked how Dhamma was for this life. . . .

'Answer my questions as you think fit, brāhman. How is it with you: do you know when you are passionate or not ?'

'Surely, Master Gotama.'

'Well, when you know it, thus Dhamma is for this life. . . . Again, do you know when you hate, are infatuated . . . or otherwise . . .; or when there is self-defilement[3] in deed, word and thought . . . or otherwise ?'

'Surely, sir.'

'Well, when you know it, thus is Dhamma for this life, for other worlds, bidding "Come see," leading onwards, knowable to the wise by its relation to self.'

'This is indeed wonderful, Master Gotama ! . . . Henceforth, till life ends, I will go to Master Gotama for help.'

§ vii (49). *Khema.*

Once, when the Exalted One was dwelling near Sāvatthī, at Jeta Grove in Anāthapiṇḍika's Park, the venerable Khema[4]

---

[1] *-dhammaṃ.* [2] The text repeats. [3] *Kāya-san-dosaṃ.*

[4] Khema does not seem to be mentioned elsewhere and the *Comy.* is silent; two Sumanas are mentioned in *Thag.* *Cf.* *K.S.* iii, 107, 'Khemaka.'

and the venerable Sumana dwelt in Andha[1] Grove, near Sāvatthī. And they went and visited the Exalted One, saluted him, and sat down at one side. So seated, the venerable Khema said to him:

'Lord, whatsoever monk is arahant, has destroyed the cankers, lived the life, done what ought to be done, set down the burden, found the highest goal,[2] destroyed becoming's bonds, and is in high gnosis released, to him there comes no thought: "There is one better than I,"[3] nor "There is one equal," nor "There is one worse."'

Thus spoke the venerable Khema and the Master approved; and seeing that, the venerable Khema got up, saluted the Exalted One and took his departure, passing him by on the right.

Now, not long after he had gone, the venerable Sumana said this to the Exalted One: 'Lord, whatsoever monk is arahant, has destroyed the cankers, lived the life, done what ought to be done, set down the burden, found the highest gain, destroyed becoming's bonds and is in high gnosis released, to him there comes no thought: "There is none better than I," nor "There is none equal," nor "There is none worse."'

Thus spoke the venerable Sumana and the Master approved; and seeing that, the venerable Sumana got up, saluted, and took his departure, passing by on the right.

And shortly after they had gone, the Exalted One addressed the monks, saying: 'Thus, monks, do clansmen declare gnosis; the goal is told, but self is not mentioned. Yet there are some foolish fellows here who declare gnosis braggingly, it seems. Afterwards they suffer remorse.[4]

---

[1] *K.S. trsl.* 'Dark Wood,' see note at i, 160 and more particularly Watters' *Chwang*, i, 397-398; Beal's '*Records*,' ii, 13.

[2] *Anu-ppatta-sa-d-attho. Cf. D.* iii, 83; *M.* i, 4; *S.* i, 71.

[3] *Atthi me seyyo*; *cf. Brethr.* 366; *Dhs.* § 1116. *Comy.* calls these *mānā*, conceits.

[4] This para. recurs at *Vin.* i, 185; *cf. A.* i, 218; *G.S.* i, 198 *n.* There is a play on the words in the text, *attho* and *attā*. *Cf.* also Mrs. Rhys Davids' *Buddhhism*, 216; *cf. Milinda*, 396.

None greater, less, the same![1]—these sway them not:
Lived is the godly life, ended the being born,[2]
And from all bonds released, they journey on.'

§ viii (50). *The senses.*

'Monks,[3] when sense-control is not, virtue perforce[4] is destroyed in him who has fallen[5] away from sense-control; when virtue is not, right concentration is perforce destroyed in him . . .; when concentration is not, true knowledge and insight are perforce destroyed in him; when true knowledge and insight are not, aversion and dispassion are perforce destroyed in him; when aversion and dispassion are not, emancipated knowledge and insight are perforce destroyed in him who has fallen away from aversion and dispassion.

Monks, imagine a tree with branches and leaves fallen away: its buds come not to maturity, nor its bark, sapwood or heart; even so, monks, when the sense-control is not, virtue is perforce destroyed. . . .

Monks, when sense-control exists, virtue perforce thrives[6] in him, thriving in sense-control; when there is virtue, concentration perforce thrives . . .; when concentration—true knowledge and insight; when true knowledge and insight—aversion and dispassion; when aversion and dispassion, emancipated knowledge and insight perforce thrive. . . .

Monks, imagine a tree with thriving branches and leaves: its buds, bark, sapwood and heart come to maturity; even so, monks, when sense-control exists, virtue perforce thrives. . . .'

§ ix (51). *Ānanda.*

Now the venerable Ānanda visited the venerable Sāriputta, greeted him and, after exchanging the usual polite talk, sat down at one side. So seated, the venerable Ānanda said this to the venerable Sāriputta:

---

1 *Cf. Sn.* 954. 2 *Sañ-jāti.*
3 See above V, § 24 and references there.
4 *Hat' upanisaŋ. Comy. -upanissayaŋ.* On *A.* iv, 99: *chinna-paccayo.*
5 *Vi-panna,* from √*pad,* to fall. 6 *Sampanna.*

'How, reverend Sāriputta, may a monk learn new[1] doctrine and doctrines learnt remain unconfused, and old doctrines, to which erstwhile he was mentally attuned,[2] remain in use and he get to know something not known?'

'The venerable Ānanda is very learned;[3] let the venerable one illuminate[4] this.'

'Well then, reverend Sāriputta, listen, pay good heed and I will speak.'

'Yes, sir,' he rejoined; and the venerable Ānanda said:

'Consider, reverend Sāriputta, a monk who masters Dhamma:[5] the sayings, psalms, catechisms, songs, solemnities, speeches, birth stories, marvels and runes—as learnt, as mastered, he teaches others Dhamma in detail; as learnt, as mastered, he makes others say it in detail; as learnt, as mastered, he makes others repeat it in detail; as learnt, as mastered, he ever reflects, ever ponders over it in his heart, mindfully he pores on it. Wheresoever abide elders, learned[6] in traditional lore, Dhamma-minders, discipline-minders, epitomists, there he spends Was;[7] and visiting them from time to time, questions and inquires of them: "This talk, sir, what, verily, is its aim?"[8]—and their reverences disclose the undisclosed, make, as it were, a causeway[9] where there is none, drive away doubt concerning many perplexing things.

In this way, reverend Sāriputta, a monk may learn new doctrine, and doctrines learnt remain unconfused, old doctrines, to which erstwhile he was mentally attuned, remain in use and he gets to know something not known.'

---

[1] *A-ssuta*, not heard.

[2] *Cetasā samphuṭṭha-pubbā. Comy. cittena phusita-pubbā.*

[3] Lit. 'has heard much.'

[4] *Cf.* above V, § 170. [5] *Cf.* V, § 73.

[6] *Āgatâgamā dhamma-dharā vinaya-dharā mātikā-dharā*; *cf. A.* i, 117. On the last *Comy.* observes: *dve pātimokkha-dharā.*

[7] *Vassam upeti*, that is the rainy season, Lent; this lasts four months, June to October, and monks then may not travel; thus it is a Retreat, but I borrow the short Sinhalese word.

[8] Or 'meaning.'

[9] *An-uttānī-kataŋ uttānī-karonti*, from √*tan* and √*kṛ*.

'Excellent, amazing, reverend sir, is all this that has been so well said by the venerable Ānanda; and we will mind that the venerable one is endowed with these six things:

The venerable Ānanda masters Dhamma: the sayings, psalms and the rest; the venerable Ānanda teaches others Dhamma in detail, as learnt, as mastered; the venerable Ānanda makes others say it; the venerable Ānanda makes others repeat it; the venerable Ānanda reflects, ponders, pores on it; wheresoever learned elders abide, there the venerable Ānanda spends Was, and he questions them: "This talk, sir, what is its aim?"[1]—and they disclose the undisclosed, make a causeway where there is none, drive away doubt concerning many perplexing things.'

§ x (52). *The noble.*

Now brāhman Jānussoṇi[2] approached the Exalted One, greeted him and, after exchanging the usual polite talk, sat down at one side. So seated, he said: 'Master Gotama, what's a noble's aim,[3] what's his quest, what's his resolve, what's his want, what's his ideal?'

'Brāhman, wealth's a noble's aim, wisdom's his quest, power's his resolve, the earth's his want, dominion's his ideal.'

'And a brāhman's, Master Gotama, what's his aim, quest and the rest . . .?'

'Wealth's his aim, wisdom's his quest, mantras are his resolve, sacrifices his want, Brahma-world is his ideal.'

'And a householder's, Master Gotama . . .?'

'Wealth's his aim, wisdom's his quest, craft's his resolve, work's his want, work's end is his ideal.'

'And a woman's, Master Gotama . . .?'

'Man's her aim, adornment's her quest, a son's her resolve, to be without[4] a rival is her want, dominion's her ideal.'

---

[1] Or 'meaning.'

[2] He lived at Manasākaṭa in Kosala; see *D.* i, 235; *M.* i, 16; *A.* i, 56; *S.* ii, 76, etc.

[3] *Adhippāya, upavicāra, adhiṭṭhāna, abhinivesa* (*Comy.* and *v.l.* also *vinivesa*), *pariyosāna.*

[4] *A-sapati-.* *Comy.* with *v.l.* *-sapatti-*, but *S.e.* *-sapati-.* *Comy.* observes: she thinks *Asapattī hutvā ekikā 'va ghare vaseyyan- ti.*

'And a thief's, Master Gotama . . .?'

'Booty's his aim, capture's his quest, a caravan's his resolve, darkness is his want, not to be seen is his ideal.'

'And a recluse's, Master Gotama . . .?'

'Patience and forbearance are his aim, wisdom's his quest, virtue's his resolve, nothing's[1] his want, Nibbāna's his ideal.'

'Wonderful, wonderful, Master Gotama! Verily, Master Gotama knows the aim, quest, resolve, want and ideal of nobles . . . brāhmans, householders, women, thieves and recluses! This is indeed wonderful, Master Gotama . . . and from henceforth, till life ends, I will go to Master Gotama for help.'

§ xi (53). *Earnestness.*[2]

Then another brāhman visited the Exalted One, greeted him, exchanged compliments and sat down at one side. So seated, he said:

'Master Gotama, is there one thing which, when made become, made to increase, embraces and establishes two weals: weal here and weal hereafter?'

'There is, brāhman. . . .''

'What is it, Master Gotama . . .?'

'Verily, earnestness, brāhman, is the one thing which, when made become, made to increase, embraces and establishes two weals: weal here and weal hereafter.

Brāhman, as the footmarks[3] of all prowling[4] creatures are admitted in an elephant's and the elephant's foot[5] is counted chief; so earnestness is the one thing which, when made become, made to increase, embraces and establishes two weals: weal here and weal hereafter.

---

[1] We should read *ākiñcañña* with *Comy.* and *S.e.* for *a-* in text.

[2] *Appamāda* ('*Appamādena sampādetha*'—*ayaŋ Tathāgatassa pacchimā vācā*); see *K.S.* i, 111 *n.* on this word; as *eko dhammo*, the one thing, *cf. D.* iii, 272 and ref. there; *It.* 16. There are six similes, hence this sutta's inclusion.

[3] *Pada-jātāni*, either 'characteristics' or 'footprints'; *cf. K.S.* and *F. Dial.* i, 133, also *A.* v, 21.

[4] *Jaṅgama*; see *K.S.* v, 34 *n.*, from $\sqrt{gam}$, with intensive *ja*; *cf. jagat.*

[5] *S.e.* with our text omits 'in size,' other texts include.

As[1] all rafters in a peaked house reach to the peak, slope to the peak, unite in the peak, and the peak is counted chief; so earnestness . . .

As a grass-cutter, on cutting grass,[2] grasps it at the top and shakes it to and fro and beats[3] it about; so earnestness . . .

As[4] in cutting mango fruit by the stalk, all the mangoes clustering thereon come away with the stalk; so earnestness . . .

As[5] every petty rajah becomes a follower of the Wheel-turning rajah and the Wheel-turner is counted chief; so earnestness . . .

As[6] the light of the stars is not worth a sixteenth part the light of the moon and the light of the moon is counted chief; so earnestness, brāhman, is the one thing which, when made become, made to increase, embraces and establishes two weals: weal here and weal hereafter.'

§ xii (54). *Dhammika.*[7]

Once, while the Exalted One was dwelling on Mount Vulture Peak near Rājagaha, the venerable Dhammika was a lodger in his native district.[8] And there were there altogether seven settlements.[9]

Now the venerable Dhammika went about insulting the monks who visited, reviling them, annoying them, nudging them, vexing them with talk; and they, so treated . . ., departed, nor settled there, but quitted the lodging.

And the local[8] lay-disciples thought to themselves: 'We're

---

[1] *Cf.* V, § 12; *S.* iii, 156; v, 43; *A.* v, 21.

[2] *Babbaja, balbaja*: *eleusine indica* (*Mcd.'s Skt. Dict.*), *K.S.* iii, 132.

[3] *S.e.* and *Comy. nicchedeti*; the latter gives the variant *nipphoṭeti*, observing: he beats it on his arm or on a tree.

[4] *D.* i, 46; *S.* iii, 156; *cf. Vism.* 356; *DA.* i, 128.

[5] *S.* v, 44; *A.* v, 22; *cf. M.* iii, 173.

[6] *It.* 19; *cf. A.* iv, 151; *J.* v, 63.

[7] He is no doubt the Dhammika of *Thag.* 303-306; *Brethr.* 185. Dhammapāla seems to have known our story but forgotten the details; he uses '*gāmakâvāsa*' for our '*jāti-bhūmi*.' He refers to the '*rukkhadhamma-jātaka*.' See below. *Vism.* 442 refers to a lay-disciple called Dhammika.

[8] *Jāti-bhūmi* and *-bhūmika*; *cf. M.* i, 145. *Comy.* is silent here, but on *M.* '*jāta-ṭṭhāna*,' observing that Kapilavatthu was the B.'s '*jātibhūmi*.'

[9] Precursors of the monastery.

ready enough with the requisites—robe, alms, lodging, medicaments—for the Order; yet visiting monks depart, nor settle here, but quit the lodging. What's the cause and reason for this?' And they thought: 'It's the venerable Dhammika! He insults the monks, reviles them . . . and vexes them with talk. Suppose we send him forth.' So they went to the venerable Dhammika and said to him: 'Sir, let the venerable Dhammika depart, long enough has he lodged here!' And the venerable Dhammika left that lodging for another.

There, too, he insulted visitors . . . and the laymen bade him go forth, saying: 'Depart, sir, you have lodged here long enough!' And he went to yet another lodging.

There, too, he insulted visitors . . . and there the laymen bade him go forth, saying: 'Sir, let the venerable Dhammika leave all seven local lodgings!'

Then thought the venerable Dhammika: 'I am sent forth by the local lay-disciples from all seven lodgings of my birthplace; where shall I go now?' And he thought: 'What if I visit the Exalted One?' So the venerable Dhammika, with robe and bowl, departed for Rājagaha, and in due time came to Mount Vulture Peak near Rājagaha; and approaching the Exalted One, saluted and sat down at one side.

And the Exalted One said to him, so seated: 'Well, brāhman Dhammika, whence come you?'

'Lord, I have been sent forth by the local lay-folk from the seven lodgings of my native district.'

'Come now, brāhman Dhammika, what's that to you? No matter where they have sent you forth[1] from, you have gone forth[1] thence to come to me!

In[2] times past, brāhman Dhammika, when seafaring

---

[1] *Pabbājenti* and *pabbājito*; there is a word-play; the latter means, also, gone forth into the Order, made a monk, ordained.

[2] This recurs at *D.* i, 222; *cf. J.* iii, 126, 267. *Comy.* says the bird was a 'quarter' crow. In the (possibly allied) story of Noah sending out birds from the ark, the raven did not return though it sighted no land. *A-tīra-dassin* was used of the untaught manyfolk, 'one who has not sighted the beyond': *K.S.* iii, 140 (*S.* iii, 164). (*J.* iii, 267 at *DA.* ii, 657 is called *Dhammika-vāyasa-jātaka*.)

merchants put to sea in ships, they took with them a bird to sight land. When the ship was out of sight of land, they freed the bird; and it flew eastward and westward, northward and southward, upward and around. And if the bird sighted land near by,[1] it was gone for good;[2] but if the bird saw no land, it returned to the ship.

Even so, brāhman Dhammika, no matter where they have sent you forth from, you have gone forth thence to come to me.

Long ago, brāhman Dhammika, rajah Koravya[3] had a king-banyan tree called Steadfast,[4] and the shade of its wide-spread[5] branches was cool and lovely. Its shelter broadened to twelve leagues, its roots spread to five and the great fruit thereof was in keeping—as big as pipkins[6] was the sweet fruit, clear and as sweet as the honey of bees.[7] And the rajah and his concubines enjoyed one portion of Steadfast, the army another; the town and country folk enjoyed one portion, recluses and godly men one portion, and one portion the beasts and birds enjoyed. None guarded its fruit and none hurt another for its fruit.

Now there came a man who ate his fill of fruit, broke a branch and went his way.

Thought the deva dwelling in Steadfast: "How amazing, how astonishing it is, that a man should be so evil as to break a branch off Steadfast, after eating his fill! Suppose Steadfast were to bear no more fruit!"

And Steadfast bore no more fruit.

Then, brāhman Dhammika, rajah Koravya visited Sakka, king of devas, and said: "Pray, your grace, know you that Steadfast, the king-banyan tree, bears no fruit?"

---

[1] Text *samantā*, but *Comy.* as well *sāmantā*.

[2] *Tathāgatako.*

[3] This may be the half-mythical Pañchāla king, Kraivya, *C.H.I.* i, 121.

[4] *Suppatiṭṭha*, *S.e.* so. Supatiṭṭha was a shrine near Rājagaha, *Vin.* i, 38.

[5] *Pañca-sākha*; see *Mcd. Skt. Dict. s.v.* $\sqrt{pañc}$.

[6] *Āḷhaka-thālikā. Comy. taṇḍulâḷhakassa bhattapacanathālikā.*

[7] *Khuddaŋ madhuŋ. Comy. khudda-makkhikāhi kataŋ daṇḍaka-madhuŋ.*

And Sakka, the deva-king, worked a work of mystic power so that there came a mighty wind and rain which smote Steadfast and overturned him. And the deva dwelling there was full of grief and despair and stood beside Steadfast, weeping and lamenting.

Then brāhman Dhammika, the deva-king, Sakka, approached the deva of the banyan tree and said: "What ails thee, deva . . . ?"

"Your grace, a mighty squall has come and overturned my home."[1]

"Came that squall, deva, whilst thou[2] keptest tree-Dhamma?"

"But how, your grace, keeps a tree tree-Dhamma?"

"Just thus, deva: The grubber takes the roots, the stripper the bark, the plucker the leaves, the picker the fruit, nor therefore is there any cause for the deva to mope and pine—thus keeps a tree tree-Dhamma."

"Your grace, I was not keeping tree-Dhamma, when the squall came and smote and overturned my home."

"Yet, deva, shouldst thou keep tree-Dhamma, thy home would be as of yore."

"Then I will keep tree-Dhamma, your grace; let my home be as of yore!"

And, brāhman Dhammika, the deva-king, Sakka, worked a work of mystic power and there came a mighty wind and rain which set up Steadfast, the king-banyan tree, and healed[3] his roots.

Did you, even so, brāhman Dhammika, keep recluse-Dhamma, when the local lay-folk sent you forth from each of the seven lodgings of your birthplace?'

'But how, lord, keeps a recluse recluse-Dhamma?'

'Thuswise, brāhman Dhammika: A recluse returns not

---

[1] *Bhavanaŋ*, haunt.

[2] *Api nu tvaŋ . . . ṭhitayā*; so also *S.e.* *Comy.* explains: *api nu tava*, and we should perhaps read *tavaŋ*.

[3] *Sacchavīni*. *Comy. samāna-cchavīni*; the *Burmese v.l. sañcharīni*; *cf. M.* ii, 216, 259.

the insult of the insulter, the anger of the angry, the abuse of the abuser[1]—thus keeps a recluse recluse-Dhamma.'

'Too true, lord, I kept not recluse-Dhamma when the local lay-folk sent me forth from the seven lodgings.'

'Long[2] ago, brāhman Dhammika, there was a teacher named Bright-Eyes,[3] a course-setter, freed of lust's passions. There were also Maimed-Mute[4] and Spoke-Rim[5] and Tiller[6] and Mahout[7] and Light-Ward,[8] all course-setters,[9] freed of lust's passions. And to each of these teachers there were many hundreds of disciples; and they taught their disciples Dhamma to win fellowship in Brahmā's world. Now those whose hearts gladdened not at the teaching, on the breaking up of the body after death, came to the wayward way, the ill way, the abyss, hell; but those whose hearts gladdened at the teaching, after death, came to the happy heaven-world.

Now what think you, brāhman Dhammika, would a man beget great demerit, were he, with ill wit, to insult, revile these six teachers, course-setters, freed of lust's passions, or the many hundreds of the disciples of their orders ?'

'Surely, lord.'

'Indeed, brāhman Dhammika, he would . . .; but he would beget greater demerit were he, with ill wit, to insult, revile a person with vision.[10] And why ? I declare, brāhman, that in the reviling of outsiders there is not so great a pit[11]

---

[1] *Cf. A.* ii, 215. *Comy.* and *S.e.* read, rightly, *rosentaŋ.*

[2] All this recurs at *A.* iv, 135; *cf.* also 103. The Dhamma taught is that of the Bodhisat, the *Amity-Dhamma*; see *J.* ii, 60; iv, 490; this is *Brahmavihāra* doctrine, *Exp.* 257 *ff.* Probably the six sages are rebirths of the Bodhisat. *Comy.* is silent.

[3] *Sunetta,* so *Comy.*; *J.* i, 35, 39.

[4] *Mūgapakkha, J.* i, 46; iv, 1; *Cariyāpiṭ.*, p. 96.

[5] *Aranemi*; refs. are lacking.

[6] *Kuddālaka, J.* i, 46.

[7] *Hatthipāla, J.* i, 45; iv, 473 *ff.*

[8] *Jotipāla, D.* ii, 230 *ff.*; *J.* i, 43; iii, 463.

[9] *Tittha-kara.*

[10] *Diṭṭhi-sampanna. Comy. sotāpanna.*

[11] *Evarupiŋ khantiŋ. Comy. attano guṇa-khaṇanaŋ*; possibly the reading is incorrect, but *S.e.* and our texts so. That *Comy.* gives the right meaning is confirmed by *akkhato; guṇa-khanaṇena* (*Comy.*) in the last line of the *gāthā.*

dug for oneself as in the reviling of one's fellows in the godly life.

Wherefore, brāhman Dhammika, train thus: We will think no ill of our fellows in the godly life. Verily, brāhman Dhammika, you should train yourself thus.

Brāhmans were Bright-Eyes, Maimed-Mute and Spoke-Rim,
A teacher Tiller and a prince[1] Mahout,
And Light-Ward, lord of bulls,[2] the seven's house-priest:
Six past-famed teachers who in harmlessness,
Not fetidness,[3] by pity freed,[4] lust's bonds
O'ercame, lust's passions purged, Brahmā's world won.

So too their many hundred followers
Unfetid and by pity freed, lust's bonds
O'ercame, lust's passions purged, Brahmā's world won.

Who with ill-fashioned wit revileth them,
Sages of other sects, lust-freed, composed—
That man shall great demerit thus beget:
But who with ill-fashioned wit revileth him,
The view-won monk-disciple of th' Awake—
That man by that demerit greater makes.

---

[1] *Māṇavo*; the *Jātakas* call him *Kumāra*.

[2] *Govinda*, *Dial.* ii, 266: 'Steward'; he was the chaplain, *purohita*, to rajah Reṇu and his six friends with whom he (Reṇu) shared his kingdom; our *Comy.* refers to this story.

[3] *Nir-āma-gandha*. *Comy. kodhâma-gandha*. However, even Light-Ward in the Dīgha story did not understand this word when used by Brahmā, the Eternal Youth! I quote the Rhys Davids translation:

'What mean'st thou by "foul odours among men,"
O Brahmā? Here I understand thee not.
Tell what these signify, who knowest all. . . .'

'Anger and lies, deceit and treachery,
Selfishness, self-conceit and jealousy,
Greed, doubt, and lifting hands 'gainst fellow-men,
Lusting and hate, dulness and pride of life,—
When yoked with these man is of odour foul,
Hell-doomed, and shut out from the heav'n of Brāhm.'

[4] *Karuṇe vimuttā*. *Comy. karuṇa-jjhāna vimuttā*; this is the second *brahma-vihāra*, godly state.

Vex[1] not the righteous, rid of groundless views,[2]
"Best man o' th' Ariyan Order" him they call;
Nor where lust's passions are but wholly stilled;[3]
Nor where the senses' edge is blunt;[4] nor where
Faith, mindfulness, zest, calm and insight sway:
Who vexes such, firstly is hurt himself;
Who hurts himself, thereafter harms another:
But who wards self, his outward[5] too is warded.
Hence ward thyself, digging no pit,[6] e'er wise.'

Chapter VI.—The Great Chapter.

§ i (55). *Soṇa.*

Thus have I heard: Once, when the Exalted One was dwelling near Rājagaha, on Mount Vulture Peak, the venerable Soṇa[7] dwelt in Cool Wood[8] near Rājagaha.

Now the venerable Soṇa, in solitude apart, communed thus in his heart: 'The Exalted One's disciples live in active energy and I am one of them; yet my heart is not detached and free of the cankers. My family is rich and I can enjoy riches and do good; what if I were to forsake the training and turn to low things, enjoy riches and do good!'

And the Exalted One, knowing in his own heart the venerable Soṇa's thoughts—as a strong man might stretch his bent arm or bend his stretched arm—left Mount Vulture Peak and appeared in Cool Wood before the venerable Soṇa. And when

---

[1] *Na sādhu-rūpaŋ āside. P.E.D.* suggests *na* should be omitted, but see *s.v. āsajja*; the meaning of *āside* here is the same as at *A.* iii, 69.

[2] *Diṭṭhi-ṭṭhāna-* (*Comy.* says 'the 62,' *D.* i, 1 *ff.*). The arahant is referred to.

[3] The Non-returner is referred to.

[4] *Cf. A.* ii, 151; the Once-returner is referred to.

[5] *Tassa bāhiro.*

[6] *Akkhato. Comy. guṇa-khananena.*

[7] This is Soṇa-Koḷivisa; see *Brethr.* 275 *ff.*; the whole sutta recurs at *Vin.* i, 179-185, where a fuller version is given; *VinA.* offers no comment on our part. Our *Comy.* explains that these thoughts arose owing to his having walked up and down (till his feet bled), without avail.

[8] Sītavana. *Comy.* says it was a cemetery.

his seat was ready, the Exalted One sat down; and the venerable Soṇa, after saluting, also sat down—at one side.

And the Exalted One said to him, so seated:

'Soṇa, did you not thus commune in your heart: "The Exalted One's disciples live in active energy and I am one of them; yet my heart is not detached and free of the cankers . . . what if I were to forsake the training and turn to low things . . . ?"'

'Yes, lord.'

'Bethink you, Soṇa, were you not, in the old days at home, clever at the lute's stringed music ?'[1]

'Yes, lord.'

'And bethink you, Soṇa, when your lute's strings were overstrung, was your lute then tuneful and playable ?'

'No, indeed, lord.'

'And bethink you, Soṇa, when your lute's strings were over-lax, was your lute then tuneful and playable ?'

'No, indeed, lord.'

'But when, Soṇa, your lute's strings were neither overstrung nor over-lax, but keyed to the middle pitch,[2] was your lute then tuneful and playable ?'

'Surely, lord.'

'Even so, Soṇa, energy, when overstrung, ends in flurry, when over-lax, in idleness. Wherefore, Soṇa, stand fast in the mean[3] of energy; pierce the mean (in the use) of the faculties; and therein grasp the real worth.'[4]

---

[1] *Comy.* quotes the following :

> *Satta sarā, tayo gāmā, mucchanā ekavīsati,*
> *Ṭhānā ekūnapaññāsaŋ, icc' ete sara-maṇḍalaŋ.*
> (Seven notes, three scales and one and twenty tones,
> Forty-nine stops,—such is the scope of music.)

P.E.D. generally omits these terms, but see *Childers s.v. sara*, quoting *Abhidhāna-ppadīpikā*.

[2] *Same guṇe patiṭṭhitā.*

[3] *Vin.* and *S.e.* read *viriya-samataŋ* with text, but *Comy. -samathaŋ*, explaining so; but see *Vism.* 129 (*trsl.* 150), *indriya-samatta-*; our *Comy.* refers to this passage. See note, *Brethr.* 277.

[4] *Nimittaŋ*, the salient feature in anything. This has nothing to do with the term in later Jhāna technique.

'Yes, lord.'

And the Exalted One, after charging the venerable Soṇa with this counsel—as a strong man might bend his arm to and fro—left Cool Wood and appeared on Mount Vulture Peak.

And presently[1] the venerable Soṇa stood fast in the mean of energy; pierced the mean in the faculties; and grasped therein the mark: and living alone, secluded, earnest, ardent, resolute, entered and abode, not long after, here amid things seen, by his own power, in the realization of that end above all of the godly life, for the sake of which clansmen rightly go forth from the home to the homeless life; and he knew: 'Birth is ended, the godly life lived, done is what was to be done, there is no more of this.'

And the venerable Soṇa was numbered among the arahants.

Then, having won to arahantship, the venerable Soṇa thought: 'Suppose I visit the Exalted One and declare gnosis[2] near him!' And he went to the Exalted One, saluted him, and sat down at one side; and so seated, he said:

'Lord, the arahant monk who has destroyed the cankers, lived the life, done what was to be done, set down the burden, won self-weal, shattered life's fetter and is freed by perfect gnosis,[3] has applied himself to six things: to dispassion, detachment, harmlessness, destroying craving, destroying grasping and to non-delusion.

Perhaps, lord, some venerable person may think: "Could it be that this venerable man has applied himself to dispassion relying on mere faith alone?" Let him not think so. Lord, the canker-freed monk, who has lived the life, done what was to be done, who sees naught in himself to be done, naught to be added to what has been done,[4]—by the fact of being passionless, has applied himself to dispassion by destroying passion; by the fact of being without hatred, has applied himself to dispassion by destroying hatred; by the fact of

---

[1] *Aparena samayena*
[2] *Aññā*, but *cf.* Thag. 632 *ff.*
[3] Read *sammadaññā-vimutto.*
[4] *Cf. Vin.* ii, 74; iii, 158; *S.* iii, 168; *A.* iv, 355.

being without delusion, has applied himself to dispassion by destroying delusion.

Or he may think: " Could it be that this venerable man has applied himself to detachment while hankering after gains, favours and flattery . . .; to harmlessness while backsliding from the true, holding rule and rite (as sufficient) . . .; to destroying craving . . .; to destroying grasping . . .; to non-delusion, holding rule and rite as sufficient ?" Let him not think so. Lord, the canker-freed monk . . ., by the fact of being without passion, hatred, delusion, has applied himself to detachment, harmlessness, destroying craving, destroying grasping, non-delusion, by destroying passion, hatred and delusion.

Lord,[1] if objects cognizable by the eye come very strongly into the range of vision of a monk, wholly freed in mind, they obsess not his mind and his mind is untroubled, firm, having won to composure; and he marks their set. So, too, sounds cognizable by the ear . . . smells by the nose . . . tastes by the tongue . . . contacts by the touch . . . and ideas by the mind . . ., he marks their set.

Imagine, lord, a mountain crag, cleftless, chasmless, massive; and a squall to come very strongly from the east: it would not shake, nor rock, nor stir that crag. Or were a squall to come from the west . . . from the north . . . from the south, it would not shake, nor rock, nor stir it. Even so, lord, if objects cognizable by the eye come very strongly into the range of a monk's vision—one wholly freed in mind—they obsess not his mind and his mind is untroubled, firm, having won to composure; and he marks their set: so, too, of sounds, smells, tastes, touches and ideas. . . .

Dispassion, mind's detachment, harmlessness,
Grasping's and craving's end, mind undeluded:
Who hath applied himself to these, hath seen
Sensations' rise[2]—his mind is wholly freed;

---

[1] *Cf. A.* iv, 404, with a different simile.

[2] *Āyatan' uppādaŋ. Comy. āyatanānaŋ uppādañ ca vayañ ca,* the rise and set.

And in that monk, calmed, wholly freed, naught need
Be added to what's done, naught due is found.
As massive crag by wind is never moved,[1]
So sights, tastes, sounds, smells, touches, yea, the things
Longed for and loathed, stir[2] not a man like that;
His mind stands firm, released; he marks their set.'

§ ii (56). *Phagguna.*[3]

Now[4] at that time the venerable Phagguna was sick, ailing, very ill; and the venerable Ānanda went to the Exalted One, saluted, and sat down at one side. So seated, he said to the Exalted One:

'Lord, the venerable Phagguna is sick, ailing, very ill. Good were it, lord, if the Exalted One were to go and see the venerable Phagguna out of compassion.'

And the Exalted One consented by silence.

Then in the evening, after he had come from solitude, the Exalted One visited the venerable Phagguna. And the venerable Phagguna saw him coming, when he was some way off, and stirred[5] on his bed; but the Exalted One spoke to him and said: 'Enough, Phagguna! Stir not on your bed. Are there not these seats here prepared already? I will sit here.' And he sat down on the seat prepared. So seated, the Exalted One said:

'I hope, Phagguna, you're bearing up, keeping going; that your aches and pains grow less, not more; that there are signs of their growing less,[6] not more?'

'Lord, I can neither bear up nor keep going; my aches and pains grow grievously more, not less; and there are signs of their growing more, not less.

Lord,[7] the violent ache that racks my head is just as though some lusty fellow chopped at it with a sharp-edged sword;

---

[1] *Cf. Dhp.* 81; *Th.* i, 643 *f.*; *Mil.* 386 (quoting).
[2] *ppavedhenti*, in the simile above, *sampavedheyya*.
[3] *S.* iv, 52.
[4] *S.* iii, 119; iv, 46; *M.* ii, 192.
[5] We should read *samañcopi*. *Comy. utthānākāraŋ dassesi.*
[6] *Paṭikkamosānaŋ*, finality of receding, viz. health; see *K.S.* iii, 102 *n.*
[7] These similes recur at *M.* ii, 193; *S.* iv, 56; *cf.* also *M.* i, 243 *ff.*

lord, I can neither bear up nor keep going; my pains grow more, not less; and there are signs of their growing more, not less.

Lord, the violent pain in my head is just as though some lusty fellow clapped a stout leather strap about it; lord, I cannot bear it. . . .

Lord, the violent stab that shoots through my stomach is just as though a skilful butcher or his apprentice gutted it with a carving knife; lord, I cannot bear it. . . .

Lord, the fever of my body is just as though a couple of lusty fellows had seized a weakling by his limbs and toasted him and roasted him over a fire-pit; lord, I cannot bear it . . . and there are signs of the pains growing worse.'

So the Exalted One instructed him, roused him, gladdened him and comforted him with Dhamma-talk, then rose from his seat and departed.

Now not long after the Exalted One's departure, the venerable Phagguna died; and at the time of his death his faculties were completely purified.

Then went the venerable Ānanda to the Exalted One, saluted him, and sat down at one side. So seated, he said: 'Lord, not long after the Exalted One left, the venerable Phagguna died; and at that time his faculties were completely purified.'

'But why, Ānanda, should not the faculties of the monk, Phagguna, have been completely purified? The monk's mind, Ānanda, had[1] not been wholly freed from the five lower fetters; but, when he heard that Dhamma teaching, his mind was wholly freed.

There are these six advantages, Ānanda, in hearing Dhamma in time, in testing its goodness in time. What six?

Consider, Ānanda, the monk whose mind is not wholly freed from the five lower fetters, but, when dying, is able to see the Tathāgata: the Tathāgata teaches him Dhamma, lovely in the beginning, lovely in the middle, lovely in the end, its goodness, its significance; and makes known the godly life,

---

[1] *Cittaŋ avimuttaŋ ahosi*, pluperfect.

wholly fulfilled, perfectly pure. When he has heard that Dhamma teaching, his mind is wholly freed from the five lower fetters. This, Ānanda, is the first advantage in hearing Dhamma in time.

Or . . . though not just able to see the Tathāgata, sees his disciple, who teaches him Dhamma . . . and makes known the godly life. . . . Then is his mind wholly freed. . . . . This, Ānanda, is the second advantage . . .

Or . . . though not able to see the Tathāgata or his disciple, continues to reflect in mind on Dhamma, as heard, as learnt, ponders on it, pores over it. Then is his mind wholly freed. . . . This, Ānanda, is the third advantage in testing its goodness in time.

Consider, Ānanda, the monk whose mind is wholly freed from the five lower fetters, whose mind is not wholly freed[1] in respect of the complete destruction of the root (of becoming); who, when dying, is able to see the Tathāgata: the Tathāgata teaches him Dhamma . . . makes known the godly life. . . . When he has heard that Dhamma teaching, his mind is wholly freed in respect of the complete destruction of the root of becoming. This, Ānanda, is the fourth advantage in hearing Dhamma in time.

Or . . . he sees the Tathāgata's disciple, who teaches him Dhamma. . . . Then is his mind wholly freed. . . . This, Ānanda, is the fifth advantage . . .

Or . . . though not able to see the Tathāgata or his disciple, ever reflects in mind on Dhamma, as heard, as learnt, ponders on it, pores over it. And as he does so, his mind is wholly freed as to the complete destruction of the root of becoming. This, Ānanda, is the sixth advantage in testing its goodness in time.

Verily, Ānanda, these are the six advantages in hearing Dhamma in time, in testing its goodness in time.'

---

[1] *Cittaŋ avimuttaŋ hoti.* *S.e.* so, but *Comy.* with *v.l. adhi-*, observing: *arahatta-phalena adhimuttaŋ hoti.* At *Sn.* 1149 we have *adhimutta-cittaŋ*; at *A.* iv, 239, *cittaŋ hīne 'dhimuttaŋ*; but I think the comment makes better sense if we read *avimuttaŋ*.

§ iii (57). *The six breeds.*[1]

Once, when the Exalted One was dwelling on Mount Vulture Peak near Rājagaha, the venerable Ānanda approached him, saluted, and sat down at one side. So seated, he said to the Exalted One:

'Lord, six breeds have been declared by Pūraṇa Kassapa:[2] the black, the blue, the red, the yellow, the white and the purest white.

Lord, here is the black breed declared by him: mutton-butchers, pork-butchers, fowlers, hunters, thugs,[3] fishermen, robbers, cut-throats, jailers, and all others who follow a bloody trade.

Here is the blue: monks who live as though with a thorn[4] in the side, and all others who profess the deed and doing [theory].[5]

Here is the red: Jains[6] and loin-cloth folk.

Here is the yellow: white-robed householders and followers of naked ascetics.

Here is the white: fakirs and their disciples.

And here, lord, is the breed of the purest white declared by Pūraṇa Kassapa: Nanda Vaccha, Kisa Saṅkicca and Makkhali Gosāla.[7]

Lord, these are the six breeds declared by him.'

'But[8] what, Ānanda, does the whole world agree with Pūraṇa Kassapa in this declaration of his?'

'Certainly not, lord.'

'Well, Ānanda, just as men might thrust a piece of meat on

---

[1] *Chaḷābhijātiyo*; see *DA.* i, 162; *Dial.* i, 72 *n.*; *K.S.* iii, 170; *D.* iii, 250.

[2] See *Dial.* i, 69; *DA.* i, 142.

[3] *Luddā.* *Comy.* *dāruṇā*, violent men. It is noteworthy that none were so 'black' as to kill cattle. This list recurs at *M.* i, 343; *Pug.* 56.

[4] *Kaṇṭaka-vuttikā.* *Comy.* *samaṇā nām' ete.* *DA.* *eke pabbajitā*; also *te kira catusa paccayesu kaṇṭhake pakkhipitvā khādanti*, which I suppose means that they 'hedge their ways with thorns'; *cf.* *Hosea* ii, 6.

[5] *Kamma-, kiriya-vādā.* See *G.S.* i, 265 *n.*; *cf.* above VI, § 38.

[6] *Nigaṇṭhā.*

[7] See *F. Dial.* i, 170, 371; they were naked ascetics. *Comy.* is silent; *MA.* ii, 285 gives no real information about them. See *Dial.* i, 73; *K.S.* iii, 61, on Makkhali.

[8] *Cf.* *M.* ii, 178, also i, 450.

some poor, needy, unwilling wretch, saying: "Here, sirrah, eat this meat—and pay for it too!"; even so is Pūraṇa Kassapa's declaration to these recluses and brāhmans, made without their consent as though by a foolish, witless numskull, lacking common-sense.[1]

I, verily, Ānanda, will declare the six breeds; hear, give heed, I will speak!'

'Yes, lord,' rejoined the venerable Ānanda; and the Exalted One said:

'And what, Ānanda, are the six breeds?

There[2] are some of black breed, Ānanda, who breed black Dhamma; some who breed white Dhamma; some who breed Nibbāna, neither black nor white: there are some of white breed who breed white Dhamma; some who breed black Dhamma; and some who breed Nibbāna, neither black nor white.

And how, Ānanda, breeds the black breed black Dhamma?

Consider,[3] Ānanda, one reborn in a low-caste clan—pariah, hunter, weaver, wheelwright, sweeper—in a poor family, where food and drink are scarce, life is hard, keep and clothing hardly come by; and he is ugly, ill-featured, misshapen and much afflicted, being blind, deformed in hand, lame or crippled; and is no recipient of food, drink, clothes, carriages, flowers, scents, ointments, bed, lodging or lighting: and suppose he wayfare in the wrong way in deed, word and thought—on the breaking up of the body after death, he arises in the wayward way, the ill way, the abyss, hell. Thus, Ānanda, some of the black breed breed black Dhamma.

And how, Ānanda, breeds the black breed white Dhamma?

Consider, again, one born in a low-caste clan . . ., who wayfares in the right way in deed, word and thought—on the breaking up of the body after death, he arises in the good way, the heaven-world. Thus, Ānanda, some of the black breed breed white Dhamma.

---

[1] *A-khetta 'ññunā*, no field-sense; at *A.* iv, 418, used of a cow.

[2] *Kaṅhâbhijātiyo samāno kaṅhaŋ dhammaŋ abhijāyati.* *Comy.* and *D.* iii read *-âbhijātiko*, but *S.e.* as our text.

[3] This is all stock; see *A.* i, 107; ii, 85; *S.* i, 93.

And how, Ānanda, breeds the black breed Nibbāna, neither black nor white ?

Consider, again, one born in a low-caste clan . . ., ugly, ill-featured, misshapen, who has his hair and beard shaved, dons the yellow robe and goes forth from the home to the homeless life—thus gone forth, he rids himself of the five hindrances, weakens the mental defilements by insight, becomes firmly fixed in the four arisings of mindfulness, makes become the seven factors of awakening, as they can become,[1] and breeds Nibbāna, neither black nor white. Thus, Ānanda, some of the black breed breed Nibbāna, neither black nor white.

And how, Ānanda, breeds the white breed black Dhamma ?

Consider one born in a high-caste clan: noble, brāhman or householder, owning stately homes, riches, wealth, domains. with gold and silver in plenty, means and service in plenty, corn and grain in plenty; and is well-formed, sightly, pleasing, blessed with a lily-like loveliness; is a recipient of food, drink, clothes, carriages, flowers, scents, ointments, bed, lodging and lighting: and suppose he wayfare in the wrong way in deed, word and thought—on the breaking up of the body after death, he arises . . . in hell. Thus, Ānanda, some of the white breed breed black Dhamma.

And how, Ānanda, breeds the white breed white Dhamma ?

Consider, again, one so born . . ., who wayfares in the right way . . . after death, he arises in heaven. Thus, Ānanda, some of the white breed breed white Dhamma.

And how, Ānanda, breeds the white breed Nibbāna, neither black nor white ?

Consider one so born . . . who goes forth and rids himself of the five hindrances and so forth . . .; he breeds Nibbāna, neither black nor white. Thus, Ānanda, some of the white breed breed Nibbāna, neither black nor white.

Verily, Ānanda, these are the six breeds.'

---

[1] *Yathā bhūtaŋ.*

§ iv (58). *The cankers.*[1]

'Monks, a monk endowed with six qualities is worthy of gifts, worthy of offerings, worthy of oblations, meet to be reverently saluted, the world's peerless field for merit. What six?

Herein, monks, the cankers to be got rid of by control by a monk are got rid of by control; to be got rid of by use, endurance, avoidance, ejection, growth, are got rid of by [these qualities respectively].

And what, monks, are the cankers to be got rid of by control, which are got rid of by control?

Monks, consider the monk who with conscious purpose[2] lives controlled by controlling the eye-faculties. Whereas, were he to live uncontrolled, the cankers, vexatious, tormenting, would arise; since he lives controlled by controlling the eye-faculties, the cankers are not. So, too, as to the faculties of the ear, nose, tongue, body, mind. . . . Whereas, were he to live uncontrolled in control, the cankers, vexatious, tormenting, would arise; since he lives controlled in control, the cankers are not. These, monks, are called the cankers to be got rid of by control, which are got rid of by control.

And what, monks, are the cankers to be got rid of by use, which are got rid of by use?

Consider, monks, the monk who with conscious purpose uses a robe just to ward off cold, heat, the bite of gadfly, gnat, wind, sun, snake, or just for a covering or loin-cloth; who with conscious purpose uses alms not for sport, enjoyment, adorning or beautifying himself, but just to maintain and keep the body

---

[1] *Cf.* the whole sutta with *M.* i, 9 *ff.* (*F. Dial.* i, 4; *S.B.E.* xi, 296); our *Comy.* is much the same as *MA.* i, 75 *ff.*; but vision, the first of seven ways of riddance, is in our sutta omitted, leaving six ('scrutiny' in the *M.* trans. does not well coincide with *dassana*). According to *M.* the four cankers—*kāma, bhava, diṭṭhi, avijjā*—are to be multiplied by the number of 'sense-doors'—in the first instance—making twenty-four cankers to be got rid of by control. Here 'cankers' are left unspecified: any baneful tendency in the religious life. See *DhS. trsl.* 292; *Expos.* 476.

[2] *Paṭisankhā yoniso*; *cf.* for a similar expression *Acts* xi, 23.

in trim, to abate (hunger's) pangs, to enter the godly life, thinking: "I'll crush out old feelings and not allow new ones to rise, and so blamelessness and comfort shall be mine!"; who with conscious purpose uses a lodging just to ward off cold, heat, the bite of gadfly, gnat and so forth, to dispel the dangers of the seasons' changes, to enjoy solitude; who with conscious purpose uses medicaments for the sick to ward off attacks of disease's pains, or on the score of healing. Whereas, were not the usage such, the cankers, vexatious, tormenting, would arise; since the usage is such, the cankers are not. These, monks, are called the cankers to be got rid of by use, which are got rid of by use.

And what, monks, are the cankers to be got rid of by endurance, which are got rid of by endurance?

Consider the monk who with conscious purpose bears cold, heat, hunger, thirst, the bite of gadfly, gnat, wind, sun and snake, the ways of speech, irksome, abusive; endures the aches and pains that surge through the body, sharp, rough, piercing, bitter, galling, deadly. Whereas, were not the endurance such, the cankers, vexatious, tormenting, would arise; since the endurance is such, the cankers are not. These, monks, are called the cankers to be got rid of by endurance, which are got rid of by endurance.

And what, monks, are the cankers to be got rid of by avoidance, which are got rid of by avoidance?

Consider the monk who with conscious purpose avoids a savage elephant, horse, bull or hound, a snake, tree-stumps, thorny brakes, ravines, cliffs, cesspools, middens; who with conscious purpose avoids the forbidden seat, haunt and evil friends—such that were he to sit there, wander in those haunts, associate with those evil friends, his fellows in the godly life might suspect him of misconduct. Whereas, were not the avoidance such, the cankers, vexatious, tormenting, would arise; since the avoidance is such, the cankers are not. These, monks, are called the cankers to be got rid of by avoidance, which are got rid of by avoidance.

And what, monks, are the cankers to be got rid of by ejection, which are got rid of by ejection?

Consider the monk who with conscious purpose allows no halt for the surge of lustful thoughts, rids himself of them, ejects them, makes an end of them, sends them to their ceasing; so likewise the surge of fell thoughts . . . of cruel thoughts . . . allows no halt for the unceasing surge of evil and wrong conditions, rids himself of them, ejects them, makes an end of them, sends them to their ceasing. Whereas, were not the ejection such, the cankers, vexatious, tormenting, would arise; since the ejection is such, the cankers are not. These, monks, are called the cankers to be got rid of by ejection, which are got rid of by ejection.

And what, monks, are the cankers to be got rid of by growth, which are got rid of by growth ?

Consider, monks, the monk who with conscious purpose grows the limb of awakening that is mindfulness, through solitude, dispassion, ending, to the fulness of release;[1] the limb of awakening that is Dhamma-testing, the limb of awakening that is energy, the limb of awakening that is zest, the limb of awakening that is tranquillity, the limb of awakening that is concentration; grows the limb of awakening that is equanimity, through solitude, dispassion, ending, to the fulness of release. Whereas, were not the growth such, the cankers, vexatious, tormenting, would arise; since the growth is such, the cankers are not. These, monks, are called the cankers to be got rid of by growth, which are got rid of by growth.

Verily, monks, endowed with these six qualities a monk is worthy of gifts, worthy of offerings, worthy of oblations, meet to be reverently saluted, the world's peerless field for merit.'

§ v (59). *The wood-seller.*[2]

Thus have I heard: Once, when the Exalted One was staying in the Brick Hall at Nādika, a householder, a wood-seller, visited him, saluted and sat down at one side. So seated, the Exalted One said to him:

'Maybe, householder, alms are given by your family ?'

---

[1] *Vossagga-pariṇāmiŋ*; see *K.S.* i, 113 *n.*, *avu* + √*sṛj*.

[2] *Dāru-kammika.*

'O yes, lord, and in this way too: such monks as are forest-gone, almsmen, rag-wearers—arahants or men won to the arahant's Way—to them, lord, alms are given by my family.'

'But surely, householder, it's a hard thing for you—a layman, engrossed in pleasures, encumbered with children, odorous with Kāsī's sandalwood, decked with flowers and scented oils, merry with silver and gold[1]—to tell which are arahants and which have won to the arahants' Way! If a forest-gone monk, householder, be puffed[2] up, proud, excitable, a mouthy speechifier, forgetful of mindfulness, not self-possessed nor composed, a scatter-brain, rude in sense-governance—he on that count is blameworthy; if he be not puffed up . . ., but upright in mindfulness, self-possessed, composed, one-pointed, controlled in faculties—he on that count is praiseworthy. So, too, of the monk dwelling on the village outskirts . . ., the almsman . . ., the guest . . ., the rag-wearer . . ., the wearer of the householder's robe,[3] if they be puffed up . . . rude in sense-governance—on that count they are blameworthy; but if the contrary, then they are praiseworthy. Nevertheless, householder, give alms to the Order. An you do so, your heart will become tranquil; and tranquil in heart, you will, on the breaking up of the body after death, arise in the good way, the heaven-world.'

'I, too, lord, henceforth from today will give alms to the Order.'

§ vi (60). *Citta Hatthisāriputta.*[4]

Thus have I heard: Once, when the Exalted One dwelt near Benares in the Deer Park at Isipatana, a number of elders,

---

[1] *Cf. A.* iv, 281; *Ud.* 65. [2] See above V, § 167; VI, § 46.

[3] *Gahapati-cīvara-dhara*, the robe *given* by a householder, not from the rag heap. *F. Dial.* i, 21, 'clad in lay attire,' and so also *P.E.D.* Bu. in both places is silent.

[4] See *D.* i, 190 *ff.*; *Dial.* i, 256 *n.* *DA.* ii, 378 says he was the son of an elephant-driver, quick at learning, and refers to the incident in our sutta, adding that the conversation was between Moggallāna and Koṭṭhita.

who had returned from alms-gathering, and fed, sat together in the round hall and talked a talk on Abhidhamma.

Now from time to time the venerable Citta Hatthisāriputta broke in on their talk. And the venerable Mahā Koṭṭhita said to him:

'Let not the venerable Citta Hatthisāriputta constantly interrupt the elders' Abhidhamma talk; the venerable Citta should wait until the talk is over!'

And when he had thus spoken, Citta's friends said: 'The venerable Mahā Koṭṭhita should not censure the venerable Citta Hatthisāriputta. A wise man is the venerable Citta and able to talk to the elders on Abhidhamma.'

''Tis a hard thing,[1] sirs, for those who know not another person's ways of thought. Consider, sirs, a person who, so long as he lives near the Master or a fellow-teacher in the godly life, is the most humble[2] of the humble, the meekest of the meek, the quietest of the quiet; and who, when he leaves the Master or his fellow-teachers, keeps company with monks, nuns, lay-disciples, men and women, rajahs, their ministers, course-setters[3] or their disciples. Living in company, untrammelled, rude, given over to gossip, passion corrupts his heart; and with his heart corrupted by passion, he disavows the training and returns to the lower life. Suppose, sirs, an ox, a meadow-browser, were kept tied by a rope or closed in a byre —would he say rightly, who should say: "Never now will that meadow-browser venture again to a meadow" ?'[4]

'No, indeed, sir, such a thing does not happen, since that ox, used to browsing in meadows, would, on snapping its rope or breaking out of the byre, venture down to the meadow again.'

'It is even so, sirs, where a person—so long as he is near the Master or a fellow-teacher—is the most humble of the humble, meekest of the meek, quietest of the quiet; but who, on leaving the Master or his fellow-teachers, keeps company

---

1 *Dujjānaṃ*, a hard knowing.

2 *Soratasorato, nivātanivāto, upasant' upasanto.*

3 See above VI, § 54.

4 *Kiṭṭha*, a stubble-field; *cf. S.* iv, 196 for simile.

with monks, nuns, lay-folk—passion corrupts his heart . . . and he returns to the lower life.

Consider again a person who, aloof from sensuous appetites . . . enters and abides in the first musing. Thinking: "I've won to the first musing," he keeps company . . . and returns to the lower life. Suppose, sirs, the rain-deva rains heavy rains at the four cross-roads, lays the dust and makes mud—would he say rightly, who should say: "Never now will dust again appear at these four cross-roads"?'

'No, indeed, sir, since along those four cross-roads men, oxen and cows might pass or the wind and heat might dry up the moisture; and then the dust would appear again.'

'It is even so, sirs, where a person enters and abides in the first musing . . . and keeps company; . . . he returns to the lower life.

Then consider a person who, suppressing applied and sustained thought . . . enters and abides in the second musing. Thinking: "I've won to the second musing," he keeps company . . . and returns to the lower life. Suppose, sirs,[1] a great lake near some village or town and the rain-deva were to rain great rains and cover the mussels and shells and sand and pebbles —would he say rightly, who should say: "Never now in this great lake shall the mussels, shells, sand and pebbles appear again"?'

'No, indeed, sir, since men, oxen and cows might come and drink from the great lake or wind and heat dry up the moisture; and then the mussels, shells, sand and pebbles would appear again.'

'It is even so, sirs, where a person enters and abides in the second musing . . . and keeps company; . . . he returns to the lower life.

Consider then the person who, free from the fervour of zest, . . . enters and abides in the third musing. Thinking: "I've won to the third musing," he keeps company . . . and returns to the lower life. Suppose, sirs, last[2] night's food please

---

[1] *Cf. D.* i, 89; *M.* i, 279; *A.* i, 9.

[2] *Cf. M.* ii, 255; our text reads *abhidosikaṃ*, *S.e. ābhi-*, *Comy. ābhidosiyaṃ*.

not a man filled with good food—would he say rightly, who should say: "Never now shall food please this man again"?'

'No, indeed, sir, that is not the case; so long as the strength of the good food remain in his body, other food shall not please that man; but when that strength has gone, then shall food please him.'

'It is even so, sirs, where a person enters and abides in the third musing . . . and keeps company; . . . he returns to the lower life.

Consider the person who, putting away ease and ill, . . . enters and abides in the fourth musing. Thinking: "I've won to the fourth musing," he keeps company . . . and returns to the lower life. Imagine,[1] sirs, a mere in a mountain glen, windless, waveless—would he say rightly, who should say: "Never now on this mere shall waves appear again"?'

'No, indeed, sir, since were a squall to come very strongly from the east, it would bring waves to the mere; so likewise were a squall to come from the west . . . the north . . . or the south. . . .'

'It is even so, sirs, where a person enters and abides in the fourth musing . . . and keeps company; . . . he returns to the lower life.

And consider the person who, paying no attention to the signs in things, enters and abides in the signless mental concentration. Thinking: "I have won to the signless mental concentration," he keeps company with monks, nuns, lay-disciples, men and women, rajahs, their ministers, course-setters and their disciples. Living in company, untrammelled, rude, given over to gossip, passion corrupts his heart; and with his heart corrupted by passion, he disavows the training and returns to the lower life. Suppose, sirs, a rajah or his minister with the four hosts of the army were to come up the high road and pitch their camp for one night in the forest and the sound of the cricket be drowned by the sound of elephant, horse, chariot and foot-soldier, by the sound of tabor, drum

---

[1] *Cf. D.* i, 84; *M.* ii, 22.

and conch—would he say rightly, who should say: "Never now in this forest shall the cricket be heard again" ?'

'No, indeed, sir, that is not the case, for when the rajah and his minister have left the forest, the cricket shall be heard again.'

'It is even so, sirs, where a person, unattentive to the signs in things, enters and abides in the signless mental concentration, and, thinking: "I've won to that,"—keeps company with monks, nuns, lay-folk. . . . Living in company, untrammelled, rude, given to gossip, passion corrupts his heart . . . and he returns to the lower life.'

And presently the venerable Citta Hatthisāriputta disavowed the training and returned to the lower life.

Then Citta's friends went to the venerable Mahā Koṭṭhita and said:

'Did the venerable Mahā Koṭṭhita discover Citta Hatthisāriputta by mind compassing mind[1] concerning the thought: "This and that state of attainment has Citta won to, but he will give up the training and return to the lower life"—or did devas tell him this thing: "Citta Hatthisāriputta, sir, has won this and that, but he'll return to the lower life" ?'

'Reverend sirs, I discovered it by mind compassing mind . . . but devas also told me. . . .'[2]

Then the venerable Citta's friends approached the Exalted One, saluted him and sat down at one side; and so seated, they said to him:

'Lord, Citta Hatthisāriputta has won to this and that state of attainment, yet he has disavowed the training and returned to the lower life.'

'Citta, monks, will ere long bethink him of renouncing [the worldly life].'

And[3] not long after, Citta Hatthisāriputta had his hair

---

[1] *Cetasā ceto paricca.*

[2] This is admitted several times by the Founder or recorded of him (see No. 62), pointing to a tradition preceding the omniscience-cult of him, but has so far not been found recorded of a disciple.

[3] All this recurs at *D.* i, 202 *ff.* *Comy.* observes: this elder went forth seven times. And why ? Because in the time of Kassapa Buddha he praised the householder's life to a monk.

and beard shaved off, donned the yellow robe and went forth from the home to the homeless life.

And the venerable Citta Hatthisāriputta, living alone, secluded, earnest, ardent, resolved, not long after, entered and abode in that aim above all of the godly life—realizing it here and now by his own knowledge—for the sake of which clansmen rightly go forth from the home to the homeless life; and he knew: 'Birth is destroyed, the godly life is lived, done is what was to be done, there is no more of this.'

And the venerable Citta Hatthisāriputta was numbered among the arahants.

§ vii (61). *The Way to the Beyond.*[1]

Thus have I heard: Once, when the Exalted One dwelt near Benares in the Deer Park at Isipatana, a number of elders, who had returned from alms-gathering, and fed, sat together in the round hall; and this talk by chance arose:

'This, sirs, was said by the Exalted One in "The Way to the Beyond," in the questions of Metteyya:[2]

"Who knows both ends—not midst[3] that sage is soiled:
Him call I 'great man'; he here hath passed the seamstress."

And what, pray, is the first end, what's the second, what's in the middle and who's the seamstress?'

Now after this had been said, one of the monks answered the elders and said: 'Contact, sirs, is the first end, its arising is the second, its ceasing is in the middle, and craving is the seamstress; for craving sews one just to this ever-becoming birth.[4] Indeed, sirs, to this extent a monk knows the know-

---

[1] *Pārâyana.*

[2] See *Sn.* 1042; *S.e.* with *Sn.* and our *Comy.* read *lippati.*

[3] 'Him first, him last, him midst and without end' (Milton, *Paradise Lost*, v, 165).

[4] *Tassa tass' eva bhavassa abhinibbattiyā.* The seamstress, *sibbanī*, recurs at *DhS.* § 1059; craving as *jālinī* occurs in *S.* (*K.S.* i, 134); *G.S.* ii, 225; *Dhp.* 180; *Th.* i, 162, 908.

able, comprehends the comprehensible; and knowing the knowable, comprehending the comprehensible, he makes an end of Ill, here now.'

And when he had thus spoken, another said: 'The past is the first end, the future is the second, the present is in the middle, and craving is the seamstress; . . . and knowing the knowable, . . . he makes an end of Ill.'

And another said: 'Pleasure[1] is the first end, pain is the second, indifference is in the middle, and craving is the seamstress. . . .'

And another said: 'Name is the first end, form is the second, consciousness is in the middle, and craving is the seamstress. . . .'

And another said: 'One's six sense-organs are the first end, the six outer objects are the second, consciousness is in the middle, and craving is the seamstress. . . .'

And another said: 'Life's bundle[2] is the first end, its arising is the second, its ceasing is in the middle, and craving is the seamstress; for craving sews one just to this ever becoming birth. Indeed, sirs, to this extent a monk knows the knowable, comprehends the comprehensible; and knowing the knowable, comprehending the comprehensible, he makes an end of Ill, here now.'

And when he had finished speaking, another monk addressed the elders and said: 'We have all, reverend sirs, replied as the matter appeared to each one of us. Let us go and visit the Exalted One and tell him. As the Exalted One declares, so will we bear in mind.'

'Very well,' rejoined the elders; and they approached the Exalted One, saluted and sat down at one side. And so seated, they told him all the words and talk that had passed between them, adding: 'Lord, who spoke best?'

'Each one of you, monks, in his own way spoke well; but as to what I spoke of in "The Way to the Beyond," in Metteyya's questions:

---

[1] See *D.* iii, 216 and ref. there.

[2] *Sakkāya*; see above VI, § 14.

"Who knows both ends—not midst that sage is soiled:
Him call I 'great man'; he here hath passed the seamstress,"

listen, pay good heed, I will speak!'

'Yes, lord,' they replied; and the Exalted One said:

'Verily, contact, monks, is the first end, its arising is the second, its ceasing is in the middle, and craving is the seamstress; for craving sews a man just to this ever-becoming birth. Verily, monks, it is to this extent that a monk knows the knowable, comprehends the comprehensible; and knowing the knowable, comprehending the comprehensible, he makes an end of Ill, here now.'

§ viii (62). *The solemn utterance.*[1]

Thus have I heard: Once, while the Exalted One walked a walk among the Kosalese with a great company of the Order's monks, he came to a Kosalan town called Daṇḍakappaka.[2] And the Exalted One stepped down from the road and sat on a seat made ready at the foot of a tree; but the monks entered Daṇḍakappaka to seek a lodging.

Now the venerable Ānanda, with a number of monks, went to the river Aciravatī[3] to bathe his limbs; and after he had bathed and had come out, he stood in one garment drying his limbs.[4]

Then a monk approached the venerable Ānanda and said:

'Ānanda, reverend sir, was it after concentrating his whole mind[5] that Devadatta was declared by the Exalted One: "Gone[6] wayward, hell-bound for a kalpa, unpardonable is Devadatta"—or was it from some deva-source (he learnt it)?'

---

[1] The text reads *udakaŋ* with *S.e.*, but one MS. *udānaŋ*.

[2] *Comy.* is silent; I find no mention of this town elsewhere. Daṇḍaka forest (*M.* i, 378; *Mil.* 130) was in the Dekkan, see *Chwang*, ii, 199.

[3] *Sāvatthī* was close to this river (? *Gandak*); see *M.* ii, 113; *Chwang*, i, 398.

[4] *Cf.* above VI, § 43.

[5] *Sabba-cetaso samannāharitvā.*

[6] *Cf. Vin.* ii, 202; *A.* iv, 160; *It.* 85.

'It was even as the Exalted One has declared.'[1]

Now the venerable Ānanda approached the Exalted One, saluted and sat down at one side; and so seated, he told the Exalted One all that had occurred. . . .[2]

(Then said the Exalted One:) 'Either, Ānanda, that monk must be new, not long gone forth, or if an elder, a witless one. How, when I have definitely declared it, can there be an alternative? I know not another person of whom this was declared by me, after full mental concentration, save of Devadatta. And so long, Ānanda, as I saw a bright spot[3] in Devadatta, even the prick-end of a horse-hair[4] in size, I declared not: "Devadatta is wayward gone, hell-bound for a kalpa, unpardonable"—but it was when I saw none, that I declared thus. . . .

'Imagine,[5] Ānanda, a cesspool, of a man's depth, brimful of dung and a man fallen in, head and all—though a man appear, ready to help, to do the friendly, to set him in safety, to lift him out; yet were he to go all round that cesspool, he would not see even the prick-end of a horse-hair of that man unsmeared with dung by which to grasp and lift him out. And it is even so with Devadatta, Ānanda, when I saw not a bright spot in him—not even the prick-end of a horse-hair in size—then I declared: "Gone wayward, hell-bound for a kalpa, unpardonable is Devadatta!"

Wouldst thou hear, Ānanda, the Tathāgata analyzing the feelings and thoughts of man?'

'This is the time, O Blessed One; this is the time, O Well-gone, for the Exalted One to analyze men's feelings and thoughts! The monks having heard will bear it in mind.'

'Well, hearken, Ānanda, pay good heed, I will speak.'

'Yes, lord,' rejoined the venerable Ānanda; and the Exalted One said:

'Suppose, Ānanda, by mind compassing mind, I know this

---

[1] See above VI, § 44, and *Comy.*'s remark there, *n.* 7.

[2] The text repeats in full.

[3] *Sukkaṃ dhammaṃ.*

[4] See *Dial.* ii, 151 *n.*; *G.S.* i, 60 *n.*

[5] *Cf. M.* i, 74; *D.* ii, 324; *Vin.* iii, 106.

of some person: "There is both good and evil in him." Then presently, by the same means, I know: "The good has disappeared, the evil is uppermost; but the root of goodness is not cut off and from that good will proceed. Thus in future he is bound not to fall."

If,[1] Ānanda, seed, neither split, rotten, nor spoilt by wind and heat, but vital,[2] well-seasoned, be thrown on well-tilled ground in a goodly field; can you say for certain: "It will yield its growth, increase and abundance"?'

'Yes, surely, lord.'

'Even so, Ānanda, by mind compassing mind, I know of some person: "There is good and evil in him"—and then: "The good has disappeared, the evil is uppermost; but the root of goodness is not cut off and from that good will proceed. Thus he is bound not to fall in future." Verily, Ānanda, thus, by mind compassing mind, the person of man is known to the Tathāgata; thus, by mind compassing mind, the feelings and thoughts of man are known to the Tathāgata; thus, by mind compassing mind, the future rise of things[3] is known to the Tathāgata.

Or suppose, by mind compassing mind, I know the converse . . . of some person. In future he is bound to fall. If seed, neither split, rotten and so forth . . . be thrown on stony ground, can you say for certain; "It'll not yield its growth, increase or abundance"?'

'Yes, surely, lord.'

'Even so, Ānanda, I know of some person . . .: "He is bound to fall." Verily, Ānanda, thus, by mind compassing mind, the person of man . . ., his thoughts and feelings . . ., and the future rise of things are known to the Tathāgata.

'Then suppose I know . . . of some person: "There's not a bright spot the size of a hair's prick-end in him"; and being

---

[1] *Cf. D.* ii, 354; *S.* iii, 54; v, 380; *A.* i, 135. We may compare the *Parable of the Sower* (*Mark* iv, 1, etc.).

[2] *Sāradāni. Comy. sārādāni gahita-sārāni, sarade māse vā nibbattāni.* See *K.S.* iii, 46 *n.*

[3] *Dhammasamuppādo.* In *K.S.* v, 323 rendered '(question of) doctrine arising,' which scarcely fits the present context.

utterly black in his evil, he will, on the breaking up of the body after death, arise in the wayward way, the ill way, the abyss, hell. Ānanda, if seed, split, rotten, spoilt by wind and heat, be thrown on well-tilled ground in a goodly field; can you say for certain: "It'll not yield growth, increase or abundance"?'

'Yes, surely, lord.'

'Even so, Ānanda, I know of some person . . .: "He will rise in hell." Thus, by mind compassing mind, the person of man, his feelings and thoughts and the future rise of things are known to the Tathāgata.'

Now, when he had thus spoken, the venerable Ānanda said to the Exalted One: 'Lord, is it possible to declare other three counterparts of these three persons?'

'It is, Ānanda,' and the Exalted One said:

'Suppose, Ānanda, by mind compassing mind, I know this of some person: "There is both good and evil in him." Then presently, by the same means, I know: "The good has disappeared, the evil is uppermost; but the root of goodness is not cut off, yet he goes about to uproot it altogether. Thus he is bound to fall in future."

If, Ānanda, burning, blazing, fiery coals are thrown on stony ground; can you say for certain: "They'll not grow, increase or spread"?'

'Yes, surely, lord.'

'Or when in the evening the sun sets, can you say for certain: "Light will go, darkness will come"?'

'Yes, surely, lord.'

'Or[1] later on, when night is part-spent and men eat; can you say for certain: "Light has gone, darkness is come"?'

'Yes, surely, lord.'

'Even so, Ānanda, I know of some person . . .: "He is bound to fall." Thus, by mind compassing mind, the person

[1] *Abhidose aḍḍha-rattaŋ bhatta-kāla-samaye. Comy.* reads *abhido,* observing: *abhi-aḍḍha-rattaŋ, aḍḍha-ratte abhimukhe bhūte. S.e.* is as our text. *Abhidose* I take to mean later on than evening, and *aḍḍha-rattaŋ* between 9 and 11 o'clock, which is when many Easterners take their meal. *Comy.* remarks rajahs and clansmen eat at the time referred to.

of man, his feelings and thoughts and the future rise of things are known to the Tathāgata.

Or suppose I know of some person . . .: " The evil in him has disappeared, the good is uppermost, and though he has not cut off the root of evil he goes about to uproot it all together. Thus he is bound not to fall in future."

If, Ānanda, burning, blazing, fiery coals are thrown on a heap of dry grass or sticks; can you say for certain: " They'll grow, increase and spread " ?'

'Yes, surely, lord.'

'Or when dawn faces night and the sun mounts up, can you say for certain: " Darkness will go, light will come " ?'

'Yes, surely, lord.'

'Or[1] later on, at midday, at meal time, can you say for certain: " Darkness has gone, light is come " ?'

'Yes, surely, lord.'

'Even so, Ānanda, I know of some person . . .: " He is bound not to fall." Thus, by mind compassing mind, he . . . is known to the Tathāgata.

Or suppose I know of some person: " There is good and evil in him." Then presently I know: " There is not in him evil amounting to a hair's prick-end, and being exceedingly pure in faultlessness, he will, here now, become completely cool."[2]

If, Ānanda, coals, cold and extinct,[3] be thrown on a heap of dry grass or sticks; can you say for certain: " These coals will not grow, increase or spread " ?'

'Yes, surely, lord.'

'Even so, Ānanda, by mind compassing mind, I know of some person: " There is good and evil in him "—then presently: " There is not even a hair's prick-end of evil in him; and being exceedingly pure in faultlessness, he will, here now, become completely cool." Thus, Ānanda, by mind compassing mind, the person of man is known to the Tathāgata; by mind compassing mind, the feelings and thoughts of man are known to the Tathāgata; by mind compassing mind, the future rise of things is known to the Tathāgata.

---

[1] *Abhidose majjhantike.* [2] *Parinibbāyissati.* [3] *Sītāni nibbutāni.*

There, Ānanda, of those first three persons, one is bound not to fall, one is bound to fall and one goes the wayward way, hell-bound: and of the last three persons, one is bound not to fall, one is bound to fall and one is bound for Nibbāna.'[1]

§ ix (63). *A penetrative discourse.*[2]

'Monks, I will teach you a penetrative discourse, a Dhamma-discourse. Listen, pay heed, I will speak!'

'Yes, lord,' rejoined those monks; and the Exalted One said:

'And what, monks, is this penetrative discourse, this Dhamma-discourse?

Monks, sense-desires must be discerned, their tie-source,[3] variety,[4] fruit, ending, and the steps leading thereto. Monks, feelings, perceptions, cankers, action and ill must be discerned; their tie-source, variety, fruit, ending and the steps leading thereto must be discerned.

Monks, it is said: "Sense-desires and so forth . . . must be discerned"—and wherefore is this said?

Monks, the strands[5] of sense-desires are five: Forms cognizable by the eye, luring, longed for, loved, enticing, lustful, impassioning; sounds cognizable by the ear, smells by the nose, tastes by the tongue, touches by the body, luring, longed for, loved, enticing, lustful, impassioning. Though these are not sense-desires, monks, in the Ariyan discipline they are called the strands of the sense-desires.

> In passionate purpose lies man's sense-desire[6]—
> The world's gay glitters are not sense-desires,
> In passionate purpose lies man's sense-desire.
> The world's gay glitters as they are abide,
> But wise men hold desire therefor in check.[7]

---

[1] *Parinibibbāna-dhammo.* [2] *DhS. trsl.* 292; *Expos.* 476.

[3] *Nidāna-sambhavo. Comy.*:*Kāme nideti*; *P.E.D.* omits. [4] *Vemattatā.*

[5] *Kāma-guṇā, Comy. Bandhanaṭṭhena guṇā, antaguṇan-ti viya.*

[6] Noteworthy here is the word *puriso* not ejected by *puggalo,* and *kāmo* in the singular; *cf.* the Upanishadic use; *Bṛh. Up.* iv, 4, 5: 'so it is said, man is wholly formed of *kāmo.*'

[7] *S.* i, 22; see *K.S.* i, 32 and *Pts. of Contr.* 216. 'Desire,' last line= *chanda.*

And what is the tie-source of sense-desires? Contact, monks.

And what is sense-desires' variety? One sense-desire is for forms, another for sounds, another for smells, another for tastes, another for touch. This, monks, is called sense-desires' variety.

And what is sense-desires' fruit? When desiring aught, one engenders just that proper state of being to partake of merit or demerit. This, monks, is called sense-desires' fruit.

And what is sense-desires' ending? Contact's ending is sense-desires' ending, monks. And just in this Ariyan eightfold Way are the steps leading thereto, to wit: right view, right purpose, right speech, right action, right livelihood, right effort, right mindfulness and right concentration. And when the Ariyan disciple thus knows sense-desires, their tie-source, variety, fruit, ending and the steps leading thereto; he knows this penetrative godly life as sense-desires' ending.

Monks, it is said: " Sense-desires and so forth must be discerned . . ."—and because of this it is said.

Monks, it is said: " Feelings must be discerned . . ."—and wherefore?

Monks, feelings are these three: feeling of ease, feeling of ill, and feeling of neither ill nor ease.

And what is feelings' tie-source? Contact, monks.

And what is feelings' variety? There are feelings of ease that are carnal,[1] there are feelings of ease that are not; so, too, of feelings of ill and of neither ill nor ease. This, monks, is called feelings' variety.

And what is feelings' fruit? When feeling aught, one engenders just that proper state of being to partake of merit or demerit. This, monks, is called feelings' fruit.

And what is feelings' ending? Contact's ending, monks. And just in this Ariyan eightfold Way are the steps leading to feelings' ending: right view and so forth. And when the Ariyan disciple thus knows feelings . . .; he knows this penetrative godly life as feelings' ending.

---

[1] *Sâmisā* and *nir*; *cf. D.* ii, 298.

Monks, it is said: "Feelings must be discerned . . ."—and because of this it is said.

Monks, it is said: "Perceptions must be discerned . . ."—and wherefore?

Monks, perceptions are these six: Perceptions of forms, sounds, smells, tastes, touches and ideas.

And what is perceptions' tie-source? Contact, monks.

And what is perceptions' variety? There is one perception as to forms, another as to sounds and so forth. . . . This, monks, is called perceptions' variety.

And what is perceptions' fruit? I say, monks, perceptions are the result of habit.[1] As one comes to know a thing, so one expresses oneself: "Thus I perceived." This, monks, is called perceptions' fruit.

And what is perceptions' ending? Contact's ending, monks. And just in this Ariyan eightfold Way are the steps leading to perceptions' ending: right view and so forth. And when the Ariyan disciple thus knows perceptions . . .; he knows this penetrative godly life as perceptions' ending.

Monks, it is said: "Perceptions must be discerned . . ."—and because of this it is said.

Monks, it is said: "Cankers must be discerned . . ."—and wherefore?

Monks, cankers are these three: canker of lust, of becoming and of ignorance.[2]

And what is cankers' tie-source? Ignorance, monks.

And what is cankers' variety? There are cankers that lead to hell, to a beast's womb, to the realm of the departed, to the world of man and to the deva-world. This, monks, is called cankers' variety.

And what is cankers' fruit? When ignorant, one engenders just that proper state of being to partake of merit and demerit. This, monks, is called cankers' fruit.

And what is cankers' ending? Ending of ignorance, monks. And just in this Ariyan eightfold Way are the steps leading to

---

[1] *Vohāra-vepakka*; *cf. Vism.* 602; *trsl.* 726.

[2] Note that we have here retained the three (not the four) cankers. So *Dial.* iii, p. 209.

cankers' ending: right view and so forth. And when the Ariyan disciple thus knows cankers . . .; he knows this penetrative godly life as cankers' ending.

Monks, it is said: "Cankers must be discerned . . ."—and because of this it is said.

Monks, it is said: "Action must be discerned[1] . . ."—and wherefore?

Monks, I say that determinate thought is action.[2] When one determines, one acts by deed, word or thought.

And what is actions' tie-source? Contact, monks.

And what is actions' variety? There is action that is experience in hell, in a beast's womb . . . in the deva-world. This, monks, is called actions' variety.

And what is actions' fruit? I say that it is threefold: It may either rise here now or at another time or on the way.[3] This, monks, is called actions' fruit.

And what is action's ending? Contact's ending, monks. And just in this Ariyan eightfold Way are the steps leading to action's ending: right view and so forth. And when the Ariyan disciple thus knows action . . .; he knows the penetrative godly life as action's ending.

Monks, it is said: "Action must be discerned . . ."—and because of this it is said.

Monks, it is said: "Ill must be discerned, its tie-source, variety, fruit, ending and the steps leading thereto"—and wherefore is this said?

Birth is ill, old age is ill, disease is ill, death is ill; grief, sorrow, misery, distress, tribulation are ill, not to get what one wants is ill—in short, (life's) fivefold bunch of clinging[4] is ill.

---

[1] *Kamma* or *karma*, considered both objectively and subjectively; see *P.E.D. s.v.* and elsewhere.

[2] *Cetanâhaŋ kammaŋ vadāmi*; see Mrs. Rhys Davids' *Buddh. Psych.* 93; *Pts. of Contr.* 225.

[3] *Ti-vidhâhaŋ kammānaŋ vipākaŋ vadāmi: Diṭṭh' eva dhamme upapajje vā apare vā pariyāye.* *S.e.* for *eva* reads *vā*. But if *tividha*, we must read *pariyāye vā* (?). *Cf.* the *fourfold effect in time* at *Cpd.* 144; *Vism. trsl.* 724; but I am not certain whether this is referred to.

[4] *Pâñc' upādāna-kkhandhā.* *Cf. Vin. Texts* (*S.B.E.*), i, 95, etc.

And what is ill's tie-source ? Craving, monks.

And what is ill's variety ? Ill that is above measure; ill that is trifling; ill that is quick to change; and ill that is slow to change. This, monks, is called ill's variety.

And what is ill's fruit ? Consider one overcome by ill, in mind forspent—he grieves, mourns, laments, beats his breast and becomes bewildered; or roams[1] abroad in search of one who knows a spell or two to end his ill. Ill yields bewilderment and search, I say. This, monks, is called ill's fruit.

And what is ill's ending ? Craving's ending, monks. And just in this Ariyan eightfold Way are the steps leading to ill's ending, to wit: right view, right purpose, right speech, right action, right livelihood, right effort, right mindfulness and right concentration. And when the Ariyan disciple thus knows ill, its tie-source, its variety, its fruit, its ending and the steps leading thereto; then he knows this penetrative godly life as ill's ending.

Monks, it is said: "Ill must be discerned . . ."—and because of this it is said.

Verily, monks, such is this penetrative discourse, this Dhamma-discourse.'

§ x (64). *The lion-roar.*

'Monks, these are the six[2] Tathāgata-powers of a Tathāgata, possessed of which the Tathāgata claims the place of the bull, roars the lion-roar in assemblies and sets a-roll the Brahmā Wheel. What six ?

Herein, monks, the Tathāgata knows as fact[3] base from base, non-base from non-base.[4] In that the Tathāgata knows this, it is the Tathāgata's Tathāgata-power whereby the Tathāgata claims the place of the bull, roars the lion-roar in assemblies and sets a-roll the Brahmā Wheel.

Again, the Tathāgata knows as fact the result, with its base and cause, of action's moulding[5] in respect of the past, present

---

[1] *Cf. D.* i, 222.

[2] See *Pts. of Contr.* 140; *M.* i, 67; *A.* v, 33.

[3] *Yathābhūtaŋ.*

[4] *Ṭhāna* and *aṭṭhāna*. *Comy. kāraṇa.*

[5] *Kamma-samādāna.*

and future. In that he knows this . . . he sets a-roll the Brahmā Wheel.

He knows the stain, purity and emergence[1] in musing, deliverance and concentration attainments. . . .

He remembers many a previous dwelling, one birth, two and so forth . . .; he remembers each in all its modes and detail. . . .

With the purified deva-eye, surpassing the human eye, he knows the faring on of men, each according to his actions. . . .

Destroying the cankers, the Tathāgata enters and abides in mind-emancipation, in insight-emancipation, canker-free. . . . In that the Tathāgata so abides, it is the Tathāgata's Tathāgata-power whereby the Tathāgata claims the place of the bull, roars the lion-roar in assemblies and sets a-roll the Brahmā Wheel.

Monks, these are the six . . .

And if, monks, others come and question the Tathāgata because of his knowledge, as fact, of base and non-base; according as the Tathāgata's knowledge, as fact, of base and non-base prevails, so the Tathāgata explains to them by knowledge as fact, when questioned.

Or if others come and question him because of his knowledge, as fact, of the result of action's moulding . . .; the stain, purity and emergence in musing . . .: previous dwelling . . .; the faring on of men . . . or because of canker-destruction . . .; according as his knowledge prevails, so he explains to them, when questioned.

Now, this knowledge, as fact, of base from base, non-base from non-base, I declare it to be the possession of the concentrated, not of the unconcentrated; so, too, the knowledge, as fact, of the other five . . ., I declare them to be the possession of the concentrated, not of the unconcentrated.

Thus, verily, monks, concentration is the Way, non-concentration the no-whither way.[2]

---

[1] See *Compendium*, 67 *ff.*

[2] *Samādhi maggo, asamādhi kummaggo.*

CHAPTER VII.—THE DEVAS.

§ i (65). *The Non-returner.*

'Monks, save one give up six things, one cannot realize the fruit of the Non-returner. What six?

Disbelief, shamelessness, recklessness, indolence, forgetfulness in mindfulness and foolishness.

Verily, monks, save one give up these six things, one cannot realize the fruit of the Non-returner.'

But if one give up these six things, one can . . .

§ ii (66). *The arahant.*

'Monks, save one give up six things, one cannot realize arahantship. What six?

Sloth, torpor, flurry, worry, disbelief and heedlessness.

Verily, monks, save one give up these six, one cannot realize arahantship.'

But if one give up these six, one can . . .

§ iii (67). *Friends.*

'Verily, monks, that a monk who is an evil friend, an evil comrade, an evil companion, serving, attending, honouring evil friends, emulating their ways of thought, shall fulfil the Dhamma-fore-course[1]—that cannot be; and that without fulfilling the course, he shall fulfil the Dhamma-training—that cannot be; and that without fulfilling the training, he shall fulfil the virtues—that cannot be; and that without fulfilling the virtues, he shall give up lustful passion, passion for the material or for the immaterial—that cannot be.

But that a monk who is good friend, comrade, companion, serving, attending, honouring good friends, emulating their ways of thought, shall fulfil the Dhamma-fore-course—that surely shall be; and that on the fulfilment of the fore-course, he shall fulfil the training—that surely shall be; and that on the fulfilment of the training, he shall fulfil the virtues[2]—

---

[1] *Abhi-sam-ācār-ika dhamma*; see above V, § 21.

[2] It seems a jumble here, that *sīlāni* should not have come first, since they must be presupposed in the foregoing. Unless the four *brahmavihāras* are meant by *sīlāni*. Possibly a corrupt recension.

that surely shall be; and that on the fulfilment of the virtues, he shall give up lustful passion, passion for form and for the formless—that surely shall be.'

§ iv (68). *Company.*[1]

'Verily, monks, that a monk delighting in company, delighted by company, absorbed in the delights of company, delighting in gatherings,[2] delighted by gatherings, absorbed in the delights of gatherings, shall find delight alone, in seclusion—that cannot be; and that without finding delight in seclusion, he shall grasp the salient fact of mind—that cannot be; and that without so grasping, he shall become perfect in right view—that cannot be; and that without becoming perfect in right view, he shall become perfect in right concentration—that cannot be; and that without becoming perfect in right concentration, he shall abandon the fetters—that cannot be; and that without abandoning the fetters, he shall realize Nibbāna—that cannot be.'

But the converse shall surely be. . . .

§ v (69). *The deva.*

Now[3] when the night was well advanced, a deva, shedding rays of far-reaching loveliness over Jeta Grove, visited the Exalted One, saluted and stood at one side; and, so standing, he spoke thus to the Exalted One: 'Lord, there are these six things that lead not to a monk's falling away. What six? Reverence for Teacher, Dhamma and Order, reverence for the training, grace in speech[4] and good friendship. Lord, these six things lead not to a monk's falling away.' Thus spoke that deva and the Teacher approved. And the deva, perceiving that the Master agreed, saluted and disappeared thence, keeping the Exalted One on his right.

Now, at the end of that night, the Exalted One addressed the monks and told them all that had passed. . . .

---

[1] Both our text and *S.e.* in the *Uddāna* omit mention of this.

[2] *Comy.* says of *Suttanta*-repeaters or fellows of his own sort.

[3] *Cf. A.* iv, 29 *ff.*; above VI, § 21.

[4] *Sovacassatā*, from *su-vācā*; *cf.* the *Epistle to the Colossians* iv, 6

And when he had spoken, the venerable Sāriputta saluted the Exalted One and said:

'Lord, the meaning of the Exalted One's brief words I thus understand in full: Suppose, lord, a monk himself reveres the Teacher and praises such reverence; he will instil such reverence in others who lack it; and of those who possess it he will speak in praise, justly, truly and timely. So, too, of reverence for Dhamma, the Order, the training, grace in speech and good friendship. It is thus I understand in full the Exalted One's brief words.'

'Well said, well said, Sāriputta, it is just as you say . . .; and, Sāriputta, thus the full meaning of my brief words ought to be understood.'

§ vi (70). *Psychic power.*[1]

'Verily, monks, that a monk, without the peace of concentration in high degree, without attaining to calm, without winning one-pointedness, shall have part in the many psychic powers: being one, he becomes many, being many, one, . . . reaches in body even as far as Brahmā's world—that cannot be; shall hear, with the purified deva-ear, surpassing man's, sounds of devas and men, far and near—that cannot be; shall know, by mind compassing mind, the thoughts of other folk, other persons: the passionate as such . . . the unemancipated as such—that cannot be; shall call to mind many a previous dwelling, one birth, two births and so forth . . .—that cannot be; shall see with the deva-eye . . . the faring on of men—that cannot be; shall enter and abide in mind-emancipation, insight emancipation, canker-free . . .—that cannot be.'

But the converse shall surely be. . . .[2]

§ vii (71). *The eyewitness.*

'Monks, if a monk be possessed of six things, he cannot become this and that, so as to be bound personally to attain, given the opportunity.[3] What six?

---

[1] The *Uddāna* omits. [2] The text repeats in full.

[3] We have here the terms hard to render of *bhabbo* and *bhabbatā*, is to, or should, become, and the abstract noun of the same. *Cf.* hereon Mrs. Rhys Davids' *Manual*, p. 128; *Sakya*, p. 324; *Khp.* vi, 11.

Suppose, monks, a monk know not as a fact: "These[1] things partake of failure," or, "These partake of stability," or, "These of distinction," or, "These of penetration," nor is he zealous nor helpful.

Monks, if a monk be possessed of these six, he cannot become this and that, so as to be bound personally to attain, given the opportunity.'

But if he be possessed of the converse six, he can . . .[2]

§ viii (72). *Strength.*

'Monks, if a monk be possessed of six things, he cannot win strength in concentration. What six?

Suppose, monks, a monk be not skilled in attaining concentration, nor skilled in maintaining concentration, nor skilled in emerging therefrom, nor is he zealous, nor persevering nor helpful.

Monks, if a monk be possessed of these six, he cannot win strength in concentration.'

But if he be possessed of the converse six, he can . . .[2]

§ ix (73). *Musing.*

'Monks, save one give up six things, one cannot enter and abide in the first musing. What six?

Sense-desires, ill-will, sloth and torpor, flurry and worry, doubt; and lust's perils are not seen clearly as such by right insight.

Monks, save one give up these six, one cannot enter and abide in the first musing.'

But if one give up these six, one can . . .

§ x (74). *The same.*

'Monks, save one give up six things, one cannot enter and abide in the first musing. What six?

---

[1] The *Comy.* refers to *Vism.*; see *trsl.* ii, 103; *cf. D.* iii, 277; *A.* ii, 167.

[2] The text repeats in full.

Brooding on sense-desire, ill-will and cruelty; conjuring up thoughts of lust, ill-will and cruelty.

Monks, save one give up these six, one cannot enter and abide in the first musing.'

But if one give up these six, one can . . .

CHAPTER VIII.—ARAHANTSHIP.

§ i (75). *Ill at ease.*

'Monks, if a monk follow six things, he will live ill at ease here now, vexed with himself,[1] troubled, fretful; and, on the breaking up of the body after death, an ill-faring is to be expected. What six?

Brooding on sense-desires, ill-will, cruelty; and conjuring up like thoughts.

Monks, if a monk follow these six, he will live ill at ease. . . .

Monks, if a monk follow six things, he will live happily here now, neither vexed, troubled, nor fretful; and, on the breaking up of the body after death, a well-faring may be expected. What six?[2]

Reflecting on renunciation, on freedom from ill-will and cruelty; and conjuring up like thoughts.

Verily, monks, if a monk follow these six, he will live happily. . . .'

§ ii (76). *Arahantship.*

'Monks, save one give up six things, one cannot realize arahantship. What six?

Conceit,[3] underrating, overrating, complacency, stubbornness and instability.[4]

---

[1] *Sa-vighātaŋ.*

[2] Text and *S.e.* omit.

[3] *Mānaŋ, o-, ati-, adhi-*, from √*man*, to think (man-like). *Māna*, pride, conveys the old English idea of 'vain conceits.' See above, p. 255.

[4] *Atinipātaŋ. P.E.D.* omits, but see *Crit. Pāli Dict.*, where the *Comy.* is quoted as 'to the base I am base.' To us it suggests the opposite error to *thambha*, since the *Comy.* meaning is a replica of *omāna*. *Cf. vv.ll.* in P.T.S. ed. of text. *Atinipāta* is 'excessive falling over.'

Monks, save one give up these six, one cannot realize arahantship.'

But if one give up these six, one can . . .

§ iii (77). *Beyond.*

'Monks, save one give up six things, one cannot realize the excellence of true Ariyan knowledge and insight, beyond man's state. What six?

Forgetfulness in mindfulness, lack of self-possession, unguardedness as to the sense-doors, lack of moderation in eating, deceit and mealy-mouthedness.

Monks, save one give up these six, one cannot realize the excellence of true Ariyan knowledge and insight, beyond man's state.'

But if one give up these six, one can . . .

§ iv (78). *Happiness.*

'Monks, if a monk follow six things, he will live here now in great happiness and contentment, and for him the mould has begun to form[1] for destroying the cankers. What six?

Herein a monk delights in Dhamma, in growth, in renunciation, in solitude, in being free of ill-will and in non-diffuseness.[2]

Monks, if a monk follow these six, he will live in great happiness. . . .'

§ v (79). *Attainment.*[3]

'Monks, if a monk possess six things, he cannot attain unattained skill in Dhamma, nor increase his skill attained therein. What six?

Herein a monk is unskilled in entering, in leaving, in approach, has no wish to attain unattained skill in Dhamma, preserves not his skill attained, nor stirs to persevere.

Verily, monks, if a monk possess these six, he cannot attain

---

[1] *Yoni c' assa āraddhā hoti.*

[2] *Nippapañcārāmo. Comy. Nippapañca-saṅkhāte Nibbāne ramati. Cf.* above for *papañca* (always a difficult rendering), p. 210.

[3] *Adhigama.*

unattained skill in Dhamma, nor increase his skill attained therein.'

But if he possess the converse six he can . . .

§ vi (80). *Greatness.*

'Monks, endowed with six things a monk shall in no long time win to greatness and growth in right things. What six?

Herein, monks, a monk has clear sight in much, application in much, zest in much, dissatisfaction in much, shirks not the burden of right things, and drives across to the beyond.[1]

Verily, monks, endowed with these six, a monk shall win to greatness and growth in right things in no long time.'

§ vii (81). *Hell.*

'Monks, following six things, one is duly cast in hell. What six?

One takes life, takes what is not given, lives carnally, lies, has evil desires and wrong views.

Verily, monks, following these six, one is duly cast in hell.'

(*But one goes to heaven if one abstain from the first four, have few desires and right views.*)

§ viii (82). *The same.*

'These six too. . . .

One lies, is slanderous, harsh, a babbler, greedy, reckless.'

(*Apply the opposite as before.*)

§ ix (83). *The chief thing.*

'Monks, if a monk be possessed of six things, he cannot become[2] one to realize the chief thing, arahantship. What six?

Herein a monk is without faith, modesty or fear of blame, is indolent, lacks insight and hankers after action[3] and life.

Monks, if a monk be possessed of these six, he cannot become one to realize the chief thing, arahantship.'

But if he be possessed of the opposite six, he can . . .

---

[1] *Uttariŋ patāreti*, a striking and unique (?) phrase.

[2] *Abhabbo.* See above, p. 299, n. 3. [3] Or 'body' (*kāye*).

§ x (84). *Day and night.*

'Monks, if a monk follow six things, come day come night, just a falling away in right things may be expected, not a growth. What six?

Herein, monks, a monk desires much, is fretful, discontented with this and that requisite: robe, alms, lodging, medicaments —is without faith or virtue, is indolent, forgetful in mindfulness and lacks insight.

Monks, if a monk follow these six, come day come night, just a falling away in right things may be expected, not a growth.'

But the converse holds. . . .

Chapter IX.—The Cool.

§ i (85). *The cool.*

'Monks, if a monk follow six things, he cannot become[1] one who realizes the cool above all. What six?

Herein,[2] monks, a monk checks not the mind when it ought to be checked; exerts not the mind when it ought to be exerted; gladdens not the mind when it ought to be gladdened; gives no heed to the mind when it ought to be given heed to; is bent on low things and finds delight in life's bundle.[3]

Verily, monks, if a monk follow these six, he cannot become one who realizes the cool above all.'

But if he follow the opposite of the first four and be bent on excellence and find delight in Nibbāna, he can . . .

§ ii (86). *The stops.*[4]

'Monks, cumbered by six conditions, though one listen to Saddhamma, he cannot become one to enter the right way of right things.[5] What six?

He[6] is cumbered by the stop of action, the stop of vice,

---

[1] *Abhabbo.* [2] See *Vism. trsl.* 284.

[3] *Sakkāya.* Above VI, § 14.

[4] *Āvaraṇatā.* [5] *Niyāma, Pts. of Contr.* 383 *ff.*

[6] *Vism. trsl.* 203. *Cf. Vibh.* 342; *Pug.* 13; *Mil.* 154. *Comy.* explains these three thus: (1) *Pañcahi ānantariya-kammehi* (see *DhS. trsl.* 267 and next sutta); (2) *niyata-micchādiṭṭhiyā*; (3) *akusala-vipāka-paṭisandhiyā vā kusala-vipākehi ahetuka-paṭisandhiyā vā.*

the stop of (action's) ripening, he is an unbeliever, lacks urge and lacks insight.

Monks, cumbered by these six conditions, though one listen to Saddhamma, he cannot become one to enter the right way of right things.'

But if one be endowed with the opposite of these six, one can . . .'

§ iii (87). *The stop of action.*[1]

'Monks, cumbered by these six conditions, he cannot become one to enter the right way. . . . What six?

(By him) his[2] mother's life has been taken, his father's, an arahant's, the Tathāgata's blood has been drawn intentionally, the Order embroiled, and he is weak in insight, a witless dullard.

Monks, cumbered by these six . . .'

But the converse holds. . . .

§ iv (88). *No desire to listen.*

'Monks, cumbered by these six conditions, he cannot become one to enter the right way . . .

He has no desire to listen, incline the ear, apply a heart of understanding, when the Dhamma-discipline declared by the Tathāgata is taught; he grasps the profitless, rejects the profitable and possesses not himself in harmony and patience.

Monks, cumbered by these six . . .'

But the converse holds. . . .

§ v (89). *To be given up.*

'Monks, save one give up six things, he becomes one who cannot realize the achievement of right view.[3] What six?

The wrong view of life's bundle, doubt, belief in the adequacy of rule and rite, passion, hate, infatuation, that lead to the ill way.

---

[1] The *Uddāna* omits to mention this sutta.

[2] *Cf.* above V, § 129.

[3] *Diṭṭhisampadā*; see *Pts. of Contr.* 269.

Verily, monks, save one give up these six, he becomes one who cannot realize the achievement of right view.'

But by giving up these, one can . . .

§ vi (90). *They are given up.*

'Monks, these six things are given up by a person who has achieved right view. What six?' (*As in* § 89.)

§ vii (91). *Cannot*[1] *be framed.*

'Monks, a person who has achieved right view cannot become one to frame six things. What six?' (*As in* § 89.)

§ viii (92). *The teacher.*

'Monks, there are these six occasions which cannot become. What six?

One who has achieved right view cannot become one who will live without respect, without regard, for the Teacher, Dhamma, the Order, the training; he cannot become one who will fall back on the view: "Nothing matters,"[2] cannot become one who will beget the eighth state of becoming.[3]

Verily, monks, these are the six.'

§ ix (93). *Any phenomenon.*

'These six also. . . .

He cannot become one who will accept any phenomenon as permanent, accept any phenomenon as happiness, accept any thing as self, do an unpardonable act, fall back on curious ceremonies[4] for purification, seek outside (the Order) for a gift-worthy.'

§ x (94). *His mother.*

'These six also. . . .

He cannot become one who will take his mother's life, his father's, an arahant's, with evil mind to draw the blood of the Tathāgata, embroil the Order, point to another teacher.'

---

[1] The *Uddāna* reads *me* for *na*, I think; *S.e.* also me.

[2] *Anāgamaniyaŋ vatthuŋ paccâgantuŋ. Comy.* guilty dread and (the sixty-two) heretical views; see above V, § 147; *A.* i, 27.

[3] *Aṭṭhamaŋ bhavaŋ. Comy. kāmâvacare aṭṭhamaŋ paṭisandhiŋ.*

[4] Above V, § 175.

§ xi (95). *Self-wrought.*

'These six also. . . .

He who has achieved right view cannot become one who will fall back on the view that weal and woe are self-wrought,[1] are wrought by another, are wrought both by oneself and another, arise by chance[2] without act of the self, or of another, or of both the self and another. And what is the cause of that?

Truly, monks, to one who has achieved right view cause and the causal origin of things are rightly discerned.

Verily, monks, these are the six.'

Chapter X.—Advantages.

§ i (96). *The manifesting.*

'Monks, the manifesting of six is hard to come by in the world. What six?

The[3] manifesting of the Tathāgata, arahant, fully enlightened, is hard to come by in the world; it is hard to come by a teacher of the Tathāgata-declared Dhamma-discipline; it is hard to come by rebirth in the Ariyan region;[4] entire sense-governance; freedom from stupidity, folly and blindness; the desire to do right is hard to come by in the world.

Verily, monks, the manifesting of these six is hard to come by.'

§ ii (97). *Advantages.*

'Monks, these are the six advantages in realizing the fruit of Streamwinning. What six?

There is certainty in Saddhamma, no liableness to fall away, none of the ill of the restricted,[5] there is the knowledge which cannot be imparted, cause is rightly discerned by one and the causal origin of things.

Verily, monks, these are the six. . . .'

---

[1] *Sayaŋkataŋ* and *asayaŋkāraŋ*; *cf. kammassaka* at V, § 57, and *attakāra* VI, § 38.

[2] *Cf. D.* iii, 138; *S.* ii, 19 (*K.S.* ii, 15); *Ud.* 69; see *J.R.A.S.*, July, 1931, p. 566 *ff.*

[3] *Cf.* above V, § 143.

[4] *Ariyāyatane. Comy. majjhima-dese.*

[5] *Pariyanta-katassa dukkhaŋ na hoti.*

§ iii (98). *Impermanence.*

'Verily, monks, that a monk who perceives permanence in any phenomenon shall live in harmony and patience—that cannot be; that without harmony and patience, he shall enter the right way—that cannot be; that without doing so, he shall realize the fruit of Streamwinning, the fruit of Once-returning, the fruit of Non-returning or arahantship—that cannot be.'

But the converse shall surely be. . . .[1]

§ iv (99). *Ill.*

'Verily, monks, that a monk who perceives happiness in any phenomenon shall live in harmony and patience—that cannot be. . . .'

§ v (100). *Not-self.*

'. . . who perceives any thing as the self. . . .'[2]

§ vi (101). *Nibbāna.*

'. . . who perceives Ill in Nibbāna shall live in harmony and patience—that cannot be. . . .'

But the converse in each case shall surely be. . . .

§ vii (102). *Without reserve*[3] *(a).*

'Monks, if a monk perceive six advantages, it is enough to establish, without reserve, the thought of impermanence anent all phenomena. What six?

"Then[4] all phenomena shall appear to me as lacking fixity; my mind shall find no delight in any world; my mind shall rise above every world; my thoughts shall be inclined towards Nibbāna; the fetters in me shall go towards their ceasing; and I shall follow the course of highest recluseship."

---

[1] The text repeats.

[2] *Kañci dhammaŋ attato.* This is not as yet exceeding the Second Utterance, which warned men that body and mind were not the self.

[3] The *Uddāna,* with *S.e., tayo anodhi saŋvutta. P.E.D.* does not notice *saŋvutta.*

[4] *Ca,*

Verily, monks, if a monk perceive these six advantages, it is enough to establish, without reserve, the thought of impermanence anent all phenomena.'

§ viii (103). *The same* (*b*).

'Monks, if a monk perceive six advantages, it is enough to establish, without reserve, the thought of Ill anent all phenomena. What six?

"Amid all phenomena, the thought of Nibbāna shall be present with me, as a slayer with drawn sword;[1] my mind shall rise above every world; I shall become a seer at peace in Nibbāna; by me lurking tendencies shall be rooted out; I shall become a doer of what ought to be done; and I shall minister to the Teacher with loving service."

Verily, monks, these are the six. . . .'

§ ix (104). *The same* (*c*).

'Monks, if a monk perceive six advantages, it is enough to establish, without reserve, the idea of not-self anent all things. What six?

Then in any world I shall become no part of it;[2] all that makes for the "I" in me shall be checked; all that makes for the "mine" shall be checked; mine shall be the knowledge that cannot be imparted; and by me cause shall be rightly discerned and the causal origin of things.[3]

Verily, monks, if a monk perceive these six, it is enough to establish, without reserve, the thought of not-self anent all things.'

§ x (105). *Becoming*.[4]

'Monks, these three spheres of becoming must be given up; and there must be training in three trainings. What three spheres must be given up?

---

[1] *Cf. A.* iv, 52.

[2] *Sabbaloke ca atammayo* (not made of that) *bhavissāmi*; see *G.S.* i, 133 *n.*

[3] *Buddh. Psych.* 99.

[4] See *D.* iii, 216 and 219 for refs.

The sphere of sense-desire, the form-sphere[1] and the formless spheres of becoming.

These three spheres must be given up. And in what three must there be training?

In further[2] virtue, in further thought and in further insight.

In these three trainings there must be training.

Verily, monks, when by a monk these three spheres of becoming have been given up and in these three trainings he in training has been trained, the monk is said[3] to have cut off craving, rolled back the bolts, and mastering pride completely, has made an end of Ill.'

§ xi (106). *Craving.*

'Monks, these three cravings must be given up and these three forms of pride. What three cravings?

The craving for lust, for becoming and for ceasing.[4]

These three cravings must be given up. And what three forms of pride must be given up?

Thinking[5] of self, thinking lowly of self and thinking muchly of self.

These three forms must be given up.

Verily, monks, when a monk has so done, he is said to have cut off craving, rolled back the bolts, and mastering pride completely, has made an end of Ill.'

Chapter XI.—The Threes.

§ i (107). *Passion.*

'Monks, there are these three conditions. What three?

Passion, hatred and delusion.

Verily, monks, these are the three. And to get rid of these three, cultivate three. What three?

To get rid of passion, cultivate the foul in it; to get rid of

---

[1] *Rūpa-bhavo*=the Brahma-world.
[2] *Adhi-*
[3] *Cf.* above V, § 200.
[4] *Vi-bhava*, ? more becoming.
[5] *Cf.* above VI, § 76.

hatred, cultivate amity; to get rid of delusion, cultivate insight.

Verily, monks, to get rid of these three conditions, cultivate these three.'

§ ii (108). *Doing ill.*

'Monks, there are these three conditions. What three? Doing ill in deed, word and thought.

Verily, monks, these are the three. And to get rid of these three, cultivate three. What three?

To get rid of doing ill in deed, cultivate doing well in deed; to get rid of doing ill in word, cultivate doing well in word; to get rid of doing ill in thought, cultivate doing well in thought.

Verily, monks, to get rid of these three conditions, cultivate these three.'

§ iii (109). *Thinking.*[1]

'Monks, there are these three conditions. What three? Sense-desire-thinking, ill-will-thinking and harm-thinking.

Verily, monks, these are the three. And to get rid of these three, cultivate three. What three?

To get rid of sense-desire-thinking, cultivate renunciation-thinking; and to get rid of the other two . . ., cultivate such thinking as is their opposites.

Verily, monks, to get rid of these three conditions, cultivate these three.'

§ iv (110). *Thoughts.*[2]

Apply the foregoing sutta, with changes.

§ v (111). *Principles.*[3]

The same with changes.

§ vi (112). *Complacence.*

'Monks, there are these three conditions. What three? The complacent view, the self-view, the wrong view.

Verily, monks, these are the three. And to get rid of these three, cultivate three. What three?

---

[1] *Vitakka*, cogitation. [2] *Saññā*. [3] *Dhātu*.

To get rid of the complacent view, cultivate the thought of impermanence; to get rid of the self-view, cultivate the thought of not-self; to get rid of the wrong view, cultivate right view.

Verily, monks, to get rid of these three, cultivate these three.'

§ vii (113). *Discontent.*[1]

'Monks, there are these three conditions. What three?

Discontent, harming others and wayfaring without Dhamma.[2]

Verily, monks, these are the three. And to get rid of these three, cultivate three. What three?

To get rid of discontent, cultivate gladness[3] of heart; and to get rid of the other two . . ., cultivate the opposite qualities.

Verily, monks, to get rid of these three, cultivate these three.'

§ viii (114). *Being satisfied.*

'Monks, there are these three things. What three?

Being dissatisfied, lacking self-possession and wanting much.

Verily, monks, these are the three. And to get rid of these three, cultivate three. What three?' *The opposite.* . . .

§ ix (115). *Unruliness.*

'These three also. . . .

Unruliness, evil friendship and being tossed about in mind.

. . . And to get rid of these three, cultivate . . .

Rule, good friendship and mindfulness in breathing in and out.'

§ x (116). *Flurry.*

'These three also. . . .

Flurry, lack of restraint and indolence.

. . . . And to get rid of these three, cultivate . . .

Calm, restraint and earnestness.'

[1] *Arati.* [2] Or 'immoral conduct.' [3] *Muditā* from √*mud.*

Chapter XII.—The Recital.

§ 117. *Contemplation.*

'Monks, save one give up six things, he cannot become one who abides in contemplation of the body as body. What six?

Delight in activity, gossip, sleep, company, being without a guard on the sense-doors and immoderate in eating.

Verily, monks, save one give up these six, he cannot become one who abides in contemplation of the body as body.'

But one surely can if one give up these six. . . .

§§ 118-130. *The same.*[1]

'Monks, save one give up six things, one cannot become one who abides in contemplation of the body as body in relation to self . . . to outside . . . to both self and outside; one cannot become one who abides in contemplation of the feelings, mind and thoughts, each as such, each in its relation to self,[2] to outside, to both self and outside. . . . What six?' (*As before.*)

But one surely can if one give up these six. . . .

§ 131. *He sees the deathless.*

'Monks, by having followed six things, the goodman Tapussa, because of the Tathāgata,[3] has gone to the end,[4] seen the deathless and has his being[5] in the realization of the deathless. What six?

Unwavering faith in the Buddha, in Dhamma and in the Order, Ariyan virtue, Ariyan knowledge and Ariyan release.

Verily, monks, by having followed these six, the goodman

---

[1] The text numbers these as one sutta. [2] *Ajjhattaŋ.*

[3] *Tathāgate.* Is Tapussa he of *Vin.*, *Mhv.* i, 4 and *A.* iv, 438?

[4] *Niṭṭhaŋ gato*; a monkish gloss, quoted by *P.E.D.*, observes: *pabbajitānaŋ arahattaŋ patta*; but here all are home-folk who are said to have won to Nibbāna, the deathless. For some not otherwise noted here see *G.S.* i, 22 *ff.*

[5] *Iriyati.*

Tapussa, because of the Tathāgata, has gone to the end, seen the deathless and has his being in the realization of the deathless.'

§ 132-151. *The same.*[1]

'These also. . . . The goodman Bhallika, Sudatta Anāthapiṇḍika, Citta Macchikāsaṇḍika, Hatthaka Āḷavaka, Mahānāma Sakka, Ugga Vesālika, Uggata, Sūra Ambaṭṭha, Jīvaka Komārabhacca, Nakulapitā, Tavakaṇṇika, Pūraṇa, Isidatta, Sandhāna, Vijaya, Vajjiyamahita, and Meṇḍaka; the lay-disciple Vāseṭṭha, Ariṭṭha and Sāragga. . . .'

§ 152. *Of passion.*[2]

'Monks, for the full understanding of passion six things ought to be made to become. What six?

The[3] sight above all, the sound above all, the gain above all, the training above all, the service above all, and the ever minding above all.

Monks, for the full understanding of passion these six things ought to be made to become.'

§ 153. *The same.*

'Monks, these six also. . . .

The[4] ever minding of the Buddha, of Dhamma, of the Order, of virtue, of liberality, and of the devas. . . .'

§ 154. *The same.*

'Monks, these six also. . . .

The thought of impermanence, of the ill therein, of there being no self in ill, of renunciation, of dispassion and of ending. . . .'

---

[1] I number differently from the text. For Pūraṇa and Isidatta, see above VI, § 44; Meṇḍaka at V, § 33; Ariṭṭha at *K.S.* v, 278, is a monk; for Vāseṭṭha see *D.* iii, 80; *M.* ii, 169; but these must be different; for Sandhāna see *DA.* i, 45; for Bhallika see p. 313, *n.* 3. Our *Comy.* mentions Tavakaṇṇika only, observing '*evan nāmako gahapati*,' which we already knew from the text! Is he connected with Tikaṇṇa of *G.S.* i, 145?

[2] *Cf.* above V, §§ 361 *ff.* and note.

[3] Above VI, § 8.

[4] Above VI, § 9.

II.—SIMILES

III.—TITLES OF SUTTAS